NO ELEPHANTS FOR THE MAHARAJA

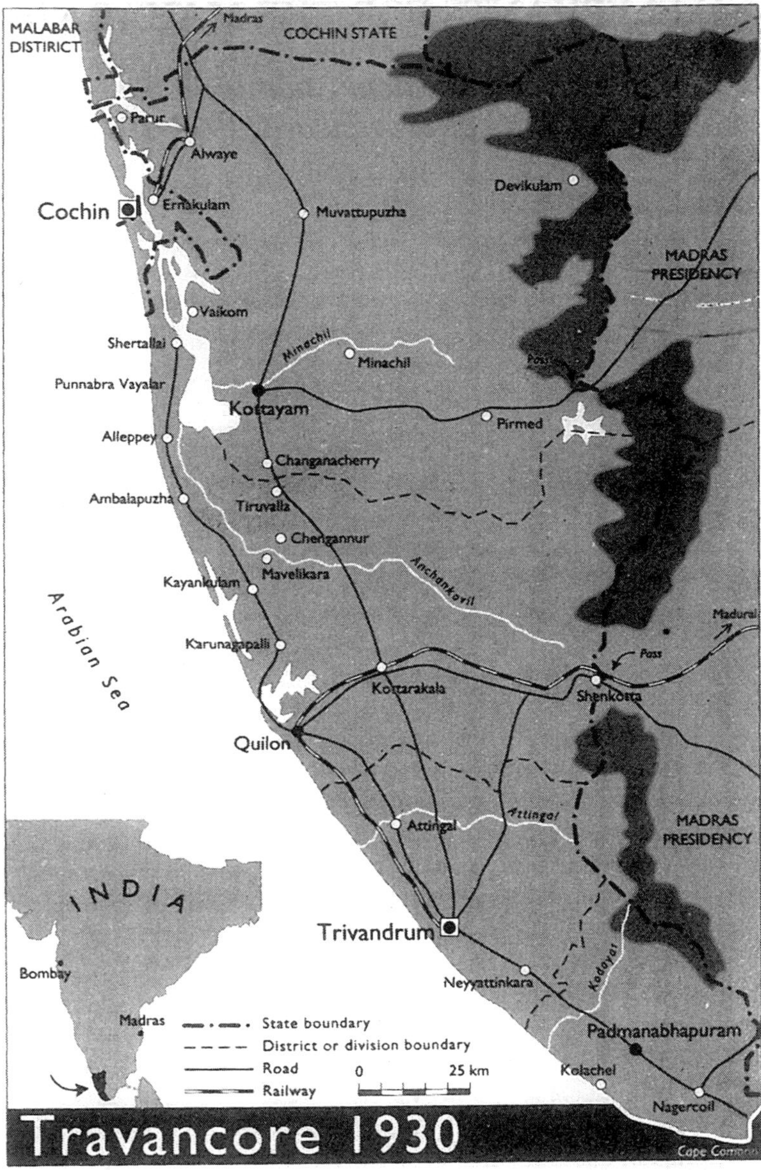

Travancore 1930

NO ELEPHANTS FOR THE MAHARAJA

Social and Political Change in the Princely State of Travancore (1921-1947)

LOUISE OUWERKERK

Edited with an Introduction by

DICK KOOIMAN

MANOHAR
2026

First published 1994
Reprinted 2011, 2019, 2020, 2021, 2023, 2024, 2025, 2026

ISBN 978-81-7304-068-9

Published by
Ajay Kumar Jain *for*
Manohar Publishers & Distributors
4753/23 Ansari Road, Daryaganj
New Delhi 110 002

Printed at
Replika Press Pvt. Ltd.

This book is dedicated to the memory of that great freedom fighter

PATTOM A. THANU PILLAI

First President of the Travancore State Congress, who, through all the dark days of persecution, imprisonment, misrepresentation and suffering, never wavered in his faith in the rightness of his cause and its ultimate triumph, the cause of democracy and civil liberty.

Contents

* Prepared by De Stichting BRON, Universiteit van Amsterdam 1993.

Introduction

Most studies on the last stand of the British Raj in south Asia tend to concentrate on the freedom movement in the directly administered territories, that is to say British India. They usually ignore the large part of south Asia that was ruled by the semi-independent, so-called Native Princes who somewhere in recent history had entered into a treaty of subsidiary alliance with the British Crown. This historiographical neglect of the Native States may be attributed to their lack of strategic importance to the Empire, the scarcity of sufficient and accessible historical sources, and the complications inherent in a freedom movement directed against a brown administration. Travancore, tucked away in the south-west corner of the Indian peninsula, was one of these states and therefore this book, originally written in 1974 by Miss Louise Ouwerkerk, is extremely valuable.

British India was established in the course of a campaign of military conquests that lasted exactly a hundred years, from 1757 to 1857. After obtaining the revenue rights over Bengal (1757-65) the East India Company extended its influence to the south and by about 1800 the last resistance of the main southern power, Mysore, was definitely broken. In a kind of circular movement the Company then pushed on along the western coast up to the north, annexing large regions like Maharashtra (1818), Sindh (1844) and Punjab (1849). The circle was more or less closed by the annexation of some central-Indian States in 1856. The violent outburst of the Mutiny in 1857, largely provoked by this aggressive expansion policy, brought the military conquests to a stand-still.

During this protracted military campaign direct annexation was not the only policy adopted by the Company. It also concluded treaties of subsidiary alliance with different kinds of Indian Princes that came its way. Under these treaties Princes were granted a semi-autonomous existence on the fringe of the emerging British-Indian empire. They were allowed to retain their own administration on the vital condition that they agreed to rule in accordance with the advice that the British government might occasionally think it necessary to offer. That gentle but binding advice was given by a British Resident or Agent, who came to assume a position of considerable importance at the Rulers' court or capital. Under the same treaties the Company agreed to furnish its well-trained troops in exchange for an annual tribute. The aim, of course was to pacify India in a quick and cheap way (Jeffrey 1978:18).

However, the status of subordinate ally did not guarantee the Princes an undisturbed continued existence: several states that had entered into a treaty relationship with the British, were as yet brought under direct rule later on, like Mysore (1831), Coorg (1834), Jhansi (1853), and Oudh (1856).

Travancore, which had emerged as the major single power in this region in the 18th century, was one of those states that entered into a military alliance with the East India Company. In 1795 and 1805 the Raja of Travancore recognized the British Paramount Power and promised to pay a substantial annual subsidy in exchange for continued military protection. Although these treaties were said to be binding "as long as the sun and moon shall endure", Travancore narrowly escaped annexation in the 1850s. Alarmed by repeated complaints of maladministration and a declining state of revenue, the Madras government warned the Raja that prompt remedial measures were needed to save Travancore from being placed under the direct management of the Company. The timely outbreak of the Mutiny proved a blessing in disguise and assured Travancore's semi-independent survival.

After 1857 Queen Victoria declared in a famous proclamation that the British government would respect the rights, dignity and honour of the Native Princes. Annexation had come to an end, but also interference by the British-Indian government in the internal affairs of the states was increasingly losing importance as an instrument of policy. Under the Viceroyalty of Lord Curzon (1899-1905) the old imperial policy flared up once again when fifteen native rulers were either forced to abdicate or temporarily deprived of their powers. But this was a temporary return to an already bygone practice. Annexation and direct intervention had become things of the past.

About two-fifths of Indian territory and somewhat less than one-fourth of the entire Indian population remained under indirect rule in states headed by Princes bearing the title of Raja, Maharaja, Nawab or Nizam. There were in all some 600 Indian States, the majority tiny and insignificant, but some like Hyderabad and Kashmir bigger than France. In the words of Sir Francis Wylie, who in 1940 became political advisor to the Crown Representative it was "surely the oddest political set-up that the world has ever seen" (Wylie in Philips and Wainwright 1970:519). Each state was allowed a certain number of gun salutes in strict accordance with a prestigious hierarchy. Only five states were accorded the maximum number of 21 gun salutes, Baroda, Gwalior, Hyderabad, Kashmir and Mysore. Travancore belonging to a slightly less glorious class of states received 19 gun salutes. The 24 states receiving salutes of 17 guns or more accounted for more than seventy per cent of the population of all states together.

For the colonial government the Indian Princes were most useful allies. Neutralized by treaties they speeded up military conquest by not halting the British siege-train and left in power, they facilitated administration which otherwise might have become a heavy burden on the Company. Paraphrasing Lord Bentinck's well-known comment on the rich landed proprietors created by the Permanent Settlement of 1793, one could summarize the British position by saying that, if security was wanting against extensive popular tumult or revolution, the subsidiary alliances had this great advantage at least, of having created a vast body of influential Indian Princes deeply interested in the continuance of the British Dominion. However, the Company's guarantee of the states' security also led to an ossification of what earlier was a dynamic political system. Whereas in the past a bad or weak Prince was removed by a violent war on the battle field or a quiet revolution in the palace wings, now British military presence and guarantees held him in his place whatever he did, as long as mismanagement went not that far as to affect the annual subsidy. In consequence of that, the states showed less social progress and economic development, although this rather general statement certainly does not apply to Travancore, as the subsequent chapters written by Louise Ouwerkerk will clearly demonstrate.

When during the last decades of the 19th century a nationalist movement slowly but irresistably began to manifest itself in British India, the Princes turned out to be equally useful allies in a different context. The British-Indian government, perceiving nationalism as the most immediate threat to the safety of the empire, openly marshalled all royal powers behind the throne of the Queen-Empress and cultivated the various Princes as the most trusted pillars supporting the imperial edifice. To ward off the dangers of a seditious national movement the government adopted a policy of non-interference in the internal affairs of the Indian States in 1909. Lord Minto formulated this non-interference policy in an often quoted speech at Udaipur in 1909, where he stated that administrative reforms in the states should not be imposed from outside, but had to emanate from the *Durbars* (State Governments) themselves in harmony with their own traditions. British officers serving in these states were reminded that it was their primary duty to respect and conserve the customs of these states.

The Princes, whose rights and privileges were thus upheld by the Crown, remained the bulwarks of British rule till far into the 20th century. Even after the passage of the Government of India Act in 1935 there were strong forces within the British government who wanted to use them as an instrument for thwarting the federation proposals and thereby maintaining some British influence in the new alignment of forces (Jeffrey 1978:1-2). The Political Department did not force political reforms on the states in the 1920s and 1930s, but by that very policy, as James Manor has argued, it virtually condemned the Princes to extinction when power had really to be transferred (Manor 1978: 306 ff.). The British preferred to uphold their alliance with the ancient rulers even when they had largely become a spent force. The leniency of the Political Department went so far as to acquiesce in the appointment of Sir C.P.Ramaswamy Aiyar as Dewan of Travancore (1936), even though it was not consulted in the matter and actually disapproved of the Maharaja's choice. When Independence drew near, the Princes changed from bulwarks into stumbling blocks.

The Indian National Congress (INC) as the main nationalist party followed a similar policy of non-interference in the internal affairs of the Princely States. That policy was primarily based on the postulate that the states were separate units and therefore not the concern of the nationalist movement. A growing political consciousness in the states after the first World War, forced the INC to gradually revise this policy. At its Calcutta session (1928) the INC assured the people of the Indian states of its sympathy with and support in their legitimate and peaceful struggle for the attainment of full responsible government. Yet, it was still assumed in this statement, that the burden of that struggle should necessarily fall on the states' people themselves. In spite of a growing concern for the states and an occasional involvement in their affairs (like the Vaikom satyagraha in Travancore 1924-25), official Congress policy remained firmly wedded to the principle of non-interference and the civil disobedience movement (1930-32) was strictly banned in the states' territory. There was an INC branch in Travancore but it existed merely in name.

On the eve of the second World War the Congress Working Committee (CWC) directed that all Congress branches in the states should function only under the direction and control of the CWC and should not engage in direct action in the name of the Congress (Wardha February 1938). For the conduct of the internal struggle of the people independent organizations should be started. About this time the Travancore State Congress was formed and it was this local Congress which so actively engaged the interest of Miss Louise Ouwerkerk. Later in the same year the Haripura session of the INC resolved to allow individual Congressmen to take part in agitations in the states in their personal capacity. At the end of 1938 the CWC went a step further and declared its support of the demand for civil liberty and responsible government in the states under the aegis of the rulers. Yet, these and similar statements, made before the war committed the INC to no more than moral support and sympathy to movements for freedom and self-expression (Jeffrey 1978:12-13, Daniel 1985:100-102). The statements were drowned in the noise of war.

A manuscript like the one that is published here, *No Elephants for the Maharaja*, has its own history and so has its author. Let us start with the latter. Miss Louise Ouwerkerk served the Government of Travancore when this state passed through a turbulent period. She was born of Dutch parents in London, Chelsea (1904) and studied at Newnham College, Cambridge University (1922-25), where she got a degree in Economics. During her college days she was actively involved in an International Fellowship which had as one of its activities mixed Sunday afternoon tea parties with Asian and African students. She also joined the Christian Student Movement at a time when Ecumenism had barely been heard of and was active in the League of Nations Union.

After going down from Cambridge Louise had difficulty in finding a job. She temporarily joined the tutorial staff of a correspondence college and then successfully applied for a teaching position at the Maharaja's Women's College in Trivandrum, the capital of Travancore State. She sailed for the East in the spring of 1929 and from her extensive correspondenc with the family at home, especially her mother, we get a spirited account of her travelling experiences and first impressions on arrival.

True to her convictions as developed at college she sought the company of the few Asian passengers and in one of her first letters she wrote that she had caused quite an upheaval aboard ship by dancing with the one and only Indian. Most of the women "cut me dead" and in a subsequent letter (28-6-1929) she wrote that the worthy ladies on board had warned her: "You wait till you get out East, then you will understand the colour bar." On arrival at Colombo she was met by what she describes as a most exquisite Indian, complete with blue flannel suit, immaculate collar and topee, who had been sent by the government of Travancore to look after her luggage. From Colombo she went north by train and crossed over to Travancore.

Arriving at her destination she was overjoyed to discover a green and leafy Trivandrum. She was definitely enraptured by her new place of residence, though it was only to be glimpsed at through its many palm trees. The people looked prosperous and contented and what struck her most was the electric street lighting extending even down little lanes and the bus services connecting Trivandrum with other municipalities. Yet, speaking about the college, her new sphere of action, she felt thoroughly disappointed.

In a first emotional outburst she complained without restraint of the inefficiency of the people she had to work with. The college was being rebuilt, half of the staff was not yet engaged, everything was in a muddle, and everybody writing polite notes to all the wrong people about it. The Director of Public Instruction was a Brahman and according to Louise he wouldn't do anything unless the day was auspicious. As far as her own job was concerned, she had applied for and been appointed to a professorship in Economics and History but after arrival she discovered to her dismay that she was required to teach Economics and Political Science instead. "Fancy, neglecting to point a little thing like that out to me... It is no joke lecturing on a subject I know nothing about, though I enjoy the struggle it means," she wrote home (28-6-1929). Her assistants at college were much older and more experienced but expected her to give a strong lead, which also created serious embarrassment on the part of the young European professor.

Lecturing started in July and after a few weeks her chief impression was that university regulations were such that for students cramming was the only possible policy to follow. Of course, she realized that for her students it was difficult to learn in a foreign language, that some of them were too poor to buy books and therefore could not do anything but take down her lectures literally and quote them back at her verbatim. It only increased her already great sense of responsibility in preparing the lectures. Yet, all these unpleasant discoveries and the general helplessness of the students came as a rude shock. Having come out with grand notions to the contrary, the change in so short a time was significant. It took some time for her to readjust.

She made the best of it and forced her way through, not least because she really liked teaching. The efforts bore fruit, as her students won many gold medals. Her many friends and admirers asserted it was because, instead of dictating lecture notes, she made her students think for themselves. She also took them out to the villages, to see for themselves how, in fact, the people in these poor villages lived — and died. Together with local INC representatives she studied village uplift work and handspinning industries and contributed articles about these subjects to *The Indian Economic Journal.*

In addition to her teaching responsibilities, Louise was for part of the time, also Warden of the Maharaja's Women's College Hostel, where she ruled with a firm hand. In 1936, when the Principal of the college went away on furlough, she became Acting Principal. In that capacity she had many interviews with irate parents who demanded admission for their children which she had to refuse since space was limited and the number wanting admission was legion.

In 1937 Louise reached the pinnacle of her academic career when she was appointed professor of History and Economics in the newly established University of Travancore. She also became Dean of the women students and remained associated with the Women's College at the same time. This accumulation of teaching obligations meant a heavy burden which was further increased by the difficult labour conditions. In the university she was head of a department in which she was the youngest and by far the most inexperienced, for after all she had only one year of advanced work, whereas her male colleagues had at least ten years, and one of them thirty years. Louise got the strong feeling that they violently resented her being there and were out to bully her. In a letter of 13-3-1938 she called the atmosphere poisonous and wrote that there was a chance of her being sent back to the Women's College while keeping her position as University Lecturer in Economics. Still she found time to study rural economics and published a paper on that subject in the *Indian Directory of Social Sciences.*

As can be imagined from this short survey of her academic career Louise had a busy time. But apart from education and research, there were many other things that occupied her time and energy. First of all there were the household duties. After her arrival she moved into a large bungalow, just across the Women's College, which she shared with Miss Grose who was responsible for organizing the new educational institution. As the two ladies did not mix well, Louise moved into her own bungalow very soon. But that created new problems, as Louise had to furnish the many rooms, to pay half a dozen servants and to maintain a car all on her own. As her salary was often overdue, she incurred many debts and on 20-7-1931 she confided to her diary in despair:

"Two *annas*, one *fanam* and four *cash* stand between me and starvation".

In spite of all these pressing duties Louise found time to take an interest in Travancore politics and after an initial period of distant observation she began to take an active part in it. In fact, she was in an excellent position to play a prominent role in public life. She was an independent and intelligent lady, full of lofty ideals and bustling energy.

In the capital Trivandrum she moved easily both in Indian and European circles and occupied a very strategic, central position in a wide network of social relations.

To begin with, she was an active member of the European Club. There she met many British people who served the Travancore administration in important positions, such as Dr. Nokes, the Public Service Commissioner who was her next-door neighbour, the Chief Engineer whom she affectionately used to address as "uncle George", members of the Legislature and many others. At the Club she talked politics with the men while the wives, in her own words, sat by glaring. She was perfectly aware of the fact that she was not popular among the women. But the discussions at the Club gave her valuable insights into Travancore politics which she later used in writing the history of this period.

She was also on friendly terms with the British Residents in Travancore. She met them at dinner parties and with C.P.Skrine, who became Resident in 1936, she visited several talkies (films). Yet, her friendship with the Residents did not prevent her from giving a very critical comment on the way they performed their official duties, as can be seen from the following pages.

Being a devout Catholic she was in frequent touch with the dignitaries of that church, both educational and ecclesiastical. The Catholic church numbered many adherents in Travancore and was a force to be reckoned with. Nevertheless, true to her ecumenical spirit, she also befriended several Protestant missionary families in Trivandrum. So she was very close with the Lefevres family who worked for the London Missionary Society and shared her musical interests. But she invited also a rather different class of people to her home, the European planters for whom she organized receptions when they came down to Trivandrum for their business meetings. In the hot weather Louise went up to Kodaikanal, where she had taken a large house and made a holiday home for her innumerable friends and acquaintances.

However, her many-sided social contacts did not remain restricted to the small European coterie in the capital. As we have seen, her teaching position at the Women's College and later the University brought her in regular touch with Indian colleagues, students and their parents. She also took an active part in the Girl Guides and through the Scouting Movement gained an additional insight in the social background of these girls and their families.

Right from the beginning and largely because of her position as a government servant Louise had regular consultations with the Dewans who headed the Travancore administration. Shortly after assuming her teaching duties she had an interview with V.S.Subrahmanya Aiyar (Dewan 1929-1932), who seems to have fully agreed with her emotional outburst that education should be more than cramming the girls up for their examinations (letter 14-7-1929), although this admission did not change matters much.

Undoubtedly the most dominating Indian politician of those days was Sir C.P.Ramaswamy Aiyar, usually referred to as Sir C.P. His towering personality loomed large not only in Travancore public life but also in the chapters of the book that Louise was going to write. Louise met him very often and was clearly impressed by his breadth of mind and unmistakable personal charm. When he assumed the office of Dewan in 1936, she called him a brilliantly clever man and expressed the hope of a more efficient administration under his direction. But gradually her admiration for the man gave way to disappointment and frustration and on several occasions she openly quarreled with him. When she was finally dismissed from government service, she suspected Sir C.P. of having been the main force behind the scenes to get her removed from the state. In her own curriculum vitae, written many years later, Louise attributed her dismissal to the anti-Christian policies of the Dewan and her disagreements with him about his treatment of the Christian women students.

Louise was also a regular visitor of the royal palace. Shortly after arrival she was presented at court to the Maharani Regent and her consort. In a letter she wrote to her mother (7-7-1929) she seems to have got the impression of a very human couple behind all the pomp of bowing attendants and the luxurious little reception room. The splendour could not hide a very shy little woman who was really more interested in her children quarreling in the adjacent room than in her visitor. A few years later she had quite a different experience when she had her first interview with the junior Maharani. "I had a fit of appalling shyness so obvious that she threw me out after 3/4 of an hour," she wrote in her diary (18-9-1931). On later visits to the same Maharani Louise fared better and had long discussions with her about the Women's College and all kinds of educational problems. "The Maharani really knows what she is talking about," Louise acknowledged, "but she wants to introduce too many changes at once which is unrealistic" (letter 28-6-1936). Apart from paying official visits to the palace Louise was invited to play tennis with the Princess or the Princess' consort and sometimes she received a whirlwind invitation to play tennis with the Maharaja.

Thus, Louise associated with Indians from all walks of life, visiting the homes of Indian students and receiving leading politicians for dinner, such as the Congressmen G.Ramachandran and C.Raja-gopalachari. These personal contacts, which went far beyond what was officially required, made many Europeans, especially the planters, frown upon her deliberate attempts to cross the colour bar (letter 11-8-1936). However, this informal disapproval did in no way deter her, but made her feel that her intermediate position as a European teacher in an Indian college might be of some practical use in establishing more harmonious relations between Indians and Europeans.

Therefore, it will come as no surprise that her interest in race relations led Louise to found the Trivandrum branch of the International Fellowship in 1930 (see Chapter VI). This larger Fellowship was founded in 1922 to bridge the social gap between British and Indians. For that purpose it organized tea parties, but as Louise was to emphasize, it was the careful selection of the guests and the provision of a definite theme for discussion that distinguished them from E.M. Forster's "bridge parties" described in *A Passage to India*. From this the Fellowship had branched out into inter-religious social service and village upgrading. Among the members of the Trivandrum branch were prominent Travancorean politicians such as T.M.Verghese, Pattom A. Thanu Pillai and C.Kesavan, but also British people, among whom were Residents, missionary families and several government servants. Membership of these Europeans seems to have been largely honorary, as the minutes of many meetings, often at Louise's bungalow, list only Indians present, apart from Louise herself.

The Fellowship worked very hard against communal hatred. Although its joint meetings of Hindus, Muslims and Christians did not yield substantial results, the fact that representatives from these communities sat together at one table was an achievement in its own right. Nevertheless, Louise often felt disappointed and complained in private that the political leaders who were members of the Fellowship still clung to their own communal organizations. In her view, they were all beating about the bush and would not face the heart of the communal problem (letter 23-11-1937).

The Dewan Sir C.P. followed Louise's political ventures very closely. On the one hand, he was most anxious to secure Louise's help in bringing about communal harmony. Yet, on the other hand he bluntly dismissed the Fellowship as a disloyal and subversive party within the state and did his utmost to destroy it. When T.M.Verghese, a Syrian Christian member of the Fellowship, took up the case of a

Hindu ex-prisoner, Sir C.P. seized upon this opportunity to unseat his enemy as Deputy President of the Legislative Assembly by pushing a motion of no-confidence against him through the House (Chapter VI.2). Louise felt thoroughly frustrated and in a letter to A.A.Paul, the secretary to the all-India organization, she wrote that the motion of no-confidence against T.M.Verghese had destroyed every effort at communal amity that had been made for years past and had put them back where they were four years ago (letter 27-11-1937).

Still she kept working along the same lines lines with unwearying energy. At the turn of the year 1937-1938 she took it upon herself to organize the meeting of the all-India International Fellowship Council in Trivandrum. The government had promised to fund it but after she sent in the budget of Rs. 2.000 she never heard anything again. On the eve of the Council meeting she received only 50% of the estimated expenditure. By threatening Sir C.P. to cancel the whole thing which would have brought public shame on the Travancore Government she got at least Rs. 1500. The Dewan was furious with her and she wondered "how they 'ill take it out of me" (letter 3-1-1938). The meeting, according to Louise, was a success, "in spite of all our divergences we established a deep unity on the basis of our common allegiance to one Father and our common brotherhood." After the meeting she had an interview with the Maharani to thank her for the Rs. 1500 grant-in-aid. "Her Highness hated being thanked for a meeting she strongly disliked and I took a devilish delight in doing it ... However, when the tension got too bad I demanded to see the Princess's baby, who received me most graciously; and the Maharani suddenly became quite human and pleasant, so I shan't be fired just yet" (letter 25-1-1938).

As far as her general political outlook was concerned Louise was very much in favour of the national independence movement as led by the INC. She considered Viceroy Lord Linlithgow's interference with the INC ministries a serious blunder and talked of Perfide Albion since the British had committed themselves to Indian self-government. Therefore, British policy to support the Native Princes against the democratic movement of the people came in for her outright condemnation (letters 22-2-1938 and 20-3-1938). In 1938 her Communal Harmony Group that had grown out the local Fellowship had joined together to demand responsible government. That little group, started by Louise, had developed into quite a considerable political party. Although it had formally dissolved all its links with the Fellowship, practically all the leaders of the State Congress, as it came to be known, still were members of the Fellowship. In her book Louise refers to this Communal Harmony Group, but she does not dwell extensively on her personal share in it, although her private papers suggest it must have been considerable.

As the 1940s drew near and the movement for responsible government was gaining momentum, there were several indications that the government was looking for a suitable opportunity to get rid of her services. Government policy to economize on salaries could offer such an opportunity. Existing salaries were frozen and the new scale of pay for professors was Rs. 200 to 300 a month, whereas Louise was getting Rs. 700 a month. Therefore, she wrote, it would not come as a surprise at all, if they were going to turn her out while she was on leave which was due in March 1939. Even before she left for Europe, the Chief Secretary requested her to vacate her bungalow, but after an indignant protest she was permitted to stay on till her departure.

Louise went on leave in the spring of 1939. During a farewell-call to the Dewan, Sir C.P. was his charming old self and agreed heartily with Louise on university affairs without touching any deeper disagreement. A few months later, on holiday in Denmark, she received a letter from the Chief Secretary to the Government of Travancore. She knew immediately what it was and wrote in her diary: "Rejoice, for it's happened! I am pensioned off!" Full of confidence she continued: "I've money saved. I have a reputation as lecturer and organizer, and I am young enough to adapt to new conditions" (Diary 30-7-1939).

Only after Independence Louise was to set foot again on what formerly was Travancorean soil. But she left behind a lasting impression on a generation of students who through her efforts were drawn into the political movement or activated into social service. One of these was M.A.Thomas, who came in touch with Louise in 1935 when he served as the first General Secretary of the Inter-Religious Students Fellowship. Later he became Director of the Christian Ecumenical Centre of India. On her death in 1989 he remembered her as one of the few Europeans who were sympathetic to the Indian freedom movement and cultivated personal friendships with many political leaders. Therefore, "she became suspect in the eyes of the (Travancore) Government and she had to pay for it." (*In Memoriam*).

Another student who remembered her with deep appreciation was M.M.Thomas. He was active in the Youth Christian Council of Action, organizing relief for the victims of the civil disobedience in Travancore 1938 and their families. In 1968 he was to become chairman of the Central Council of the World Council of Churches. In a *In*

Memoriam he wrote: "The fact that she had the leadership among the students created problems for her, since the Government authorities, especially the Dewan, Sir C.P. Ramaswamy Aiyar, felt that she was awakening people to their social responsibilities. I would say, she was one of the formative influences in my life, as well as in many other lives, while we were in Trivandrum."

As she had already observed in her diary, Louise was young enough to make a new start after her dismissal from Travancore. Back in India she was offered the post of principal of Government Women's College in Bangalore, the Princely State of Mysore. She started in May 1940 but by the next November she was interned under the Defence of India Rules, as a result, she maintained, of fabricated information from the Travancore Government. The charges were never revealed and there was no appeal tribunal. Owing to the personal efforts of Sir Maurice Gwyer, Chief Justice of India, she was released from the internment camp one year later but prohibited from teaching. She refused to return to England unless she was deported and, financed by the Maharani of Vizianagram, she continued her research on rural reconstruction.

Between 1942-1946 she worked for the Government of India, serving as expert on Indian affairs at the Foreign Publicity Office in Delhi under the leadership of Col. Geoffrey Wheeler. In that capacity she wrote articles to inform British troops on Indian life and customs and completely rewrote a *Manual for Troops* that dated from the last century and cleared it from its most flagrant racist overtones. At the same time, she helped to found the Delhi branch of the East-West Fraternity with Lady Wavell as its patron.

After Independence Louise returned to England. We need not pause to describe her manifold activities since then. Suffice it to say that she resumed teaching and that from 1954-1963 she served as head of a primary, secondary-modern and new secondary school in present-day Nigeria. But she could never forget India and so, we come to the history of the manuscript.

In 1963 Miss Louise Ouwerkerk returned to India to assume a part-time post in the International Girls' School at Ooticamund in the Tamilnadu hills. There she hoped to find time to write a book on the freedom movement in Travancore. However, she was soon asked to take over the headship of the school and that took all her time and energy. In 1967 she was teaching in England again in order to raise money for a longer period of research in India. Three years later she gave up teaching altogether to concentrate on writing the book she had in mind. By then, a great deal of classified information had been released under the '30-

years rule' and at the Public Record Office in Kew and the India Office in London she studied the Political Department files covering the period of her own active involvement in Travancore politics. A grant from the Leverhulme Trust enabled her to spend one year of research in India and to visit many old friends who gave her their reminiscences, their views, their private papers and their hospitality. They are all mentioned in the notes and bibliography. In 1974 she finally completed her manuscript that was entitled *No Elephants for the Maharaja.*

Unfortunately, her manuscript was never published. From her correspondence I understand that the publishers who saw her manuscript called it an admirable history and excellently written. But they were doubtful about the commercial prospects for a book like this, as it might be difficult to persuade the public that its interest and implications transcended the one small Indian State which was its immediate topic. Later, the Indo-British Historical Society in Madras accepted her manuscript for publication, but after its chairman died in 1978 the new Board was reluctant to commit itself to new ventures and the agreement lapsed. In the end Louise gave up and when she died in Banstead, Surrey, in 1989, the manuscript was collecting dust in a drawer.

During one of my research-visits to the India Office Library in London where I was working on Travancore's history, I happened to come across the Ouwerkerk Papers. After Louise's death in 1989 her surviving sister Miss Petronella Ouwerkerk had decided to transfer all her remaining papers to the India Office. Among this collection of papers I found her unpublished manuscript *No Elephants for the Maharaja* which considers the period from the investiture of the last Maharaja till Independence. In this work, with special emphasis on themes like communal harmony and State Congress, she unfolds the thesis that the movement for freedom and responsible government in Travancore was a truly indigenous one, stemming from local grievances and not artificially fostered from outside. In this respect she disagrees with Robin Jeffrey who holds the view that nationalism was essentially a movement that spread from British India to the States (Jeffrey 1978: 12).

The manuscript is not free from deficiencies. First of all, since the text was written almost twenty years ago, it has not benefited from the many studies and research findings that have appeared since its date of completion. The treatment of the earlier history in which the author had no personal part is rather weak. Furthermore, her study does not excel in theoretical or comparative analysis and her list of references and bibliography is chaotic and far from complete.

Nevertheless, the manuscript is still a most interesting and valuable contribution to this period of Travancore history and throws considerable light on the emergence of a movement for responsible government in a Princely State. Louise knew the place and the people intimately and in the mid-1970s her study could rightly claim to be a sequel to Robin Jeffrey's *The Decline of Nayar Dominance.* In 1981 she wrote in one of her letters: "I was one of the very few persons who was in contact with all aspects of the freedom movement in Travancore and therefore I am in a position to give an impartial account (or nearly so) of a turbulent period." And the reader will have to agree that Louise, in spite of her own active involvement and strong personal feelings, has succeeded in keeping that critical distance which makes reading her history both entertaining and rewarding. Her manuscript still stands as a major piece of research by a keen, contemporary eyewitness and makes excellent reading as narrative history, rich in its description of local personalities and developments.

What is quite exceptional is that many of the documents, interview notes and press reports on which her study is based are available in the same Ouwerkerk Papers. This enables the researcher to test the author's conclusions by referring to her own sources, a situation that seldom occurs in ordinary circumstances. A look at these papers taught me, among other things, that she made much more use of these sources than she actually acknowledged in her notes.

Several people have been most helpful in bringing this manuscript into print. I owe them a lot of thanks and mention their names in gratitude. First of all Dr. Richard Bingle of the India Office in London who drew my attention to the Ouwerkerk Papers. Dr. Hans Schenk suggested that I might edit the manuscript and after some hesitation I accepted his suggestion though he himself may have forgotten he ever made it. The necessary permission for publication was kindly granted by Louise's surviving sister Miss Petronella Ouwerkerk, who received me with great hospitality at her Banstead home. Dr. David Blake of the India Office lent his assistence in producing a manuscript copy and collecting some old pictures that have been included in this book. The Netherlands Organization for Scientific Research (NWO) gave me a research grant to visit the India Office to collect material for writing this introduction and awarded a subsidy for the publication of this book. Wietske Wielenga-Hockey M.A. improved the English wording of the introduction, Josée Netten M.A. assisted in the proof-reading and

Dr. B.N. Teensma, a relative to the Ouwerkerk family, prepared the index. Very important moral support was received from my colleagues, Prof.Dr.K.K.N.Kurup of Calicut University and Dr.K.K.Kusuman of Kerala University in Trivandrum who followed my editing work with great interest. Finally, Mr.Ajay Kumar Jain of Manohar Publishers & Distributors had sufficient confidence in this book about one small Indian State to face the market.

Miss Petronella granted me permission for publication on the strict condition that nothing was altered, added to, or deleted from the original manuscript. However, in consultation with her, I was allowed to effect some amendments in the organization of the text. So, I changed the chapterization, as some chapters of the original manuscript had too many sections and others none at all. I also inserted some notes where I thought some clarification might be useful and omitted others which seemed superfluous. The present subtitle has been added by me and was not part of the manuscript, though it has been taken from her own text (Chapter I.1). A major problem was that the references to books and articles left much to be desired. Her quotations from contemporary daily papers and journals are usually based on her own scrapbooks and paper cuttings which often remained undated. Apart from that, the bibliography was badly organized. I have tried to arrange the references and bibliography in a more systematic way and corrected shortcomings to the best of my knowledge. For those readers who want to be updated on Travancore historiography I have added a short list of the main publications that have appeared since the beginning of the 1970s Finally, I wrote an introduction to give the manuscript and its author some background. The body of the text underwent only a few minor changes and remains very much Louise Ouwerkerk's own work.

SOURCES

1. *The Ouwerkerk Collection* (The British Library, Oriental and India Office Collections, European Manuscripts)

Diaries 1-45. Forty-five small booklets, covering the period 1931-1983 but 1933-1939 are missing. They may have been lost, but it is more probable that they were seized by the police when she was interned in the Satara camp in 1940.

Papers 46-59, arranged chronologically, containing files, documents, paper cuttings, etc., on village uplift, local politics, the State Congress, the Travancore National and Quilon Bank, Christianity in Travancore, the East-West Fellowship, including her correspondence with the Dewan Sir C.P.Ramaswamy Aiyar and other political leaders.

Correspondence 60-70, mainly with family and friends.

Typescripts 71- 78, with drafts of books like *No Elephants for the Maharaja* and *I too was a Jailbird*, about her internment during the war.

Printed Materials 79-92, a collection of books and pamphlets.

Photographs 93-95.

Louise Ouwerkerk, Curriculum Vitae, undated (1984), and *In Memoriam* (1989).

2. Bibliography

(A short list of more recent studies on Travancore and Kerala history)

Baak, Paul E. 1992. "Planters' Lobby in late 19th Century: implications for Travancore", in *Economic and Political Weekly*, XXVII: 33, pp. 1747-1753.

Bayly, Susan. 1989. *Saints, Goddesses and Kings: Muslims and Christians in South Indian Society 1700-1900.* Cambridge: Cambridge University Press.

Chiriyankandath, J.L.1985 "Social Change and the Development of 'Modern' Politics in Travancore: from the late nineteenth century to 1938." unpublished Ph. D. dissertation University of London.

——— 1993. "Communities at the Polls: electoral politics and the mobilization of communal groups in Travancore", *Modern Asian Studies,* 27: 3, pp. 643-665.

Daniel, D. 1985. *Struggle for Responsible Government in Travancore 1938-1947.* Madurai: Raj Publishers.

George, Alex. 1990. *The Militant Phase of Pulaya Movement of South Travancore 1884-1914.* Amsterdam: CASA Werkdocumenten Nr.22

George, K.C. 1975. *Immortal Punnapra Vayalar.* New Delhi: CPI Publ.

Gladstone, J.W. 1984. *Protestant Christianity and People's Movements in Kerala: a study of Christian mass movements in relation to neo-Hindu socio-religious movements in Kerala, 1850-1936.* Trivandrum: The Seminary Publications.

Isaac, T. M.Thomas & P.K.Michael Tharakan. 1986. *An Enquiry into the Historical Roots of Industrial Backwardness of Kerala: a study of the Travancore Region*. Trivandrum: Centre for Development Studies, Working Paper No.215.

Jeffrey, Robin. 1976. *The Decline of Nayar Dominance: Society and Politics in Travancore, 1847-1908*. New Delhi: Vikas.

———1977. "A Sanctified Label: 'Congress' in Travancore Politics, 1938- 48", in D.A.Low (Ed.) *Congress and the Raj: Facets of the Indian struggle 1917-1947*. London: Heinemann.

———(Ed). 1978. *People, Princes and Paramount Power: Society and Politics in the Indian Princely States*. New Delhi: Oxford University Press.

———1981. "Religious Symbolisation of the Transition from Caste to Class: the Temple Entry Movement in Travancore 1860-1940", *Social Compass* XXVIII: 2-3, pp. 269-291.

Joseph, K.V. 1988. *Migration and Economic Development of Kerala*. Delhi: Mittal Publications.

Kooiman, Dick. 1989. *Conversion and Social Equality in India: the London Missionary Society in South Travancore in the 19th century*. New Delhi/Amsterdam:Manohar/Free University Press.

———1993. "Political Rivalry among Religious Communities: a case study of communal reservations in India", in *Economic and Political Weekly*, XXVIII: 7, pp. 287-294.

Kusuman, K.K. 1976. *The Abstention Movement*. Trivandrum: Kerala Historical Society.

Mahadevan, Raman. 1991. "Industrial Entrepreneurship in Princely Travancore: 1930-1947," in S.Bhattacharya (Ed.), *The South Indian Economy: Agrarian change, industrial structure & state policy, c. 1914-47*. New Delhi: Oxford University Press, pp. 159-207.

Mammen, P.M. 1981. *Communism vs. Communalism: A study of the socio- religious communities and political parties in Kerala 1892-1970*. Calcutta: Minerva.

Manor, James. 1978. "The Demise of the Princely Order: a reassessment", in *People, Princes and Paramount Power*. Edited by Robin Jeffrey, pp. 306-329.

Mathew, George. 1989 *Communal Road to a Secular Kerala*. New Delhi: Concept Publishing House.

Nayar, N.S. 1984. *History of Travancore Legislature*. Trivandrum: Kerala Historical Society.

Pandian, M.S.S. 1990. *The Political Economy of Agrarian Change: Nanchilnadu, 1880-1939*. New Delhi: Sage Publications.

Philips, C.H. and Mary D.Wainwright (Eds.). 1970. *The Partition of India: Policies and Perspectives, 1935-1947*. London: George Allen and Unwin.

Rangaswami, Vanaja. 1981. *The Story of Integration: a new interpretation in the context of the democratic movements in the Princely States of Mysore, Travancore and Cochin, 1900-1947*. New Delhi: Manohar.

Saradamoni, K. 1980. *Emergence of a Slave Caste*. New Delhi: People's Publishing House.

Schenk, Hans. 1986. *Views on Alleppey: Socio-historical and socio-spatial perspectives on an industrial port town in Kerala, south India*. Amsterdam: Netherlands Geographical Studies Nr. 4.

Sreedhara Menon, A. 1987. *A Concise Political History of Modern Kerala (1885- 1957)*, Madras: Viswanathan Publisher.

Tharakan, P.K.Michael and George Tharian, K. 1986. "Penetration of Capital into a Traditional Economy: the case of tea plantations in Kerala, 1880-1950," in *Studies in History*, N.S. II:2, pp. 199-229.

Tharamangalam, J. 1984. "The Penetration of Capitalism and Agrarian Change in South-West India, 1901 to 1941: a preliminary analysis," in *Bulletin of Concerned Asian Scholars*, XVI:1, pp. 53-62.

NO ELEPHANTS FOR THE MAHARAJA

PROLOGUE

1938. A great crowd lines the road from the Sri Padmanabhaswami temple, in the heart of the old city of Trivandrum, capital of the ancient Indian State of Travancore, down to the sea beach, a distance of four miles. Its murmurs are muted and hushed, as the head of the religious procession comes into view. Its march is silent; the gorgeous caparisoned elephants, seven of them, move without a sound, the men who make up the procession are barefoot. First come the State Army, dressed in 18th century uniforms and carrying ancient flintlocks of the same century. Their uniforms are a reminder of the fact that in 1729 the Travancoreans won a great victory over a Dutch fleet and captured an Admiral* who, with true Dutch adaptability, took service with his captors and became Captain-General of the army, putting them in European uniforms and training them in European methods of warfare. Next come the high Hindu officials of the State, dressed as for hunting– a white loincloth, a green hunting cap, swords in their hands, barefoot and silent, so as not to disturb the animals in the forest. This procession is in part a commemoration of the old hunting parties which the Maharaja gave twice a year to his officials, which has now changed into a temple ceremony. Last of the officials is a small middle-aged but vigorous man, wearing the sacred thread of the Brahman, balding, the heavy lids half-closed over his eyes, hiding whatever his feelings may be. He is Sir C.P.Ramaswamy Aiyar, K.C.I.E., K.C.S.I., etc., etc., once a member of the Viceroy's Executive Council, Indian representative to the League of Nations, Adviser to the Princes at the Round Table Conference, now Dewan of Travancore. He is followed by a sturdy lad of fourteen, open-faced, grinning with excitement at his first *Arhat* procession, waving irreverently to his European friends on the

---

* Note by the Editor: The "admiral" was Eustach de Lannoy (1715-1777), a French soldier in the service of Dutch East India Company who deserted the Dutch before their defeat at Colachel in 1741.

balconies of the houses along the road. He is the *Elaya Raja*, younger brother of the Maharaja. Then comes a slighter figure, a young man, bareheaded as well as barefooted to show his humility before the great God, wearing only a loincloth but also a great collar of four rows of emeralds and one of diamonds: His Highness Sir Bala Rama Varma, Sri Padmanabhadasa (servant of the god *Padmanabha*), Maharaja of Travancore. He is taking the gods for their twice-yearly bath in the sea. Blood has been shed in the temple where the hunt has taken place and it must be purified. The hunt has taken place in the temple courtyard; a forest of branches was erected in the courtyard and a coconut tied to one of them. With a silver bow and arrow His Highness has shot the coconut; at a range of six inches he has never been known to miss. He is serious, absorbed in his religious duty, but has an occasional twinkle for a friend. The gods follow – small images of them carried shoulder-high by the temple priests in litters laden with jasmine garlands. The procession winds its way to the sea; His Highness sprinkles a few drops of sea water on the images of the gods, then gets into his waiting Rolls-Royce and is driven to his new palace on the hill above the town.

Chapter I

PRINCES AND PEOPLE

Why was the transition from autocracy to democracy in the Native States of India at Independence in 1947 and their integration into the Indian Union achieved so swiftly and easily? The main answer is that the foundations for the change had been laid in earlier popular movements in the states, which were easily suppressed at the time but which threw up leaders who could carry the people with them in effecting the sweeping changes at Independence. These movements were strongest in the more progressive states.

The Native State of Travancore, in the southern most part of India, was one of the most progressive, both in social reform and in political advancement. Long before Independence it had developed representative institutions, though these stopped short of responsible government by a ministry chosen from and responsible to the Legislature on the Westminster model. This is a study of Travancore's social and political changes during a period covering roughly the quarter of a century preceding Independence. It is a story worth the telling for its own sake; it was one of the most fascinating corners of India and the personal story of the chief actors in the drama could provide the theme for a Shakespearian tragedy or a Gilbert and Sullivan opera, according to the point of view of the reader. But it is at the same time a case history of the states showing how local events generated their own popular movements, which merged into the national movement, so that at Independence Travancore swiftly and easily became part of the Indian Union.

I.1 The All-India Framework

To understand the significance of the social and political changes in Travancore, and the impact of British Indian developments on the states, it is important to place local events in their All-India framework.

India under British rule was divided into two: British India, divided into Provinces, which were directly ruled by the British Government of India; and the Native States, directly ruled by their own Princes who were under the suzerainty of the British Paramount Power. They were those parts of India which had not been taken over by the British but had been left under existing rulers who had made their peace with the British. The relation between them and the Paramount Power was essentially one of subordinate alliance.

There were 597 Native States, some ancient, some of recent origin. Some were very big; the largest of them, Hyderabad, was bigger than France; some were only a few hundred acres. They were at varying stages of social progress and political development. Divergent as they were, they had certain things in common: first, their treaties or agreements with the British Power; secondly, the British government assumed responsibility for their external relations and their internal and external defence; thirdly, they were themselves responsible for their internal administration, finance and justice. The British were not concerned with their internal administration, unless there was such gross mismanagement or such crime that British intervention was called for.

In the eyes of the British rulers, British India and Indian India were separate ; but they had a geographical, historical and cultural unity. It was therefore impossible for the people in the Indian States to remain unaffected by what was happening in British India.

I.2 Progress to Self-Government

It had long been the intention of the British to associate Indians more and more with the government as they became more accustomed to Western ways. As early as 1833, in the debate in the British Parliament on the Government of India Act of 1833, Macaulay had said: "Having become instructed in European knowledge, (our Indian subjects) may in some future age demand European institutions. Whenever such a day comes, it will be the proudest day in English history." The more far-seeing realized that India would eventually become self-governing; and with the spread of Western education Indians themselves began to demand a greater share in the government of their country and eventually complete independence. The Indian National Congress, later the spearhead of the Indian national movement, was founded in 1885.

The British policy was one of gradual advance (far too slow for Indian politicians). A summary of the major stages in that advance may be useful in indicating the influences on the people of the Native States.

At the assumption of direct rule by the Crown in 1858, government was purely by officials in a Central Council and the Provincial Councils, which also made the laws. Non-officials were gradually introduced into the Councils. and the first Indians were nominated to them. In 1892 the Councils were made bigger, and representative bodies like Chambers of Commerce, Universities and Landholders' Associations could recommend members for nominations.

In 1908 the Morley-Minto Reforms introduced the principle of direct election, though on a very limited franchise. In 1917 a Declaration by the Secretary of State for India, Mr.E.Montagu, defined the aim of British policy to be "the gradual development of self-governing institutions with a view to the progressive realisation of responsible government in India as an integral part of the British Empire." This was followed by the Montagu-Chelmsford Reforms of 1919, which gave a limited form of responsible government to the Provinces and reformed the Central Legislature, providing for greater participation by Indians at all levels of government. But the Central Executive remained in the hands of the Governor-General and his nominated Council. A review after ten years was promised.

It must be made clear that all these reforms applied only to British India and that the Native States were outside the process of constitutional advance except where the Princes initiated them. But as time went it was recognized that they were also concerned, and the Montagu-Chelmsford Report was the first to discuss their position. This was at the insistence of a group of Princes who had put forward their own views on constitutional progress in British India. The result was the setting up in 1921 of a Chamber of Princes which could provide them with a forum for discussion and the representation of their point of view.

In 1928, well before the ten years were up, pressure from Indian politicians brought about the appointment of the Simon Commission to review the situation. At this time Indian politicians began to assume that they would inherit Paramountcy when India became self-governing, and the Princes became alarmed; they therefore sought legal counsel to affirm what they claimed to be their sovereign rights. But the British Government appointed a committee under Sir Harcourt Butler to examine the issue, and this came down firmly on the side of the British Government and against the Princes' claim to sovereignty. Its viewpoint was summed up in the famous phrase, "Paramountcy must remain paramount." The position of the Princes as one of subordinate alliance was restated. The Princes were however assured that, whatever the form of Government in India, their rights and privileges would be upheld by the Crown.

After protracted negotiations at the two Round Table Conferences of 1930 and 1931, at the first of which the Princes favoured some form of federation between their States and the British Indian Provinces, and the publication of a White Paper by the Joint Select Committee on Indian Constitutional Reforms, the Government of India Act of 1935 finally emerged. The first part, giving full responsible government to the Provinces, came into operation at once. The second part provided for a Federation of the States and the Provinces, which would involve far-reaching changes in the Central Government; this was to come into operation when a sufficient number of Princes had consented to join it.

I.3 The Princes and the Reforms

From the time of the Round Table Conferences, when the issue of federation was first raised, British policy towards the Princes was directed towards the implementation of the federal provisions of what became the Government of India Act of 1935. These provisions envisaged what Sir William Barton called "a delicate balance of forces" by which the conservative elements of the Princes and the Muslims were to be balanced against the more progressive Indian National Congress. The structure of the proposed Federation showed this clearly: although the population of all the states put together was less than a quarter of the whole of India, the states were allotted 104 seats out of 260 in the Central Council and 125 seats out of 375 in the Federal Legislative Assembly. The representatives of the states moreover were to be nominated by the Princes. If therefore the Congress were to capture power at the centre, necessary to achieve that effective independence which they sought, they had either to ally themselves with the conservative Muslim minority (which was proving less and less likely) or to obtain control of the representatives of the states – and this could only be achieved by the institution of popular governments in the States which would control the selection of states' representatives to the Federal Legislature. (It must be added that the population of most of the Indian states was Hindu, as were most of the Princes – so that any popular movement in the states would presumably be mainly Hindu also, and so more than likely to favour the Hindu-dominated Congress.)

If then the British formula for the balance of forces in India was to work, the Princes should remain in control of the nomination of the states' representatives; therefore the development of popular movements in the States, which if successful would lead to some form of democratic selection of the federal representatives, was viewed with alarm and suspicion by the Paramount Power.

And here we have the essential dilemma of British policy in India at that time. Their general policy was one of ever-widening democracy and self-government in British India, but they had of necessity to uphold Princely autocracy in the states against the danger of popular forces capturing real power and sending Congress-oriented representatives to the Central Legislature, thus upsetting the carefully-devised "delicate balance". The British Raj had therefore the complicated task of presenting a somewhat different face to the Princes on one side and to the British Indian politicians on the other. In order to persuade the Princes to join the Federation, they had to reassure them that their treaties with the Crown would remain "inviolate and inviolable"; there would be no intervention in their internal affairs, with the exception of cases of gross misgovernment; on the contrary, the Paramount Power would come to their assistance in case of violent disorder. The Crown Representative (as the Viceroy was called in his relations with the Princes) both in his public utterances and through his agents with the Princes, tried to forestall any intervention by the Congress by continually exhorting them to reform and improve their administrations, and to give their people a greater say by granting them representative institutions. But the Paramount Power would put no pressure on them; the rulers were to be the judges of the extent and timing of any constitutional advance. Finally, the Princes were assured from time to time that under no circumstances would Paramountcy be transferred to any popular government that might be set up in British India.

At the same time the British had to reassure the politicians of British India that they were not upholding black reaction and supporting misgovernment in the Princely States, that after all the traditional forms of Princely rule was indigenous to India and enshrined an important element of Indian culture. It was partly to prevent the Congress "capturing the initiative" in the States by clamouring for long overdue reforms that there was a spate of exhortations to the rulers to mend their ways.

The inauguration of Provincial Autonomy was the beginning of the end for both the British Raj and the Princes. The people of the states observed the greater degree of self-government in the provinces, and asked themselves why they too should not have greater self-government; and this inevitably led to unrest in the states.

Indeed, as early as 1927 a States People's movement had come into being. Its first conference was held in Bombay in December 1927, and a permanent organization was set up. It was not a Congress body, but it was loosely connected with the Congress and individual Congressmen took a leading part in it. From the first it stood for democracy in the states in the form of responsible government under the aegis of the rulers, civil liberties, a federation of the states and the provinces, and an effective voice for the people of the states in the drawing up of any new Constitution for India.

And with the imminent coming of Independence, the pressure from the people of the states, encouraged by the Congress, became overwhelming. It made the accession of the states to the Union, sweeping constitutional reforms, and their eventual absorption in the Union inevitable.

Travancore, then, provides a case history of the changes in the Princely States during the turbulent decades before Independence. In many ways it is not typical (if such a thing as a typical Native State could be said to exist), but nonetheless it provides a study of the impact of changes in the British Indian Provinces upon the social and political life of one of the Princely States.

Chapter II

THE NATIVE STATE OF TRAVANCORE

The former Princely State of Travancore was the southern third of that area of India known to history as Kerala, which now forms the political entity of the Indian Union known as the state of Kerala. The other parts of Kerala were formerly the smaller Princely State of Cochin and the former British Malabar which was part of British India, directly under the control of the Government of India. Travancore itself included to the south a small Tamil-speaking area which was transferred after Independence to the mainly Tamil-speaking state of Tamilnadu.

Kerala is unique. It is unique in its geography and its climate. It is unique in its social structure, in some of its castes and communities which have no exact parallel in any other part of India. It is unique in its language, Malayalam (by far the most difficult of all Indian languages) which is why it became a separate linguistic state in 1951.*

The former Native States of Travancore and Cochin shared that geographical and social uniqueness. For a century-and-a-half before Independence they had a different polity and a different relationship with the British overlords from those of Malabar. The latter was annexed to British India after the wars of the later part of the 18th century and directly administered by the British, first by the East India Company's governmental machinery, and later by the very similar machinery under the Government of India. Travancore and Cochin, however, made treaties with the East India Company and became subordinate allies of the British; so they retained their own Rajas and their form of internal government. In every respect these two Native States were similar. For example, the succession in the ruling families was matriarchal,** not patriarchal; in both the highest caste of Brahmans only permitted the oldest son to marry. Both had a large and

---

* Note by the Editor: In fact, only in 1956 the former Princely States of Travancore and Cochin and the former British district of Malabar were merged in one united linguistic state of Kerala.

** Note by the Editor: Actually, the kinship system was matrilineal more than matriarchal: the line of descent and inheritance was traced along the maternal line, but authority vested in the senior male member of the family.

important community of Syrian Christians who claim that their Brahman ancestors were converted by St. Thomas the Apostle at the beginning of the Christian era.

Both were among the most advanced sections of India as a whole in literacy, college education, the freedom of women. The traditions of their Ruling Houses were similar; they interpreted their duties in the light of the best Hindu traditions, and served their countries for the most part faithfully and well. It must be added that any tendency to tyranny was kept in check by a lively and intelligent feudal class of warriors, the Nayars - and in their last half century, as literacy increased, by a lively press and well-organized popular opinion.

But in the latter years their political and social histories diverged and led to markedly different developments. These differences were due mainly to the different personalities of the rulers and their ministers. While Cochin progressed relatively quietly towards ever greater democratisation under a wise old ruler and an astute but unobtrusive Dewan, Travancore's affairs were, in the crucial two decades before Independence, in the hands of strong and flamboyant personalities, which led to a violent explosion — at least it was "non-violent" in intent and more or less so in fact — which makes the story of Travancore's progress to freedom and democracy of unique interest.

II.1 Geography and Climate

The area which formed the old Princely State of Travancore lies between the mountains of the Western Ghats and the Arabian Sea. It is 174 miles long from North to its southernmost tip at Cape Comorin (now called Kanyakumari), 75 miles wide in the north and 30 miles wide in the south. Its shape has been compared with that of an unpeeled prawn.

It has three geographical regions which lie side by side from north to south in long, narrow strips. To the east lies the almost unbroken barrier of the Western Ghasts, rising in the north to mountains over 8,000 ft. high, and descending in the south in a series of jagged peaks looking like a dinosaur's back to the rocky promontory and islands which form Cape Comorin. There are only three passes through the mountains and they are easily defended; invaders have come round the southern tip of the mountains or through the wider lowlands to the north. This mountain barrier has helped to preserve the uniqueness of Kerala's culture but has by no means prevented cultural influences coming into Kerala from outside or Keralan influences, for that matter, spreading beyond its borders.

The central strip is low country. It is a region of small, rounded hills of varying shapes and sizes, intersected by long narrow valleys and a large number of rivers, mostly small. These valleys are for the most part filled with terraced rice fields, while the slopes of the hills grow tapioca, palms, mangoes, jackfruit, cashew nuts.

The coastal strip is of recent geological origin, consisting of alluvial soil and sand laced with a series of lagoons and lakes which, linked by backwaters and canals, provide almost continuous water transport from north to south. This is the area of fish and coconuts; along practically the whole beach strip are fishermen's huts, while from the very fringes of the beaches to far inland are countless millions of coconut palms.

The climate is tropical tempered by the presence of the sea. It is never very hot and never cold at all (except in the higher mountain areas); Travancore gets two monsoons, the south-west monsoon from June to September, and the less heavy north-west monsoon, coming across the mountains, from October to December. The dry season is relatively short and may itself be broken by thunderstorms. There is therefore abundant water for cultivation throughout the year; rainfall ranges from about 35" per annum in the south to over 200" in the mountains of the north-east. Consequently it is possible to grow two crops a year everywhere — even three in some favoured places.

The Travancore area is rich in natural resources. With its fertile soil, abundant rainfall, and lack of extremes of temperature, agriculture is the most important occupation; rice, tapioca, coconuts, fruits, ginger, pepper, cardamoms are the chief lowland crops; tea grows in the mountains and rubber on the lower slopes and in the lowland country. The country is prosperous; there is little abject poverty, a failure of rains is almost unknown, famine a rarity. If it has occurred in the past, it has been due to the diversion of agriculture from food crops to cash crops which meant that Travancore had to import a large proportion of its food supplies from outside, and any interruption to trade constituted a threat to the food supply.

It has considerable mineral wealth of an unusual kind; its "black sands" are rich in the rarer metals such as ilmenite, thorium, titanium. Of the commoner metals there are only small quantities, but the hydro-electric potential is enormous, and it was already beginning to be exploited in the reign of the last Maharaja. Hydro-electricity is the basis for industrial development, which also became the policy of the Government of Travancore in the thirties.

North-south communications are excellent. I have already mentioned the water communications by lagoon, backwater and canal; later roads and railways were also developed, though the mountains are inevitably a barrier; but about half-way along the Western Ghats is the Shencottah Gap, which has long carried a road, and through which a railway was built towards the end of last century. There is a pass over the mountains in the north which carries a road but is unsuitable for a railway, and towards the dinosaur's tail is the Aramboly Pass, three miles long, which has seen numerous invasions in olden days.

Perhaps the most remarkable feature of Travancore, and indeed of the whole of Kerala, is the absence of villages in the accepted sense of the word. You can describe Kerala either as having no villages or as consisting of one vast scattered village. The villages, such as they are, are slightly denser groupings of houses at crossroads where markets have sprung up. Nowhere (except in the inaccessible mountain areas still inhabited by wild elephants, tigers, leopards and a handful of tribal people) are you away from human habitation and human beings along the roads or in the fields. Let your car get bogged down on the remotest road and in ten minutes a crowd will have materialized to dig it out and build a temporary road surface with branches. Geography is responsible for this phenomenon. There is so much water that there is no need to combine for the purposes of irrigation, as in other parts of India, and each man can have his own assured water supply. The shape of the land is such as to break up the cultivable areas into relatively small units, with some wet land for rice cultivation and some dry land for other crops available for each homestead. The result is that homesteads are separate, each surrounded by its own paddy fields in the long green valleys, coconut groves, tapioca fields on the hillsides, each house standing in a compound surrounded by mud walls, within which grow the mangoes, jack fruit trees, vegetables and spices used by the family.

The social consequences of this physical structure of society are incalculable. Each farming family can live practically independently, supplying the bulk of its own daily needs from its own farm. There are no tight village groupings such as are characteristic of the rest of India. This leads to a lack of social cohesion which is one of the problems of Kerala. The Malayali is above all an individualist, used to going about his business regardless of anybody except the members of his own family, tenacious of his personal rights, quarrelsome, difficult to organize for any continuing purpose. There is a saying in Kerala which may be relevant here, as it certainly is to the main theme of this book:

"Take one Keralan: you have a politician;
Take two Keralans: you have a political party;

Take three Keralans: you have two political parties."

At the same time, geography has had beneficial effects. Life has been easy; very little cultivation will yield an assured and abundant harvest, and the people have had plenty of leisure to develop a very high level of culture. They are distinguished by a great liveliness of intelligence, a keen interest in religion, politics, literary pursuits. No part of India has spawned such an output of newspapers, good, bad and indifferent, or such a large proportion of newspaper readers and listeners; surveys show that every newspaper is read by or read to, an average of ten persons.

For a long time the interests of this lively, intelligent, pugnacious people lay in their own affairs, which usually gave them enough to think about — and if they had no real reasons to quarrel, they invented them. But the time came when they too were swept into the great tides of social reform and political change which were flowing over British India. It was in vain that their local king Canutes* ordered the waves to stand still.

II.2 Origins of the State of Travancore

In ancient times when the gods walked the earth, Parasurama (Rama of the axe) in fulfilment of a vow, stood on Kanyakumari, the southernmost point of India, where the Arabian Sea meets the Bay of Bengal, and threw his axe northwards along the west coast, and the land of Kerala rose out of the sea. Parasurama then brought Brahmans from the north, and gave them the land and the overlordship over the other people who settled there.

So runs the legend of the origin of Kerala. Unquestionably, it enshrines a geological fact, that the coastal strip of Kerala is of very recent geological origin, composed as it is of alluvial soils and sand — whether brought down by the 240 rivers of Kerala or pushed up by some volcanic or seismic disturbance, geologists have not yet agreed. More arguably, it probably contains a germ of historic truth. The highest caste of local Brahmans, the Nambudiris, are both considerable landowners and the chief priests of the local temples, and scholars agree that they had their origins across the Western Ghats. They probably penetrated Kerala before the Christian era, bringing Hinduism with

---

* Note by the Editor: a reference, most probably, to Canute, King of Denmark and Norway, who ruled the waves and conquered large parts of England (11th Century).

them, and established their supremacy over the local people, becoming both the spiritual leaders and considerable landowners.

When Kerala began to emerge from the mists of legend, at the beginning of the Christian era, it formed part of the two bigger empires in South India, those of the Cheras and Pandyas; but these broke up into a number of petty kingdoms perpetually at war with each other. These ancient kingdoms, separated to some extent from the rest of India by the mountains, were nevertheless open to the wide world on their seaward side. Their trade was great; they sent their pepper and spices as far as Rome on one side and China on the other. It was probably from Kerala that Solomon got his ivory, apes and peacocks. Jews fled there from Roman persecution, Christians from persecution in Persia. Arabs later brought Islam. According to a well-authenticated, though unwritten tradition, St. Thomas the Apostle preached the Gospel there in the first century of the Christian era. The Hindu kings welcomed them all, gave them land and charters to trade, and even permitted them to have their own armed forces.

In these petty kingdoms, society was feudal, organized for war and administration. A martial caste, the Nayars, developed, the men of which were trained to the use of arms from the age of seven. The Nambudiri Brahmans undertook this training, and turned their schools into gymnasia for the Nayar boys and youths. The Nayar nobles became feudal barons owing allegiance to the king, and bound to supply the king with troops in time of war; their fighting men in their turn held land on condition of military service. Inevitably, as happened in Europe during its feudal ages, the nobles kept private armies, with which from time to time they could defy the king. The administration was also feudal; the Nayars were organized into territorial groups, largely for revenue collection. These units were based on the number of fighting men they could provide — e.g. such as units of 300 Nayars, or 600 Nayars.

In theory the king was all-powerful; in practice he could be kept in check by his feudal nobles on the one hand and by the people on the other. It was the immemorial right of the people to approach the king directly with their demands and grievances, and stories of great gatherings of people approaching the king abound in Travancore history. A strong king could keep the Nayars in check; a weak king was usually faced with disorder stirred up by these lively and turbulent warriors.

Travancore itself had its origins in a petty kingdom Venad lying to the south of Quilon and stretching to Kanyakumari; it took shape round about the 9th century A.D. The rulers of this kingdom, from whom the ruling family of the later Travancore were descended, claimed descent from the ancient Chera kings; their claim may well be justified, and there is no doubt that theirs was one of the most ancient dynasties in India.

The little kingdom suffered all the vicissitudes of a feudal polity for some nine centuries, during which there were periods of peace and prosperity and also periods of disturbance when the feudal nobles fought with their ruler. From the 16th century onwards a new force entered the complicated politics of Kerala, the traders form the West, the Portuguese, the Dutch, the French, the British. Like the Romans and the Chinese, their chief interest lay in the trade in spices and pepper. It was the British and Dutch in particular who interested themselves in the southern kingdom, which had not only a high output of pepper, ginger and cardamoms, but a number of useful ports.

In the first half of the 18th century a powerful ruler arose; he was Marthanda Varma, founder of modern Travancore, who ruled from 1729 to 1758. When he became Raja, the kingdom had been disturbed by thirty years of clashes between the royal tax-gatherers and the tenants of the temple lands, whose cause was championed by the feudal nobles, who held the real power. But Marthanda Varma was a man of "blood and iron", and he began by engaging mercenaries from the Tamil country to crush the nobles. When he was well established on his throne, he dismissed the mercenaries and built up his own standing army. As we have seen, the fighting men of the area had been Nayars, trained to fight from their youth, but Marthanda Varma included Christians, Muslims and untouchables in the ranks of his army, and won their unquestioned loyalty. He also built up a navy, with which he defeated a Dutch fleet in the battle of Colachel in 1741. A Flemish mercenary, Admiral de Lannoy,* was taken prisoner, and was so well treated by his captors that he took service with them. He eventually became Captain-General of the Travancore army and reorganized it on modern European lines. With this powerful force Marthanda Varma embarked on a career of conquest and enlarged his kingdom to the boundaries it retained until 1949, when it was merged with Cochin on its northern side.

Marthanda Varma paid attention to administrative reforms also. The whole revenue system was overhauled, a proper land settlement made and for the first time in history an annual budget was drawn up.

---

* See Editor's note on page 20.

Customs, excise, the prevention of smuggling, new roads and canals, the rebuilding of palaces, temples, forts, all received his attention. In short, he laid the sound foundations of an efficient administrative system on which his successors built just as soundly.

Perhaps his most remarkable act was the dedication of the State to the deity of the great temple in Trivandrum, *Sri Padmanabha*, in 1750. In a great ceremony in that temple, Marthanda Varma gave his sword of state to the god, and received it back from him in trust. He also transferred all his lands to the deity. He proclaimed himself the servant of the god, *Sri Padmanabhadasa*, henceforth to rule the state— not as his own possession but as vice regent of *Sri Padmanabha*, to whom it now belonged.

It is easy to see this ceremony as a shrewd political move, which placed him and his lands above the control of the erstwhile rebellious nobles and won over the powerful temple priests to his side. This it undoubtedly was; but its effects were more far-reaching than a political manoeuvre. *Sri Padmanabhadasa* became the proudest title of the Rajas; they inherited a tradition of total dedication to the service of Travancore. Their lives were simple, their wants modest, their devotion to duty exemplary; and this tradition persisted until the last Maharaja retired into private life in 1950, lamenting that he could not serve his god and his state to the end. This sense of dedication, so strongly felt by the rulers of Travancore during the two centuries that followed Marthanda Varma's ceremony, is the major reason why Travancore was for long among the best ruled and most prosperous Princely States in the whole of India.

II.3 Relations with the British

The first Englishman to visit the coasts of Kerala was Master Ralph Fitch in 1583, but regular trade with the East India Company did not develop until the middle of the 17th century. In the northern part of Kerala they encountered the hostility of the Dutch, and so turned their attention to the southern part, that is, the area which was to become Travancore. A trade treaty was concluded between the East India Company and Travancore in 1723. Whereby, significantly the East India Company promised to help the Raja in suppressing the turbulent feudal nobles.

It was the invasions of Kerala by the Mysore rulers, Haider Ali and Tipu Sultan, in the latter half of the 18th century, which brought Travancore into closer relations with the English and brought about their eventual subordination to them. The English had their own reasons for checking the aggressions of the Mysore rulers, who were in alliance with the French. When therefore Tipu Sultan marched on Travancore in 1789, the English entered the war on the side of Travancore, and attacked Tipu Sultan's headquarters at Srirangapatam. Tipu Sultan had therefore to withdraw from Kerala which was freed from the invaders. The whole of Kerala was freed; the English brought the northern part of it, which had been administered by Mysore for a quarter of a century, under their direct rule; but they made separate treaties with the rulers of Travancore and Cochin, who thus became subordinate allies.

By the Treaty of 1795 between the East India Company and Travancore, the latter was forced to accept a contingent of Company troops and to pay for their upkeep; at the same time Travancore undertook to have no dealings with other foreign powers and the Company undertook not to interfere in the ruler's internal administration.

But internal disorders changed the situation and led to a second treaty with different terms. The event is worth recording because it threw up a national hero, whose name was on everybody's lips a century-and-a-half later at another crisis; moreover the revolt which he led was one of the earliest examples of a vast popular agitation at which the Travancoreans have been adept ever since.

From 1798 to 1810 Travancore was ruled by a weak Raja, who chose for his advisers three corrupt and unpopular men who proceeded to make private fortunes out of the state. In 1799 one of the Nayar landholders, Velu Thampi, refused to pay the extortionate taxes on his land, collected an army of villagers (who according to one account were joined by some of the Raja's own soldiers), and marched on the capital to demand the dismissal of the three ministers. The Raja sent envoys to hear the people's grievances, but the citizens claimed their ancient right to present them directly to their sovereign master. He was therefore forced to face his people and hear their complaints. Consequently the three rascals were driven out, the heavy taxes remitted, and Velu Thampi himself appointed Dewan.

He was an able administrator but his rule was too strict;the result was a mutiny of the *Raja's* troops which had to be put down with the aid of Company troops from Cochin. This gave the East India Company the opportunity to make a second treaty with Travancore, that of 1805, which governed the relations of Britain with Travancore until the lapse of Paramountcy in 1947.

The terms were somewhat different from those of the Treaty of

1795, and there was an important new clause. The East India Company undertook to defend the Raja and his territory; the Raja in return was to pay an annual subsidy of 8 lakhs of rupees (£ 50,000). He was to have no dealings with foreign powers, nor to employ any foreigners without the consent of the Company.

The main difference lay in the right which the Company obtained of intervention in internal affairs. This was contained in Clause 9, and its exact wording is of interest because it demonstrates how delicately the Company refrained from a blunt statement that the Raja was now subject to them. Paramountcy was left undefined and indeterminate, and could in fact be made to mean whatever the Paramount Power wished it to mean.

"His Highness promises to pay at all times the utmost attention to such advice as the English Government shall occasionally judge it necessary to offer him, with a view to the economy of his finances, the better collection of his revenues, the administration of justice, the encouragement of trade, agriculture and industry, or any other object connected with the advancement of His Highness's interests, the happiness of his people, and the mutual welfare of both States."

In effect, Travancore lost its independence. Its external sovereignty was entirely lost, and it only retained control of its internal affairs so long as its policy met with the approval of its English overlord. A British Resident was stationed at the Raja's court with power of "advice", and the advice was invariably taken.

In the event, the relations between Travancore and the Paramount Power were remarkably pleasant; but there was one flare-up before Travancore settled down to its subordinate position.

The first Resident, Col. Macaulay, who was appointed to both Travancore and Cochin, was an unfortunate choice. He was proud, high-handed and hasty, and was soon at loggerheads with the equally proud Dewan, Velu Thampi. He insisted on the prompt payment of the tribute at a time when the state was in financial difficulties. In 1809 one of the three former unpopular ministers of the Raja was in arrears with his land taxes and Velu Thampi ordered the attachment of some of his lands. Col. Macaulay cancelled the order. Velu Thampi raised the standard of rebellion, and issued a proclamation denouncing the treaty with the East India Company and calling for resistance. At the same time rebellion broke out in Cochin as a result of Col. Macaulay's high-handed actions there. There were widespread disorders; but the British forces were called in and proved too powerful for the rebels, and the rebellion was stamped out. The Raja, who had been inclined to support the rebels, made his peace with the British, and sent his own troops to seek out and capture Velu Thampi. But faced with the certainty of capture, Velu Thampi committed suicide as the troops surrounded the house in which he had taken refuge.

He is now doubly a folk hero: he defended the people against the misrule of the Raja, and raised a rebellion against the British power. Now his statue stands, proud and defiant, in front of the Secretariat in the capital city, Trivandrum.

Travancore soon settled down. The Raja's Nayar army was disbanded and a British subsidiary force undertook the defence of the state. Col. Macaulay was replaced by Col. Munro, who was so able and so popular that he was invited to become the Dewan of Travancore and Cochin as well as their Resident. He introduced a system of administration modelled on that of the British (the very files are bound with red tape of the British kind) and launched Travancore on its career as the model state of India, peaceful, progressive, prosperous, loyal to the British connection.

Even the Nayars settled down, took up modern education and entered the professions. So peaceful was the state that in 1830 the British forces were withdrawn and the Nayar Brigade was revived, this time with British officers. Its functions were mainly ceremonial; there were neither external enemies nor internal rebels to engage its attention. Two years later the British Resident wrote in his report: "That war-like, refractory and turbulent temper for which the Nayars of Travancore were once remarkable has totally disappeared. They are now convinced that their safety depends essentially on the stability, support and friendliness of the British Government."[1] So outstanding was the progress in the state that the British, in recognition, conferred the title of Maharaja on its ruler. This was in 1866.

It was not untill the last decade of the British Raj in India, in the reign of the last Maharaja, that the spirit of Velu Thampi moved again.

II.4 The Social Structure

The history and politics of Travancore (or indeed of post-independence Kerala) cannot be properly understood without a study of the compartmentalization of society into castes and communities.

Society is organized into castes, which are mutually exclusive groups, which are tightly organized by the fact that marriages are arranged within the caste (with some curious exceptions as we shall see). A man is born into his caste, marries within it, brings his children into it, dies in it. It follows that in order to preserve the exclusiveness of the caste his social life is largely spent within it — or was so until western education began to undermine the old institutions. Even the Christians, Muslims and Jews, whatever their religious beliefs, are tightly organized into groups analogous to castes, and these have the same place in the whole structure of society as the castes of the Hindus themselves.

The politics of Travancore in the troubled years from about 1921 were very largely based on these groupings, which either formed political parties like the Muslim League, or formed pressure groups within the non-communal parties like the Congress. But the varying social groups of Kerala are fascinating and worth studying for their own sake. Kerala, for instance, is the only part of India south of the Himalayas where matriarchal groups are to be found; the Syrian Christians also have no counterpart in the rest of India.

The communal problem of Travancore was also totally different from that of British India during the same period. It was not a Hindu-Muslim problem but a Hindu-Christian problem, and never had anything like the acerbity of the British India problem. According to the figures given in the Census of 1931, Hindus formed 62% of the population and Christians 31%, while Muslims were a mere 7%.

Both the Hindus and the Christians were divided into many groups, of which three played the biggest part in the complicated politics of Travancore, namely the Nayars, of whom we have already heard, the Syrian Christians (an ancient community dating back to the early years of the Christian era), and the Ezhavas, an untouchable group which was nonetheless rapidly rising in the social scale and becoming a force in politics. Of these groups the Nayars and Syrian Christians were educationally and economically the most advanced, and the main confrontation was between them, with the Ezhavas moving sometimes towards the Nayars as fellow-Hindus, and sometimes towards the Syrian Christians as fellow-sufferers in their exclusion from the specially favoured position of the caste Hindus.

But I anticipate, and must return to the description of the chief groups which formed the ingredients of this witch's brew of communal disharmony.

Among the Hindus the Brahmans form the apex of the social scale. These are divided into two groups , the larger being the Malayalam-speaking Nambudiri Brahmans who are indigenous, and the smaller the Tamil-speaking Brahmans from across the mountains.

The story of Parasurama probably gives in legend form the

explanation of the origin of the Nambudiri Brahmans as Hindu missionaries from the North, who became spiritual leaders and substantial landowners. This latter characteristic is explained by the fact that much of the land traditionally belonged to the temples which they controlled. Their marriage customs are curious. Only the eldest son is permitted to marry within the caste, to carry on the line. This custom probably derives from the need to keep their large properties intact. Other sons form alliances with the castes below them, usually the Nayars, and the offspring are absorbed into the Nayar community. This is the only Hindu group indigenous to Travancore which traditionally observes *purdah*, understandable when you consider the large number of unmarried women among them.

The Tamil Brahmans constituted a small group in Travancore. They were well-educated, clever and industrious, and first came to assist the Rajas in the administration. Marthanda Varma used them in preference to local people because they were dependent on him and unlikely to side with the troublesome Nayars. His able Dewan Ramayya was a Tamil Brahman. They usually retained their roots in the Tamil country and rarely identified themselves with the local people. Some rose to high positions by intelligence and industry; if they became too important they roused the jealousy of the local people. They were rarely popular.

There was only a handful of Kshatriyas, about 3,000. Most of them were connected with temple worship. A few were relics of the old princely families conquered by Marthanda Varma, claiming descent from the emperors of the ancient Chera dynasty. Some of the Kshatriyas follow the matrilineal system of inheritance.

The Nayars are by far the most important of the Hindu groups of Travancore. Indeed, it is sometimes questioned if they can be called a caste at all. "Nayars were not a caste", writes K.M.Panikkar in his *History of Kerala,* "they were a race. Every kind of caste with varying social pretensions existed among them."[2] They are Dravidians with a considerable admixture of Aryan blood, owing to their close and peculiar association with the Nambudiri Brahmans. One theory of their origin is that they were initially hill dwellers and hunters, but attracted by its fertility, migrated to the low country and became farmers. But the land was easy to work, water supplies from the heavy monsoon rains and the countless rivers were abundant, so they left the actual farming to the women and turned to fighting as their chief occupation and past-time.

The origins of their matriarchal customs are obscure and this theory offers a possible explanation; certainly matriarchy has been a Nayar institution for countless centuries. Property passes, not from father to son but from mother to daughter; the joint family consists of the women of the family living together, and husbands go to their wives' houses to live. But the property is actually administered by the senior male member of the matriarchal family who may be the brother or maternal uncle of the female head of the family but never her husband. In a sense husbands are only visitors to their wives' family houses and have their permanent interest in their own maternal family home. Children therefore under this system are brought up by their uncles rather than their own fathers. The system was women's liberation with a vengeance: divorce was easy; it is said that a woman had only to place the sandals of her former husband's supplanter outside the door and the husband knew that he had to retire. Polyandry was not unknown, though the extent to which it was practised is a matter of dispute among scholars.

Under the stress of modern conditions the pattern of the Nayar family is changing. Professional men tend to live in towns and sometimes to move away from Kerala altogether; they take their wives and children with them, and so the patriarchal family begins to emerge. This tendency became so strong that it was recognized by the Nayar Regulation of 1925, which permitted the break up of the old matriarchal properties, and the substitution of the patrilineal form of inheritance.

But Nayar women have remained free and influential, as they have been through the centuries. They were among the first women in the whole of India to take up western education, and they play a large part in the professions and government service. Even in the old days in the ruling families which followed the matriarchal customs, the senior woman of the family always acted as regent while the ruler was a minor, and these regents were without exception able rulers. Some ruled in their own right, for instance the queens of Quilon and Attingal; and great was the surprise of English and Dutch merchants when they found themselves negotiating trade treaties with bare-bosomed but dignified and capable Indian queens. Though the private army of the Rajas of Travancore was crushed and disbanded after the troubles of the first decade of the 19th century, the martial traditions of the Nayars did not entirely die out. From 1830, when the Raja was again allowed to have his private army, it was composed entirely of Nayars, and remained so as the Nayar Brigade until 1936, when it became the Travancore State Forces, which in turn became a unit of the Indian Army. They regarded the administration of Travancore as almost their own preserve; their ancestors had shared the ruling of the country with the Rajas and they wielded the pen and the typewriter instead of the sword. Whatever they do they will not do manual labour; even those who live on their own farms, however small, employ agricultural labourers of the depressed classes to do the actual hard work for them. Their gymnastic traditions, which in the old days were the foundation of their dexterity with weapons, live on on the tennis court, hockey and football fields.

Nayars are scattered all over Kerala, but in Travancore itself they were chiefly concentrated in the southern portion, in what had been the ancient kingdom of Venad. Trivandrum itself, the old capital, is a Nayar stronghold; and many of the old aristocratic families are still concentrated there.

The problem of defining the "depressed classes" is one that has exercised Census Commissioners for decades. They are "untouchables", yes; but, as pointed out by the Census Commissioner for Travancore in 1931, "untouchability exists not only between the depressed and the non-depressed but also to a certain extent between the different castes of the latter." He suggested that for census purposes the depressed classes could be defined as "those who lack the right to enter temples." As this touches on what became a burning political issue, not only for Travancore but for the whole of India, it is an excellent one for the purpose of a socio-political study.

Chief of the depressed classes of Travancore were the Ezhavas, of whom there were some 870,000 in 1931. The traditional theory of their origin was that they had come to Kerala from Ceylon during the early centuries of Buddhism (i.e. some time before the Christian era) bringing with them the cultivation of the coconut and possibly also the Buddhist religion. To this day they are in the main a farming class who specialize in coconut cultivation and in the crafts connected with it — toddy tapping and the making of toddy (fermented juice of the coconut palm) and the spinning and weaving of coir. Their position as a depressed class has been explained by the supposition that they were comparative late-comers to Kerala and as such had no place in the caste structure. Another theory of their origin is that they were indigenous people who had accepted Buddhism; but when the Brahmans set out to re-establish Hinduism and its caste structure, many people refused to give up Buddhism, and also their habits of eating meat and drinking toddy and other intoxicating drinks frowned upon by the Brahman priests. For these habits they were denounced as unclean, refused the use of the village wells, and driven out of the villages as untouchables. Later, as

Buddhism died out, they became Hindus again but were not fully taken back into the Hindu fold. Dr.Ambedkar, the great leader of the untouchables, put forward this theory as explaining untouchability in the whole of India[3]; and it can be applied to the Ezhavas. In fact they bear a strong resemblance to Nayars both in their appearance and their customs; the majority of them are matriarchal, and in their domestic ways, their cooking, the manner of serving food are practically identical. They too have martial traditions; it is known that Marthanda Varma recruited Ezhavas for his royal army.

The Ezhavas are no longer simply an agricultural community; in spite of opposition from the caste Hindus they have taken up modern education and entered the professions and business. The community has thrown up outstanding leaders; they have long been well-organized and run their own educational institutions and newspapers. By 1930 they were a force to be reckoned with.

There are many other depressed class groups, numbering roughly 900,000 in 1931. Together with the Ezhavas, then, they comprised over half the total number of Hindus in the state, some 35% of the population. But most of the depressed classes, apart from the progressive and well-organized Ezhavas, were agricultural labourers, — the most neglected and poverty-stricken section of the whole population. They were literally untouchable; their touch polluted. Some were unapproachables and there were strict rules about the distance these unapproachables had to keep from members of various Hindu castes. At the bottom of the scale there were even "unseeables", people so low that the mere sight of them involved pollution; they had to move about at night, or if they were obliged to move in the daytime they dared not use a main road and had to hide themselves if caste people came within sight. (Though by the Census definition of 1931 Europeans were depressed classes in that they were debarred from entering Hindu temples, the "unseeables" regarded them as caste people and scuttled away at their approach.)

In the remote forests there were a considerable number of tribal people, probably the remnants of the earliest inhabitants, mostly negrito in type, living primitive lives, hunting, fishing scratching the soil for bare subsistence, some of them building their houses in the trees to be safe from elephants, tigers, leopards and snakes.

The groups were innumerable (the 1931 Census received returns of nearly 500 castes and sub-castes), their gradations and the archaic rules that regulated their relationships all but incredible. No wonder Swami Vivekananda, the great social reformer, who visited Travancore in

1892, exclaimed, "Travancore is a madhouse of castes and communities!"

The Christians, who formed an integral part of the social structure of Travancore, had acquired a little of that particular form of lunacy. In 1931 they formed 31% of the total population, and were rapidly increasing both by conversion and by natural increase. At the 1921 Census they had formed 25% of the population, so that the increase was relative as well as absolute;* and this was one of the facts of political life in Travancore to be borne in mind.

There were three major divisions: the Syrian Christians, the Latin Catholics, and the Protestant Christians.

Of these, the Syrian Christians were by far the most important, in weight of numbers, in antiquity, in their high social position, in wealth, in education, and therefore ultimately in political importance. They formed about 17% of the total population.

There is one, and only one tradition of their origin. The old Syrian families claim that their ancestors were Nambudiri Brahmans who were converted by St. Thomas the Apostle, who arrived in Kerala in 52 A.D. There is a strong tradition that he built seven churches on lands given to him by Nambudiri converts; the sites of these churches are identifiable. (There is a chapel at Niranom, next to the family house of the Elanjikal family, which they claim is on the original site given to St.Thomas by their Nambudiri ancestors.) There are no written records of this early missionary effort; but as there is no other account of their origin, and as it is known that there was a Christian community in Kerala by the second century A.D., there is a high degree of probability that the story is true. It is not inherently improbable; there had been trade relations between the west coast of India and the Middle East for a thousand years previously and there was considerable trade with Rome in the first century of the Christian era. The community was reinforced in the 4th century A.D. by a group of Christians under a Thomas of Cana; and it was this group that introduced Syriac as the language of the liturgy. It is from this connection that the name "Syrian Christian" derives.

The Christians were welcomed by the Hindu kings and were given land and the right to trade; indeed they were given special trading privileges and the right to bear arms and regulate their own affairs. In short they were given a high place in the hierarchy of caste. And for

* Note by the Editor: According to the Census, the proportion of Christians in the population of Travancore was 26,4% in 1911, 29,3% in 1921 and 31,5% in 1931.

centuries they behaved like a Hindu caste. They held to their faith, it is true, but they made no attempt to spread the Gospel. "In order to maintain its own social status, in the midst of a vast Hindu population", write C.P.Mathew and M.M.Thomas in their study of the Indian Churches of St.Thomas, "the community reserved the Gospel to themselves, and did not seek to share it with the downcast, the depressed and oppressed, or to receive converts from among them in their midst. They learnt to look down on lower castes, and to expect the privileges of the Brahmins from whom they claimed descent. Their exclusiveness, their lack of prosyletising zeal, were necessary for survival. It was only in recent years, when under the influence of Western missionary zeal the bolder spirits among them went forth to make converts, that the community was attacked and persecuted."[4]

They were no more united in their faith than are western Christians, and being Malayalis they quarrelled with zest. Many groups arose among them. The Portuguese were responsible for the first great split at the end of the 16th century when they were the dominant influence on the west coast; they tried to force the whole community to submit to Rome and to adopt the Latin rite. Half a century later, however, the bulk of the Syrian Christians rebelled against Roman and Portuguese domination, and swore to return to the Syriac rite and offered their allegiance to the Patriarch of Antioch. Many were later won back to Rome but retained Syriac as their sacred language. They are known as the Romo-Syrians.

Further splits occurred in the 19th century. The strongly evangelical missionaries of the Church Missionary Society, who began work in Travancore in 1814, objected to the elaborate rituals of the orthodox section as savouring of Rome, and tried to win them over to the Anglican communion; a few of them joined it. Later in the century a reform movement arose within the Orthodox Church, reminiscent of the Methodist movement in the Church of England in the 18th century, and this led to another split and the formation of the relatively small but progressive Mar Thoma Church. This group used the vernacular in its services, stressed Bible reading and study, undertook social service, held great revival conventions and most important of all from the point of view of the relations between the communities of Travancore, developed a zeal for preaching the Gospel among the non-Christians.

But whatever deep division they had among themselves, they remained for centuries a very distinctive community. Unlike the Nambudiris, Nayars and Ezhavas who are scattered all over Kerala, they are concentrated mainly in central and northern Travancore and the sister-state of Cochin. The high social position which they claimed was confirmed by the attitude of their Hindu neighbours; for instance, until recently if a Hindu temple had been polluted by the presence of an untouchable, a Syrian Christian priest would be sent for to purify it. Under the influence of the missionaries of the 19th century, the Syrians took up western education, entered the professions, took up planting, business, banking and journalism, and became the most thriving community in Travancore. But the bulk of them have remained farmers.

They might quarrel among themselves; but they united at any threat to their rights and privileges. Let there be any threat to their educational institutions, be it by anti-Christian Hindu or anti-religious Communist, and they spoke with one voice. In political matters they acted as one.

The Latin community is of more recent origin, having begun with the conversions of St.Francis Xavier, who worked particularly among the fishing communities along the coast. They are mostly, though not entirely, from the depressed classes. By the 20th century the Catholic mission was run by Carmelites, mostly Flemish, though a native priesthood and native conventual orders were being rapidly built up. There was among them a handful of highly-educated and influential Anglo-Indian families; their women in particular played a pioneering part in education and medicine.

It is worth observing that more than half of the Christians owed allegiance to Rome, for these included both the Latin Christians and the Roman-Syrians. When their educational institutions were threatened the ensuing rumpus echoed far beyond India.

The Protestant Christians were the result of still more missionary efforts from the beginning of the 19th century. The Church Missionary Society by no means confined its efforts to the Syrian Christian community but made converts among the depressed classes; while the London Missionary Society worked among the depressed classes in south Travancore. It was their work among the very lowly Shanars in south Travancore that sparked off the famous controversy in 1835 about the right of the Shanar women to wear an upper cloth above the waist which Hindus claimed was the right of high caste women only. The Shanar women won the right to dress modestly. It was the first sign of the untouchable worm turning.

There were many smaller groups: the Salvation Army, famous as ever for magnificent medical and social work, Missouri Lutherans, Children of the Assembly of God, and many more. All these worked among the depressed classes and were regarded by some with cynicism; it was said that these poor and underprivileged people only became

Christians for the material advantages they gained — education, jobs, status. But whatever the motives that inspired the converts, their conversion profoundly affected the traditional shape of society as moulded by Hinduism.

In Travancore itself the Muslims were a relatively small number. The original Muslims came as traders from Arabia, who made some converts. They were mostly petty traders and were on the whole backward; indeed their women were very backward and still in *purdah* in the thirties with one or two striking exceptions. But higher education was spreading among them; some were entering the professions and government service, and they were beginning to become politically conscious.

Jews are worth mentioning only as a curious survival from ancient migrations. Tradition has it that some fled from Roman persecution in the first century A D., had been given charters to trade and formed an important trading community. A later wave of refugees, this time from Portuguese persecution, came in the 16th century. The earlier immigrants had acquired the local complexion and were known as the "Black Jews". The later immigrants were fair and known as the "White Jews". By the 20th century they had all but disappeared as the younger people were migrating to Palestine.

It may be observed that there was nothing in the Hindu social structure of Kerala to correspond with the merchant or Vaisya caste. But the role of the merchants was to some extent taken by the Syrian Christians and the Jews, and to a smaller extent by the Muslims.

II. 5 Relations between the Communities

Travancore was always considered a Hindu state; the ruling family and the great majority of the population were Hindus. But for centuries past the Hindu rulers followed a policy of complete toleration. A welcome was given to Christians, Jews and Muslims. They were permitted to practise their religion freely; they were given land for their churches, mosques and synagogues and their burial grounds; they were given charters to trade and to control ports and market places. No obstacle was placed in the way of their making converts if they wished to do so.

Each community was governed by its own moral code based on its religious books. K.M.Panikkar, in his *History of Kerala*, describes Kerala as a "social system of parallel societies." "The Hindu society with local rulers at its head formed the orthodox 'pays legal'. Parallel to it was a Christian society, perhaps not more than five per cent at the time (the 16th century) living under their own bishops around their churches. A small Jewish community. . . lived the life prescribed by the Torah. . . Arab Muslim traders had their warehouses and settlements. A local Muslim community grew up around these settlements."[5]

The good relationship of the various religious groups was to be found not only in the towns, where each group had more or less its own quarter, but also in the villages, where the unique village structure of Kerala helped good relationships. In particular, Hindus and Christians lived interspersed with each other, each extended family living on its own land, but meeting in friendly contact in market places and along the roads. Hindus, as we have seen, borrowed the services of Syrian Christian priests to counteract ritual pollution; Syrian Christians borrowed temple elephants for their religious procession with no sense of incongruity. But caste rules were kept and the Christians kept theirs too; the different groups never ate together, and of course there was no inter-marriage.

Very occasionally there was friction. Caste Hindus disliked Christian converts from depressed classes getting education and giving themselves airs. There occasionally were (and still are) clashes between rival groups of fishermen — Hindus, Christians, Muslims— which took a religious turn. But these were rare occurrences. Travancore has never known a real communal riot.

The communal issue was never serious until recent times. Modern education and social ferment broke the rigidity of Travancore's Hinduised social structure. Different groups became rivals for government posts, and looked to their community organizations to back their demands. Representative institutions developed, and the question of the proper representation of the various groups in the legislature arose to bedevil their inter-relations, and in the course of time became a burning political issue. But behind the tumult and the shouting the communal problem resolved itself into a matter of the loaves and fishes of government posts; and it was almost entirely a matter for the educated urban classes. There was hardly any trouble of a communal kind at the village level, where the old amity prevailed. Above all it was not, in Travancore itself, religious.

The ruling family was the apex of the whole social structure. Their caste position and their relationship with the other castes and religious groups were of great importance.

Their caste position was unique (or almost so; the Cochin ruling family observed the same customs). They were Kshatriyas but matriarchal; the head of the family was not the Raja but a woman, the Senior Rani, in fact there were always two Ranis, the Senior and the Junior. They had their own estate at Attingal, some 25 miles north of Trivandrum, and the Royal Princes were those whose mothers were princesses of the Attingal family. The oldest male member of the family became the Raja who ruled the whole of Travancore, though the Senior Ranis administered the Attingal estate and claimed its revenues as their own right. The Ranis always married into other Kshatriya families; after the conquest of Marthanda Varma they married into the families which had ruled the petty kingdoms which he had added to Travancore.

Whom the Rajas married was not of great importance as their sons had no claim to the throne. The Rajas in fact invariably married Nayar women, usually of the old Trivandrum Nayar families. Their sons were called Thampi (meaning younger brother); they took their mother's caste and were absorbed into the Nayar community.

One important consequence of this custom was that there was a very close association between the ruling family and the Nayar community. The palace officials and servants were almost always Nayars; the relatives of the Raja's consort (she was never termed his wife) could exercise a great influence. This close association was yet another reason, besides their traditional position in the old feudal structure and in the fighting forces, for the predominance of the Nayars in the governing of the country. It was to escape their undue influence that the Rajas, from Marthanda Varma onwards, so often chose Tamil Brahmans for their Dewans.

The last Maharaja, then, in appointing a Tamil Brahman as his Dewan, was only following a well-established custom; and the people, in trying to get rid of him, were also following a well-established precedent. The details of the story are, however, unprecedented.

Chapter III

THE MODERNIZATION OF TRAVANCORE

III.1 Hindu Reforms and Christianity

In Travancore as in British India, the national awakening embraced both social reform and political awakening. They were inseparable, for both flowed from a common source of ideas from the West. The demands for political democracy and national independence were therefore closely linked with the attack on the rigidities of the caste system, especially that of untouchability, the fight for women's freedom, concern for the uplift of the poor, equal opportunities for all.

The West was itself undergoing a great transformation of ideas and institutions in the 19th century. It was the age when the cry of the French Revolution for "Liberty, Equality, Fraternity" was still influencing European thought, when Socialism and Communism were born, the working class movement developed, slaves were liberated and the women's movement began, and Christians began to preach the Gospel in a modern context. In essence the social revolutions of the West proclaimed the dignity of the individual, his right to "life, liberty and the pursuit of happiness", in defiance of all the institutions of Church, State and Society which had once given him his unalterable place in society. One of the basic rights was to live under a government of his own choosing; this involved not only political democracy but nationalism.

It was inevitable that India should be influenced by these ideas. English had become the language of business and administration; education in English was essential to the upper and urban classes. Those who received higher education studied English literature, British history, British law; their minds were moulded by British concepts, superimposed upon their traditional Hindu or Muslim culture. The officials brought essentially English ideas to their administrative and judicial tasks. The missionaries brought the social teachings of the Bible.

It has been said, and with some truth, that the concept of social reform is incompatible with basic Hindu ideas. But Hinduism means so many different things that such a sweeping statement may be rash. However, it is important to examine it at this stage. In the first place, the whole Hindu idea of the transmigration of souls and of *karma* explains why a people so cultured and so kindly could accept the injustices and barbarities of their traditional social system. Secondly, Travancore had remained a museum of ancient customs well into the 20th century, and when the social revolution came it had to blow up great fortresses of rock-hard obscurantism before it triumphed.

We may say that the basic concept of Hinduism, common to all its forms, is that of the individual soul seeking liberation from self and absorption into the All, the ground of all Being, through countless successive lives. Linked with this is the concept of *karma*, the result of one's deeds, running through all these lives until the final release from the prison of the self into the bliss of union with *Brahma*. Good deeds in one life earn a better reincarnation into the next; evil deeds earn a worse reincarnation. For instance, it was traditionally considered that a young wife whose husband dies has deserved her fate because of her evil deeds in a previous incarnation, and by her patient acceptance of her consequent sufferings she is expiating those deeds and earning a better reincarnation. It is this attitude that explains the acceptance of caste inequalities, a certain indifference to poverty and suffering, the lowly position of women. To the strictly orthodox Hindu there is no injustice in such inequalities; indeed, to attempt to put them right would in a sense interfere with the workings of *karma*.

Christianity carried forward the Judaic social gospel but gave it a world-wide relevance. It preached a gospel of love, of service to the poor and unfortunate, of the equal worth of all human beings in the eyes of God here and now, on this earth, to be continued through all eternity, not through the absorption of the individual into the All, but in loving communion between the individual soul and God.[1] It is in essence a revolutionary religion: even before its inception, even before its Founder was born, his mother had sung:

> "He has pulled down princes from their thrones, and exalted the lowly,
> The hungry he has filled with good things, the rich sent empty away." (The Gospel according to Luke 1:52,53)

It is true that for centuries society accepted injustices such as serfdom and slavery and preached resignation to them; but the care for the poor never ceased, and the revolutionary and egalitarian implications were never entirely forgotten. They emerged during the 19th century in the forms of social reform and Christian socialism, and in the social teachings of the Roman Catholic Church. The great missionary movements of the 19th century were in fact part of this awakening.

The missionaries sought out the poor and depressed in India, not only because they were the most easily converted (which was true) but simply because they were poor and depressed and in need of help. To them the gospel of Christ gave a new life and a new dignity, not only in the hereafter but on earth. They could hold up their heads and face their oppressors; they could get education through mission schools, treatment for their diseases in mission hospitals, a better standard of living through mission industries, and through the jobs which their better education made available to them.

The Christian teaching was a challenge to Hinduism, and the best of Hinduism accepted the challenge. Relatively few of the students in the mission high schools and colleges became Christians — the main groups of converts were always from the depressed classes — but even those who could not accept Christ as the unique Saviour were profoundly influenced by His ethical teachings. Mahatma Gandhi himself claimed to have founded his social philosophy on Tolstoy and the Sermon on the Mount.

Hinduism has a genius for renewing itself by absorbing ideas from outside into its many-faceted teachings. A consequence of the challenge of Christian democratic ideas was the emergence of important Hindu reform movements. One such was the Brahmo Samaj movement, a reformed Hindu sect which did not recognize caste, was monotheistic, and devoted much energy to social and educational reform. Its founder, Raja Ram Mohan Roy, was successful in getting the horrible custom of widow-burning abolished in 1829. Another important reform movement was the Ramakrishna Mission, a monastic group which owed much in its organization to the Franciscan Order. While orthodox in many ways, it did not recognize caste, and its monks devoted themselves to social service and education, particularly of the poor. The Theosophical Society, which aimed at a synthesis of all religions, also set its face against caste, and while its appeal was limited to a few, it had considerable influence on the educated classes.

III.2 Social Reform in Travancore

Just as Travancore was the home of the most rigid caste exclusiveness carried to the absurd limits of unapproachability and unseeability, so also it witnessed some of the most dramatic attacks on evil customs. The country was to some extent isolated behind its mountains, and it was some time before the social revolution reached it. One British official, commenting on the caste rioting of 1859, wrote, "The pride and the intolerance of caste prejudice prevails with greater intensity in Travancore than in any other part of India because that province has never come under direct foreign control."[2] Moreover, right through the 19th century Travancore rejoiced in a succession of devoted rulers and able Dewans who were progressive in outlook and brought the state to a degree of advancement unparalleled in British India. But they reformed from the top, and for the most part left the traditional social structures untouched, until there was sufficient clamour for their reform.

That clamour developed in time. The Roman Catholic missionaries worked mainly among the depressed classes everywhere; but they accepted the social structure as it was and did not pose a challenge to the Hindu caste system. The Protestant missionaries began to come in the early 19th century and proved a more disturbing influence. The Church Missionary Society worked in the Syrian Christian districts of the north, where they concerned themselves largely with converting the untouchables, and also with building up schools and colleges teaching in English, which attracted Syrian Christian boys and girls in large numbers. The London Missionary Society worked in the south among the untouchables there; they also built up educational institutions as well as medical work and cottage industries. The new Hindu movements came across the mountains bringing new ideas; the Ramakrishṇa Mission established houses in a few places in the early years of this century, and there were a few members of the Theosophical Society. But it was the general tide of change, reform and revolution which swept in from British India into the state. It was the most advanced part of India in English education, and the ideas which were changing the country across the mountains began to change Travancore also. It threw up its own reforming leaders, such as Sri Narayana Guru, the Ezhava leader, and Abraham Malpan of the reformed branch of the Syrian Christian Church. In the 20th century Gandhian ideas of social and political revolution made their impact in course of time. When the social and political revolutionary movements came to a head in the thirties of this century, the upheaval was all the more violent and dramatic for having been delayed. The local revolution joined the national revolution, and those who tried to stem the flood were swept away.

The first mutterings of the great storms which abolished untouchability were heard not long after the London Missionary Society opened up a mission at Nagercoil in the south of Travancore in 1816. They worked particularly among the Shanars a caste of toddy tappers closely related to the Ezhavas. Hitherto the women of the untouchable classes by ancient custom wore nothing above the waist; but the Christian converts began to cover their bosoms with jackets. The Hindu Shanar women understandably began to copy them, but the caste people objected so violently that in 1829 the Rani Regent issued an order forbidding "the wearing of cloths on their bosoms as do the Nayar women." Thirty year later the agitation was renewed; serious riots occurred in which the caste people burnt mission schools, chapels and some huts of the Shanars, and troops had to be sent to quell the disturbances. There were other grievances: the Travancore Durbar had abolished slavery in 1853, which deprived the land-holders of free and subservient labour, and the Christian converts refused to work on Sundays. The Raja was an enlighted man, and issued a proclamation "abolishing all rules prohibiting the covering of the upper parts of the person of Shanar women, with the simple restriction, that they do not imitate the same mode of dress that appertains to the higher classes." It was the first victory in long war.[3]

But the salvation of the untouchables of Travancore was to come from one of their own number, a man whose life and work are one of the glories of Travancore history, Sri Narayana Guru. He was born in 1854 of an Ezhava family and was highly educated, even taking higher studies in Sanskrit. (Sanskrit is the sacred language which traditionally only Brahmans were permitted to learn — it was a sin for an untouchable even to hear it, let alone learn it.) He became a wandering ascetic, seeking enlightenment, and after some years settled on the bank of a river not far from Trivandrum, where the villagers brought him food, happy that a holy man had chosen to live among them. It was there that he had a great mystical experience, of that ultimate union which all Hindu devotees seek. But, like the Buddha millenia before him, the effect of his experience was to send him back into the world he had left, to concern himself with the needs of those around him. He became a practical reformer, a great founder of institutions, a propagandist for a better way of life for the poor. His central inspiration remained religious; he was primarily concerned with the purification of Hinduism, the abolition of superstition and evil practices, the abolition of caste. His battle cry was always "One God, one religion, one caste." He fought for the simplification of temple worship, the abolition of animal sacrifice. He also campaigned against drunkenness, took an interest in diet reform, preached greater cleanliness of one's person and surroundings. (His pet aversion was spitting.) He founded schools, reading rooms, temples without idols, hospitals. He organized a band of *sanyasis* for social service.

The effects of his activities were felt mainly by his own community. In 1902 an association for the propagation of the principles of *Sri* Narayana was founded - the Sri Narayana Dharma Paripad Yogam, universally known as the S.N.D.P. Yogam. It was meant for all, but it attracted chiefly those who were suffering from religious and social disabilities, and within a short time, contrary to the intentions of its founder, it became the exclusive organ of the Ezhava people, who turned it into a powerful weapon in their fight for the removal of their disabilities and the promotion of their communal interests.

Sri Narayana Guru died in 1928. Towards the end of his life he took part in a conference of all religions at Alwaye, performed the marriage ceremony of an Ezhava young man with an English girl in the teeth of the criticism of the older men and women, helped to found an Ezhava women's association in Trivandrum devoted to social work among women and children, and gave his blessing to the Vaikom satyagraha. He lived to see his people move into the modern age well-organized, progressive, ready to fight for equality of status with the caste Hindus. They were to become a powerful political force whom caste Hindus had to learn to respect. Sri Narayana Guru must be reckoned one of the founders not only of the Ezhava movement for equality, but of the whole of modern India.

The right to enter temples and worship in them was the crux of the fight for equality of the untouchables with the caste people. If an untouchable entered a temple, according to long-established custom, it was polluted and unfit for the worship of the gods, and had to be purified with elaborate and costly ceremonies. So powerful was the grip of the Hindu caste system and the appeal of Hindu ideas that relatively few untouchables left Hinduism altogether to become Christians or Muslims or Sikhs or Buddhists, all of which groups rejected caste. Some solved the problem, as had Sri Narayana Guru, by setting up their own temples served by their own priests: you found them in the outcaste quarter of the villages, along the roadside, in the forests, in the appalling stinking tenements in the industrial cities into which this religious apartheid herded the outcaste factory workers.

The question assumed political overtones. In a country in which the voters were grouped according to their religious affiliations, every matter of religion became bedevilled by politics. In the Hindu-Muslim struggle going on in British India, it was important for the caste Hindus to be able to count on the sixty million untouchables (scheduled castes became the polite name for them), as part of their voting strength.* But how could they be so reckoned when they were not considered fit to worship in the Hindu temples? And so a mixture of motives, a deep and sincere concern for the rights of the underprivileged, mixed with shrewd political calculation, moved Mahatma Gandhi to make temple entry one of the main planks of his socio-political platform. It was to have its repercussions on Travancore, although at no time was the complex communal problem of Travancore further complicated by communal electorates as such .

Travancore had its own problems. The prohibition related not only to the temples but to the very approach roads surrounding the temples. Christians, Muslims, cows, goats and dogs could use these roads, but not the untouchables.[4]

The right of Christians to use the roads round temples had been fought for and won as early as 1886, in a small and forgotten incident. In southern Travancore a Christian wedding procession had passed close to a temple, the local police had stopped it and the bridegroom had been beaten up. The Christians, who were converts from the Nadar (Shanar) caste, petitioned the Resident, who inquired of the Dewan, who received a report from a local official describing the Christians as of low caste. The Resident's comments were freezing: "Now whether or not according to Hindoo religious tenets, contact between classes or castes may cause pollution to one or other of those castes, it would not do to permit such a doctrine to be admitted as a State policy so as to debar Christians or any other class of the population from using public ways, or exercising any right open to other classes of the people. . ." "I could not admit," he added, "that Her Majesty the Empress or any person holding the Christian faith should be called 'low' caste because of the religion they hold."[5] The British lion had given a small roar; Christians continued to use the roads to the temples.

In 1923 a leading Ezhava, T.K.Madhavan, attended the Cocanada session of the Indian National Congress with the special aim of interesting Gandhi in the untouchables of Travancore. The following year the battle was joined for the right of the untouchable Hindus to use

* Note by the Editor: The argument is correct, but it should be borne in mind that under the India Act of 1935 the franchise based on property qualifications was extended from 2.8% to 11% of the population only.

the roads round the temple at Vaikom in north Travancore. This was the famous Vaikom satyagraha, and Gandhian methods were adopted. The satyagraha was initiated by caste Hindus, but supported by hundreds of volunteers of all castes. For twenty months the agitation was kept up; volunteers fasted before the temple, caste Hindus brought outcastes with them onto the forbidden roads; a great *jatha* (demonstration march) of the caste Hindus from Vaikom to Trivandrum was led by the founder of the Nayar Service Society, Mannath Padmanabhan, to place the demand before the Maharani Regent. Gandhi himself came to Trivandrum to plead the cause of the untouchables with the Regent, and it was his intervention that finally secured the victory. At first it applied only to Vaikom, but within the next four years the approach to temples all over Travancore was thrown open to Hindus irrespective of caste.

There are two points of interest, in the light of subsequent developments, which are worthy of comment at this stage. The first is that, unlike so many "civil disobedience" movements, the whole agitation was strictly non-violent from start to finish. C.F.Andrews, who came to see for himself, commented that the satyagrahis did not even break the barriers which the police set up; they patiently squatted outside them in all weather. The absence of violence was probably due to the careful selection of the demonstrators: educated caste Hindus and Harijans who defied the police orders in small numbers. It was mass civil disobedience which almost always degenerated into violence after the leaders had been jailed for breaking the laws; news of arrests caused mob violence and there were no powerful leaders to control it.

The second point of interest is the misinterpretation of the events of the Vaikom satyagraha by the Political Department. Sir William Barton's book, *The Princes of India* gives a very inaccurate account of the whole affair. Apparently unaware that it was a leading Ezhava, inspired by Sri Narayana Guru, who had initiated the agitation, he writes: "It was typical of Mr. Gandhi's methods that he should have chosen Travancore, a stronghold of caste, as the stage for his first massed attack on untouchability. The Civil Disobedience led to serious rioting, but ultimately the Government gained control of the situation." The usual Fortnightly Confidential Reports from the Resident to the Political Department give no accounts of riots — only that at one religious festival "there might have been serious trouble but for the tact and resourcefulness shown by the Police Commissioner."[6] Presumably peaceful disobedience to government orders looked like serious rioting to a member of the Political Service; but it was the Maharani Regent who gave way, and the whole episode was regarded locally as a victory for everybody except the obscurantists.

The Vaikom satyagraha is rightly regarded as a turning point in the emancipation of the Harijans (children of God), as Gandhi was now calling them. It was recognized as the preliminary step towards the major objective of opening the temples to the untouchables, an objective which was to be achieved after a further struggle of more than a decade. But for Travancore itself it was much more: it was the first step which the people of Travancore took towards joining the national movement. There had been great public excitement about the struggle, and all castes and communities joined in — even the Syrian Christians caught the excitement and a few became Gandhians. It was the first time that Gandhi had visited Travancore; and although the mass of the people were still pretty contented under their traditional rulers, his visit and his successful intervention in what had started as a local dispute had an important impact upon Travancoreans.

The Vaikom satyagraha was the combined effort of all the Hindu communities (with some unscheduled help from Christians); but most of the social reform of Hinduism was carried out by numerous community organizations. In the circumstances of Kerala this was inevitable: the social structure with its rigid caste and sub-caste divisions practically forced reformers to begin with their own group. Moreover, each group had its own peculiar problems of harmful social customs which had to be solved before its members could look beyond.

The Nayars were of course the most numerous and also the most influential of the caste Hindu groups. But they were hampered by ancient customs, such as the ruinous expenses of marriage ceremonies. The ancient matriarchal system also was not working well. It had been acceptable in the days when most people were static on their own land, and produced nearly all their own requirements from it. With the growth of urban civilization, western education, entry of Nayars into the professions and administrative services, there was a growth in mobility, and men moving to jobs tended to take their wives and children with them. Consequently the family unit — certainly in the towns — grew to be the nuclear partiarchal family of father-mother-children, and not the old one of the female relations together with their husbands and children, looked after by the *karanavan*, the oldest male member of the matriarchal family. Another difficulty was the division of the whole caste into a large number of sub-castes (the 1901 Census Report lists 116) with little social contacts and no inter-marriage.

Leaders of the community realized the need for reform, and began to form special Nayar associations. In 1914 a young Nayar schoolteacher, actor and playwright, Mannath Padmanabha Pillai, formed the Nayar Service Society, pledged to serve the community as a whole and the Nayars in particular. It was to become the main association of the Nayars, and he himself was to dominate it for half a century. Whatever the original intentions of its founder, it was in the main a frankly communal organization for Nayar interests. It played a large part in improving the education of Nayars, founding many schools and colleges. It attacked the division of the community into sub-castes — only three were listed in the Census Report of 1931. Mannath himself had a wide vision of the well-being of Hinduism as a whole; it was his concern over the loss to Hinduism of converts to Christianity that led him to take a prominent part in the Vaikom satyagraha. He was not however a Gandhian, and was in general opposed to Congress, until the final struggle in 1947 when all differences were dropped to fight that final battle for democracy and freedom for Travancore within the Indian Union.

The Nayar Service Society also brought a change in the laws regarding marriage and inheritance. A prolonged agitation brought about the passing of the Nayar Regulations of 1925, which permitted the break-up of the old joint matriarchal family properties, and deprived nephews of any claim to the property of their uncles. It also made polygamy illegal. A similar Act was passed to reform the marriage and property laws of the Ezhavas, which had also followed the matriarchal system of inheritance.

The Nambudiri community, although by far the most conservative group in the complex social structure of Kerala, were also affected by the desire for social change. The younger male family members in particular wanted the right to marry into their own community, and as early as 1908 a *Yogakshima* (Union) was formed to agitate for the reform of their marriage customs, the abolition of *purdah* among Nambudiri women, and the promotion of English education. It was a long time, however, before these reforms took effect.

Even the lowest untouchables, the "unapproachables" and the "unseeables", began to clamour for equality. The Pulayas had a tradition that they once ruled Travancore, but had been reduced by successive waves of invaders to unskilled agricultural labourers, slaves and serfs of the caste people. They too produced a twentieth-century leader, Ayyankali, who founded an untouchables' union on the model of the S.N.D.P. Yogam with branches all over the state. Its main achievement was to win the right of Pulayas to use the public roads; it also promoted education of the lowest classes and took a share in the agitation for temple entry.

All religions as well as groups of Hindus were affected by the new currents. The Muslims of Travancore were a relatively small and backward community, their women in *purdah*, their standard of education low; but they too began to work for social reform and the promotion of English education. Their great reformer, Abdul Khadi Maulavi, was himself a scholar learned in Arabic, Persian and Urdu; he urged his co-religionists not only to become better Muslims but to join all progressive movements. He founded a number of journals to propagate his ideas. He founded the Travancore Muslim Mahajana Sabha, on the same model as the S.N.D.P. Yogam and the Nayar Service Society.

The Census of 1931 summed up the reform movement: "Most of them (i.e. the communities) have organized associations on caste or communal lines for the betterment of their social, economic, religious or political conditions. At present there is hardly any caste or community in the State without an association of its own for self-advancement in the social and political spheres."

As long as these associations confined themselves to social, religious and economic reforms they deserved nothing but praise, and the good they achieved in these spheres is immeasurable. But the drawback lay in the political sphere. These organizations had the unfortunate effect of sharpening communal consciousness; for instance, the movement started by Sri Narayana Guru for the uplift of all was narrowed down to the uplift of the Ezhava community. In the political sphere they created antagonistic organizations designed to improve social conditions which were used to secure sectional advantages — it might be a share of the loaves and fishes of government posts; it might be special representation in the legislative bodies; it might be land for schools and colleges, special educational grants, special fee concessions or scholarships reserved for backward communities. So ultimately these well-intentioned communal organizations contributed to the growth of communal tension which bedevilled public life in the twenties and thirties.

In discussing social reforms among the Christians of Travancore, we must always draw a distinction between the ancient Syrian Christian community and the communities formed by more recent missionary endeavours.

Among the more recent converts, it might well be said that the Churches themselves constituted the organizations for social reform. The foreign missionaries were after all the chief carriers of the new ideas; they gave the Gospel to their converts, the bulk of them poor and outcaste, and the Gospel in itself gave them new concepts of their own human dignity. The missionaries also brought them education and medical services (though these were of course open to all, Christian and non-Christian alike); they promoted cottage industries which raised them above starvation level; the Y.M.C.A. under the great Rural Extension Secretary, Spencer Hatch promoted a programme of rural reconstruction aimed specifically at "the poorest, the lowliest and the lost".

Associations for men, women, children, proliferated. Some were purely religious: the Children of Mary, the Bible study groups, Women's Fellowship, Mothers' Unions. In time groups developed which were more directed to social problems: the Y.M.C.A., the Y.W.C.A., the Catholic Young Men's Society. The Student Christian Movement with its full-time paid secretaries was a particularly lively body.

The Latin Catholics were most easy to organize, well-disciplined as they were under their parish priests and bishops. When Margaret Sanger came to Trivandrum in 1935 preaching birth control, the Catholic women were organized by the formidable Miss Watts literally overnight. Woe betide any reformer, Hindu or communist, who touched their parish schools! The potential for a fiercely communal group in the political sense was there.

The position of the Syrian Christians was of course completely different. They could be described as a caste which happened to have Christianity as their personal religion; they considered themselves to be a high caste, and were accepted as such by their Hindu neighbours. Like the high-caste Hindus they accepted the whole caste structure — they kept the rules of untouchability and unapproachability. Their different sects resembled the sub-castes of the Nayars; there was no social intercourse or inter-marriage between them. They regarded the Church as identical with the Syrian Christian community and made no effort to preach the Gospel to the heathen around them. This socially exclusive casteism and lack of missionary zeal were mutually dependent. It was in a sense the condition of their survival among the far more numerous and powerful Hindus of Kerala.

The impetus for change came first from the missionaries of the Church Missionary Society. They brought with them not only Evangelical devotion to the Scriptures and aversion from elaborate rituals, but Evangelical fervour for social improvement. They made converts among the untouchables whom the caste-ridden Syrians had neglected for centuries. They set up printing presses and translated the Bible into Malayalam. They founded schools and colleges using English as the medium of instruction and Syrian boys and girls flocked to them in large numbers. The reforming Mar Thoma Church took up the work of social reform. Above all it was missionary-minded. The Mar Thoma Evangelical Association, founded in 1888, undertook missionary work among the untouchables, especially in central Travancore where the Mar Thoma sect was the strongest and converted several thousands. The converts were however organized in separate churches, known euphemistically as "the new churches," and had to worship apart. The Romo-Syrians, who also began to work among the outcastes in the 19th century, found a different solution; their converts attended the old caste churches but – rain or shine – had to sit outside, where the priests brought them their Communion. These caste practices were fiercely attacked by the younger generation in the 20th century, as they came under the influence of Gandhian ideas, and integrated services became more common. But the caste divisions only finally disappeared after Independence, when the Constitution of India made the practice of untouchability in any shape or form an offence.

Not content with preaching the Gospel in their own area, the Mar Thoma sect began to look across the mountains. In 1905 the National Missionary Society was founded in Serampore in Bengal, to lay upon Indian shoulders the task of evangelizing India, and the Mar Thomas Association cooperated with it. A number of missionary centres were established outside Travancore; now they go as far afield as Nepal. In course of time other branches of the Syrian Church took up extended mission work; there are Syrian missions even in Thailand.

Progressive Syrian Christians' interest in the outcastes extended beyond winning converts among them. They developed an interest in their material welfare. The Union Christian College, a joint venture of the different sects of the Syrians, founded the Alwaye Settlement for work among the rural poor, enlisting the services of the College students. The Oollannore Rural Reconstruction Institute, which lifted a whole rural district out of abject poverty, was founded by a Syrian Christian, though it served all communities. Gandhi's compaign against untouchability, and particularly the Vaikom satyagraha of 1924, in an area where the Syrian Christians formed a large proportion of the population, constituted a challenge. "It was in this context that groups of Syrian Christians in Kerala (though not the Syrian Churches as a whole) awoke to their responsibility to participate in movements of political, economic and social liberation, and made attempts to relate this sense of social responsibility to the dynamic of the Christian Gospel. . . . Several young leaders of the Syrian Church became spiritually challenged by Gandhi's combination of religion, nationalist politics, social passion and the techniques of non-violence."[7]

Down to the political tornado of 1938, however, the bulk of the Syrian Christian community remained inward-looking, hardly touched by the wider vision which was challenging the young leaders. When it came to defending their sectional interests against rival groups, they could be as fiercely communalist as those other groups.

The beginnings of an Industrial Revolution in Travancore called forth a corresponding labour movement. The chief source of production of goods was that of cottage industries; but by the twenties there was a modest development of factory industry in the coastal towns of Alleppey and Quilon, along the sandy littoral where coconut palms grew in millions. The major activity of these small factories was the manufacture of coir mats and matting; a textile mill also started up in Quilon and saw mills and tile factories also developed.

The workers were mostly Ezhavas, who were untouchables and poor; and in Alleppey there were also numbers of poor Muslims. There was another group of poor workers whom it proved easy to organize: these were the boatmen who poled the great canoes along the backwaters between Quilon and Ernakulam in Cochin state - their centre also was Alleppey. All these workers were badly paid and worked very long hours.

Like the trade union movement in Britain, in which the social activities of the Methodist Church played so large a part, the trade union movement of Travancore had a religious origin. The S.N.D.P. Yogam, which worked for the uplift of poor Ezhavas everywhere, organized the first Travancore Labour Association in 1922. Its founder, P.K.Bava, was an Ezhava, and a bright young Ezhava lawyer, V.K.Velayudhan, became its first General Secretary. By 1926, when it first attracted the attention of the press, it had 800 members, not all Ezhavas however; it ran a night school and reading room, and an employment bureau.

On May 26th the All-Travancore Labour Conference was held in Quilon. Its president was a prominent Ezhava Congressman, T.K. Madhavan; it was he who had drawn Gandhi's attention to the plight of the untouchables of Travancore at the Cocanada Congress in 1923. Over 1,000 attended and the proceedings opened with prayer. Resolutions were passed demanding the introduction of an eight-hour day, that employers should provide schools for their workers' children, that all workers should join the Association. There were political resolutions also, demanding universal franchise and special representation of labour in the Legislative Council and the Popular Assembly.[8]

The movement spread and attracted workers of all communities. It doubled its numbers in four years, and its demands became more specific. By 1930 it was demanding, as well as higher wages, improved factory conditions and a complete overhaul of factory legislation.

The soil of Travancore was ripe for a labour movement. Literacy was higher among the factory workers of Travancore than anywhere else in India with the possible exception of Bombay, and each literate worker read out his half-*anna* newspaper to a group of illiterate fellow-workers. The efficient organization of the S.N.D.P. Yogam had awakened social consciousness among the poor factory workers and boat crewmen; they rapidly became politically conscious also.

III.3 Constitutional Developments

Travancore was the pioneer in constitutional developments among the Indian states, as it had been in the promotion of English education; and it was profoundly influenced by the constitutional developments in British India.

But there was not, until after Independence, any break with tradition. For by tradition the ruler was the source of all power in the state, and this tradition had been confirmed and strengthened by the action of Marthanda Varma in dedicating the state to the god Sri Padmanabha.. The *gaddi* (throne) was surrounded by an aura of sanctity; the Raja was regarded as the Vice-Regent of the Deity, and any action against him was regarded as close to sacrilege. The practice grew up that the Raja ruled through a Dewan, who was the head of the administration and took full responsibility for all government actions. In important matters he sought the formal sanction of the ruler, and even this was not directly given by the ruler himself but conveyed by his Private Secretary. The convention grew up that the ruler never withheld his sanction; but of course private discussions had preceded the formal application for the ruler's sanction to government measure. So strong was the tradition that the ruler stood above the actual business of administration, that although his consent to the carrying out of a death sentence was necessary, the death warrant was always signed by a special palace official, so that the wrath of the gods would not fall on the Raja.

The ruler was also the fountain of justice. By tradition he was the supreme judge and lawgiver. By tradition also, Hindu law, as set out in the ancient Hindu law books, was applied to all his subjects regardless of their personal religion. But in the course of the 19th century a separate judiciary modelled on that of British India was developed. A High Court was set up in 1834, the Judges being appointed by the ruler. The Travancore High Court gained a very high reputation for learning, integrity and independence. The laws were also modified to meet modern conditions. Col. Munro had introduced law-making by proclamation; for instance, a proclamation was issued in his time exempting Syrian Christians and recent converts from temple service. With the introduction of the new courts, new legal codes were drawn up, again modelled — sometimes word for word — on the legal codes of British India. (It is an interesting point, however, that in this land where women were freer than anywhere else in India, they were exempt from the death penalty.)

The system was autocratic, but by no means tyrannical. The rulers, profoundly influenced by their dedication to Sri Padmanabha, hard-working, simple in their habits, were responsive to the feelings and wishes of their people. The ancient right of the people to have direct access to the ruler to lay their petitions and grievances before him was a living tradition, and we have seen how Velu Thampi had drawn on it in 1798 when he led the people to petition for the removal of the corrupt and unpopular advisers to the ruler.

In the 19th century English education and the development of modern vehicles of communication changed the method but not the spirit of this traditional freedom. English was made the language of the administration in 1855, and this gave an additional impetus to the learning of English. A lively local press in both Malayalam and English developed. Travancore became a nation of newspaper readers — and hearers. Debate on government actions was open and vigorous, and the Travancoreans early developed the art of agitation through the press, the public platform, the formation of pressure groups, and the presenting of petitions. "The great national indoor sport of Travancore", commented Dr.G.D.Nokes, the Public Service Commissioner, in 1936, "is the holding of public meetings."

The government set limits, of course. In 1881 three students were expelled from the Maharaja's College for publishing articles criticizing the administration. One of them, G.Parameswaran Pillai, fled to Madras and became an outstanding journalist and social reformer. But the limits were not tightly drawn, and the time was becoming ripe for the development of institutions through which this lively political consciousness could be guided into constructive channels.

In 1885 the year in which the Indian National Congress was founded, a young man ascended the *gaddi* of Travancore who was destined to guide the country through vast changes in the course of a reign of nearly forty years. He is usually known as Sri Mulam Thirunal (Travancore rulers were sometimes referred to by their personal names, such as Marthaṇda Varma, sometimes by the names of their guiding stars.) In later years he was always referred to as the "old" Maharaja in contrast to the "young" Maharaja who succeeded him in 1924 at the age of twelve. Sri Mulam Thirunal combined strict religious orthodoxy with progressive views. The Resident, reporting approvingly of him shortly after his accession, wrote: "He is fond of European society, dances quadrilles and such-like dances with European ladies, and joins in lawn tennis. . . He is decidedly intelligent and possesses very good commonsense. In my opinion he is likely to prove an excellent ruler."[9]

One of the earliest results of the new Maharaja's sound sense was the institution of the Legislative Council in 1888. Such Councils existed in British India but Travancore was the second Native State to copy them (Mysore had instituted one in 1881).* The Maharaja realized the need for a closer association of the people with the government. Since the insurrection of 1809 the last vestiges of the old popular bodies had been removed; the Dewans were all "foreigners" in the eyes of the people, the old customs were dying out, and new laws were necessary to deal with the new ways of thinking and living.

The new Legislative Council consisted of eight members, six officials and two non-officials, all nominated by the Maharaja. The Dewan had wanted only official members but the Maharaja overruled him. His Highness included a Christian, hoping to forestall criticism — one Mr. Frank Watts, a Eurasian—but the criticism of inadequate representation of Christians was voiced nonetheless. The Council's functions were strictly limited to the tendering of advice and the drawing up of draft legislation for submission to His Highness. Its members were increased to 15 by a law which the Council itself had passed; but it remained a nominated body, in spite of frequent requests for at least some elected element.

Consequently, whatever its value (and it was great) the council was not a channel for the voicing of popular demands. But these rapidly developed in the next decade. In 1891 the Malayalee Memorial,

* Note by the Editor: The Mysore Council actually dated from 1892.

organized by the irrepressible G.Parameswaran Pillai, and signed by more than 10,000 persons of all communities was presented to the Maharaja. Their chief complaint was "the denial to the Malayalees of a fair share in the Government of the country and their systematic exclusion from the higher grades of the service." The country had been ruled by foreign Dewans (as Tamilians were reckoned foreign), and these had "regularly and systematically without exception introduced their relatives, castemen and friends into the State." The complaint had been voiced before; it was to be voiced again with far greater emphasis. The Maharaja sent a soothing reply conveyed to the petitioners by the Dewan: His Highness would be happy to consider natives for the higher posts but he had also to consider educational and other qualifications, and there was an advantage in recruiting from beyond the borders of the state in obtaining a wider view. What he diplomatically refrained from saying was that an outsider stood free of the communal problem in the state. The agitation died down.

But is was an important step forward. It was the first of a series of popular agitations organized by the educated classes. It was particularly important because all communities joined in; there was nothing communal about it. "It was," remarks R.Ramakrishnan Nair, "the first political expression of a new class—the middle class growing in strength in society."[10]

In 1896 an even bigger Memorial, signed by over 13,000 Ezhavas, was presented to the Maharaja. Under the inspiration of Sri Narayana Guru, and impelled by their own energy and determination, the Ezhavas were struggling upwards, but they suffered great disabilities. They were denied entry into government schools and colleges. A particularly scandalous case was that of the first Ezhava to qualify as a doctor, Dr. Palpu, who had been refused a post in the Travancore Medical Service, and went to Mysore where there were no restrictions against him. He returned to organize the Ezhava Memorial. It petitioned the Maharaja to confer on the Ezhavas the same rights and privileges as those of their caste who had become Christians. The Maharaja retained his orthodox attitude, and the Memorial had no immediate effect.

In 1904 the Maharaja set up an institution, unique in India, of which the purpose was to acquaint the government with the people's wishes. This was the Sri Mulam Popular Assembly. It consisted of 100 members, whose only powers were to put questions to the Durbar, each member being allowed two questions. The members were not at first directly elected, but were nominated by various bodies, heads of districts, municipalities, certain representative associations. The government nominated ten members. The Dewan presided and heads of government departments answered questions concerning their own department. It had no law-making powers and no control over the administration, and was known among the irreverent as "the monkey-house" because it did nothing but chatter. But it did good work in bringing the needs of the people before the government; roads and bridges, hospitals and schools were built as a result of members' questions; discriminative actions against backward communities were brought to light. The personal contact between government and people, for which it had been established, was effectively achieved.

From the first the Assembly wanted more powers. It very soon got the right to elect four members of the Legislative Council, and itself became an elected body, though on a high franchise which favoured the property-owning high-caste Hindus. In 1914, in a confidential note to the Resident, the then Dewan (himself a Tamil Brahman) commented on the disproportionate number of Nayar members who dominated the Assembley; the Christians, Ezhavas and Muslims were complaining of this and he saw a danger that these dissatisfied communities might join together to secure the redress of their grievances.[11] It was a prescient comment.

The big changes introduced in British India by the Government of India Act of 1919, by which partial self-government was introduced in the British provinces, had their inevitable repercussions on the politically conscious state of Travancore. The Maharaja issued a proclamation reforming the Legislative Council. The numbers were increased to 25, 11 of whom were to be non-officials and 8 were to be elected. The franchise qualifications were high and the elected members would represent the propertied classes in the state.

The organs of public opinion went into action at once. There was criticism in the press and on the public platform; a memorandum was drawn up and a deputation, representative of all communities, waited on the Dewan. The agitation was organized by a leading Nayar lawyer, Changanacherry Parameswaran Pillai — we shall hear more of him as a great social reformer and Congressman. The chief complaint was that the measure did not go far enough, not nearly as far as the reforms in British India. The elected element was still in a minority; the powers of the Council were still restricted to legislation. The lawyers criticized the method of promulgation of the reforms by proclamation instead of by legislative action of the Council itself, as had been the case with earlier reforms; they put forward the argument that the very establishment of a Legislative Council was a "permanent delegation of legislative authority by the Sovereign." On this point the Dewan firmly rebuked the petitioners; he emphasized "the ancient and undoubted right of the Sovereign to make laws concurrently with, or in supersession of, any passed by him when submitted by a non-sovereign legislature like our Legislative Council."[12] Put simply, the Council had no real rights and the Maharaja in the last analysis, remained all-powerful. The petitioners went away dissatisfied.

Nonetheless, another Regulation, that of 1921, was promulgated by proclamation, far in advance of the Regulation of 1919. It closely followed the Government of India Act of 1919 as it applied to the Provinces. A Council of 50 members was to be set up; there were to be 28 elected and 22 nominated members, of whom seven were to be non-officials. The Council's rights were extended: it could discuss and vote on the budget, it obtained rights of interpellation and of moving resolutions; in short, it obtained the right of criticizing the administration. But the Dewan was still its president; there were provisions for certifying the budget if it was thrown out by the council; questions and motions could be ruled out of order. The Maharaja's right of legislation by proclamation remained untouched. The executive remained independent of the Legislature.

This Regulation could not be promulgated without the consent of the British. At that time the southern states came under the control of the Government of Madras (they were transferred to the direct control of the Political Department of the Government of India in 1923); so the Dewan had to approach the Governor of Madras through the Resident to the Madras State, and the Governor of Madras had to signify his approval.

Mr. H.M.Burkitt, the Resident, gave a strong recommendation for its acceptance.[13] He considered that the people of Travancore were the most advanced in India (with the exception of those of Cochin) in respect of literacy, higher education and culture; moreover "practically every member of the intelligentsia is politically-minded." If the people of British India are qualified for a big measure of political advance, those of Travancore are ten times as well qualified. The reforms in British India are having a profound effect; there is discontent because they know that they are better qualified for reform than British Indian subjects.

He next considers the position of the ruler: His powers remain intact. His position is strengthened by the existence of a communal problem: the Christians and Ezhavas are at variance with the predominent Hindu caste, the Nayars. "To put the matter crudely, the sovereignty of the ruler is secured by the factions among the people, rendering any combination directed against the Durbar improbable in the extreme." It was a delicate phrasing of the policy of 'Divide and rule.' As regards the Paramount Power, he envisages no difference. In any case communal factions will cause the people to wish for a continuance of the ultimate control of the Paramount Power.

The Regulation was discussed in Madras by the Governor's Council. They endorsed Mr.Burkitt's recommendation; the Law Member commented that while substantial concessions had been given "the position and prerogatives of His Highness are amply safeguarded." The Governor passed an order that there was "no objection" to the proposed reforms, and they were duly enshrined in a proclamation and became law.

There are a number of points to be noted about the whole process introducing these reforms. First, at no time did the Maharaja give away the essence of power. Secondly, it was the concern of the Political Department and of the Government of Madras that he should not do so. The great confrontation with the Indian National Congress had hardly begun, and it certainly was not yet affecting relations with the states; but the later federation policy, in which the Princes were to be built up as a counterweight to the Congress, was already faintly outlined. Thirdly, the Travancore Durbar, internally sovereign, had yet to obtain the consent of the British government before making constitutional changes. This remained true even down to 1946, shortly before Independence, when that great constitutional lawyer, Sir C.P.Ramaswamy Aiyar, submitted his "American Model" constitution for Travancore to the Political Department before proceeding with it.

Finally, the people were never satisfied with what they were given. Sri Mulam Thirunal, instituting his Legislative Council in 1888, was setting up an institution far in advance of his time. He could not have foreseen that he had launched Travancore on that slippery slope which, everywhere in the British Empire and the Commonwealth was to lead ineluctably from nomination to election, on an ever-widening franchise, from there to the demand for full legislative power, control over the budget, control over the executive, until finally full responsible government based on adult franchise is achieved. A great many king Canutes were to be overwhelmed on the way.

III.4 The Regency

Sri Mulam Thirunal died in 1924. The new Maharaja, Sri Chitra Thirunal, destined to be the last Maharaja of Travancore, was twelve years old when he mounted the *gaddi*, and was invested with full ruling power in 1931, just before his nineteenth birthday. As was the centuries-old custom in matriarchal ruling families, the Senior Maharani became the Regent.

The seven years' Regency was a transition period between the mostly calm and happy reign of the "old" Maharaja and the stormy years of the "young" Maharaja's reign. On the whole the Regency partook of the happy, peaceful character of the previous reign, but storms were blowing up, presaging those great storms that were to sweep away the ruling family of Travancore altogether.

The storm-centre was the relationship between the Senior and Junior Princesses. The old Maharaja had no sisters, and so he adopted two children from a collateral branch of the family as his nieces, and they became the Senior Maharani and Junior Maharani. They were first cousins, the Junior was two years younger than the Senior, and they were brought up together by a remarkable Eurasian woman, Miss Doris Watts (daughter of Frank Watts, who had been the first Christian to hold the post of Chief Secretary to the Government) as their tutor. Miss Watts was a staunch but broad-minded Catholic and she did her best to instill solid principles and a progressive and tolerant outlook in the minds of her royal pupils. They turned out entirely different.

Now there was a legend that, centuries ago, a beggar had approached the palace when the two little princesses of the ruling family were playing in the garden, and begged for food. The Senior Princess laughed at him but the Junior Princess brought him food. So he cursed the Senior and blessed the Junior, and prophesied that all Senior Princesses would bear only daughters from henceforth, but the Junior Princesses would bear sons and thus become the mothers of Rajas. And so it turned out generation after generation.[14] Our Senior Maharani had only daughters, the Junior Maharani had two sons and a daughter. Her son therefore became the Maharaja, and her daughter, married off quickly before the Senior's daughters could be married, bore a son who was third in succession to the *gaddi*. Here was the cause of tension. The Senior became Regent by right. But the Junior felt that, as mother of the Maharaja, she should have been appointed Regent, or at least a Council of Regency should have been appointed of which she would be a member.

Another cause of tension was the Maharani Regent's apparent preference for Christians. To everyone's astonishment she appointed Miss Watts' brother Maurice as Dewan. He was the first non-Hindu Dewan to be appointed since Colonel Munro — and a despised Eurasian at that! He was even more able than his sister, and was an excellent administrator. The Regent also appointed a Syrian Christian as Chief Secretary to Government. The fat was in the fire. The Junior Maharani turned to the Hindus for support, particularly the Nayars, who had expected to get the plums of government office for themselves. She enlisted the help of one of India's ablest lawyers, Sir C.P.Ramaswamy Aiyar, to draw up petitions and memoranda with which she bombarded the Viceroy. All they achieved was that the Regency was shortened by a year, and Maurice Watts fell a victim to the intrigues of the caste Hindus.

The Regency, in spite of the mutterings of storm, was a constructive period and also a period of social reform. Her Highness began by dealing with the Vaikom satyagraha. The marriage and inheritance laws of the Nayars and Ezhavas were reformed. The *Devadasi* (temple prostitutes) system was abolished, as were animal sacrifice in the state temples. Miss Watts, enthusiastically backed by the Regent and her own brother, founded the Women's Degree College and started the Trivandrum branch of the All-India Women's Conference.

Her Highness earned the unstinted love and respect of her people. Maurice Watts, opening the 1928 session of the Sri Mulam Popular Assembly could speak with complete sincerity of 'Tranquil Travancore.' "Set in the centre is our Maharani, radiating wisdom, courage, goodness and a warm love for her people. Her Highness rules. And so a blessing rests on this land."[15]

Chapter IV

THE COMMUNAL PROBLEM IN POLITICS

The year 1931 was a turning point in the history of Travancore, as indeed it was for all the Princely states. The Round Table Conference had brought the question of a federation between the states and the British India provinces to the forefront of discussions on the future of India, and the Princes were henceforth committed to dealing with British India and British Indian politicians in a totally new way. And in 1931 the reign of the last Maharaja of Travancore began.

IV.1 The Last Maharaja and the Triumvirate

On 6 November 1931, His Highness Bala Rama Varma, Sri Chitra Thirunal, descendant of the ancient Chera dynasty, servant of the god Sri Padmanabhaswami, before a distinguished assembly, was invested with ruling powers by Lt. Col. Pritchard, the Agent to the Governor-General, representing the Viceroy. Colonel Pritchard read out the Viceroy's proclamation of recognition and investiture, the Maharani Regent formally renounced control of the administration of the state and passed quietly out of the assembly, and the new Maharaja formally assumed his ruling powers. He made his first speech as Maharaja immediately after, pulling the paper out of the pocket of his cloth-of-gold coat with a boyish grin and reading it with a clear but expressionless voice.[1]

The speech contained all the expected sentiments, respects to the Viceroy and Lady Willingdon, tributes to his aunt the Maharani Regent, his intention to devote himself to the service of his people. But it also contained two announcements of great importance. Having referred to the "far-reaching political and constitutional changes now being debated on", he announced: "In view of these developments I have decided to avail myself of the services of Sir C.P. Ramaswamy Aiyar, who is a trusted friend of my family, as my legal and constitutional adviser." Even that well-bred and well-schooled assembly gasped. After paying a tribute to his mother, "whose watchful solicitude and unparalleled devotion" to him would always be available to help him in his task, he announced that the Sri Mulam Popular Assembly was to be placed on a statutory basis with enlarged powers and functions.[2] His Highness had begun his reign by calmly announcing that he had sown a crop of dragons' teeth.

For nearly the whole of Sri Chitra Thirunal's reign, three people shared power: the Maharaja himself, his mother and Sir C.P.Ramaswamy Aiyar, who was Legal and Constitutional Adviser from 1931 to 1936, and Dewan from 1936 until his sudden and ignominious departure from the state in July 1947, three weeks before Independence.[3]

His Highness was a charming boy, an excellent tennis player, and a delightful host at his tennis parties which he ran himself, full of a quiet sense of humour. He was sincerely and deeply religious, and scrupulous in the performance of his many ceremonial duties as the servant of the tutelary deity of his family Sri Padmanabhaswami. But he was so closely associated with his mother that he could never be said to express any opinion of his own; asked his opinion out of the blue, he evaded an answer until he had "thought it over". He never married.

The Junior Maharani (or "The Maharani of Travancore" as she later came to be called), was a woman of keen intelligence, wide interests, restless energy and boundless ambition. It was a tragedy that she was a Princess, and a Junior Princess at that, for her position continually frustrated her. She was married as a child to a shy and retiring scholarly Prince of the right family whose chief interest was Sanskrit, who had no social graces and no wish to acquire them. She wanted to travel, to meet intelligent and interesting people, to shine in the new mixed society of cultured progressive India that was now developing. Inevitably they separated and she led her own life, having a gay time in the hill stations and taking the little Maharaja with her. That her quiet, retiring and orthodox cousin became Regent was a bitter blow to her, that she won the love and respect of her people was still more bitter. When her son was invested with ruling powers she determined to exercise power in the background, and like a more amiable Catherine de Medici, to rule through her son. This was fully recognized by the local people; it was to the Maharani they went for favours, for jobs or promotions for themselves and their relatives. Inevitably she was surrounded by sycophants and flatterers who warped her judgement. She was capable of far better things. When the Yuvarani* of Mysore (who still kept *purdah*) refused to preside over the 1935 session of the All-India

* Note by the Editor: Yuvarani lit. means a junior queen.

Women's Conference at Trivandrum, because we refused to provide *purdah* arrangements for her, the Junior Maharani offered to take her place, and performed her functions with such enthusiasm, efficiency tact and good sense that we were immensely proud of her.[4] Had she been free of her position, she would have been a tower of strength to the women's movement in India.

What can one say of Sir C.P.Ramaswamy Aiyar, that complex and fascinating character? He was to dominate Travancore for sixteen years. What manner of man was he?

Like Napoleon a small man, he was yet larger than life. His outstanding characteristic was his brilliance of intellect; a rapier-keen mind, prodigious learning, an incredible ability in marshalling facts and deploying arguments, brilliance in oratory and conversation, made him India's outstanding constitutional lawyer. Born in 1879 and educated in Madras, he was drawn into nationalist politics as a young man; at one time he and Jawaharlal Nehru were joint secretaries of the Indian National Congress. But he differed sharply from Gandhi's politics of non-cooperation, and left the Congress in 1921 to become an ornament of the Indian Liberal Party. The Willingdons (Lord Willingdon was then Governor of Madras) befriended him and he became Advocate-General of Madras. The remainder of his career until Independence was spent in the orbit of the British rulers of India. At the same time he interested himself in the problems of the Princely States, spoke for some of them at the Butler Committee sessions, and was Chairman of a committee appointed by the Chamber of Princes in 1933 to consider the proposed constitutional changes. He held one distinguished post after another—Indian representative at the League of Nations, member of the Viceroy's Executive Council in 1932. An Indian could not rise higher. Yet in 1936 he left the scene of all-India politics to become Dewan of a state at the remote southernmost tip of India, far away from the centres of power.

There was much speculation about his motives. Some said he had ruined himself financially (for he was extravagant) and had come to recoup his fortunes. Some said it was his devotion to the ruling family, developed when he was helping the Junior Maharani in her intrigues against the Regent, which brought him so far south. A few shrewd observers said that he saw in the ancient Syrian Christian community the greatest force for the conversion of India to Christianity (for the foreign missionaries could be swept away after Independence) and therefore the greatest threat to Brahman domination, and he had come to Travancore to crush them. It might be however that he was attracted by the prospect of almost unlimited power which service in a Native State offered, untrammelled by British superiors who would always be above him in British India; moreover as a representative of an Indian State he could progress to even greater power at the centre when Federation came, as come it must.

Whatever his motives, it was power that attracted him. He had not only a brilliant intellect, but outstanding administrative ability. But he had to dominate; criticism, opposition, infuriated him. He had a supreme contempt, which he did not trouble to conceal, for the people of Travancore; he saw them as responding only to the meanest motives. They could be manipulated, flattered, bribed, bullied, threatened. He did not believe that any of them had integrity, honour, or the capacity to suffer and sacrifice for higher ends. He was puzzled, baffled, infuriated when he met steadfastness in his opponents and always looked for their ulterior motives, which he could somehow use for his own ends. His enemies he pursued with vindictive hatred; no strategem was too crooked, no lie too gross, to bring them down. Yet, when he was defeated by some enemy, he bore no malice but acclaimed him as his "good friend."

"In friendship false, implacable in hate,
Resolv'd to Ruin or to Rule the State."

He was alleged to be corrupt, but of this there is no proof; the Resident, Mr. C.P. (later Sir Clarmont) Skrine, went into the question thoroughly in 1938 and concluded that he was above corruption - his lust was for power, not money.[5]

Above all he was a Brahman with all the virtues and faults of the Brahman—an immense pride, a profound sense of the importance of the spiritual, a sensitiveness to beauty, and a conviction that the Brahman, if not born to rule (for that was the caste function of the Kshatriya) at the least was born to influence men's minds and lives, to be the power behind the throne. He reminded me of nothing so much as a Renaissance Cardinal. And when he was confronted with men who demanded responsible government in the state and the ending of his own authority, he reacted like a Renaissance Cardinal confronted with democratically-minded Calvinists.

And yet he had immense charm—a width and depth of culture, a knowledge of several languages and their literature, a keen enjoyment of the cut and thrust of witty conversation. He had an ugly reputation as a womaniser, which may have been somewhat undeserved; for he took a Shavian delight in the company of lively women intelligent enough to appreciate his brilliance, and had a number of platonic friendships with such women. Among his close women friends he counted Mrs. Annie Besant, Lady Willingdon, and of course the Junior Maharani of Travancore. He was the perfect dinner partner.

Into this complex character were woven two threads of pure gold. One was his deep and sincere devotion to the Hindu religion. He cared passionately for its teachings and for its purification from the corruption that had grown round it. In his later years he became not only personally deeply religious but tolerant of all religions, even of Christianity, against which he had once waged war. The other, of great political importance, was his unshakable devotion to those he had elected to serve—the ruling family of Travancore—and to his own immediate family and immediate circle of friends and dependants. However false he might be to those he used for his own ends, whatever motives had impelled him to take service with them, he remained true to the task he had undertaken to serve the Maharaja and Maharani of Travancore. He was not a free agent: he supported their policies—even those that were foolish and impracticable, he announced them as his own—defended them, worked them out, took the blame for what went wrong, braved the storms of hatred and calumny and threats to his life. He was indeed a "daring pilot in extremity". At no time, either at the height of his power or after his fall, did he cast the blame for disastrous policies where it belonged.

"His honour rooted in dishonour stood,
And faith unfaithful kept him falsely true."

Sir C.P.'s appointment as Legal and Constitutional Adviser was unpopular from the start. A group of Trivandrum Nayars at once organized a meeting to protest against the appointment; he was denounced as an unprincipled adventurer out to exploit the state. It was asked why such an appointment was necessary when in other states the Dewans were performing his work along with their administrative duties; and why he should draw a salary of Rs. 72,000 a year (about £5,000) for a part-time post which was double that of the Dewan.[6] As time went on he became more and more unpopular, as it became clear that he was interfering in internal matters that were outside his province, and indeed that he and the Maharani were running the state while the Maharaja stayed in the background and the Dewan was almost out of the picture.

The Dewans could not stand it; the Maharaja had three Dewans in the first five years of his reign. The Dewan who had served the Maharani Regent, a local Brahman, retired soon after the investiture. Sir C.P. suggested to Lord Willingdon, then Viceroy, that a British

I.C.S. officer from Madras, who would know something of the local problems but stand free of them, should be appointed. Mr. Thomas (later Sir Thomas) Austin I.C.S. was appointed early in 1932 on a two-year contract. When he had thankfully returned to Madras, Sir Mohammed Habibullah, a distinguished Muslim with long service in British India, was brought in largely to deal with the growing communal problem. He too was broken by the continual intrigue and interference from Sir C.P., and in July 1936 offered his resignation.

The Political Department busied itself about finding a successor. By Article 9 of the Treaty of 1805 the Travancore Durbar had to consult the Resident who in his turn would consult the Political Department in Delhi before he would advise on the appointment of a new Dewan, which advice he was bound to accept. The officers of the Political Department were discussing finding some other appointment for Sir C. P. so that he could sever his connection with Travancore and a Dewan with some authority could be established.[7] But by the end of August the Maharaja informed the Resident that he had decided on the appointment of Sir C.P. "in view especially of the forthcoming discussions regarding Federation". The Political Department was solidly against the selection and the Resident was instructed to remind His Highness of his obligations under the Treaty of 1805. But on September 10th the official announcement of his appointment was published, without any consultation with the Political Department, and Sir C.P. took charge as Dewan on October 1st.

There was no protest meeting; he was all-powerful now. Instead, a public meeting was organized to welcome him, a terrific *tamasha*[*] with two bands playing at once and fireworks. After outlining his policies for the state, he declared he would have no mercy on communalism, corruption and administrative delays; and his enemies cringed before him.[8]

IV.2 The Development of the Communal Problem

It was universally recoginzed that the communal problem was the most serious facing the young Maharaja; and it was to dominate politics for some seven years after his assumption of ruling powers. It is appropriate therefore at this point to examine it more fully than I have done hitherto.

---

[*] Note by the Editor: a *tamasha* is a spectacular and elaborate public celebration.

His Highness Rama Varma, Maharaja of Travancore in his riding costume. Reproduced with permission, from *The Madras States Directory 1930,* Cochin: Pearl Press 1930, the British Library, Oriental and India Office Collections.

His Highness Setu Lakshmi Bai, Maharani Regent of Travancore.
Reproduced with permission, from *The Madras States Directory, 1930*,
Cochin: Pearl Press 1930, the British Library, Oriental and
India Office Collections.

The communal problem of Travancore was unique in India, except for the very similar problem in the sister state of Cochin, which had a very similar social structure. In the greater part of India it was a Hindu-Muslim problem, centuries old, based on deep religious differences, expressing itself from time to time in bloody communal riots and leading to political divisions so irreconcilable that only superhuman wisdom could have averted the partition of India.

Not so the problem of Travancore and Cochin. It was not religious. Over the centuries the people of the different religious groups had lived amicably in their "parallel societies". If there were religious disputes they were amiable discussions among intellectuals, a dialogue rather than a confrontation. Communal troubles do not, and never did, touch the mass of the people.

Nor was the communal problem Hindu-Muslim as in the rest of India; it was rather Hindu-Christian, or more accurately a question of the privileged caste Hindus opposed to the underprivileged groups of the Christians, the Muslims and the depressed classes, chiefly the progressive but still untouchable Ezhavas. It was a question of status, and religion only came into the question as an adjunct to status.

The privileged position of the high caste Hindus, the Nayars and Brahmans, was a matter of history; Travancore was after all a Hindu state, with a Hindu ruler whose functions were bound up with the Hindu religion. Its original area in the southern part of Travancore was predominantly Nayar. Although the old feudal system had been finally broken after the rebellion of Velu Thampi in 1809, the Nayars retained their dominant position; but the Rajas brought in Brahmans from the Tamil country, largely to counterbalance the Nayars. In the palace the Raja was surrounded by Nayars; the servants, the administrative staff, his aides-de-camp, were almost without exception Nayar.

Another preserve of the caste Hindus was the Nayar Brigade; the Nayars had traditionally fought the Raja's wars, (when they were not fighting against him); and when the force was reconstructed in 1830, it was once more the preserve of the Nayars. Their duties for the ensuing century were largely ceremonial and included temple duties, which could be undertaken only by caste Hindus.

Colonel Munro, who was the Dewan-Resident in the early years of the 19th century, unwittingly contributed to the later communal problem, by what seemed a wise measure at the time. The Hindu temples were in the hands of trustees who had often been centres of Nayar disaffection; the temples were very wealthy, owning large areas of the land, and many of them were mismanaged. In 1812 therefore the government took over the management of several hundred temples, and a Temple Management Department, known as the *Devaswom* Department, was set up. Since the temples owned most of the land of the State, the *Devaswom* Department was combined with the Land Revenue Department, and the temple accounts were merged with the State accounts. Traditionally, all over India, the Revenue Department collectors of the land revenue were also the administrative heads of districts, and this system was adopted in Travancore. Obviously only caste Hindus could manage temples; consequently only caste Hindus held responsible posts in the district administration, and could expect to be promoted to the higher posts in the Secretariat. And since there was no system of open competition by examination for any posts whatever, and administrative heads appointed their own subordinates, Hindus held every kind of post from Revenue Commissioner to messengers and night watchmen.

There were two major reasons why this position, accepted as a matter of course in Colonel Munro's day, became intolerable in the course of the 19th century. One was the rise of the oppressed lower classes and their demand for equal status. The other was the conquest of central and north Travancore by Marthanda Varma. By so doing he added to the population a very large number of Syrian Christians. This community, progressive, well-educated, roughly equal in number to the Nayars, and just as conscious of its position as a high caste, was bound in the course of time to claim its share of the privileges of the caste Hindus.

In the 19th century the problem had been mainly one of the fight of the oppressed classes for recognition. The Shanar riots were caused, not so much by the objections of the caste Hindus to the actual change of religion of their helot classes, as to their consequent claims to a higher status. In the 20th century, as has been pointed out by the Communist leader, E.M.S.Nambudiripad, the character of the conflict changed. "The conflict of the post-1921 years," he writes, "had the character of conflicts between the upper class elements of various castes for their respective share in government jobs and other spoils of office."[9]

There were two aspects of this problem. One was the direct problem of the "loaves and fishes" of government jobs, to which E.M.S Nambudiripad refers; the other was the question of representation of the different communities in the legislative bodies of Travancore. This was closely bound up with the loaves and fishes aspect, as regrettably most legislators were more concerned with serving the interests of their community than in legislating for the welfare of the country as a whole.

It was only slowly that the deprived communities began to be introduced into the public services. Christians however were numerous in the medical and educational services, because of their advanced education; Christian women were pioneers in both fields. The "old" Maharaja had appointed Francis Watts as Chief Secretary to Government, and this appears to have roused no antagonism. The chief battle was of course for the administrative posts in the combined Land Revenue and *Devaswon* Department. In 1921 a combination of Christians, Ezhavas and Muslims submitted a memorial to the Maharaja putting forward their claims to a reasonable share of government posts. As a result, a Government Committee was set up which recommended the formation of a separate *Devaswom* Department; this was done in 1922, so that it was now possible for Christians and other communities to join the Land Revenue Department.[10] But of course the caste Hindus were well-entrenched in all its grades, and it would take a long time and much agitation to achieve an equitable distribution of the loaves and fishes of government posts among all the communities.

The opening of the Nayar Brigade to all communities was done more easily, and was not the subject of much agitation, though entry into the armed forces was always mentioned in the agitations. In 1936 the Travancore Army was integrated into the Indian Army and renamed the Travancore State Forces; cadet officers were recruited from all communities, from the Brahmans to the Ezhava, on a strict basis of merit as a result of a public examination; and a third battalion was started for which recruitment was opened to all communities. But the first two battalions were still called the Nayar Infantry, were composed only of Nayars and were available for temple duties.

The Nayar influence in the palace, however, remained as strong as ever.

IV.3 The Legislature

It may well be asked: if the Legislature had very little real power, why did the various communities attach so much importance to adequate representation in it? The answer is that it was at once a form of agitation and a base for influence in the capital. The comment in 1933, of the Joint Political Congress, a body composed of Christians, Ezhavas and Muslims, is relevant to the whole history of representative bodies from their inception: "Communalism is so strong and deep-rooted that a community which has not its own champions in the representative institutions in the country can hardly hope to have its claims satisfied and its disabilities removed or to protect itself against the communal aggressiveness of others."[11]

The predominance of the caste Hindus in the Legislature was an old problem. In 1891 the Resident, reporting to the Governor of Madras, wrote: "The Native Christian Community which comprises one fifth of the population have complained that they are quite unrepresented."[12] The same complaint was voiced about the Sri Mulam Popular Assembly; in 1911 the native Christians had only one representative in it although they were 26% of the population. There were no Ezhavas at all. In a confidential report the Dewan forecast an alliance of the disgruntled communities of Christians, Ezhavas and Muslims against the Nayars.

Under the Constitution of 1921, the problem became even more acute. The reason for the Nayar predominance were clear: the rules governing elections. Wearyingly complex in detail, their effect in giving the Nayars predominance can be simply explained. First, the franchise was based on a land tax, and the Nayars had the largest number of holdings. Secondly, they were favoured by the delimitation of constituencies, which were based for administrative convenience, on existing revenue divisions. As the Nayars were widely distributed all over the state, they could, given their advantageous franchise, secure a number of seats. The Syrian Christians were concentrated in only a few divisions, so could count on getting only a few seats. The other Christians, Muslims and Ezhavas were widely scattered, and in any case relatively few of them qualified for the franchise owing to their poverty, so their chances of getting elected were slim. In fact, throughout its seven years of life, the Nayars held more than half the elected seats in the Legislative Council under the 1921 Constitution, the Christians about a fifth, and the Ezhavas and the Muslims* none at all.[13]

At the outset of Sri Chitra Thirunal's reign many factors aggravated the problem. With the depression on the one hand and the spread of higher education on the other, there was growing unemployment of the better educated; government jobs offered the safest prospects and the struggle for them became keener than ever. There was the prospect of a new Legislature, promised by the Maharaja at his investiture, with enhanced powers; this made the fair representation of all communities all the more important. There was a strong suspicion moreover, fostered

* Note by the Editor: The Muslims captured one seat in the 1928 Council elections; see Joint Political Congress 1934:21.

by unhappy events during the Regency, that the Junior Maharani and the new Legal and Constitutional Adviser, and in consequence the new Maharaja, favoured the Nayars. Already the seeds of suspicion, that Sir C.P.Ramaswamy Aiyar was anti-Christian, were beginning to sprout.

It was therefore with keen interest and anxiety that all communities awaited the promulgation of the new Constitution, and the rules governing electoral procedure.

The first step in bringing the new Constitution into being was the issue of a communique on 2 June, 1932, setting out the purposes of the new Constitution and sketching the main outlines.[14] The press note stressed the need for change in relation to developments in India. "Special attention will be paid to the trend of Reforms in India as well as to the constitutional machinery in countries possessing a representative form of Government. The aim of the Government will be to secure adequate representation of all interests and all points of view and to fit the institution into the scheme of Federation now under contemplation in India."

The Legislature was to be bicameral. The old Sri Mulam Popular Assembly was to be replaced by the Sri Mulam Assembly, a chamber of 72 members of whom 48 would be elected on a wide franchise, 14 would be nominated by government to represent various minority interests, and ten would be officials. It would replace the former Legislative Council as the main legislative body; but a new body, to be called the Sri Chitra State Council, with only 37 members of whom 27 would be elected on a higher franchise*, would be set up to act as a Second Chamber. Both houses would have legislative functions, and all bills had to pass both Houses and receive the Maharaja's assent; and the budget would be presented in the Assembly which would vote on it in detail. But the Dewan would have powers of certification if the budget was rejected. The Maharaja also retained the power of legislation by proclamation. The Dewan was to be the President of both Houses, but the Assembly obtained the right to elect its Deputy President. Both Houses would have the right to discuss government policy and administration through interpellations, debates and adjournment motions; but the Dewan-President had the right to rule any question or motion out of order.

The communique also dealt with the burning question of communal

---

* Note by the Editor: The State Council had 27 non-official members of whom 22 were elected. So, the total number of elective seats in both Houses was 70, see also page 87.

representation. The government ruled out communal electorates or any system of reservation of seats in joint electorates on a communal basis. It was felt that members of different communities would in fact get elected from the general constituencies, and the government proposed to use its powers of nomination to secure the representation of under-represented communities.

The draft of the new Constitution had to secure the approval of the Paramount Power, and so it was submitted to the Political Department for scrutiny. The Political Department considered a new Constitution designed to fit in with the proposed scheme of Federation "a little premature", as His Majesty's Government had not yet expressed its views on, say, communal representation in India. The Political Department expressed no opinion on the arrangements of the Government of Travancore for the representation of their communities - the point which most passionately interested Travancoreans. Having criticized the use of the word "the Sovereign" when "His Highness the Maharaja" would have been used (the King of England being the only sovereign concerned), they decided that there was nothing in the draft constitution to which exception could be made, and the draft was approved.

Its reception in Travancore was anything but enthusiastic. The Nayar press criticized the proposals as promising no real devolution of power. Bodies representing various groups of Christians, and the great Ezhava organization, the S.N.D.P. Yogam, concurred in thinking that any real representation of the minority communities would not be secured by government nomination. The Muslims joined in this criticism. Suggestions for adult suffrage, proportional representation, reservation of seats in multi-member constitutencies, were canvassed, and there was a widespread feeling that a Round Table Conference of the different communities should be called to consider the proposals.

On the Maharaja's birthday, 20 October 1932, the Constitution was promulgated by Royal Proclamation as a birthday gift from His Highness to his people. The next day the government issued a lengthy communication explaining the electoral rules. In particular the question of the minorities was examined, and special attention was paid to the Ezhavas (the best organized group and the most clamorous about their disabilities.) The government kept to the system of direct election combined with nomination; it was expected that they would get some seats by direct election in districts in which they were in large numbers; but if they did not, the government would examine the situation and provide at least four seats for them by nomination. In the same way two seats would be provided by nomination to the Muslims. Other minority interests "will be adequately represented by suitable nominations by Government."

IV.4 The Formation of the Joint Political Conference[15]

The Christian bodies, the S.N.D.P. Yogam, the Muslim Service League, all immediately entered their protest. They held meetings, passed resolutions, sent deputations to the Dewan, but they all met with a cool reception and discouragement. The government was not prepared to change.

As a result, their common interest threw the Christians, the Ezhavas and the Muslims into each other's arms. On 17 December 1932, the three communities formed the All-Travancore Joint Political Conference, with a Syrian Christian (Jacobite) president, a Syrian Christian (Catholic) secretary, and two joint secretaries, an Ezhava and a Muslim. It was a turning point. Their interests were still frankly communal, but it was the first sign that the leaders were prepared to rise above the narrowest communal interests to a somewhat wider vision, and to cooperate fully with those of other communities.

The Executive Committee worked out that, assuming that voters voted for members of their own community (as was still to be the case for many years to come) then by the proposed electoral rules the Nayars would get at least half the seats, the Christians would get a handful, and the Ezhavas and Muslims none at all. The Joint Political Conference decided to press for reservation of seats in multi-member constituencies, and sent a deputation to the Dewan on 9 January, 1933. But all he would discuss was a redistribution of constituencies, which would go only a very little way to meet their grievances. The question of fair representation for all communities was ignored.

On 25 January the Joint Political Conference took a momentous step: they launched the Abstention Movement.[16] At a crowded public meeting, having first expressed their loyalty to His Highness the Maharaja, and reiterated their stand on reserved seats in multi-member constituencies, they declared that "no useful purpose will be served if only a few members of these communities (i.e. Christians, Ezhavas and Muslims) manage to get into the new Legislature", and resolved to abstain from voting, standing for election, or accepting nominations to seats in the new Legislature, "as a legitimate protest."

The Abstention Movement threw Travancore into a ferment of

political excitement, especially in central and north Travancore, where Christians were numerous and influential. The reported figures were no doubt exaggerated, but attendance at meetings certainly ran into thousands. A fresh newspaper war broke out descending to fresh depths of scurrility. The Nayar press in general condemned the movement as non-cooperation in another form; the Joint Political Conference repudiated the charge, and claimed they were law-abiding and within their rights. One Nayar newspaper went so far as to claim that the Christians had a secret plot to abolish the Hindu dynasty and turn Travancore into a Christian State, and "the senile Lord Willingdon" (then Viceroy of India) would be sympathetic. Sir C.P.Ramaswamy Aiyar gave a statement to the Associated Press of India: he too could see no distinction between non-cooperation and abstention. "No Government," he added, "could view the attitude of non-cooperation with equanimity." Howls of protest arose from press and platform; in what capacity, they asked, had Sir C.P. chosen to make this statement? He was interfering in the internal administration of the state; he did the state no good and the Travancore Government should dispense with his services as Legal and Constitutional Adviser.

Worse was to come from that quarter. A group of influential and moderate Christians, led by K.C.Mammen Mappillay, editor of the leading Malayalam daily, the *Manorama*, was ready for compromise. The Dewan, the genial and able Mr. T. (later Sir Thomas) Austin, I.C.S. got in touch with them and an agreement was made that if the elections proved patently unjust to the protesting communities, the Legislature would be dissolved. On March 24th, the evening before the very day on which the group was to meet the Dewan to hammer out the final form of a government communique on the matter, Sir C.P. Ramaswamy Aiyar literally descended on Trivandrum, having flown from Delhi, saw the Dewan, and went off again; and when the group met, the Dewan announced government had said its final word and abruptly left the meeting. (The Resident, in his confidential reports to the Viceroy, blames the Christians for the whole uproar, but makes no mention of Sir C.P.'s intervention.)

From now on every meeting of the Abstentionists began with expressions of loyalty to His Highness the Maharaja and ended with demands for the dismissal of the Legal and Constitutional Adviser. The long war had started. But Sir C.P. was temporarily out of it. Their Highnesses went off to Europe for a couple of months, and he accompanied them.

The elections were due to be held in mid-June 1933, and the Joint

Political Conference planned to go on with its compaign. A few monster meetings were held, but in the first week of April the district magistrates prohibited public meetings and the distribution of pamphlets as threatening to disturb public peace and foment communal discord, and these orders were maintained until a fortnight after the election. Newspapers supporting the Abstention Movement were threatened with the cancellation of their licences. The Joint Political Conference adopted tactics which were to be repeated on a far larger scale in the far more serious Congress agitation five years later; they moved their campaign to the other parts of Kerala, Cochin and British Malabar, where there were the keenest interest and sympathy, and launched their speeches and newspaper articles from those relatively safe havens. All government orders were scrupulously obeyed, however, and there was no physical violence.

The results of the elections to the two Houses of the new Legislature were as follows: out of 70 elective seats, 36 were won by Nayars, 15 by other high-caste Hindus, 10 by Christians, 3 by Ezhavas, 3 by Muslims. In a vitriolic but well-documented memorandum, published from Calicut by the Joint Political Conference, shortly after the elections, it was alleged that there had been extensive interference with the elections. The Christians, Ezhavas and Muslims who obtained seats were unknown men (this was certainly true; no well-known leader stood for election) and they were returned unopposed (which was also true) because, it was said, all other candidates had been bribed or bullied into withdrawing their candidature so that the government-sponsored nobodies could be elected. The vitriolic campaign continued. In 1935 the general secretary of the S.N.D.P. Yogam, C. Kesavan, was so violent in a speech attacking the Nayar community and Sir C.P. Ramaswamy Aiyar that he was charged with sedition and jailed for two years. We shall hear more about that.

Meanwhile the Government of Travancore had already taken steps to remedy one grievance by appointing a Public Service Commission. This appointment had been promised by the Maharaja soon after his investiture, but was only made in 1933.[17] Its report recommended that the Superior Service should be selected by competitive examination, and the lower services according to community.* In 1934 Dr.

---

* Note by the Editor:

This Public Service Commission, which according to the Fortnightly report of the British Resident had been set up in August 1932, listed 14 major communities which had to compete for 90% of the posts in the Superior

G.D.Nokes, an English judge of the Travancore High Court, prepared a more detailed report, the recommendations of which followed the same principles, and he became the first Public Service Commissioner.[18] His scheme worked well and allayed a lot of the agitation, though naturally it was a good many years before the under-represented communities were adequately represented in the senior ranks of the services. Moreover, the *Devaswom* Department and the Nayar Brigade remained the preserve of the caste Hindus, and the reform of the military arm was unnecessarily delayed until 1936. From time to time also the palace by-passed the Public Service Commissioner to slip some favourite into a well-paid post; as this however irritated everybody it promoted communal disharmony rather than the reverse.

The question of the electoral rules was taken up by a new Dewan. Mr. Austin had served his two years and returned happily to Madras service. The new Dewan, Sir Mohammed Habibullah, appointed a Brahman as Commissioner for Franchise and Delimitation, patiently listened to complaints, and on August 17th, 1935, the government published new electoral rules which made very big changes.[19]

The State Council was left as it was; it was a revising Chamber and was working well. Extensive reforms were made in the rules for elections to the Sri Mulam Assembly. All persons owning land assessable to a tax of one rupee or more were enfranchised, so were persons in municipal areas who paid any tax at all. (The fishermen, a large but very poor community, could be qualified if they held a certificate for fishing; many were Muslims and Sir Mohammed had a special concern for them). The provision raised the enfranchised percentage of the population from 3% to 10-12%.

The system of constituencies was completely changed.[20] The whole state was divided into 17 multiple-member electoral divisions returning 43 members between them for the Assembly, and ten divisions returning 16 members for the Council. Within these divisions certain seats were reserved for under-represented communities - 10 for Ezhavas, 4 for Muslims, 4 for Latin Catholics. Government would still nominate members from entirely unrepresented communities; there was provision for instance for the nomination of two women to the Assembly. It will be noted that there was no special representation for the Syrian Christians; but it was rightly calculated that the lowering of

Services and share all the posts in the Inferior Services in proportion to their numerical strength.

the franchise qualification would bring in a sufficient number of Syrian Christian voters to secure them adequate representation. Another Brahman was appointed Electoral Polls Officer to draw up the new voting lists.

The proposals were widely welcomed, the extension of the franchise universally so. There was of course a general complaint that universal adult franchise had not been granted, and the Nayars of course complained that they would now be under-represented. But Christians, Ezhavas and Muslims hailed the reforms as a real advance. The Joint Political Conference had particular reason to be pleased; it was their own scheme, put forward at their first meeting, which had been accepted.

The proof of the pudding was in the eating. The elections of May 1937 were held in a tranquil atmosphere; there was a striking absence of communal tension. The returns to the Assembly were: Nayars 12, Syrian Christians 12, Protestant Christians 1, Ezhavas 8, Muslims 3, Latin Christians 1.* At the final session of the outgoing Assembly, one speaker could say with a fair measure of truth: "The first session of the Assembly met under a black cloud of misunderstanding that was the result of unhappy communal rivalry in the State. Now the session closes in the bright and happy sunshine of communal amity and concord all round".[21]

It was not altogether true. The verbal warfare had left not merely scars but festering sores; suspicions remained active, Christians and their partners in the Joint Political Conference could still see Nayars and Brahmans favoured in appointments and promotions. And they were particularly suspicious of the influence of the new Dewan Sir C.P. Ramaswamy Aiyar.

I have already said that the formation of the Joint Political Conference was the real turning point in the process of political change. Their joint action and the victory they won had results far beyond their immediate achievements. For centuries the Nayars had been the dominant element in the State of Travancore, only held in check from time to time by the Brahmans whom the Rajas imported from the Tamil country for that very purpose. But now the Syrian Christians, the

* Note by the Editor: Reports about the election results are confusing both in the Ouwerkerk manuscript and in other sources. The reason is the complicated system of seat distribution involving general and special constituencies, nominated and elected seats and reserved and non-reserved seats. The main result undoubtedly was that the Joint Political Conference became the largest single party in the Legislature.

Ezhavas and the Muslims could look the Nayars in the face and treat with them on equal terms. They had learned the value of mass agitation and developed the techniques of conducting it even in the face of government oppression. They had learned to work together across the boundaries of communalism. It is true that their aims were the promotion of the interests of the different communities involved and to that extent they deserved the accusation of "rank communalists" which was the favourite term of abuse of Nayar press and platform. But the alliance lasted, as did the personal friendships formed; indeed the Conference changed its name to the Samyuktha Party (which is Sanskrit for "yoked together") for the purpose of action in the Sri Mulam Assembly as a recognized party. And two men, T.M.Verghese in the Assembly, and C.Kesavan in his prison cell, were already dreaming of a wider alliance which would have no flavour of communalism.

It was on the basis of the Samyuktha Party that the later Travancore State Congress was built, with a leading Nayar as its president, T.M. Verghese as its vice-president, and C.Kesavan as one of its chief spokesman; and it was the State Congress which at the end won democracy for Travancore.

Chapter V

THE TEMPLE ENTRY PROCLAMATION

If the names of Sri Chitra Thirunal and Sir C.P.Ramaswamy Aiyar go down in history at all, it will be as the authors of the Temple Entry Proclamation of 1936, which was rightly acclaimed as one of the greatest revolutions in Hinduism.

To understand its full significance it must be seen against the background of all-India developments. The untouchables (variously called the depressed classes, the Scheduled Castes, and by Mr. Gandhi the Harijans or children of God) still suffered from every kind of social, economic and religious disability, and were disillusioned with the Indian National Congress which was dominated by caste Hindus and which, while paying lip service to the uplift of the depressed classes, had in fact done very little to help them, certainly down to 1932. Some of them had been rising in the social scale, and they had produced a great leader, Dr.B.R.Ambedkar, who was anti-Congress, anti-Caste Hindu, and finally anti-Hindu. He was invited to the Round Table Conference as a representative of the depressed classes, and there fell foul of Mr. Gandhi, who claimed in his own person to represent the masses of India. There was a quarrel in the Minorities Sub-Committee about the separate representation of the depressed classes under the proposed Constitution, Mr. Gandhi claiming that they were Hindus and Dr.Ambedkar maintaining that they were a separate community. No settlement could be reached, and so the British Prime Minister undertook to make an Award, which could be altered if all the parties agreed to an alteration. The Communal Award of August 1932 recognized the existence of the depressed classes as a separate community, and they were given two votes, one for their own representatives in special constituencies and one for the general constituencies. Mr. Gandhi started a "fast unto death" against the Award; so it fell to Dr. Ambedkar to save the Mahatma's life by negotiating a new arrangement. Separate seats for the depressed classes were retained, but now they lost their second vote and all the electorate voted for the depressed classes' candidates. Dr. Ambedkar saw this as a device for the caste Hindus to interefere in the elections of depressed class candidates, and was further embittered against Mr. Gandhi and the Congress.

About this time the All-India Anti-Untouchability League was founded to combat untouchability in all its forms and to fight for civil rights, but Mr. Gandhi took it over and changed both its name and its character. It became the Harijan Sevak Sangh, the Society for the service of Harijans, and it now adopted the Gandhian constructive programme for their uplift and dropped the fight for civil rights on which Dr.Ambedkar had set his heart. It became an organisation of caste Hindus serving the outcaste; the Mahatma explained that it was "a kind of penance which Hindus have to do for the sin of untouchability". Only caste Hindus served on the governing body, and the funds were collected only from caste Hindus.

Dr. Ambedkar left the organisation (which he had helped to found), and now turned entirely against Hinduism. On October 13th, 1935, at a huge conference of the depressed classes held near Nasik, he advised his hearers to abjure Hinduism and embrace some other faith that would give them an equal status, a secure position and rightful treatment. He mentioned Islam, Sikhism, Buddhism and Christianity.[1]

V. 1 The Campaign for Temple Entry in Travancore

The problem of the untouchables was particularly urgent in Travancore. They comprised two-fifths of the population. On the one hand it was the land with the strictest orthodoxy in India, with the most rigid and complicated rules about distance pollution, which still practised "unseeability" in spite of its legal abolition; on the other hand it contained the most progressive, well-educated and highly organized untouchable community in India, the Ezhavas, clamouring for equal status and equal rights with the caste Hindus. The political implications are obvious.

The right to worship in the temples was the test of their acceptance. Laws for their social and economic uplift might be passed, their civil rights might be safeguarded, but as long as they were excluded from the temples they were not fully accepted. Even those who, like C.Kesavan, turned against religion altogether, were aware of the importance to the untouchables of the right to temple entry.

Under the inspiration of Sri Narayana Guru the Ezhavas had built their own temples; nonetheless their big organization, the S.N.D.P. Yogam, passed resolutions demanding temple entry at every conference. In 1921 the Ezhava leader T.K.Madhavan, who was a member of the Sri Mulan Popular Assembly, raised the question there; the Dewan replied that government could not interfere in a purely religious matter.[2] In 1924 came the Vaikom satyagraha, which confined itself only to the right of the untouchables to walk on the roads surrounding the Vaikom Temple. One of the most striking things about the agitation was the very big part played by caste Hindus, especially the Nayars. It should be observed also that the Hindus who conducted it were mostly politically-minded, and many of them were Congressmen, either at the time or later. To say it was a political move would be totally unjust; these Hindu leaders were religious men with a burning sense of social justice. But under the influence of the Mahatma, religion and politics had even by 1924 become so enmeshed that it is impossible to separate them.

Although the Maharani Regent had carried out many reforms, she remained strictly orthodox; and it was not until the young Maharaja took up the reigns of government, and the real power fell into the hands of those two highly unorthodox people, the Junior Maharani and Sir C.P.Ramaswamy Aiyar, that sweeping changes became possible. "England-returned" Hindus were polluted and excluded from the temples, prayers had to be said on the sacred soil of India. (One Maharaja took a box of the sacred soil about with him on which to say his prayers—a simple but inconvenient solution). Almost the first order passed by the Maharaja, in his capacity as a trustee of the Sri Padmanabha Temple, was to permit "England-returned" Hindu officials to take part in the ceremonies there. In 1932 his mother paid a visit to England, and in 1933 the entire ruling family went to Europe. After all, the Maharaja was a sacred person, a servant of the gods; and even the most rigidly orthodox Nambudiri Brahmans conceded his right to alter the sacred *Smritis*.

Within a year of his investiture he appointed a Temple Entry Enquiry Committee, under the chairmanship of the retiring Dewan, Mr. V.S.Subramanya Iyer, himself an orthodox Brahman. It included an Ezhava Mr. M.Govindan, a retired district judge who was the first Ezhava to rise so high in the Judicial Service , and a retired High Court judge, Mr. Changanacherry Parameswaran Pillai, a man of the highest integrity and independent judgement, universally respected, with a very active interest in social reform. The Committee were to go into the whole question, to tour the state and assess public opinion, and to make recommendations. Cochin, which was faced with the same problem, was invited to cooperate in the enquiry; but the Maharaja of Cochin was old and very orthodox, and would only consent to informal consultation. The enquiry was only directly relevant to the 1500 temples under state management for which the government had the power to legislate; there were over 500 temples in the hands of private trustees which could make their own rules.

The committee reported in January 1934; its report is one of the most fascinating and illuminating documents of the time.[3] Its first chapter describes the structure of a temple: there is an inner shrine, a holy of holies where the image of the god is kept, which is approached by steps, also very holy; this is surrounded by courtyards and halls of ever-diminishing holiness, the whole surrounded by a wall. Different classes have different degrees of access: only Brahmans and Kshatriyas can go to the inner shrine for worship. Vaisyas and Sudras may go as far as the steps leading up to it—and "unapproachables" (the term significantly used in the report) have to worship outside the walls.

The Committee then discusses the teachings of Hinduism concerning worship in temples. The real power resides in the image, and this power is kept alive by ceremonies which can only be performed by qualified Brahmans. But the power can be lost be defilement and can then only be restored by elaborate ceremonies. Defilement can come about in a number of ways which include the presence of unbelievers and outcastes; a polluted temple pollutes all who enter it. It was agreed, however, that the ancient writings allow for changes in these rules if they are sanctioned by sufficiently learned bodies.

The Committee's report on the feeling in the country shows that practically all the *Avarnas** agreed that worship in the temple, which would give them *darshan* (sight) of the image was more efficacious than worship outside it. The feeling of the Brahmans was overwhelmingly against temple entry, particularly among the Nambudiri Brahmans; but the Nayars were in favour of temple entry by a large majority.

The Committee's majority report made a number of proposals which were a compromise; they included proposals to allow the *Avarnas* inside the temple walls but not so far as the inner halls and court- yards; to throw open a few temples to the *Avarnas*; to build new temples for common worship; to open all public roads, tanks and wells to the *Avarnas*, and to abolish *theendal* or distance pollution. The two stalwarts of social reform, Mr. Parameswaran Pillai and Mr. M. Govindan, submitted a minority report recommending the immediate

* Note by the Editor: *Avarnas* are those who do not belong to one of the four major caste categories or *varnas*, i.e. the untouchables or depressed classes.

and unconditional opening of all temples to all Hindus.

The government at once carried out the least controversial recommendation: all public roads, tanks and wells were thrown open to the *Avarnas*, and distance pollution was abolished completely. Mr. Gandhi happened to be touring Travancore at the time, and expressed his delight at this measure.

The rest of the report was shelved. The Maharaja's chief adviser, Sir C.P.Ramaswamy Aiyar, was at that time not in favour of temple entry. Commenting on the temple entry satyagraha then going on for the temple at Guruvayur, he had said that although he himself did not observe caste rules, he realized the strength of the feeling among orthodox Hindus that the system of temple worship and its details were governed by divine ordinance. "The problem could only be gradually solved by a process of mental adjustment which would preserve the solidarity of the Hindu community. Shock tactics", he concluded, "will not answer the purpose."[4]

But the agitation went on; all conferences of Nayars and of Ezhavas passed resolutions demanding temple entry. The chief weapon in the hands of the reformers was the Kerala branch of the Harijan Sevak Sangh, which had started work there in 1933. It had a powerful board; its president was Mr. Changanacherry Parameswaran Pillai, and Mr. M. Govindan, that other stalwart of the minority report of the Temple Entry Enquiry Committee, was a very active member. Mr. Gandhi sent one of his ablest lieutenants, G.Ramachandran, to be its general secretary.

"G.R." was a local man, a Nayar although he never used his caste appellation; but he had been educated at Santiniketan, where he fell under the influence of Rabindranath Tagore and C.F.Andrews. He resolved to devote his life to serving the poor—a resolution which he kept throughout his life. He worked for some years under C. Rajagopalachari in the villages round Salem, and was for two years one of Mr. Gandhi's secretaries. Under all these influences he developed a burning passion for social justice, a tender love for the poor and an indefatigable zeal for very hard work. Although a Congressman and a member of the All-India Congress Committee, his interest was far more in the Gandhian "constructive" programme of social service than in politics as such. With G.R. as its driving force, the Kerala Harijan Sevak Sangh started schools for Harijans, night schools, dispensaries, hostels for Harijan students, persuaded caste doctors to give Harijans medical care, took up legal cases, broke down caste prejudices, got the cooperation of caste Hindus and caste Christians in their work. They also organized meetings and conferences which continued to press for temple entry.

The impact of Dr.Ambedkar's advice to the Harijans to leave Hinduism was sensational. The Christian missionaries had been making converts among them for more than a century, and by this time the Christians of untouchable origin numbered about 50,000.[5] But now the Ezhavas began to consider a mass migration to some other religion. Although Sikhs and Arya Samajists sent missionaries to Travancore, and Mohammedanism was already there, the Ezhava leaders were attracted to Christianity largely because of its social teachings. They had also worked with Christians in the Joint Political Conference and liked them. Some were undoubtedly attracted to the person of Christ. At a meeting in January 1936, a number of Ezhava leaders, doctors, lawyers, teachers and journalists, decided to leave Hinduism and take steps to become Christians; and they approached some leaders of the Church of India (as the Anglican Church was known in India). They freely admitted that their motive was social rather than religious, but they were willing to be instructed. They made it clear however that they wanted to come over in a body, not as individuals. The Anglican Bishop of Kottayam, Bishop Moore, was not prepared to accept a whole community; he was interested only in converts who became Christians for truly spiritual reasons. A number of missions, however, were started among the *Ezhavas*. The Mar Thoma community of the Syrian Christians, at that time the most missionary-minded of their churches, enrolled a hundred young volunteers to do evangelistic work in central Travancore, where the Mar Thomas were strongest and the Ezhavas also were numerous.

Dr. Ambedkar's advice and the decision of leading Ezhavas to leave Hinduism in order to take their community into the Christian fold acted as an "electric shock" to the workers of the Kerala Harijan Sevak Sangh, as also to the caste Hindus.[6] Many, following Mahatma Gandhi's lead, were sincerely convinced of the wrongness of leaving the religion of one's birth. Others, looking at the arithmetic of it from the political angle, added the 16% of the Ezhava population to the 30% of the Christian population, and were appalled at the answer. The Hindu character of the state was in danger. Sir C.P.Ramaswamy Aiyar was undoubtedly one of those who did this simple sum, and decided on the shock tactics he had formerly deplored. (Some Syrian Christians were of the opinion that it was this prospect that decided him to become Dewan of Travancore in 1936, but this is speculation. Let us return to facts).

The Kerala Harijan Sevak Sangh swung into action. They prepared a plan, got the approval of the Central Board of the All-India Harijan Sevak Sangh, and G.Ramachandran was put in charge of a "hurricane compaign" under the direction of Mahatma Gandhi. A huge All-Kerala Temple Entry Conference was held in Trivandrum in May 1936, addressed by a leading Congresswoman, Mrs. Rameshwari Nehru, and a deputation went from the Conference to the Maharaja. Another deputation of caste Hindus plus the genial Mr. M.Govindan toured Travancore to collect signatures from caste Hindus to a monster petition for temple entry. *Jathas*, always led by a caste Hindu, went from village to village collecting more signatures. Public meetings were held all over Travancore attended by enthusiastic crowds. By May 1936, G. Ramachandran was able to write in Gandhi's weekly *Harijan*: "In Central Travancore, where the movement among the Ezhavas for migration to Christianity was strongest, there is clear evidence that the Ezhava masses have been considerably impressed by our sincerity, and therefore the conversion movement is beginning to collapse."[7] Leading Congressmen like A.V.Thakkar, chairman of the Central Board of the *Harijan Sevak Sangh*, and G.D.Birla, visited Travancore and called on the palace to press the cause of temple entry on their Highnesses.

V.2 *The Proclamation (1936)*

On November 3rd the deputation appointed by the All-Kerala Temple Entry Conference waited on the Dewan, to present their petition for immediate and unconditional temple entry; it had 50,522 signatures of caste Hindus. The Dewan was sympathetic. His Highness was enthusiastic; he swept aside all half-measures and compromises, and insisted on what in his youthful enthusiasm he called "the whole hog".

And so, on November 12th 1936, on the Maharaja's birthday,* came the Temple Entry Proclamation which shook the whole of India:

> "Profoundly convinced of the truth and validity of Our religion, believing that it is based on divine guidance and on an all-comprehending toleration, knowing that in its practice it has,

---

* Note by the Editor: The Maharaja's birthday wavers uncertainly between the third week of October and the second week of November. This is not the result of indifferent or inaccurate chronology but of a complicated way of fixing the auspicious day by the moon and the stars. For that reason the date varies every year.

> throughout the centuries, adapted itself to the needs of changing times, solicitous that none of Our subjects should, by reason of birth or caste or community, be denied the consolations and solace of the Hindu faith, we have decided and hereby declare, ordain and command that, subject to such rules and conditions as may be laid down and imposed by Us for preserving their proper atmosphere and maintaining their rituals and observances, there should be henceforth no restriction placed on any Hindu by birth or religion on entering or worshipping at the temples controlled by Us and Our Government."

The place went mad. There were meetings and processions and congratulatory addresses. There were proposals to erect a statue of the Maharaja in Trivandrum, in Madras, of his mother, of the Dewan. Mahatma Gandhi, after being reassured that the "rules and conditions" only related to such matters as cleanliness of dress and orderliness of conduct, hailed the Temple Entry Proclamation as one of the greatest revolutions in the history of Hinduism.

In January he came to Travancore and was made a state guest. He addressed endless mass meetings, including a huge meeting in Kottayam specially for Christians. He visited endless temples in the company of Harijans. He was emphatic that the motive behind the Temple Entry Proclamation was not political but purely religious.

C.Rajagopalachari, a great fighter for the Harijans, and a much-loved patron of the Students' Inter-religious Fellowship, came from Madras specially so that he too could visit temples in the company of Harijans, and the students, who swarmed shouting to meet his train at the railway station. That day was the public thanksgiving for temple entry; the outcastes formed a great procession, with drums and banners and elephants , and stormed into the palace grounds and up to the very windows of the palace itself. They had illuminated the grounds and floodlit the palace, and fantastic shadows of men and banners were flung on the white palace walls, dwarfing the tiny figures of the Maharaja's family on the balcony, as the procession passed before the great flooding lights. To an onlooker it appeared a portent, the writing on the wall—the lowest of the state towering over the highest, a spiritual Fall of the Bastille.[8]

The tumult and the shouting died, and in time one could assess the results.

A blow had been struck at Hindu religious obscurantism from which it never recovered; but this was not apparent at first. The untouchables invaded the state temples in large numbers at first, but once their curiosity was satisfied they returned to worship in their own temples under their own priests. Many of the orthodox Brahmans stayed away from the state temples which they considered polluted by the presence of *Avarnas*, and the government found it necessary to issue a confidential circular to its caste Hindu officers that they were expected to attend temple services regularly, and they had to sign a register of attendance for some months.[9] The Maharaja of Cochin refused to allow Nambudiri priests who had entered the polluted temples of Travancore to officiate in the temples of Cochin, causing a quarrel which went on for five years. But many even among the orthodox recognized the right of the ruler, by ancient laws, to alter the regulations governing temple worship, and over the years the caste Hindus became reconciled to the non-caste Hindus in the temples, and the distinction became blurred.

What is more, Sir C.P. embarked on a course dear to his heart, a kind of counter-reformation in the state temples. He insisted on the training of priests in the Hindu scriptures, one and two-year courses were instituted for the thorough study of Sanskrit; a Central Religious Library was set up in Trivandrum, and popular services with the singing of *bhajans* (hymns) and discourses were introduced into the temples.

A Hindu Mission was set up to reconvert those who had gone over to Christianity. School fee concessions to depressed classes were withdrawn from those who became Christians, and they were encouraged to abandon their Christian names and to return to their Hindu names. There was even a certain amount of harassment of converts falling not far short of persecution; though such cases were not common. The missionary societies reported however that on the whole the recent converts stood firm and refused to abandon their new religion in spite of its material disadvantages. The threatened mass movement to Christianity of the Ezhavas never materialized, but a steady trickle of individual conversions continued.[10]

The political effects were incalculable. The campaign had been conducted almost entirely by Congressmen (apart form Mr. Govindan, who was non-political); both during the campaign and after the proclamation prominent Congressmen had visited the state and been made much of. Congress ideas of all kinds, not only the eradication of untouchability, flooded into the state. The shake-up of the foundations of society jolted the people of Travancore out of their complacent isolation, and opened the way for widespread social and political unrest. If Sir C.P. had chased one of his bogeymen, Christian domination of

Travancore, out of the door; he had opened the window wide for his other bogeyman, the revolutionary spirit of the Indian National Congress.

Chapter VI

COMMUNAL HARMONY

By October 1936, the major causes of communal bitterness had been tackled and solutions found, although they still had to be worked out in practice. A Public Service Commission had been established, with clear rules. The electoral rules had been drastically altered to secure fair representation of all communities in the Legislature. The reorganization of the Nayar Brigade, once the preserve of the Nayars, and its transformation into the Travancore State Forces which would be recruited from all communities, had been taken in hand. Sir Mohammed Habibullah, during whose Dewanship these changes had been effected, could thankfully say his "Nunc Dimittis."

Yet bitterness remained. The savage verbal warfare of the past four year had left scars and festering sores that could not be healed overnight, and skirmishes still went on. The political parties, such as they were, were organized on communal lines—except the Communist Party, at that time no bigger than a man's hand. Sir C.P. in his first speech had publicly stated that one of his aims was the abolition of communalism —a statement received with sycophantic applause but widely disbelieved. The Christians in particular were sharply suspicious of him, and the Nayars and Brahmans hoped to continue to benefit from his patronage.

Communal bitterness could only be overcome by bringing together the leaders of the Joint Political Conference, who had after all partially overcome it, and the leaders of the Nayars, and prevailing on them to put the interests of the whole country above their narrow communal interests. The instrument by which this was achieved was the International Fellowship.[1]

VI.1 The International Fellowship

This amiable talking shop, devoted to tea parties, picnics and endless and inconclusive debates on religion, politics, international affairs, race relations, social reform and Indian culture had been started in Madras at a time of great tension in 1922. The founder and general secretary for three decades was a Syrian Christian landowner from north Travancore, A.A.Paul. He had been general secretary of the Student Christian

Movement of India, Burma and Ceylon; in that capacity he had travelled widely, and everywhere he found the same social gulf between Indians and Englishmen, the all but complete failure to meet in friendship and to hear each other's point of view, let alone understand it. He therefore began, with the aid of some English missionary friends, to hold tea parties for a carefully selected mixed group of Indians and Englishmen, at which they could meet quite informally to discuss matters of common interest. It was the careful selection of the members of the group and the provision of a definite theme for discussion that distinguished them from E.M.Forster's "bridge parties" described in *A Passage to India*; they were so successful that a definite organization, the International Fellowship, grew out of them, proclaiming the brotherhood of man under the Fatherhood of God, with its motto "Under Heaven One Family." The movement spread all over India, and Paul now gave his whole time to it. It appealed strongly to thoughtful Indians and to European and American missionaries; its work was quiet and unostentatious, and except in Travancore its influence cannot be assessed. As communal tension mounted in India, it became more and more preoccupied with inter-communal harmony rather than with racial harmony, though it never lost sight of the wider world view. The organization was non-political though inevitably politics was much discussed; its chief interest lay in inter-religious understanding and in the promotion of social service on an inter-religious basis. It developed an All-India Council which met every two years, and in 1936 the Council started a Rural Service branch under that remarkable American Dick Keithahn (who had left his wealthy mission to live as one among poor villagers) and a Student Inter-religious Fellowship under an equally remarkable young Indian, M.A.Thomas, (later founder and director of the Christian Ecumenical Centre of India).

Mr. Gandhi was so impressed by the value of its quiet work that he became a member of the All-India Council of the Fellowship, and it says much for Paul's strength of character and independence of mind that the Mahatma never succeeded in capturing it. Dr.Zakir Hussain (later President of the Indian Union) and C.Rajagopalachari (later Governor-General of India) were also members of the All-India Council, both were very active in their respective branches. The Fellowship therefore was not a Congress organization, though many Congressmen belonged to it, particularly those who, like G.Ramachandran, were at heart more interested in Gandhian social reform than in Congress politics.

The Trivandrum branch was founded in 1930. All sorts of people belonged to it, from the Resident to humble school teachers and journalists. One teacher, a small landowner, was so fired by what he learned through the Fellowship that he started a highly successful Rural Reconstruction Centre in central Travancore, the Oollannore Rural Reconstruction School, giving the whole of his six acres of land to it. The Trivandrum branch supported it. M.A.Thomas fixed his headquarters in Trivandrum; together with M.M.Thomas (later Chairman of the Central Council of the World Council of Churches) he ran a Waifs and Strays Home in a stinking slum inhabited by the Municipal scavengers, and prevailed on the Students of the Inter-Religious Fellowship to help. The Senior Branch supported this effort financially. The Senior Branch itself was an innocuous social group, of apparently no importance whatever; but it was at least conspicuously successful in bringing people of different races, religions and political persuasion together in an atmosphere of tolerance and friendship.

A.A.Paul combined a world outlook with an intense love for his native Travancore, and in 1936 he decided to take a hand in the solution of its communal problem. The elections under the new rules were due; the Joint Political Conference members were jubilant, the Nayars resentful at the curtailment of their former dominance; communal tension was increasing instead of diminishing. He was the right man for the task. He was deeply religious, totally dedicated, completely without personal ambition. Although a Syrian Christian, he stood right outside the communal structure in Travancore, belonged to no political party or pressure group. He had a genius for friendship.

So he proposed an informal conference of communal leaders to discuss ways of reducing communal tension and of saving waste of money in the forthcoming elections. What he proposed was an electoral pact by which the two major communities who had no reservation of seats guaranteed to them, that is, the Nayars and Syrian Christians, should allot certain seats to the two communities—13 for the Nayars and 12 for the Syrian Christians—and agree not to contest elections in them. Twenty-nine leaders came to the meeting, in itself a hopeful sign.[2] Many agreed with the idea, but it broke down on the implacable hostility of some leading Nayars to the electoral reforms; and this hostility was confirmed at a conference of the Nayar Service Society, which resolved that the reforms were unjust to the Nayars and that they would not cooperate with the Joint Political Congress.* A.A. Paul,

---

* Note by the Editor: The Joint Political Conference later came to be known as the Joint Political Congress.

however, went on working with the silent persistence of a white ant at undermining the foundations of communalism, and kept in touch with those who had agreed with his ideas.

The elections of 1937 under the new rules were, as we have seen, peaceful. Paul's estimate had been roughly correct;[3] the Nayars and Syrian Christians each got 12 seats. But though the elections themselves had been peaceful, as soon as the Sri Mulam Assembly met communalism raised its head.[4] The Joint Political Conference, now the Samyuktha Party, had 24 members; the caste Hindus drew together to form the Travancore Nationalist Party with 22 members. The first excitement arose out of the election for the Deputy President, whom the members visualized as holding a position analogous to that of the Speaker of the House of Commons. The Dewan-President laid down the rule that only the elected members should vote for the Deputy President, and that the government and nominated members should refrain from voting. Consequently the leader of the Samyuktha Party, Mr. T.M.Verghese, was elected. The first session, held in July 1937, was comparatively peaceful, but there was an undercurrent of discontent that the government was demanding grants for big schemes such as a new University of Travancore, while the Dewan did not allow the Assembly to debate them; such schemes, said members of all parties, should have been presented in the form of bills before the House. And every question had a communal edge to it.

In August 1937, between the first and second sessions of the Sri Mulam Assembly, the International Fellowship held an All-Travancore Conference in central Travancore. By now there were branches in Kottayam, Alleppey and Nagercoil. A.A.Paul came from Madras to take the chair. The communal questions came into every discussion, no matter what the subject. Late on the last evening, T.M.Verghese suddenly appeared, and we scrapped our final programme to listen to his appeal that the Fellowship—myself in particular—should tackle the communal question again. I was a government servant and refused on those grounds, but Paul and Verghese went over my head to the Dewan himself to ask for my services. Sir C.P. was enthusiastic and gave me permission to meet the communal leaders in an effort at conciliation. "After all", he said, "you aren't even English—the most independent person in the State. But don't let them talk about Responsible Government." I refused again; under my roof they should feel free to discuss anything they liked, and I would respect their confidence and his, and give him only an agreed report of what was said. But if they turned political I would throw them out. Sir C.P. agreed to my conditions and we went ahead; A.A.Paul came from Madras for the meetings, which were an instant and unqualified success. Most of the leaders joined the International Fellowship. (Not C.Kesavan: his bitterness against Hinduism had made an atheist of him and he could not bring himself to accept its religious basis. But Paul, friendliest of men, prevailed on him to moderate his language against the Nayars - and that was more important than you might think.). The Maharaja took a keen interest, and invited the All-India Council of the Federation of International Fellowships to hold its biennial meeting in Trivandrum, where they would be state guests.

Of course they talked of responsible government. Paul had long ago privately expressed the view to me that this was the only solution to the somewhat arbitary rule of the "Palace"; Pattom Thanu Pillai, the Nayar who had at once taken the lead in the meetings, was outspoken on the subject that, once the details of the remaining communal grievances were settled, they should, all together, work for responsible government. They would have to meet elsewhere than in my house, I said; but there seemed no further need of meetings. The back of the communal problem was broken. After the second full meeting of the group, I could report to th Dewan on 17 November that they had been a success.

At this point Sir C.P. appeared to change his mind about the desirability of communal harmony. I say "appeared" as one never knew whether he was thinking and acting on his own initiative or as a result of pressure from "the Palace." In either case the threat to his own position and power from a non-communal political party, possibly linked to the Indian National Congress, was obvious. He moved swiftly to stir up communal passions again and break up the Communal Harmony group.

VI.2 The Kesavan Affair[5]

The Kesavan affair gave Sir C.P. his opportunity.

We must go back two years to C.Kesavan's conviction for sedition. He had made a speech when presiding at a conference of the Joint Political Conference, in which his immoderate language was not only directed against the Nayars but extended to Sir C.P. himself (at that time Legal and Constitutional Adviser to the Maharaja.) Kesavan denounced him as "an intolerable burden to the country" and demanded that he be sent away from the state. Criticism of the Maharaja's servant was considered criticism of the Maharaja himself, and Kesavan got two years for sedition. The Resident, in his confidential report to the Viceroy, commented: " His conviction will have a salutary effect." But he had reckoned without the character of the man himself or of the people supporting him. He had been made a martyr, and as steps were taken to meet the grievances of the Joint Political Conference, the three communities did not forget their martyr and felt grateful to him for the sacrifices he had made on their behalf.

But the extent and fervour of the welcome accorded on his release from jail in September 1937 staggered everybody. He was the hero of the new Samyuktha Party. On October 3rd there was a great reception for him at Alleppey, where the Ezhavas were numerous; a crowd estimated at 100,000 came to meet him—not by any means all Ezhavas; there was even a Nayar on the platform. All the leaders of the Samyuktha Party were there; he was greeted with a salute of 101 guns. T.M.Verghese welcomed him "on behalf of the 51 *lakhs** of people of Travancore." The editor of the *Malayala Manorama*, K.C. Mammen Mappillay, whom we have met before as one of the founders of the Joint Political Conference, acclaimed him as "the uncrowned king of Kerala." He and his wife were bowed down with the weight of the garlands hung round their necks; purses and cheques were showered upon them.

The *Malayala Manorama* became lyrical; the Nayar Press condemnatory. The government published a stiff press note expressing disapproval. A salute of 101 guns was reserved for His Majesty the King Emperor; the expression "uncrowned king" was criticized, as were references to the establishment of responsible government; utterances had been made purporting to be on behalf of the entire population of the state of 51 *lakhs* acclaiming him as the chosen leader of all the people. The government condemned these utterances as "wholly subversive and dangerous", and warned that action might have to be taken against newspapers giving them publicity. The *Malayala Manorama* in particular was warned.

Nothing daunted, Kesavan's supporters organized another meeting at Quilon on October 9th. About 20,000 people came to it. This time it was a leading Nayar doctor who welcomed the hero; T.M.Verghese took the chair and repeated all the offending expressions. He added a new note, that "Kesavan has to be congratulated on coming forward to work for the whole community without consideration of caste or creed." It was a challenge to those who sought to divide and rule.

---

* Note by the Editor: One *lakh* = 1,00,000

The second session of the new Sri Mulam Assembly met on November 22nd.[6] The atmosphere had subtly changed; there was now a possibility, with the success of the communal harmony talks, of an alliance between Pattom Thanu Pillai and the Samyuktha Party, and it was to the interest of the palace to break it up.

The communal bomb exploded on November 25th. A Nayar member of the Travancore National Party rose to move a vote of No-Confidence in the Deputy President, on the ground of the prominent part he had played in the demonstrations to welcome a convicted criminal. T. M. Verghese's claim to speak on behalf of the 51 *lakhs* of the people of the state was condemned; he could only have based such a claim in his position as the Deputy President of the Sri Mulam Assembly, and this was an abuse of his position. The debate raged for two days; on one side were the Samyuktha Party, on the other caste Hindus of the National Party. It was a display of virulent communal passions. The only balanced speech came from Pattom Thanu Pillai. He felt that the Deputy President ought to keep out of party politics as far as possible, although entitled to his personal views; the Assembly was a young body and there was a need to develop healthy precedents. However, the point having been made, the No-Confidence motion could very well be dropped.

The voice of common sense was not allowed to prevail. Sir C.P. Ramaswamy Aiyar, as Dewan-President, was in the chair throughout the whole of the debate, and on the second day he summed up. After learned references to parliamentary procedure and the need for establishing precedents, he concluded: "As the President of this House, I feel that the Deputy President ought not to have used words which claimed he spoke on behalf of 51 lakhs when he had no right to speak on such an occasion with reference to such a topic." It was a threat.

There was a brief interval before the vote was taken. In that interval the official members were ordered to vote for the motion and the nominated members "advised" to do so, in defiance of the precedent set up by the Dewan-President himself in July that only elected members should vote in the election for the Deputy Presidentship. The motion was carried by 42 votes to 24, the Samyuktha Party voting solid against it. T.M.Verghese resigned and another Deputy President was elected—a *Nayar* this time Had the voting been confined to the elected members the motion would have been lost by 22 votes to 24.[7]

The affair caused a roar all over the country; what was debated was not only the matter of the motion but the manner in which it had been passed. It was felt that the palace party had triumphed and that the forces of progress and communal harmony had been routed. And it left a bad taste in everybody's mouth, for it was realized that this kind of manipulation of the voting in the Assembly made a mockery of its pretension to be a step on the way to greater democracy. Even the Nayars were disgusted.

A.A.Paul's Communal Harmony group lay in ruins. How could they believe in the Dewan's good faith after the deliberate use of the worst communal passions to get rid of a critic?

The defeated T.M.Verghese however remained peculiarly undefeated. There was a big wedding two days after the debate. Mr. K.C.Eapen, brother of K.C.Mammen Mappillay, a banker, a founder member of the Trivandrum International Fellowship, Vice-President of the Trivandrum Y.M.C.A., gave a huge garden party to celebrate the marriage of his son, to which he invited everybody who was anybody in Trivandrum—including all the members of the Legislature. T.M.Verghese arrived late—and in Pattom's car; the pair linked arms and walked right through the stunned and silenced gathering and refused to be separated all evening. (It might be said they only separated nine years later over the question whether the best way of ridding Travancore of its incubus was by violent or non-violent means.) The whirring of thoughts as the Assembly took in the significance of the gesture was almost audible.[8]

VI.3 The Fellowship Council Meeting [9]

It was inevitable that the Dewan (or was it the palace?) should attempt to cancel the meeting of the Council of the All-India Federation of International Fellowships, but we had taken the precaution of getting out the invitations very early and it would have been too embarrassing to stop it. The Dewan and the palace accepted the situation with good grace; the Dewan gave the inaugural address, and their Highnesses gave a garden party to the delegates at which they were their most gracious and charming selves.

The delegates were a very mixed group. There was a large number of local people, mostly Fellowship members; eight of the Communal Harmony group, the three stalwarts of the Temple Entry Campaign, some local missionaries. The Mahatma was ill and could not come; but he sent in his stead a leading Congressman, Dr.Bharatan Kumarappa, a Harvard graduate in Philosophy who was living on Rs. 10 a month in Gandhi's ashram and was assistant secretary of the All-India Village Industries Association. Another leading Congressman was Brahmachari Ramachandra, a highly-educated Brahman who was leading a life of devoted social service in the slums of Bangalore. These two, together with our own G.Ramachandran, represented those Gandhians who were dedicated to the uplift of the poorest members of the community rather than to political action (though all of them had jail records for political offences.) There were learned Hindus and Muslims, prominent Indian Christians, English and American missionaries. The keenest and best of our local student group acted as volunteers, led by the indefatigable M.A.Thomas. Brother Dick Keithahn, rural secretary of the Fellowship, organized everything in the background.

Sir C.P.Ramaswamy Aiyar set the high intellectual tone of the Conference with a learned address on Science and Religion. In conclusion he praised the Fellowship for its spirit of charity and comprehension, and stressed the need for overcoming the communal differences in the state. "During the four or five years I shall be in Travancore to carry out the work entrusted to me by His Highness", he concluded, "I hope to labour at the task and before I leave the State, I should rejoice if I could say that there are not and will not be fundamental divergences and differences between community and community". Those who had recently taken part in or followed the battle of the No-Confidence motion could be forgiven for feeling a trifle cynical.

But the rest of the conference was an eye-opener to the local people. The conference theme was: "Fellowship in the Sphere of Religion, the Social Sphere, the Sphere of Economics, the Sphere of Politics." Religion was treated, not as a label for quarrelling politicians, but a discussion of the different ways of approaching eternal truth. The social sphere dealt with the uplift of the poverty- stricken masses, abolition of caste, the freedom of women. Economics led to heated arguments about Gandhian village industries. Politics looked beyond communal groups and sectional interests to the national interest. Even G.Ramachandran's burning patriotism was rebuked by wise old Mr.M.Govindan who stressed the need to look on the needs of the whole world for peace. They were caught up in a quite different dimension of public and political life; they had put before them—by men who had cheerfully sacrificed careers, comfort, wealth—not Congress politics as such, but the Gandhian programme of care for the poor and the underprivileged as the children of God (the Harijans); the group discussed the deep spiritual basis of that programme expressed so simply in the Fellowship motto "Under Heaven One Family". And there was true deep fellowship in the meals together, in the prayers, the social contacts, the laughter and teasing and use of first names. They were torn loose from their moorings and launched—for a time at least—onto the broad-stream of the Indian National awakening.

Pattom Thanu Pillai in particular was profoundly influenced. He had long been interested in the Congress; henceforth he was a Gandhian committed unalterably to non-violence, and he kept to it through all the turbulent decade that was to follow.

Chapter VII

THE TRAVANCORE STATE CONGRESS

The year 1938 was one of growing unrest in the Indian states. Under the Government of India Act of 1935 the provinces of British India had become self-governing, and there were Congress governments in six of the eleven provinces. They were on the whole making a success of their governments, and gaining experience if nothing else. The state people watched the provinces running their own affairs and saw no reason why they should not run theirs.

At the same time, the prospect of Federation which would include the states demanded a reappraisal of the conditions prevailing in the states. The essential problem—evaded though it was by British officialdom—was that of combining the democratically run provinces with the autocratically-run states. Faced with this the people of the states broadened their demands; they not only wanted responsible government and civil liberty in their own states, but a voice in the shaping of the All-India Federation through elected representatives. The various states' peoples' organizations, some confined to individual states, some based on groups of states, began to clamour for the Indian National Congress to take charge of the movements in the states so as to present one broad united front.

The attitude of the Congress to the people of the states had been consistent. They had throughout expressed sympathy with the aspirations of the states people, and as early as 1920 had called upon the Princes to grant full responsible government in their states; but they maintained that they could not actively interfere in the internal affairs of the states, in which conditions were very varied and always different from those in British India, which was their chief concern. In view of the prospect of Federation, however, Congress examined the question afresh at its meeting at Haripura in February 1938. Its resolution on the states was considered so important that it is frequently referred to simply as "the Haripura resolution".

"In view of the fact that owing to the growth of public life and the demand for freedom in the Indian states, new problems are arising and new conflicts taking place, the Congress lays down afresh its policy in regard to the states... The Congress stands for the same political, social and economic freedom in the states as in the rest of India, and considers the states as integral parts of India which cannot be separated". With regard to Federation, it went on: "The only kind of Federation that can be acceptable to the Congress is one in which the states participate as free units, enjoying a measure of democratic freedom as the rest of India. The Congress, therefore, stands for full responsible government and the guarantee of civil liberty in the states".

It was not however in a position to work effectively within the states: "In view of the different conditions prevailing in the states and the rest of India, the general policy of the Congress is often unsuited to the states and may result in preventing or hampering the natural growth of a freedom movement in a state. Such movements are likely to develop more rapidly and have a broader base, if they draw their strength from the people of the state... and do not rely on extraneous help and assistance on the prestige of the Congress name. The Congress welcomes such movements, but in the nature of things and under present conditions, the burden of the struggle for freedom must fall on the people of the states". The Congress would extend its good will and support to such struggles. Individual Congressmen, however, would be free to render assistance in their personal capacity.

The Congress therefore directed that Congress committees in the states should not launch any direct action; any struggle should be undertaken by independent organizations, which should now be started, or continued where they already existed.

This resolution called forth strong criticism from the states peoples' organizations, which felt they were being abandoned. But there was wisdom in this policy, and none saw it more clearly than Gandhi, or foresaw more clearly what would be the result. His comments to "a friend from the states"[1] were set out in *Harijan* of 5th March 1938.

"The states resolution", he said "is a call to the states people not to go to sleep but to start work in right earnest. We want the states people to carry on ceaseless work in the states, but not in the name of the Congress... let them work with the moral support of the Congress but avoid the Congress name. The real job", he concluded, "is to build up your own organizations. You may continue to be members of the Congress, attend it and keep in touch with it. But your real work will lie in the states".

And this is exactly what happened. Everywhere organizations sprang up, but they were called *Praja Mandals* (Peoples' Unions) and not Congress bodies. (The Travancore state Congress had been founded a week prior to the Haripura resolution and saw no reason to change its name.) The states people flung themselves into the movement, often with the help of local Congressmen, and the flame of direct action went from state to state like a forest fire. Down to 1947 there was no direct organizational link between the Congress and the states peoples' movements; but the actual links were close. Gandhi himself directed a number of the states movements; the states leaders made their pilgrimages to Gandhi's *ashram* at Wardha to consult him and for the most part took his advice. In his *History of the Indian National Congress,* Dr.P.Sitaramayya compares the two movements to two trains running on parallel tracks—"and Gandhiji was the driver of both trains". Moreover, Jawaharlal Nehru, himself from the Native state of Kashmir, took a deep interest in states' affairs, and accepted the Presidentship of the All-India states Peoples' Conference at Ludhiana in February 1939.

It was no wonder that the British authorities saw in this almost simultaneous outbreak of unrest in the states, which increased in 1938, a deep Congress plot. They developed the theory that the states movements were engineered by the Congress with the deliberate intention of capturing the seats allotted to the states in the proposed Federation, and thus upsetting that "delicate balance of forces" (to quote Sir William Barton) which would keep the Congress in check. This theory was expounded most eloquently by Sir C.P.Ramaswamy Aiyar, in a brilliant memorandum which he submitted to the Political Department in December 1938.[2]

There was perhaps no state to which the theory had less relevance than the very state of which he was Dewan. The causes of the unrest in Travancore were local, and stemmed largely from his own administration. The form which the Travancore agitation took was influenced by Congress ideas and techniques, and of course Mr. Gandhi took advantage of it. But there was no question of its being "engineered from outside". It was primarily a local affair.

VII.1 Congress in Travancore before 1938

To understand the evolution of Congress in Travancore it is necessary to get the flavour of life in the state capital, where most of the political action took place, and which was dominated by the palace and the Dewan. Until 1938 public life and political activity were confined almost entirely to the English-speaking middle classes of the capital, local men who had been locally educated. Most of them were lawyers and journalists—many of the journalists also had legal qualifications; they had usually taken a degree in History or English, the former including courses in British Constitutional History and Political Science. They could—and did—quote Burke and Rousseau, John Stuart Mill and Abraham Lincoln. The parliamentarians among them knew Erskine May's *Parliamentary Procedure* by heart, for was not the British Parliament the Mother of Parliaments, and was not their ideal to copy the British parliamentary form of government? They were in touch with the other English-speaking groups, the higher officials (English being the language of administration) and the staffs of the colleges (English being the medium of instruction.) Politics was on communal lines, and had been ever since the Legislative Council developed; there was also the important aspect of palace favour to consider. So it was a narrow inward-looking society, full of intrigue, squabbles, gossip; yet it was a cosy society once you understood the unwritten rules, with a charm of its own, particularly if you regarded it (as did some of its British officials, and indeed some of its Oxford and Cambridge Indians) as a sort of Indian version of "The Mikado". And there were better elements, men and women of high principles who eschewed communalism, who cared for the poor and set up social service institutions, who gave their energies to activities like the Harijan Sevak Sangh, the Y.M.C.A. and Y.W.C.A, the Waifs and Strays Home, the Friend-in-Need Society, who campaigned for social reforms. There were also those who cared for Kerala culture, who organized the great annual Arts Festival, who revived the ancient Keralan *Kathakali* dance-drama and encouraged Indian music and Malayalam literature. In the atmosphere of a Princely capital, it was rather the idealistic element who took an interest in Congress - for they had nothing to gain by it.

It is striking that, down to the thirties, most of the men and women who played a large part in public life were Nayars, with a handful of Brahmans. Striking, but not surprising, because Trivandrum was a Nayar stronghold. Having lost their feudal powers, they turned, as did the feudal elements in English society, to the peaceful pursuit of influence and power, first through the law and public office, later through the representative bodies set up by the far-seeing Sri Mulam Thirunal. They were moreover closely associated with the palace (except for a brief period during the Regency) and benefited from palace favour.

Congress therefore was initially the activity of a small group consisting mainly of Nayars, with a sprinkling of Brahmans and a handful of progressive Ezhavas. The local Christians took very little part; in any case there were relatively few Christians in Trivandrum of any standing, and they were mostly in government service. The Syrian Christians throughout Travancore were not interested in Congress (with the remarkable exception of George Joseph); for one thing they were inclined to regard it as a Hindu affair, a view to which some of the Mahatma's utterances lent colour. Secondly, like the Ezhavas and Muslims, they were too busy fighting for their rights, i.e. their share of the local loaves and fishes to bother much with non-communal politics. It took a huge convulsion to turn the minds of Travancore Christians towards the Congress.

In its earlier years the Indian National Congress had confined itself entirely to British India; but in 1921 there was a complete re-organization of the Congress machinery. It was at this time that the small and powerful working Committee was set up, and also the All-India Congress Committee. India was divided into linguistic provinces each with its own Congress organization. Kerala, the Malayalam-speaking area of the West Coast, was made into one of these linguistic provinces, with far-reaching results. It brought together into one organization a British province, British Malabar, and the two Native states of Travancore and Cochin. It was welcomed by the politically-minded who thought in terms of the cultural unity of Kerala, as did indeed many who were not politically-minded, whose main interests were cultural. The closely-linked but independent bodies that promoted Gandhi's "constructive programme", the All-India Spinners' Association, the Harijan Sevak Sangh, were also organized on an all-Kerala basis, and were of course run by Congressmen. The few in the two Native states who were active in Congress were thus brought into close contact with the very active Congressmen of British Malabar, and strong links were forged. This wider all-Kerala outlook, based on cultural affinities, was of great importance therefore in the development of the Congress movement and, we may add, in the development of communist influence at a later stage.

Travancore was made a district, in which Trivandrum City was one branch, and there were other branches in smaller places, such as Quilon and Alleppey. The Travancore Congress Committee was formed in 1921; its two secretaries were Nayars, A.K.Pillai and V.Achyuthan Menon, who were active in the Congress movement throughout the whole period.[3]

The first real impact of the Congress movement on Travancore occurred with the Vaikom satyagraha of 1924. As already related, Gandhi himself visited Travancore and negotiated the settlement, which was a triumph for the satyagrahis. According to the Resident, who took a keen interest, he did not draw large crowds, but there was some increase in the wearing of *khaddar** and of hand- spinning.[4]

We have seen that there was an increase in communal tension during the Regency, since the palace appeared to favour Christians, while the Junior Maharani enlisted the aid of the Nayars in her compaign for a Regency Council. The result was an outbreak of scurrility in the Nayar press, and the publication of a strict Press Regulation in 1926. This Regulation was strongly resented by public men in Trivandrum, especially by the Nayars, and it led to a heated debate in the Legislative Council, which objected to the manner of its promulgation by a palace decree instead of by a law duly passed through the Legislature. Public meetings of protest were held, and in August there was a two-day political conference which attracted large crowds. It was decided to start an All-Travancore Political Association to work for "the establishment of Responsible Government in Travancore and for the safeguarding and development of popular interests". This, it must be observed, had nothing to do with the Congress as such, though A.K. Pillai was one of the leading and most intemperate speakers. As usual it was largely a Nayar affair.

The success of the first meeting of the All-India People's Conference, held in Bombay in December 1927, inspired the local people to organize the South India states Subjects' Conference, which took place in Trivandrum in January 1929.[5] Like its parent body, it was not a Congress organization, though some Congressmen took an active part in it. It was an eminently respectable affair. The president and chief speaker was a distinguished public figure, Sir M. Visveswarayya, who had been Dewan of Mysore. The Travancore Government gave full cooperation, and Sir M.Visveswarayya was made a state guest while the other visitors were accommodated in government buildings. The president of the reception committee was a highly respected lawyer and member of the Legislative Council, Mr. Pattom A.Thanu Pillai; its chairman was the only active Congressman among the leaders, Mr.A.Narayana Pillai, an advocate and journalist. Sir C.P. Ramaswamy Aiyar sent a telegram of good wishes.

There were about 900 delegates, 850 of them from all over Travancore. Some 1,000 people flocked to the meetings which were held in an enormous *pandal* lent by the government.

Discussion centred on three main topics: the establishment of responsible government in the states, the right of the states people to

---

* Note by the Editor: *Khaddar* or *khadi* is handwoven/handspun cloth.

send elected representatives to a Federal Government for the whole of India, and the safeguarding of civil rights in the states. The conference favoured Dominion Status for India and a Federal Constitution to embrace both the British Indian provinces and the states. In his presidential address, Sir M Visveswarayya, after he had gone fully into the whole question of the relationship of the states with the Paramount Power, uttered a warning: "There is also one thing to remember; when the British provinces become autonomous, as they must within a few years, there is no manner of possibility of keeping the states people content with any form of absolute monarchy. So even on the lower ground of ordinary prudence, it will be in the interest of the Princely Order to deal with the situation in a liberal, if not wholly generous, spirit".

The conference ended by setting up a permanent executive committee to carry out propaganda and to cooperate with the All-India states Peoples' Conference in Bombay. It held a few meetings and then faded out. A *khaddar* shop was opened in Trivandrum, but the local politicians normally wore the cheaper mill-made cloth and kept their *khaddar* for special occasions, such as a visit from the Mahatma. They turned once more to their local communal squabbles. The whole Conference had apparently sunk without leaving a ripple on the surface.

The Salt Satyagraha of 1930, which roused enormous excitement all over India, even affected Travancore. It is true that there was no civil disobedience within the state, for the agitation was directed against the British Raj and not against the rulers of the states. But the Trivandrum City branch became active; some public meetings were held, and a group of twelve volunteers under K.Kumar and G.Sreedhar went off to join the makers of illegal salt on the beaches of Cannanore in British Malabar. This they did, but they were not arrested and returned home somewhat disheartened. So Trivandrum sank back into its old isolation; though *khaddar* became briefly somewhat more popular among the students.

There was more activity in the smaller towns such as Alleppey and Quilon. Budding Congressmen found in the new labour movement a field of activity which at once satisfied their desire to be politically active and their desire to carry out the Congress constructive programme. In 1930 there was much picketing of foreign cloth shops and some promotion of the wearing of *khaddar* (though the factory workers themselves could not afford it). "Congress" wrote the Resident in his Report for August 1931, "is now supporting labour and encouraging the move for a strike for better wages. It is the European firms who are most affected and the reason is obvious".

But the growing activity of the Princes in relation to Federation stirred up growing activity in their subjects, and at the end of 1930 a small group in Trivandrum made a determined effort to build up a Congress organization afresh. This time that much-respected legislator Pattom Thanu Pillai was put in the chair at a big public meeting. In his speech he strongly criticized the ruling Princes, put forward the usual demands for responsible government and the guarantee of civil liberties, and the eradication of untouchability. He added a new note, however, of high relevance—a plea for the promotion of communal harmony. There was a flurry of activity in the forming of branches all over Travancore; but after a few months interest focussed on local politics again and Congress seemed forgotten.

There was a temporary revival of interest with the arrest of Gandhi on his return from the Round Table Conference in January 1932. In Trivandrum a few shops closed and protest meetings were arranged; but the District Magistrate banned them, and four young volunteers who tried to hold a meeting in contravention of the ban were arrested and were given a fortnight's imprisonment. The city Congress Committee, frightened by this display of firmness, hastily issued a statement that they were only conducting peaceful picketing; they were of the opinion that there was no necessity for civil disobedience in Native states, and they all resigned in a body. The Resident reported that the students hooted them in the streets. There was more activity in the smaller towns; in Alleppey A.Narayana Pillai organized the picketing of foreign cloth shops, and delivered a speech in defiance of a prohibitory order, for which he got a month's rigorous imprisonment.

No wonder the Resident could report month after month "There is little Congress activity now". The communal row, which led to the Abstention Movement and the forming of the Samyuktha Party, was brewing up it burst out in January 1933 and absorbed the interest of the politically-minded for the next four years. Gandhi toured the state in 1934 collecting for the Harijan Welfare Fund; he attracted big crowds but little money.

But the "constructive" programme went on. As was frankly admitted by the Working Committee of the Indian National Congress, "it is carried on in the states by All-India organizations doubtless affiliated to, but more or less independent of, the Congress". This work kept a number of Congress workers busy in the states; Kerala had its *khaddar*-clad G.Ramachandran, dashing on his bicycle from meeting to meeting, or leaping into buses to remote parts of Kerala, to remind us of the existence of Congress. The All-India Spinners' Association was not very important, but the All-Kerala Harijan Sevak Sangh was, since it touched a pressing local problem.

The Temple Entry Proclamation marked a watershed in Travancore public life. This was not entirely due to its own impact, important though that was, but it preceded by a few months a great revolution in the political sphere, the inauguration of Provincial self-government in British India. Congress became respectable as Congressmen took office in six of the eleven provinces, and became ministers; and British officials who had previously put them in jail now worked under them This was particularly noticeable in Madras where the premier, C.Rajagopalachari and practically all the Cabinet ministers were ex-jailbirds; the Madrassi had a keen sense of humour and shared the humour of the situation with their British civil servants. Travancore had very close links with Madras; after all Sir C.P. was himself a Madras Brahman and had been a Congressman before 1921, when he differed with Gandhi on such matters as non-cooperation and *khaddar*. In the relaxed atmosphere he renewed his old friendships. He had already won the high regard of Congress with the Temple Entry Proclamation; he visited Madras in August 1937 and gave a party to the Congress ministers in his Madras home.

Leading Congressmen and women visited Travancore and were freely welcomed. There was an All-Kerala Hindu Women's Conference in Quilon in August, which was dominated by two Congresswomen, members of the Madras Legislative Assembly. The Junior Maharani visited it in order to receive a congratulatory address on her part in the Temple Entry Proclamation. Apart from that the resolutions related mainly to the Congress constructive programme, the abolition of caste, the prohibition of liquor in the state, and the compulsory teaching of Hindi in the schools. The Young Kerala Society was founded, its chief office-bearers being Congressmen; its first conference was addressed by a Congressman, a member of the Central Legislative Assembly; he said that in consonance with the spirit of the Temple Entry Proclamation Travancore should give the lead in establishing responsible government in the state and guaranteeing civil liberties. Students swarmed round him wherever he went. The government encouraged the use of products of local manufacture, and Sir C.P. was seen wearing *khaddar* (of the finest quality) in his own home.

"Now that the rulers of the state themselves have begun to flirt with the Congress", wrote the Resident in his confidential report for the first half of September 1937, "the public have not been slow to note the change of attitude. At a meeting of prominent workers held at Trivandrum on the 12th inst. an influential committee of about 50 members has been constituted to revive the Congress movement in the state". The president was Changanacherry Parameswaran Pillai, retired High Court judge and president of the All-Kerala Harijan Sevak Sangh; the secretaries G.Ramachandran and G.Sreedhar of Salt Satyagraha fame.[6] When the newly-constituted Committee met on November 3rd, it resolved to carry out the programme of the Indian National Congress, particularly the "constructive" programme. It adopted the attitude of the National Congress in rejecting the proposed Federal scheme, as a federation should be one of self-governing units; it undertook to work within Travancore for responsible government and fundamental civil rights, and to tackle the evils of communalism. There was not a whisper of criticism from the authorities and the Congress honeymoon in Madras appeared to have reached Travancore.

VII.2 Causes of Local Discontent

There was however no mating of Princely rule with popular feeling in Travancore. On the contrary, Prince and people were being driven apart by the growing unpopularity of the Prince's Dewan, Sir C.P. Ramaswamy Aiyar. It was this unpopularity, rather than any hopeful breezes from across the Ghats, which caused the growing demand for responsible government. He was fully aware that the first act of any popular ministry would be to get rid of him, so the louder the clamour for responsible government, the more unbending his attitude; the more repressive his policy; the more unpopular he became, the louder the clamour, until the whole state was in an uproar.

Let the Working Committee of the Travancore state Congress speak: "No Dewan ever started his term of office under better auspices than Sir C.P.Ramaswamy Aiyar. He enjoyed the utmost confidence of His Highness. The historic Proclamation relating to the temples made a profound impression everywhere creating a favourable atmosphere. But it did not take long for the new Dewan to squander these invaluable assets. He should have followed up this great social reform with equally important political reforms.... Responsible Government was the natural expectation of the people... but the Dewan is adopting an unjustifiable attitude of open hostility to their legitimate and modest demands".

This popular discontent had far deeper causes than his refusal even to discuss responsible government. He had been unpopular ever since he emerged during the Regency as the supporter of the Junior Maharani against the Maharani Regent; and this unpopularity increased when he became Legal and Constitutional Adviser to the Maharaja. There were three main reasons for his unpopularity in those earlier days, and his conduct as Dewan did nothing to dispel them.

In the first place, he was suspected of fostering disharmony between the Nayars and the Christians; the Constitution he devised in 1932, and his blatant encouragement of communalism at the time of the No-Confidence Motion in November 1937, are but two examples of an attitude which gave force to the suspicion.

The local people suspected him of corruption. Nothing was ever proved against him; there was at no time an impartial inquiry, rumours were persistent and the state Congress demanded an inquiry. The Resident, Mr. C.P. (later Sir Clarmont) Skrine, in his confidential report in October 1938, "Impressions of Travancore", was of the opinion that Sir C.P. was "incorruptible by money—his weakness is for power and fame, not money[7]." But the political fact was that the rumours were believed, and formed the basis of some of the accusations in the notorious Memorandum to the Maharaja praying for his dismissal and an inquiry into his administration.

Perhaps the major cause of his unpopularity was his relationship with the ruling family. His friendship with the Maharaja's mother had given rise to gossip for two decades; the rumour may have been completely unfounded, as some closest to the family maintained; but the political fact was not their truth or untruth but the fact that they were universally believed. The Ruling House of Travancore had stood out among other Ruling Houses for its simplicity of life, purity of morals and devotion to duty; and the people were saddened by the blot on its reputation. The Maharaja's own reputation was above this kind of gossip; but it was widely realized that his mother had a dominating influence over him and interfered in matters of state where he ought to have been acting on his own initiative. But Travancoreans were too loyal to their ruler to attack his mother openly; and so they attacked the Dewan instead—and he, intensely loyal to his exalted mistress and her son, accepted the responsibility for all that was done, good and bad alike.[8] The loyalty of the people to their Maharaja never swerved and was invariably expressed in terms of the deepest respect; it was the Dewan who bore the odium.

One of Sir C.P.'s worst faults was his utter contempt for the people he ruled, which he did not trouble to conceal. The Resident, in his "Impressions of Travancore", wrote: "He is a 'superior person' domineering and contemptuous of the common herd.... His methods are Machiavellian; he rules by dividing, he bribes with office and other favours, he sets traps for his critics and plays on the weakness of his enemies. No wonder the man in the street does not love him". His contempt for the Legislature, the constitution of which he had himself devised, angered its members. The most important measures were passed by proclamation, and only submitted to the Council and Assembly as a fait accompli. It was useless to resist; funds refused by the Legislature could be certified by the Dewan. He manipulated votes to suit his purpose.

The scheme for a separate University of Travancore was a favourite project of Sir C.P. and the Maharani. At that time there were a number of colleges in Travancore affiliated to the University of Madras, which incidentally had given an honorary degree to the Maharani Regent in recognition of her services during the Regency but had ignored the Junior Maharani. There were grandiose schemes for promoting Malayali culture and for building up courses in Applied Science geared to the industrial development of the state which was also planned. Sir C. P. first approached the government of India through the Resident on the scheme.[9] The Political Department was less than enthusiastic; there was already a surfeit of universities in India, the scheme was financially unsound, the aims could be achieved by expansion of the existing institutions, the Science College and the Sanskrit School. The local people were also unhappy about the scheme. It is true that they had clamoured for a university separate from that of Madras for a matter of thirty years; but it was an all-Kerala university which they wanted, and there was an unofficial committee (which the Travancore Government completely ignored) sitting even then to draw up a scheme for it. The Christians were particularly unhappy; they feared Hindu domination and the undermining of the freedom of their excellent Christian colleges in regard to religious education and religious and social activities. The Sri Mulam Assembly, which had its first chance to discuss the scheme only in a debate of the budget provisions for a university, were also critical of it: it was too ambitious, would be too small to be efficient, and what is more, they too wanted a Kerala University. But their chief complaint was the failure to present a bill to the House. Pattom Thanu Pillai was particularly scathing; he suggested secondary education (which was bad on the whole) should be tackled first, and ended his speech: "I take objection to the fact that the University was considered an accomplished fact by the Government even before the Legislature discussed the questions".[10] The Durbar swept aside all the objections, and the university was inaugurated by proclamation on the Maharaja's birthday in November 1937.

The state Transport scheme was equally unpopular. In itself it was an excellent scheme; there was a large number of private buses plying erratically, in dangerous competition with each other. At the same time much of the state was not covered by the railway, and good bus and lorry transport was a necessity. There was one large and flourishing concern operating between Trivandrum and Nagercoil with some degree of efficiency, owned by one Kumaraswamy Pillai; the rest were inefficient. But the State Transport scheme was unpopular. The legislators objected that it ought to have been embodied in a bill to allow for full discussion. It was strongly suspected the Dewan had made a lot of money out of the contracts for the buses (which according to the Chief Transport Officer, an Englishman new to the state, was quite untrue). The private bus owners feared for their livelihood. Sir C.P. chose to take over the only route which was working well for its first venture, that from Trivandrum to Nagercoil. And when Kumaraswamy Pillai asked for compensation the Dewan refused to consider the request on the grounds that his income tax returns had shown a loss on the bus service for the previous two or three years. The Resident sensibly suggested that Kumaraswamy Pillai should be given compensation with one hand and have it taken back in the shape of income tax with the other—a procedure which would have appealed both to the sense of justice and the sense of humour of the Travancoreans; but the Dewan was not listening.[11] He announced that the bus conductors would be graduates; this would be a contribution to solving the graduate unemployment problem, but it put an equal number of Kumaraswamy's bus conductors out of work. It was not surprising, therefore, in the disturbances later that year, that state buses were the object of the mob's peculiar hatred, and a large number were burnt.

The same kind of suspicion attended all the schemes for industrialization, although they were good and necessary in themselves. But the local people seized on one complaint, that too many contracts were given to outsiders, especially to Tamil Brahmans; and they felt cheated.

Another cause of complaint was the mania for self-advertisement displayed by the Dewan and the ruling family. In 1932, when Sir C.P. became Legal and Constitutional Adviser to the Maharaja, a bureau of the Associated Press of India was set up in Trivandrum, with a subsidy of Rs. 24,000 a year, which gave a lot of publicity to the doings of the ruling family, the Dewan and the Dewan's supporters. The ruling family made a trip to the then Dutch East Indies in 1936, and took with them a reporter from the *Madras Mail*; his glowing descriptions earned him the newly-created post of Director of Public Information. It was a palace appointment, made over the heads of the Public Service Commission; and it created a lot of local bad feeling.

It was no wonder then that when the Dewan extolled the wonderful constitutional progress of Travancore, and pointed to the Sri Mulam Assembly and the Sri Chitra state Council, with their powers of legislation, budget discussion, debate and interpellation, thoughtful people were somewhat cynical about the reality of the alleged progress to greater democracy.

The last straw was a veritable straw—the Dewan, in September 1937, changed the school hours, which since time immemorial had been from 10a.m to 4p.m. for a Monday-to-Friday week, to 7.30 to 11.30a.m.* for a six-day week. The hours of working for government offices were similarly changed. It seems ludicrously trivial but it caused an uproar. The Congress Government in Madras were contemplating this change, and Sir C.P. thought to steal a march on them. But Madras is much hotter than Travancore, where the temperature rarely rises above 85^0 and all-day work is not oppressive as it is in Madras. The change meant changing traditional habits, especially in the country districts where the children might have to walk five or six miles to school and back daily; now they would have to make the return journey in the heat of the day. Small as it seems, the change brought home to the remotest village that a foreigner ruled their lives.[12]

VII.3 The Erosion of Civil Liberties

It should be borne in mind that the whole states peoples' movement from its inception in 1927 was as much concerned with civil liberties as with constitutional reform. The latter touched the educated classes; but civil liberties touched everyone. The record of Travancore was better than that of most states in this respect. There was no *begar* or forced labour, widespread in the northern Princely states. The courts were well organized and had a high reputation for integrity; there was a clear code of law copied from the Indian Penal Code. The police were no better and no worse than their counterparts in British India.

---

* Note by the Editor: Other sources mention a six-day week from 7.30 a.m. to 0.30 p.m. which makes more sense as its total number of 30 hours equals established practice.

Travancore was a nation of newspaper readers and listeners, and there were over a hundred newspapers in the thirties. There were a series of press regulations which were the cause of long-standing dissatisfaction, but in view of the capacity of some of the newspapers for scurrility beyond the bounds of decency, these were a necessary safeguard. At worst, editors had been threatened with the cancellation of their licenses; but the press was reasonably free.

Towards the end of 1937, however, as the outlines of a truly non-communal movement began to appear, it became clear that civil liberties were under the threat of attack. The Kesavan affair, two years earlier, had been a warning. In November 1937 the newspaper license fee was raised from Rs. 500 to Rs. 1,000. This was sharply criticized in the state Council; the new regulation was condemned as a threat to the freedom of public opinion.[13] It was pointed out that there was adequate provision in the Penal Code for such offences as sedition or causing enmity between the various sections of the people of the state, and those accused had the protection of the courts, whereas there was no appeal against the cancellation of a license. Members of all parties joined to condemn the new regulation. Already the sense of a threat to personal liberty was strong, already the lines were being more clearly drawn. Those who supported the resolution then emerged as members of the new state Congress Party three months later.

On January 19th, 1938, the little world of Trivandrum was shocked to hear that two respectable middle-aged journalists had been attacked by hooligans in broad daylight in the streets. Both had been warned earlier by an official against publishing anti-government matter in their journals, and this attack appeared to be the result of their refusal to apologize.[12] Amid great public excitement, both Pattom Thanu Pillai and T.M. Verghese put down an adjournment motion in the Legislative Assembly on an urgent matter of public importance, namely the feeling of insecurity among the public because of these assaults. The Dewan-President ruled them out of order: "assaults on individuals", he said, "are prima facie private matters".[14]

It was the case of A.Narayana Pillai which put the match to the accumulating tinder and set the whole state ablaze. Narayana Pillai was a Congressman of long standing, who had served one prison sentence already in 1932 on a political charge. He was by no means a firebrand, and was a member of the Trivandrum International Fellowship and of their Communal Harmony group. On January 19th a mild article appeared in his weekly, suggesting that Nayars should stop grumbling about the disappearance of their old predominance in the public services and ask for their own communal quota like all the other communities; then all communities could join their sister communities to make common cause against abuses—for, he warned, while they were squabbling, Brahmans with no interest in the country were getting the jobs.

For this mild article, with however a sting in its tail, Narayana Pillai was threatened by the Chief Secretary to government with a prosecution for sedition, for "transgressing the limits of legitimate criticism of Government and promoting feelings of enmity and hatred between the communities of the country". He made a spirited reply on February 1st; the article was clearly meant to promote communal harmony, and in its criticism of government was fair and legitimate. "If in spite of its clear meaning the Government takes action, I shall of course defend it in vindication of popular rights and in the public interest".

Before discussing the momentous consequences of his defiance, a word about the progress of his case may not be out of place here. He was arrested but given bail by the magistrate; the bail was cancelled by the Chief Justice and the case transferred to another court; he was not permitted to call defence witnesses; when a noted barrister, Mr. K.F.Nariman, a leading light of the Civil Liberties Union, came from Bombay to defend Narayana Pillai, he was not allowed to plead in the Travancore courts on the grounds that he was an ex-convict (i.e. a Congressman who had been convicted for taking part in civil disobedience). With ex-convicts ruling six of the British provinces as His Majesty's ministers, this episode attracted nationwide interest, and amid a blaze of publicity Narayana Pillai was given 18 months' imprisonment.[15]

VII.4 The Demand for Responsible Government

The rising discontent made the question of responsible government even more pressing, and the matter raised in a debate in the Legislative Assembly was of such importance that it led to a question in the British House of Commons, and elicited an important policy statement by Lord Winterton, Under-Secretary for India.

On 2nd February 1938 T.M.Verghese, leader of the Samyuktha Party, put an adjournment motion to discuss "the urgent need for immediate steps being taken by the Government for the establishment of Responsible Government in this state subject to the powers and prerogatives of His Highness the Maharaja".*

The Dewan-President at once stated that the rules of the House put the motion out of order as the relations of the state with the Paramount Power were outside its competence; but in view of the great interest in the matter it would not be wise or expedient to rule out discussion. He then made his own position perfectly clear. The Maharaja was the sole source of authority, and the Travancore constitution "exhibits the characteristics of a fully responsive as differentiated from a responsible form of Government". But he gave the real reason for the inability to change the constitution as the obligations of the ruler to the Paramount Power under the treaties of 1795 and 1805, which appertained to all fields of administration. "Legally therefore it is not possible without the active concurrence of the British Government for the Ruler to divest himself of his undivided authority and jurisdiction over the governance of his state in favour of any other authority".

It was a weak argument and T.M.Verghese demolished it in his opening speech. These was no necessary conflict between responsible government and the Maharaja's prerogatives; nor would it affect His Highness's relations with the King-Emperor. Responsible government was necessary because "sooner or later this state will have to link itself with a greater India", and if the representatives were nominated by the Maharaja the implication would be that the people of Travancore were unfit to gevern themselves. V.K.Velayudhan, the Ezhava leader, pointed out that the people of Travancore were more educated and fitter to govern themselves than the less well-educated people of the British provinces. Pattom Thanu Pillai, made, as ever, a thoughtful speech. He warned the Dewan that the time was ripe for advance, and the people of Travancore were sharing the thoughts and aspirations of the people across the Ghats. He too did not believe that the Paramount Power would raise difficulties in the way of granting responsible government; if it did, the Government of Travancore should press for it. He ended with an appeal, "not across the Ghats, but across the seas".

"Let us approach the Paramount Power and tell them: 'Here is a state where people are educated at great cost, and are given some political education also, who want to manage their own affairs. Will you Britishers who are so well-known throughout the world and

* Note by the Editor: A few weeks earlier Lord Lothian in a statement to the press had agreed with the Congress view that constitutional reforms in the Indian States were a necessary condition of their entering any form of federation with British India.

through the centuries for your love of freedom, help them in their attempt to get responsible government.?' "

The debate raged all day, and was talked out without a vote.[16]

The answer came across the seas. On February 21st, a question was asked in the House of Commons by one Captain Heligers of the Under-Secretary of state for India, drawing attention to Sir C.P.Ramaswamy Aiyar's statement that the power of the ruler of an Indian state to grant measures of responsible government is restricted by the necessity of obtaining the explicit consent of the Paramount Power, and asking what the policy of the British Government was in this matter. Lord Winterton, replying, said: "It is not the policy of the Paramount Power in ordinary circumstances to intervene in the internal administration of full-powered states. In particular, I can assure Captain Heligers that the Paramount Power would certainly not obstruct proposals for constitutional advance initiated by a Ruler". Pattom Thanu Pillai had his answer; and it was unequivocal.

Before Lord Winterton made his historic pronouncement, events in Trivandrum moved to a climax. A.Narayana Pillai had written his defiant letter to the Chief Secretary to Government, and made it public. The Chief Secretary passed it on to Sir C.P., who passed it on to the Advocate-General with his instructions how to conduct the case scribbled in the margin. When this leaked out public indignation reached boiling point. Narayana Pillai had not yet been arrested, and on 18th February a meeting was held in his office attended by many of the leading public figures: members of both Houses of the Legislature, leading lawyers and journalists—Nayars, Christians, Ezhavas, Muslims. Communal divisions were forgotten; they were blazing with indignation at the high-handed interference of the Dewan with the freedom of the press, the independence of the judiciary, the suspected violation of personal security. There was only one remedy, responsible government; only one way of attaining it, the formation of a party which would work for it; only one party in India pledged to the same aims as these men found they had in common. A resolution was proposed and carried unanimously that those present should form the Travancore state Congress.

Pattom Thanu Pillai, who had taken the chair, was unanimously elected president and T.M.Verghese deputy president. Two joint secretaries were appointed, one Nayar and one Christian; a Working Committee was elected which included C.Kesavan, V.K.Velayudhan (then general secretary of the S.N.D.P. Yogam); two leading Muslims, some more Christians who included both Catholics and Protestants, one woman (a Latin Catholic and a lawyer).

Apart from Brahmans, it was a cross-section of the major communities of Travancore.[17]

And so communalism was swept away on a tide of patriotic enthusiasm, and Travancore itself was swept into the national movement.

Chapter VIII

EVENTS LEADING TO CIVIL DISOBEDIENCE

The lines were now drawn between the opposing parties. It was a division on principle, no longer on communal lines; indeed "communalist" became a favourite term of abuse, freely used by both sides against each other. On one side were those who cared for civil liberties and the right of the people to have an effective voice in the government of their own country-men and women who hated what they considered to be an evil foreign influence at the palace, fomenting communalism, crushing freedom of expression, stooping to use hooligans to harass respectable citizens. On the other side were the supporters of palace and Dewan—some, it is true, were toadies and place-hunters, but many were sincere upholders of Princely rule. They recognized Sir C.P. as a Dewan of exceptional ability, and shared his belief that "responsive" government was more suited to the conditions of Travancore, with its quarelling communal factions, than "responsible" government. Many Nayars believed moreover that the recent reforms in the Legislature and the public services had placed their community at a disadvantage vis-à-vis the communities comprising the Samyuktha Party, considered the Travancore state Congress was but the Samyuktha Party writ large with the addition of a few disgruntled Nayars, and opposed it in all sincerity in the interests of their community. Both sides had their share of real trouble-makers, hot-heads, misguided idealists, or simply people out to get what pickings they could out of disturbance.

VIII.1 state Congress Leadership

From the outset, however, the Travancore state Congress contained a considerable proportion of the leading citizens who were free to take part in political activity: members of both Houses of the Legislature (not that that was necessarily a guarantee of respectability), leading lawyers, journalists working for reputable papers, the principal of the Jacobite Theological College. They were men who had a lot to lose, and were ready for sacrifice. They had no illusions.

We have met most of the leaders already. The president, Pattom A. Thanu Pillai, was one of the most respected public figures. Born in 1885, of one of those Trivandrum Nayar families from whom the higher officials were mostly drawn, he had been locally educated in the Maharaja's College and the Trivandrum Law College. He quickly became a prominent lawyer; he was an elected member of the Trivandrum Improvement Committee (which was the forerunner of the Trivandrum Municipality) and in 1927 was elected to the Legislative Council from the Trivandrum Urban Constituency. In 1933 he was elected to the Sri Mulam Assembly under the reformed Constitution, and was one of its leading members. When the University of Travancore was formed he was elected by the Assembly to be its representative on the Senate. He was the least communal of Nayars, and was never a member of the Nayar Service Society (their most important organization), though he joined in any activity when he felt the interests of the community needed it. Nor was he a Congressman before 1938, apart from a brief flirtation with Congress in 1930 which soon ended; he was too much of a monarchist and constitutionalist. He was the president of the reception committee of the South Indian States' Subjects Conference in 1929; but this was not a specifically Congress activity, and its aims, of responsible government under the aegis of the rulers, and the defence of fundamental civil rights, were after his own heart. It was only when he was faced with the contempt for civil liberties of a high-handed Dewan that he finally turned to the Congress.

Pattom's election to the presidency of the state Congress was unanimous. The group which formed the state Congress were largely members of the old Samyuktha Party, though there was a goodly sprinkling of Nayars even then; and they realized that they needed a Nayar as president if they were to shake off the label of communalists. But he was in any case the obvious choice because of his public position and his qualities of leadership. They were sure, too, that he could not be bought over; he (as also the Christian leader of the Samyuktha Party, T.M.Verghese) had been offered a post as Judge of the Travancore High Court, and had refused it.[1] Through all adversity he remained impervious to bribes and threats, and his faith in the rightness of his cause and its ultimate triumph was unshakeable.

He was new to the politics of revolution, which was really alien to his conservative nature and monarchist traditions. he therefore accepted Gandhi's lead—not always wisely or with the special conditions of Travancore in mind. But non-violence appealed to him; he had a hatred of violence and extreme measures, and became a leading advocate of non-violence. His was always the voice of moderation.

T.M.Verghese, who was elected vice-president, belonged to the Mar Thoma sect of Syrian Christians, which was the most progressive and the most missionary-minded. It was the Mar Thoma youth who had taken up the conversion of the Ezhavas with enthusiasm in 1935, and were the special object of Sir C.P.'s hatred. T.M.Verghese had been moreover the real leader of the Abstention Movement, and the initiator of the communal harmony talks which had led indirectly to the founding of the state Congress. He was an exceptionally able lawyer with a clear mind, and an excellent debater. He was strikingly good-looking, somewhat vain, well-dressed (to whom, gossip said, the wearing of *khaddar* was a real sacrifice). He found Gandhian ideas difficult to understand and did not take readily to the philosophy of non-violence; but he was realist enough to know it was the only weapon available to the oppressed, and stayed loyal to the state Congress and its Gandhian policies until just before the end of the struggle. His personal relations with Gandhi were excellent and he was always a welcome visitor to Wardha.

C.Kesavan was the third member of the unshakeable triumvirate of the state Congress. He was an Ezhava of a humble family of weavers and had earned his first school fees by weaving.[2] He worked his way through school and college, helped by his wife who was a primary school teacher, and finally took a law degree. But it was journalism that attracted him, and he worked for the leading Ezhava newspaper the *Kaumudi*, and finally became its editor. He was a very active member of the S.N.D.P. Yogam, and strongly anti-Nayar. For this reason he flung himself into the Abstention Movement and became one of its leaders. A fearless fighter, violent and abusive in his language, he almost deserved his two year sentence for sedition. Cooperation with Christians and Muslims in the Joint Political Congress cured him of the narrower form of communalism, and he came out of jail to declare his intention of working for the good of all communities. Like T.M.Verghese, he did not take readily to Gandhian ideas. His hatred of orthodox Hinduism made him anti-religious. He was Sir C.P.'s most outspoken opponent, and as far as is known Sir C.P. never even tried to win him over.

Two of the younger leaders, one a Syrian Christian and one a Nayar, who became close associates, deserve mention as showing the kind of young man who was attracted to the new movement. We have already met G.Ramachandran in his capacity as general secretary of the Kerala Harijan Sevak Sangh. After a little hesitation (for he waited to see if the new state Congress was as non-communal as it claimed to be) he flung himself into local politics and became a great orator and writer for the state Congress. He was the hero of the students.

E.John Philipose came from one of the ancient aristocratic Syrian Christian families of north Travancore, who claimed that their Nambudiri Brahman ancestors had been converted by St.Thomas the Apostle in the first century A.D. and had given him land for one of his seven chapels. (The family chapel still stands on that land.) He was the son of E.J.John, the doyen of the Trivandrum bar, from whose house in Trivandrum both the Abstention Movement and the earlier Communal Harmony talks had been launched. Educated at the Madras Christian College and the Trivandrum Law College, he proved as able a lawyer as his father. He was elected to the Sri Mulam Assembly in 1937 as a member of the Samyuktha Party and at once made his mark as a speaker. His special interest was Constitutional Law.[3]

Another personality we have met before, who only became a member of the Travancore State Congress later, was the president of the Kerala Harijan Sevak Sangh, Changanacherry K. Parameswaran Pillai. As early as 1913, as a very young member of the Sri Mulam Popular Assembly,* he had advocated responsible government for Travancore, and around 1921 became an ardent Congressman. He had been weaned from agitation by being made a Judge of the High Court of Travancore; but when he retired in 1932, he went back to public life by fighting for all good causes; and when the Trivandrum branch of the Indian National Congress was revived in 1937 he became its president. The mere fact that he was a retired High Court Judge gave him great prestige, which his own strength of character, integrity and independence of mind supported. People often said: "What does Changanacherry think?" He stayed aloof from the State Congress at first, not only because he thought of it as basically communal, but also to keep himself free, if need arose, to act as conciliator between the opposing parties. At the same time any attack on civil liberties found him in the forefront of the protestors, quite literally, for he headed numerous processions and took the chair at public indignation meetings. His position as an honorary prison visitor gave him opportunities to act as a go-between. When, therefore, he joined the State Congress nearly a year after its foundation in a blaze of righteous indignation, the effect was all the more impressive.

---

* Note by the Editor: The Sri Mulam Popular Assembly (1904-1932), preceded the Sri Mulam Assembly instituted under the reformed constitution.

He was not the only Congress-minded Travancorean who hesitated. The point at issue was: was the State Congress communal, as its enemies declared it to be? This question exercised the minds of a group of intellectuals, mostly young, who had founded the Young Kerala Society in 1937, in order to study and pronounce on social and political questions. Theoretically non-political, it had many Congressmen in it and also some young Christian leaders; Changanacherry was its president, G.Ramachandran its secretary, K.Kumar, that seasoned Congressman, and K.A.Mathew, secretary of the Kerala Student Christian Movement, among its members. In March 1938 it issued a statement on the political situation in Travancore, which welcomed the emergence of the State Congress, but expressed their dissatisfaction with the failure of its members to cut their affiliations with communal organizations. The Indian National Congress demanded that its members should not belong to any communal organization whereas the constitution of the Travancore State Congress was silent on the point. It was a serious criticism in view of the abuse hurled at it by its enemies. But in the conditions of Travancore it would have been an impossible requirement; communal organizations were social and educational bodies as well as political. The State Congress could not ask its Ezhava members to abandon the S.N.D.P.Yogam or its Catholic members their various Catholic societies. It had to accept the structure of Kerala society as it was, or become a small and ineffectual group. Its structure remained inter-communal but its policies were non-communal. Ramachandran soon became satisfied that it was truly non-communal in its aims and actions, and joined it in May 1938. K. Kumar remained unconvinced and never joined it, though he was not won over to the other side.[4]

The State Congress won the support of labour. As elsewhere in India at this time, the organizers of the trade unions were mainly politicians, educated men, and the presidents of the All-Travancore Labour Union were the Muslim P.K.Kunju and the Ezhava lawyer V.K.Velayudhan. They had been leaders of the Samyuktha Party and were members of the Legislative Assembly. They were two of the original members of the Working Committee of the State Congress. As the huge reception given to C.Kesavan in Alleppey on his release from jail had shown, the organized workers were already politically conscious. In their annual conference in May 1937, presided over by a great labour leader and Congressman, V.V.Giri (later president of the Indian Union) they had passed a resolution demanding responsible government for Travancore. P.K.Kunju and V.K.Velayudhan brought the labourers into the State

Congress en bloc.

Needless to say the students, already much influenced by the Congressmen who had been visiting Travancore since the temple entry campaign, were solid for the Congress—even the Brahmans among them. They were wildly enthusiastic and a thorough nuisance.

There was considerable interest outside Travancore in the new movement. The Narayana Pillai case had caught public attention, and the Indian Civil Liberties Union suggested to the leaders of the State Congress the formation of a Trivandrum branch, which, as it was non-political, might be acceptable to the state authorities. The general secretary of the All-India States Peoples' Conference took keen interest, though its president, Dr Pattabhi Sitaramayya, was worried about the "communal character" of the organization, and appealed to them to "get rid of the communal taint".[5] Malayalis, scattered all over India and beyond, were thrilled with the new developments, and branches of the Travancore State Congress were established in Madras, Bombay, Delhi and Calcutta, and even in Colombo.

But the Dewan was also building up his own party. He had a group at hand, the old National Party of the Sri Mulam Assembly who had helped him attack T.M.Verghese in the no-confidence motion of the previous November, and had spoken against the motion in favour of responsible government in February. Out of this rump he formed the Travancore National Congress. For its president he found a man of a different stamp, Mannath Padmanabha Pillai, president of the Nayar Service Society, and one of the grand old men of Travancore public life. He was nobody's jackal. Like C.Kesavan a boy from a poor family, who had worked his way through school, he became the life and soul of the Nayar Service Society and eventually its president. Ardent worker for his community though he was, he was no narrow communalist; he believed passionately in the abolition of untouchability, had been one of the leaders of the Vaikom satyagraha and a supporter of the 1936 temple entry campaign. But he too believed the State Congress to be nothing but the old Samyuktha Party plus a few disgruntled Nayars, and a menace to the Nayar community. When Sir C.P. suggested he should become the president of the Travancore National Congress he readily accepted.[6] But this group had almost no support outside Trivandrum though its activities were given much publicity from the Associated press of India. When they sent a delegation to meet the Mahatma, it found G.Ramachandran and John Philipose already there.[7] The Mahatma was good at separating sheep from goats and gave them polite words.

By March 1st the new State Congress was ready to go into action.

An office had been set up under an ebullient young journalist, M.M.Varkey: copies of rules, leaflets, receipt books for membership fees were ready printed. A statement was issued to the press announcing the aims of the State Congress to be "the attainment of Responsible Government under the aegis of His Highness the Maharaja by all peaceful and legitimate means".

There was an immediate and enthusiastic response. Letters poured in from all over Travancore and from members of the old community organizations declaring support, announcing the formation of local committees, asking for copies of rules and receipt books, and yet more receipt books, please, by return post, and asking for visits from members of the Working Committee. Many writers expressed their joy that a really national party had come into being to replace the old communal parties with their narrow sectional outlook. The Travancore Committee of the Indian National Congress met, and in the light of the Haripura Resolution advised its members to join the Travancore State Congress, and dissolved itself.[8]

In face of all this enthusiasm, the Dewan might well have blenched. But he had all the resources of the state at his command—the officials, the law courts, the police, and in the background, the state Forces. He had almost illimitable powers of patronage and control of funds such as university grants to educational institutions, which could be used as inducements to communal organizations. Above all, he had the unquestioning backing of the palace. He was well equipped for battle and confident of a swift and crushing victory.

VIII.2 The First Skirmishes

Battle commenced on March, 7th 1938.

Two days previously, when I went to see Sir C.P. on matters connected with the International Fellowship, I found him tremendously excited about the Travancore State Congress. "It's the best thing that has happened in Travancore in years!" he exclaimed. "Responsible Government is the aim, but Travancore is not ready for it. The State Congress is all in the right direction; but I am playing the role of persecutor, for they must be prepared to be in the wilderness before they are fit for self-government".[9]

On March 7th the District Magistrate of the Trivandrum district prohibited all meetings of the State Congress in the district for two months, on the grounds that a rival party was likely to resent the meetings and cause a breach of the peace. The State Congress promptly issued a statement that in that case it was the duty of the authorities to restrain the troublesome rival party (on whose existence they cast doubts) and not to ban meetings of peaceful citizens; and Pattom Thanu Pillai petitioned for the rescindment of the ban on the ground that it was an infringement of the fundamental rights of speech and organization of loyal and law-abiding citizens. The petition was rejected. Similar prohibitory orders were passed in all districts of Travancore except the High Range, the mountainous area inhabited by planters and their workers and wild animals.[10]

Recruitment to the State Congress was stimulated by repression. From Quilon a young man wrote to the secretary: "This letter is the result of that unwanted order. Blood boils and I can no more keep silent. . . Please send me bills, forms and receipts. In six months you can see all young men of this place as members of the Congress". From the High Range, where branches were being formed on the tea estates, one organizer writing for a fresh supply of receipt books, said: "There are so many young men who have the courage even to court arrest". From the outset neither the leaders nor their followers were under any illusion about the price they would have to pay. "All the people", he added in a later letter, "are privately in favour of the Congress and are eager to see it grow. But for fear of consequences of joining it they keep aloof".[11]

The government's repressive policy extended to the labour movement. The Dewan did not want labour trouble on his hands as well; an order prohibiting public meetings in Alleppey for two months was passed on March 16th, on the grounds that plans were being made for a general strike which would occasion breaches of the peace. There were no such plans, and the labourers assembled on March 21st in front of the Alleppey Police Station were dispersed by a *lathi* charge in which several persons were injured and one man died; the secretary of the Travancore Labour Association claimed that the man had died from *lathi* cuts, the government that he was trampled on by the crowd. There was no public enquiry, although the Labour Association pressed for one; the refusal of the government to hold one led to a savage feeling of resentment, which several months later exploded into a general strike and violence. The labour movement henceforward supported the State Congress though some of its activities were independent.

The press was controlled still further. The Ezhava papers, the daily and the weekly *Kaumudi* had their licences cancelled on the grounds that they had reprinted an article by George Joseph (one of Gandhi's closest disciples from Travancore who had just died) on responsible government. It had appeared 19 months earlier without arousing comment; now it was seditious. Other newspapers received warnings against printing seditious matter. The freedom of the press was undermined; a number of smaller newspapers ceased publication and others became cautious in their reporting and their comments.

On April 4th the Dewan's term of office was extended by five years. It was a warning to his critics that he had the backing of the palace and intended to stay in the saddle.

Unable to make themselves heard on the platform or in the local press, the State Congress sent a strong delegation to the freer and friendlier city of Madras, now under a Congress government headed by C. Rajagopalachari.[12] A.K. Pillai, one of the founders of the original Trivandrum branch of the Indian National Congress in 1921, was now a successful barrister in Madras, and he had already organized a branch of the Travancore State Congress in the city, and organized meetings for the delegation. The politically-minded citizens of Madras had heard (Sir C.P. had a well-organized grape-vine extending far into British India) that the new body consisted of penniless young agitators with nothing to lose, and were surprised to encounter a group of solid respectable citizens. Two well-attended meetings were held by the Congress, and the Civil Liberties Union held another, for they had been shocked by the Narayana Pillai case and the gross interference with the rights of the accused. Now they learned that the peaceful demand for responsible government had been met with instant repression and wide spread interference with civil liberties. It was difficult for leading Congressmen such as "Rajaji" (the Premier's widely-used name) and the president of the Madras Civil Liberties Union to associate Sir C.P., once the life and soul of the Home Rule League and the hero of the Temple Entry Proclamation, with the repression of a moderate and constitutional movement for responsible government; but the facts were incontrovertible. The Premier was on the horns of a dilemma—the basic dilemma which by now British policy towards the states had created: on the one hand he sympathized with liberating movements, on the other he was in charge of a great province and took a different point of view on matters of law and order from that of his days as a freedom fighter, and was cautious towards anything that might lead to a breach of the peace. Besides, Sir C.P. was an old friend and a fellow-Brahman.

The delegation was invited to Bombay and Delhi to speak to the groups that had been formed in these cities; but as the prohibitory orders in Trivandrum were due to expire on May 7th, and recruitment to the State Congress was going on apace, they decided to return to

Travancore to build up their organization, and by the beginning of May they were back in Trivandrum and busy organizing a tour.

They returned to more trouble. True, the ban on their meetings had been lifted, but they were subjected to personal harassment, and many meetings were broken up by rowdy trouble-makers. A pattern emerged which was followed right down to 1947: State Congress members went to address a meeting, rowdies turned up and created a disturbance (or began one while the meeting was going on peacefully) while the police stood by; later they moved in and troubled the speakers and not the rowdies; the crowd got restive in spite of appeals for calm by the speakers, who asked them to disperse, not always successfully; the police then charged the crowd with *lathis* and the meeting broke up in disorder. The government and the State Congress then issued contradictory statements, the government blaming the inflammatory speeches of the State Congress for inciting the crowd to violence, the State Congress declaring their adherence to non-violence and accusing the police of putting the rowdies up to create a disturbance so that the police had an excuse to move in and break up the meeting. It is certainly true that where the police were absent, State Congress meetings were peaceful. Meanwhile recruitment of State Congress members continued and new branches continued to be formed.

A Congress meeting held at Chenganoor, on June 25th, in central Travancore where Congress was strongest, proved the climax of the campaign and led to a sharp exchange between Sir C.P. and Gandhi.[13] A full account by G.Ramachandran was published in *The Hindu*; and as G.R. was Gandhi's close disciple and incapable of telling a deliberate lie, this may be taken as substantially true. A number of the leaders went there to address an open-air meeting, and found a huge crowd already assembled at the bus station, and the police already beating up people along the road to the meeting place. The leaders determined to hold the meeting, but when they got to the meeting place the platform was already occupied by rowdies who attacked them. That young aristocrat, John Philipose, was beaten with a slipper (in India the worst possible insult) and almost lost self-control; but even he submitted to the beating. The leaders appealed to the crowd to remain peaceful; but the police, who had made no attempt to protect the speakers, charged the crowd with *lathis* and did considerable damage. At this the crowd lost patience and began to pelt the police with stones and chased them down the road to the police station. The leaders linked arms across the road to stop the crowd harassing the police and urged the crowd to disperse. But after they themselves had gone back to Trivandrum the police renewed their *lathi* charges and inflicted damage on some of the crowd.

G.Ramachandran concluded his account of these happenings with the statement: "The problem now facing us in Travancore is far more fundamental than political reform. The question is whether peaceable citizens are to be persecuted for the exercise of fundamental civil rights by organized hooliganism".

Mr. Gandhi telegraphed the Dewan to protest: "Hope state will recognize altered times and allow full play expression public opinion". The Dewan telegraphed back: "Greatly regret you should have arrived at conclusion without reference to other side stop sorry Ramachandran's statement ignores injuries sustained by Hindu Loyalist League stop your assertion no provocation not accurate stop Travancore Government have no desire to interface with legitimate political activities"

Not only were peaceful meetings broken up but individual State Congress members were attacked. The case of Miss Anne Mascarene, the only woman on the State Congress Working Committee, aroused much comment both within and outside Travancore. She was one of three women advocates of the Trivandrum bar, and a keen member of the Trivandrum branch of the All-India Women's Conference, where her fiery speeches roused some amusement but an honest straight-forward lass and a devout Roman Catholic. On the night of April 29th, when she had just returned tired out after a strenuous tour, she was awakened by the flashing of a torch in her eyes, and found she had been robbed of everything she possessed except the small suitcase under her bed which she had not yet unpacked, so at least she had a sari to wear when she went to the police station. The police were extraordinarily dilatory about finding the robber, although Miss Mascarene had a good notion who he was; and when she complained of the delay and appealed for protection, she was served with a notice threatening her with prosecution for defamation of character of the Inspector of Police. Her reply was so spirited that the case was dropped—but the robber was never arrested. "Indian Womanhood Insulted", "Our Women's Honour Unsafe", the local papers roared with it for weeks, and it made headlines in papers in British India. She was safe for the time being.[14]

Two more members of the State Congress were physically assaulted, one being one of the general secretaries of the State Congress, K.P. Nilakanta Pillai. On June 19th, as he was walking along the lonely road that leads to his house, he was set upon by three rowdies and his arm broken; his shouts attracted a crowd who caught one of his assailants and took him to the police station; another one was pulled in shortly after. (It is an interesting point that these assailants, caught by members of the public, were the only ones brought to book for their assaults on State Congress members.)

Public indignation now boiled over. Next day a public meeting of protest was organized. Judge Changanacherry Parameswaran Pillai led a procession from the Congress office to the great square outside the new Railway Station; at that time it had no garden or railings, so it formed an open space which could - and in those times often did—accommodate some 20,000 people. G.Ramachandran, who had just come from visiting K.P.Nilakanta Pillai in hospital, was the chief speaker, and the meeting passed a resolution protesting against the failure of the government to secure adequate protection to peaceful citizens.

Travancore affairs were now receiving such publicity that the government issued a press note on July 1st, putting the blame for the disturbances in the state on the subversive activities of the State Congress, which were strongly resented by important sections of the public. The State Congress issued an equally strongly worded reply, which mainly blamed the police with failing to control the rowdies who broke up peaceful meetings, and with charging crowds who had not been ordered to disperse. They claimed that their movement was perfectly constitutional, and that they were pledged to non-violence.

A bye-election at the beginning of June provided another occasion for clashes. The leader of the National Party in the Legislature had just been given the post of Legal Remembrancer to Government, causing a vacancy. The State Congress decided to put up a candidate, but the rival candidate had government backing, which included that of government officials and the police. There was a good deal of rowdyism and rough handling of electors, particularly on election day. The government candidate obtained two thirds of the votes, but local people resented the result which they felt was no measure of the support for the State Congress. Such blatant police and official interferences, they said, made a mockery of the so-called democratic institutions of Travancore.[15]

Meanwhile the Dewan continued his efforts to weaken the State Congress. His aim seems to have been to isolate the Christians, for he addressed himself to the Hindu groups and attempted to stir up communalism among them. The Nayars were already a split community; some of them felt they were now an underprivileged minority community, while others followed Pattom Thanu Pillai into the State Congress precisely because it was above communalism. There was a big Nayar conference in May at which there was a serious division among the delegates and a number of them walked out. To those who remained, Sir C.P. promised support for a proposed Nayar College in Trivandrum for the promotion of Kerala arts and literature; in his message to the conference he stated that the university was prepared to encourage the scheme.[16]

For the Nayars, gifts; for the Ezhavas, who stood solid behind the State Congress, threats. Their great organization, the S.N.D.P. Yogam, had been founded by Sri Narayana Guru for the social, religious, educational and economic welfare of the community, and held its license of incorporation in those terms. But it had undoubtedly strayed into politics, first in its support to the Abstention Movement and the Joint Political Conference, and more recently in its deep involvement in State Congress politics. On June 3rd, therefore, the government issued a notice to the general secretary, V.K.Velayudhan, asking the Yogam to show cause why its license should not be revoked, as it had engaged in political activities unconnected with its declared objects. The Board of Directors asked for time to call a general body meeting; but V.K.Velayudhan privately told the Dewan that if the threats to revoke the license were carried out, the Board would promptly dissolve the Yogam and turn its thousand branches (there were actually 700) into a thousand branches of the State Congress.[17] The matter was dropped.

VIII.3 The Memorial and the Memorandum

For the first three months the State Congress campaign was fought on the closely-related issues of responsible government and civil liberties. Though they clamoured for the immediate introduction of responsible government, they knew perfectly well it was an aim for the future; it was the issue of civil liberty which aroused the deepest passions among the local people and the widest interest outside—for it was direct, personal and immediate.

At the end of May, however, the State Congress made a new move, an attack on the Dewan himself. It took the form of a Memorial addressed directly to His Highness the Maharaja, petitioning for the establishment of responsible government, accompanied with a Memorandum setting forth at length the reasons for this petition. It was signed by 21 members of the Working Committee of the Travancore State Congress; a twenty-second name was appended of a member unable to sign personally: "A.Narayana Pillai (in jail)".

The Memorial was brief and dignified. "His Gracious Highness's humble and loyal subjects" requested "a Cabinet of Ministers responsible to the Legislature;"* secondly, adult franchise; thirdly, a declaration of fundamental civil rights, freedom of speech and of the press, freedom of religious worship, freedom from arbitrary arrest or imprisonment, a guarantee of a living wage; fourthly, the restoration of the independence of the judiciary and finally, the dismissal of Sir C.P. Ramaswamy Aiyar from the service of the state and an independent inquiry into his acts as Dewan.

The Memorandum was a much longer document. The first part was a dignified and restrained statement of the need for responsible government to replace the present system of administration which was corrupt and inefficient. The recent reforms had overcome the former communal differences, and the Travancore State Congress had united all communities in the demand for responsible government.

The second part contained the direct attack on the Dewan. The existing Government was the greatest obstacle to the attainment of responsible government, because of its policy of crushing a peaceful constitutional movement. The responsibility for the unpopularity of the government and the corruption of public life was placed squarely on the Dewan's shoulders. The Memorandum listed a number of shady business transactions in connection with public enterprise, cases of nepotism, the bribery of party leaders with highly paid government posts. The only remedies were the establishment of responsible government, the termination of Sir C.P.Ramaswamy Aiyar's contract, and an independent inquiry.

On May 30th these documents were sent to the private secretary to the Maharaja for presentation to His Highness. His Highness passed them on to the Dewan without comment; and officially they disappeared. It is not known if the Maharaja so much as read them. But as they remained totally unacknowledged, the Working Committee decided to publish them in book form. This book, printed in Cochin state, appeared at the end of June under the title *Travancore Today* (1938), and contained not only the Memorial and Memorandum, but also many relevant appendixes, concerning such matters as the Narayana Pillai trial, attacks on the State Congress leaders, police interference in public meetings and the bye-election, the suppression of newspapers. Its import into Travancore was of course at once forbidden but within a few weeks everybody of any consequence in the state had read it,

* Note by the Editor: The Memorial emphasized that the Cabinet of Ministers should not only be responsible to the legislature, but also "subject to the powers and prerogatives of His Highness the Maharaja".

secretly and avidly.

The signatories had looked forward to being arrested for sedition; the trial would have given them an All-India audience and created a far bigger sensation than even the Narayana Pillai case. They had their brief prepared. Astute lawyers like T.M.Verghese and public men of high integrity like Pattom Thanu Pillai would never have put their signatures to allegations which they could not prove up to the hilt. But there was no trial. The charges were never proved nor disproved. Sir C.P.'s energies were rather devoted to persuading the signatories to withdraw the Memorandum. The Resident for months pressed Sir C.P. to have the trial for sedition, or else submit the matter to a special tribunal under a judge from British India, so as to clear the matter up once and for all, and he went to endless trouble to find the right man. Sir C. P. first displayed enthusiasm for the idea; but later, in a series of long letters to the Resident, gave reasons for not proceeding with the inquiry, but proposed to try the signatories in the Travancore courts.[19] But he redoubled his efforts to get the Memorandum withdrawn, mainly by trying to persuade Mahatma Gandhi to put pressure on the signatories. So the allegations were never examined and the signatories at no time had the opportunity to produce their evidence in court. The accusations against the Dewan hung like a black cloud over all subsequent dealings between the Travancore State Congress and the Dewan, and made any kind of compromise, let alone reconciliation, impossible.

The Memorandum remains a subject of fierce debate. G.Ramachandran would not touch it, and it kept Changanacherry from joining the State Congress for months, even though he was the strongest critic of the Travancore Government in the matter of civil liberty. The veteran Congressman A.K.Pillai, who knew the mind of Pattom Thanu Pillai, stated that it had been intended as a confidential memorandum for the Maharaja's eye only and was never meant for publication; and it was only when the petition was ignored that the Working Committee decided to publish it.[20] Most important, Gandhi thought it was a mistake, because it sullied the purity of the motives of the Travancore State Congress by bringing in personal attacks. The issues should have remained at the level of the great principles of freedom and democracy. The State Congress leaders (speaking privately) justified their attack on Sir C.P. by their need to exploit Sir C.P.'s unpopularity in order to win mass support.

The historian has the advantage of hindsight in judging motives and actions. I consider Mr. Gandhi was right in calling the Memorandum a mistake. During the first three months of the State Congress campaign, they had been borne along on a tremendous wave of popular enthusiasm for the non-communal character of their movement, the demands for responsible government, and their defence of fundamental civil rights. They had the decency and good sense not to bring in Sir C.P.'s private life, although it was the subject of universal gossip and an underlying if unmentioned cause of the disgust with which he was regarded; they did not need openly to attack his alleged venality and nepotism to stir up hatred against him. His suppression of civil rights won the sympathy for the state's citizens throughout India and considerable interest abroad. Then Roman Catholics in particular had the ear of Roman Catholic Members of Parliament and could well have arranged for a "Question in the House", as long as it was a matter of civil liberty.* But a personal attack on an Indian politician who upheld the British policy of balancing the Princes against the Congress was the wrong ground of attack.

On the other hand, once the Memorandum was published, the mischief was done. Gandhi's first reaction was to denounce it as a mistake; at the same time he considered, as did the Resident, that the charges should be openly refuted. But later he dropped his demand for an open inquiry and confined himself to urging the signatories to withdraw the charges unconditionally. For a long time he could not bring himself to believe that the author of the Temple Entry Proclamation was less than noble,[21] and he was overpersuaded that there was no evidence for the charges because it was not produced, and ignored the fact that they were never given the opportunity to produce it. He accepted Sir C.P.'s opinion of the signatories that they were irresponsible agitators making unfounded accusations, In this matter the Mahatma, usually so shrewd, had the wool pulled over his eyes by Sir C.P., to the fury of the younger Congressmen in particular. But more of that in its proper place in the narrative.

VIII. 4 The Bank Crash[22]

Sensation followed sensation in those crowded months of mid-1938. After the sensation of the publication of the Memorial and Memorandum came the sensation of the failure of the Travancore

---

* Note by the Editor: Earlier Lord Fitz Alan had raised questions in the House of Lords about what he saw as the threatened position of the Travancore Christian Community.

National and Quilon bank. It was no ordinary crash, for it had wide repercussions on the political situation.

To sketch in the background: in June 1937 two successful banks, the Travancore National bank and the Quilon bank, both founded by Syrian Christians and largely run by them, had amalgamated to form the Travancore National and Quilon bank. The first had been founded by the family of K.C.Mammen Mappillay, that same leading Syrian Christian who had taken a prominent part in the founding of the Joint Political Conference, and had welcomed C.Kesavan on his release from jail. He became Chairman of the new joint bank. In the twenties he had been a member of the Legislative Council and had served on various government committees. The Chairman of the Quilon Bank was C.P.Matthen, whose father had founded it; he was a highly successful businessman, not involved in politics, but he too had served on government committees. Both banks had been very successful, and when they amalgamated most of their business was outside Travancore. Sir C.P. took a keen interest in the amalgamation, and although their biggest field of activity was in Madras, he insisted on the new bank being registered in Travancore. In return, he promised them a large government deposit and a share in government financial business. The bank, moreover, was anxious not to appear a purely Christian concern and invited some Hindus onto the Board of Directors; Sir C.P. himself suggested one K.S.Ramanujam, a former official of the Imperial Bank of India.

But early in 1938 there were growing rumours about the bank's unsoundness. The suspicion grew that Sir C.P. himself was at the bottom of these rumours, and this was confirmed when it leaked out that on April 25th the Commissioner of Police had issued a confidential order to all police officers "for strict compliance": "In view of the large deposits withdrawn from the National Quilon bank, the solvency of the institution has to be seriously questioned. The public should be warned against the danger involved in having pecuniary transactions with the bank".[23] Confidential communications in Travancore rarely remained confidential, and there was a run on the bank. It survived, though with difficulty. The Resident tried to persuade the Dewan to offer help, but he would only do so if the directors refrained from all political activities. (They had taken no part in the State Congress movement.) The directors appealed to the Reserve bank in vain. The pressure continued and finally the bank closed its doors on June 21st. In the announcement of the closure, the Chairman, K.C. Mammen Mappillay, specifically stated that the bank's troubles were due to "the persistent inimical and malicious propaganda" carried on by Sir C.P., and the board were in a position to prove it. Attempts were made to reconstruct the bank, but Sir C.P. insisted on his pound of flesh. He persuaded the Resident to issue an extradition warrant ordering the directors, who were in Madras, to be arrested and brought back for trial in Travancore. K.S.Ramanujam, Sir C.P.'s nominee, turned approver and gave evidence for the prosecution, and went scot-free. After a trial in which much of the evidence for the defence was withheld, the Travancore High Court gave the accused, all Syrian Christians, excessively long sentences.

The case was very complex. The bank had unquestionably sinned against banking practice, invested too much in fixed assests; and the balance sheet of December 31st, 1937, had unquestionably been doctored. But the bank was basically sound and could have been rescued; after it was wound up it still could pay its creditors 13 *annas* in the rupee (of 16 *annas*).

We are not here concerned with the rights and wrongs of the bank case so much as with its political effects. Sir C.P. had made martyrs of the directors, for everybody from the Viceroy downwards blamed the attack on the Dewan. The Syrian Christian community, and also their allies in the State Congress, saw the attack on the bank as primarily an anti-Christian move. Far from splitting the communities, the bank affair knit them more closely than ever in opposition to the foreign tyrant.

The major political effect of the bank crash was to swing the powerful, wealthy and well-organized Syrian Christian community solid behind the Travancore State Congress, and through that brought them into the national movement. Christians as a whole had been suspicious of the Indian National Congress (like the Muslims though not to the same fanatical extent) as a Hindu-dominated organization; and many of them had been inclined to look to the British to protect them from Hindu encroachment. The Syrian Christians in particular had been more interested in their position within Travancore than in national politics. The bank crash came as a tremendous shock. The directors had appealed to the Resident in vain for help. Now the whole community became the most ardent supporters of Congress; Christian money, Christian drive, Christian organization, kept up the fight through the blackest days. Christian contacts kept the outside world informed. Sir C.P. was wrong in stigmatizing the whole movement as a Christian one, "financed by the fraudulent bankers to take Travancore over and turn it into a Christian state"—it was a combined effort of all the communities. But it was his own actions that awakened the national ardour of the Syrian Christians.

If Sir C.P. had calculated that his anti-Christian propaganda would induce Mahatma Gandhi to withdraw his support from the Travancore State Congress, he had misread the Mahatma's mind. Gandhi was not anti-Christian as such; many of his most trusted workers, such as Rajkumari Amrit Kaur, the Kumarappa brothers, Samuel Aryanayagam, were Christians. He was rather against foreign missionaries whom he tended to regard as emissaries of a foreign culture, and he was critical of any kind of conversion which he thought unnecessary as all religions led to the same truth. There is no doubt that his contacts with Syrian Christians, who could justly claim that their Christianity was far older in India than Islam and had developed a truly indigenous Christian culture, modified his attitude markedly.

VIII. 5 The Budget Session

The Budget Session of the Legislature in July and August 1938 brought all the politicians to the capital. As the Dewan was president of both Houses, and the high officials were members of both, they took place consecutively in the Assembly in July and the state Council in August.

Trivandrum was by now in an angry mood, buzzing like a disturbed beehive. Police high-handedness was one cause; there had been that great protest meeting against the assaults on Congress leaders, followed by the indignation over the Chenganoor *lathi* charge. The closing of the bank had affected hundreds, and many inclined to believe its Chairman's direct accusation of the Dewan's responsibility. Moreover, the students were now back from their long vacation. There were about two thousand of them in Trivandrum's five colleges. Many of them had been swept up into the Congress movement, ready to cheer the State Congress leaders and boo the Dewan and his supporters. *Khaddar* was the fashionable wear, and since the minimum age for membership of the Congress was 18, hundreds had enrolled as actual members. It was an explosive mixture.

The angry mood was exacerbated by the contrasts of repression in Travancore with progress in the neighbouring state of Cochin and Mysore, to which much publicity was given. Cochin had taken the first step towards responsible government by appointing one member of its Executive Council from the Legislative Assembly, to be responsible to the Assembly for the administration of his department. A well-known

Congressman had been chosen; the Congress was recognized and cooperated happily with the Cochin Government. The Paramount Power had presumably given its blessing to the experiment—at any rate the British Resident attended all the functions inaugurating this constitutional step forward. In Mysore, ruled by a saintly old Maharaja and his able Dewan, Sir Mirza Ismail, there had been on outbreak of violence; in April the police had attacked a Congress meeting, torn down the Congress flag and fired on the crowd, killing fifteen; within four days Sir Mirza Ismail had set up an inquiry under an independent judge from British India, a leading Congressman Sardar Vallabhbhai Patel had come to make peace, a Constitutional Committee was set up on which Congress was represented. The families of those killed were compensated. The Dewan undertook that Mysore's representatives on any Federal body would be selected in accordance with popular wishes. Peace and goodwill reigned; after all this Sir Mirza continued his benevolent autocratic rule just as before with general support. If such things were possible in other states, no more advanced and enlightened than Travancore, people asked each other, why not in Travancore too? The bees buzzed louder.

The Sri Mulam Assembly opened on July 10th in a tense mood. The Samyuktha Party, of which all the members had joined the State Congress, dissolved itself. The Travancore State Congress was now organized as a parliamentary party with Pattom Thanu Pillai as its leader and T.M. Verghese as its deputy leader. They created a sensation by arriving in procession all dressed in *khaddar* with Gandhi caps on their heads. It must be noted that the Jubilee Town Hall, in which the sessions were held, is on the main road and adjacent to the big Science College with its 800 students, in which students from other colleges tended to gather. At the end of the Assembly session the students came out to cheer their heroes and boo the unpopular Dewan and his chief secretary.

After a week of this behaviour the Dewan decided to teach the students a lesson. On Friday July 15th police officers ordered the principals of the government colleges to warn their students not to go to the Town Hall as they were proposing to use violence against them (a warning calculated to send all two thousand of them trooping there to see the fun). By four in the afternoon the police were on all side roads armed with *lathis* while the students were at the Town Hall end of the Science College compound booing and cheering; meanwhile in the side road at the other end young ragamuffins were collecting road metal and dropping it over the wall into the college compound. Also on the side roads were Congressmen patrolling the streets trying to persuade students from other colleges, in the name of non-violence, to turn back. Also present, the improbable figure of the Commandant of the state Forces, Col. Harold Watkis, doing his weekend shopping, who realized something was up, parked his car, and went across to pacify the students. Suddenly the ragamuffins entered the compound, collected their ammunition and began to throw stones from behind the students. At this police poured into the compound and began to beat the students, smashing tennis racquets and bicycles in their zeal. The Pro-Vice-Chancellor arrived on the scene to find the police arresting some innocent tennis players behind the building who had imprudently taken refuge in the tennis court instead of taking to their heels; when the Pro-Vice-Chancellor protested, a police officer said, "We must make *some* arrests". Colonel Watkis charged in, rescued a badly-injured fourteen-year-old schoolboy, took him to hospital, and then ordered out the Maharaja's bodyguard to play the part of mounted police, to keep not the students, but the police, in order.

Nothing so aroused public anger as this *lathi* charge on the students in the very heart of the capital. It was widely believed that the trouble had been deliberately stirred up by the Dewan so that he could accuse the State Congress—as he did, in every statement about their methods—of fostering violence "in order to bring about contempt of lawful authority and in particular of fostering student unrest". These allegations were contradicted by a thousand indignant young witnesses who told their story all over the state and beyond. That the victims—four of whom were detained in hospital and an uncounted number received minor injuries—were students and schoolboys added fuel to the flames.

If the intention had been to overawe the students the exercise was a failure. They were raging; they wanted a week's strike and demonstrations and a public protest meeting. A committee quickly formed itself, led by a forceful young Muslim, Mohammed Basheer, who was prominent in the Students' Inter-religious Fellowship and therefore in touch with the brightest sparks in all the colleges. They went to the Congress office to ask the leaders for their cooperation. G. Ramachandran prevailed on them to adopt the Gandhian method of a day's *hartal*, to stay at home on the following Monday with fasting and prayer. The lads also agreed, in the name of non-violence, not to demonstrate at the Town Hall any more. Next day the Dewan, uncomfortably aware of the severe criticism of Col. Watkis and the Resident (who had also been doing his weekend shopping) of the police excesses, gave a small lunch party for the leading members of the University and Col. Watkis to discuss the situation; as a result his guests went off to the Congress office to ask for the cooperation of the leaders in restoring peace. They agreed to enrol no more student members, and to allow a week to elapse before calling a public meeting. Col. Watkis proposed a hockey match, Army vs. University, to restore good humour. Peace was restored; the lecturers lectured to almost empty classrooms on Monday, but on Tuesday all the colleges were working normally.*

The promised public meeting was held the following Saturday at the Railway *Maidan*. It was almost a blood-bath. The Dewan was determined to put down criticism with a strong hand and ordered out the state Forces to police the meeting and put down disorder. But the Resident was kept fully informed of what was going on and prevailed on the Dewan to withdraw the orders. There was a huge rally; parents had travelled from al over the state to voice their protest. The speeches were strong but there was no disorder. It was resolved to appoint an unofficial committee of distinguished citizens to inquire into the police attack on the students. Changanacherry Parameswaran Pillai was its secretary.

The Committee met and asked for government cooperation. The committee were told that they had no kind of official standing; moreover the government were appointing their own Committee in the University to inquire into the student disorders, and government officials and students were forbidden to give evidence before the unofficial Committee. It had to give up. No government committee was ever appointed and no inquiry was held.[24]

The Resident put the blame squarely on the excesses of the police, and pressed for the resignation of the Commissioner of Police. But he

---

* Note by the Author: I have given a full account of this episode, partly because it was an important part of the Dewan's case against the State Congress that they had fostered unrest among the students, partly because every account I have read of it is garbled. So much flowed from this incident that it is important to get the facts right. I was in a position to know. The principal being conveniently absent that weekend, I as Senior Professor of the Arts College was in charge; it was to me that the students came with their stories, their broken heads, bicycles, tennis racquets. I also got full accounts from Col. Watkis, G.Ramachandran, and Mrs. Sally Handley, wife of the adjutant, whose bull terrier pup had got mixed up with the melee as she was returning from her weekend shopping. Later I got a clue as to the identity of the ragamuffins, as I shall relate in its proper place.

was a favourite at "the Palace" - an amiable but rather ineffective Brahmin; and it was not until lives were lost that the Resident was able to get an efficient special police officer appointed to deal with riot situations.

At the beginning of August it was the turn of the Sri Chitra state Council to hold its budget session.[25] Meanwhile meetings of the Travancore State Congress and the Youth League had been banned because of the rising excitement. The state Council also had its Congress group. Its leader, N.V.Chacko, set the tone in his remarks on the Dewan's budget speech; he thanked the Dewan for extracting from the British Government the assurance that they would not stand in the way of Travancore or any other state introducing responsible government. (The Proceedings record: "president: 'Order order. That is an irrelevant remark.'") The Congress members fought the Dewan every step of the way: through adjournment motions which were disallowed by the Dewan-President, through questions, also disallowed, through discussions on every grant, particularly that for the police. Finally, the Dewan-President was stung into making the pronouncement: "As the Government is carried on by the agents of His Highness, any criticism of the Government is criticism of His Highness, and the Penal Code puts them on the same basis" If this were true, any criticism of the Dewan was subversive and disloyal; but the Congress members claimed the right and the duty of criticism and continued to speak out fearlessly.

Matters were now moving swiftly to the crisis. As soon as the latest prohibition of meetings was issued, the Working Committee met, and resolved not to submit to prohibitory orders any longer. The government, they pointed out, was giving the Travancore National Congress full freedom to carry on propaganda for responsible government, and there was no reason why the State Congress should be muzzled. Pattom Thanu wrote to the Chief secretary conveying the Working Committee's resolution to assert its right of public meeting, and its intention, if the ban were not withdrawn, to defy it in certain selected places on the first day of the Malabar New Year (August 15th).* The government were adamant: the State Congress were subversive and disloyal and the ban could not be withdrawn.

At this point Mahatma Gandhi intervened; he asked the State Congress to stay its hand as he proposed to send an "Ambassador" to

---

* Note by the Editor: The Malabar year began on August 15th and the Malabar era in 824 A.D. The year 1114 M.E. was therefore 1938-1939 A.D.

make peace.

The Youth League however refused to wait. It had made its own plans to hold a conference on August 20th in defiance of the ban on its meeting. It should be noted that this Youth League was not strictly a Congress organization; it had been founded in 1931 at a time of national excitement, had become quiescent but had recently sprung into activity again. It was socialist but not at this time communist. The League invited that socialist firebrand, Kamaladevi Chattopadhyaya, to preside. The government prohibited her entry into Travancore; but as the Railway was British India property over which the Government of Travancore had no jurisdiction, she came along it as far as Trivandrum, where she delivered a speech on Liberty on the station platform. She then came out of the station, was arrested by the Travancore Police amid the cheers of the crowd, rushed off by police car and released again across the frontier in British India. There were demonstrations and a few of the leaders of the Youth League were arrested.[26]

Meanwhile Gandhi's "ambassador" had arrived. She was one of his closest followers, Rajkumari Amrit Kaur. Of the Christian branch of the ruling family of the Sikh state of Kapurthala, she was the ideal person for the situation. She could deal on equal terms with the Maharani; she spoke with the authentic voice of the Mahatma, and she was acceptable to the large Christian element in the State Congress, to whom she was well-known for her devoted work for the Y.M.C.A. Rajkumari was in Trivandrum from August 18th to 25th; she saw the Dewan at once and several times later, she visited the Maharani, she saw both the State Congress leaders and the leaders of the National Congress; she had personal talks with her old friend G.Ramachandran and her new friend Pattom Thanu Pillai. She wrote a very long "aide memoire" for Gandhi and also took him a letter from Pattom setting out the State Congress point of view.

The Dewan, she reported, appeared obsessed with the menace of Christianity. He began the first interview with a statement about "the definite attempt by the Christians since time immemorial to capture Travancore and make it a Christian state". Later he gave as one reason for his opposition to responsible government that "it would definitely mean a Christian oligarchy". (One presumes that these statements were intended to impress the Mahatma on the assumption that he too was anti-Christian, and that Sir C.P. reckoned on neither the Mahatma nor his ambassador knowing enough of Travancore history to recognize their absurdity.) He made a sweeping condemnation of the Travancore State Congress as "proven liars, men of no standing, with no stake to lose, most of them unemployed or briefless barristers", communalists, disappointed place-hunters, openly subverting students and promoting violence. It was the theme on which all his subsequent statements about the State Congress were to be but variations. The Youth League preached communism, the State Congress insulted the ruling family.

Rajkumari, "probing a little deeper", found the Travancore National Congress "the real communalists, too communal-minded to want Responsible Government". She had long sessions with the State Congress, who refuted all the Dewan's charges, using those arguments which they had already used in so many public meetings and in the Assembly. Pattom was able to add that the educational authorities had sought their help with the students and acknowledged their restraining influence. She realized that "part of the strength of the movement derives from personal dislike of Sir C.P". She attempted to negotiate a settlement; she proposed that the State Congress should be permitted to function normally if the allegations in the Memorandum were withdrawn, but "there did not seem to be any real desire on the part of the Dewan to come to a settlement" and she left disheartened to report her failure to Gandhi.

Now it was open warfare. Pattom issued a long statement on their reasons for defying the ban on their public meetings. "The immediate issue is wholly one of civil liberties. Every other issue pales into insignificance before this one".

On August 25th, the same day that Rajkumari left Trivandrum, the Maharaja issued a Proclamation, called the Criminal Law Amendment Regulation, "for the prohibition of associations dangerous to the public peace". The government could, by notification in the Government Gazette, declare any association unlawful which had for its object interference with the law, or the maintenance of public order, or constituted a danger to public peace. The Travancore State Congress and the Youth League were forthwith declared unlawful associations.

The State Congress immediately issued a manifesto declaring the Regulation "an iniquitous law" which it was their duty to break, and the plans formulated on August 3rd were carried out. On August 26 they held a meeting on Trivandrum Beach, which some 20,000 attended. Pattom Thanu Pillai and T.M.Verghese spoke a few words appealing for calm, and were arrested. The vast crowd went home, in a silence more menacing than the noisiest demonstrations.[27]

In Quilon, Kottayam and Alleppey, on the same day, other leaders broke the ban in the presence of vast crowds and were arrested. The whole state was caught up in the movement.

Chapter IX

A YEAR OF STRUGGLE

IX.1 Civil Disobedience

Among those going to the beach in Trivandrum on 26 August 1938 was the Congress office manager, M.M. Varkey. But having strict orders to avoid arrest, he dodged back to town, and fled through the night to Ernakulam, capital of the Native state of Cochin. There he was received by enthusiastic helpers, both Travancoreans and Cochinites, and set up an Action Council to direct the Travancore campaign. Money, cars, printing presses, were put at his disposal; newspaper licences were easy to come by.[1] The Dewan of Travancore complained to the Dewan of Cochin (who had recently given some degree of responsible government to the state) about the vilification campaign directed from Cochin; the Government of Cochin issued a stern warning that it would take "a serious view of attacks on the administration of a neighbouring state"; and there the matter rested.[2] Meanwhile, as each president of the Travancore State Congress was arrested, he nominated his successor to be "Dictator" of the movement and temporary president; he issued a statement from Cochin and went forth to be arrested. They had got to their twelfth president in two months.

But, as always happened in mass "non-violent" campaigns inspired by Mahatma Gandhi, violence broke out as the leaders went to jail and their restraining influence was removed. Already on August 29th a second meeting was held on Trivandrum beach; but when the speakers were arrested, the police began to hustle the crowd which became restive, stoned the police and burnt the District Superintendent's car. Worse was to happen at Neyyattinkara, 15 miles south of Trivandrum, where a large crowd demonstrating against the arrest of a local leader got out of hand, shut the local police up in their police station, and took to burning state Transport buses. G.Ramachandran, whose family home was in Neyyattinkara, rushed down to attempt to control the mob, and got some buses safely through.[3] A platoon of the state Forces under Colonel Watkis also went down to rescue the police and restore order. The crowd proved uncontrollable and attacked the platoon with big stones till nearly all were injured. Colonel Watkis ordered the troops to fire, three were killed and the crowd melted away. G. Ramachandran was arrested that night for fomenting a riot, so another restraining hand was removed.[4]

The Resident again placed the blame for the beach riots on the police, and after lives had been lost at Neyyattinkara he was able, though still with difficulty, to bring in an experienced police officer from British India as Special Officer. Khan Bahadur Abdul Karim had experience of riot control, and quickly brought better discipline into the Travancore police force.

There were more riots that week in Quilon, where again state Transport buses were burnt and the leaders were unable to control the crowd. Col. Watkis and Abdul Karim took down detachments of troops and police and the crowd were fired on. But they had encountered the third president, V.K. Velayudhan also rushing to Quilon, who took the initiative in starting peace talks. V.K. Velayudhan the much respected Ezhava leader, was able to disperse the crowd, telling them the masses were not yet ready to carry on the campaign non-violently and sending them home ashamed of themselves. No Ezhava had yet been sent to jail as Sir C.P. still hoped to detach them from the State Congress (the local joke was that the Ezhavas were demanding communal representation in jail); so Velayudhan was free to approach the Dewan in a renewed effort for peace. But Sir C.P. was adamant that the Memorandum should first be withdrawn and the signatories tender their apologies. The abortive negotiations failed, Ezhavas began to get their "communal representation in jail" and the Resident began to press the Dewan for an open sedition trial of the signatories.[5]

Rioting and shootings occurred in half a dozen other places, and altogether some twenty persons were killed and 120 injured. One police constable was among the killed; but it was in a riot about excessive market tolls which had nothing to do directly with the Congress movement except insofar as unrest is infectious. But the violence died down, and by September 24th both Col. Watkis and the Dewan were able to report to the Resident that the situation was completely under control.

The agitation itself never stopped. Two things had happened. People had learnt the importance of remaining non-violent. There was only one serious outbreak in October at Chenganoor in central Travancore, where the story got round that the police had laid hands on a schoolgirl, and the local people ran amuck. Secondly, the police themselves were now under stricter discipline. But every day meetings were held and speakers were arrested somewhere in Travancore. When the towns were quiet, speakers cropped up in the villages; when the villages were quiet, speakers cropped up in the towns. When Trivandrum appeared back to normal at the end of September, a sensation was caused by the arrival of a special train carrying Mrs. Annamma Kuruvilla, daughter of a retired member of the Mysore Executive Council (who had paid for the train). She stopped at every station in Travancore to make speeches to delighted crowds, but of course could not be arrested by the Travancore police as she was on British territory; she made speeches from the balcony above the entrance to the Trivandrum railway station with impunity, then came out to court arrest and was taken to the Central Jail.

The students, both college students and schoolchildren, kept up the agitation on their own account. In the capital there was trouble when the students returned from their fortnight's *Onam** holiday in September. The government put it about that Congressmen and unemployed bank officials were paying fishermen from the beach to throw stones at the students. They were in fact paid by the police, and as early as August principal K.K.Kuruvilla had asked a question in the state Council about their part in the student demonstrations in July.** So the students were brought to college in state buses to "protect" them—inevitably shouting State Congress slogans, and police stood at th gates to "protect" them further, which meant they beat those who shouted slogans. It was very difficult to persuade the authorities to stop this nonsence, pacify the students, and get down to solid work.

But in central and north Travancore the schools and colleges never got back to normal working throughout the civil disobedience movement. In these largely Christian areas the people were almost solid for the Congress, partly because this was the area which had suffered most from the bank crash; the students and school children spent their time in strikes and demonstrations. The missionaries, who were thick on the ground in this part of the state, were in a quandary; if they closed their empty educational institutions, they were in danger of losing their government grants; if they kept them open, they lost local support.

Jathas or demonstration marches also came from outside to support

---

* Note by the Editor: *Onam* is the most important Malayali harvest festival, taking place in August/September, according to the moon.

** Note by the Author: My informants were the Flemish nuns who worked among the fishermen at the Beach Convent. Their parish priest, on learning they had taken police bribes, denounced them as Judases in a hell-fire sermon. The Flemish missionaries had no interest in politics. I have no doubt the ragamuffins of the July incident also came from the beach.

the State Congress. There was one from British Malabar, led by A.K. Gopalan, the communist leader, one from Cochin, even one from Ceylon. But they played an insignificant part in the whole agitation. The *jatha* launched from Madras held so many public meetings en route that the political prisoners were all out of jail by the time it got to Trivandrum.[8]

The outward appearance of calm was enhanced by the rigid control of the local press. Editors were warned of serious consequences if they published anything unfavourable to the government, and a number of papers had their licenses cancelled and their presses attached.

The leading local paper, the *Malayala Manorama*, published from Kottayam, was suppressed. Its owner and editor-in-chief was K.C.Mammen Mappillay though in practice it was run by some of his sons. It was threatened with closure because it had given publicity to the government's repressive measures. An unconditional apology did not save it. The press was seized one Saturday night, not however before the editor (having had a tip from the district magistrate, a fellow-Christian, to remove his "personal belongings") had removed the entire back files to a secret place. Two days later a new paper, also called the *Manorama*, appeared in Cochin state; the headline of its first edition ran: "The Manorama is dead; long live the Manorama!" It continued until printing was resumed in the old press after Independence; and it is the boast of the family that they have the complete files of the paper from 1885 when it was founded. The news staggered the citizens of Travancore, and Changanacherry Parameswaran Pillai, who was too important to be arrested, went off to take the chair at a huge protest meeting on the Kottayam *maidan*.[9]

The Native States were attracting a good deal of attention at this time in India; as Gandhi had shrewdly foreseen, the Haripura resolution had put the people of the state on their mettle, and there was much popular agitation and unrest in the states. The movement in Travancore was particularly dramatic and unexpected, for Sir C.P. had long been a prominent liberal, and his connection with the Temple Entry Proclamation had earned him a reputation for progressive views. The civil disobedience movement was widely discussed, particularly in the Madras newspapers. The Madras *Indian Express*, a Congress newspaper, was so sharply critical of the Travancore Government that its import into Travancore was forbidden. However, the Travancoreans could always buy it at the railway stations.

Harijan, Gandhi's weekly, gave a good deal of space to Travancore. Gandhi's opinion was of great importance; the Travancore leaders looked to him for guidance, while Sir C.P. looked to him to put pressure on them to withdraw their Memorandum. Gandhi wrote that he was "inundated" with telegrams about Travancore and got endless reports and deputations. He was much too well informed to believe the news put out by the Associated press of India, busy earning its large subsidy from the Travancore Government, and freely denounced the savage repression in Travancore. He took the line that the demand for responsible government was perfectly constitutional and could see no evidence that it was "subversive" and disloyal'. While he accepted Changanacherry's reports that the violence was instigated by agents provocateurs, he appealed to the Travancore State Congress to see that no violence was done by its supporters, but to go on "till the Travancore Government relents or the last man is accounted for". At the same time he appealed to Sir C.P. to follow the example of the Dewan of Mysore and to appoint an outsider of "unimpeachable integrity" to inquire into the violence, instead of importing a Special Officer to carry on repression.

On October 8th he wrote that he had again appealed to the imprisoned leaders to withdraw the Memorandum, but received the reply: "The Working Committee feels that the Dewan's continuance in office is detrimental to the people's interests. The withdrawal of the Memorandum may unmeritedly discredit the State Congress and cause an irretrievable setback to the movement". By this time the Mahatma had been led to believe that they were "without the ability to prove the charges", and that it was therefore their clear duty to withdraw them.*

Another would-be peace maker was the president of the Madras branch of the Civil Liberties Union, who went to Trivandrum to offer his good offices. But he found the Congress leaders, whom he met freely in jail, concentrating on responsible government, and the Dewan concentrating on the withdrawal of the Memorandum, and he came away convinced the Memorandum should be withdrawn, and the issue of civil liberty was forgotten.[10]

From out of the fog of conflicting versions of events and conflicting solutions came one clear voice, that of Rabindranath Tagore. He sent a message to the press of India: "Along with the whole country I have felt grievously hurt that an enlightened state like Travancore should have initiated a regime of fascism with its techniques of shootings.

---

* Note by the Editor: Already on 3-9-1938 Gandhi had written in *The Hindu* that the State Congress was "making the most serious charges unsupported by any evidence against the able *Dewan*. . ."

denial of the elementary rights of freedom and deliberate persecution of the Congress. Whatever the provocation or the nature of the dispute, the methods that have been pursued to exert authority are without justification".

Sir C.P. was being driven into a corner. On October 5th, on his way to Delhi to see the Viceroy he issued a statement to the press in Bombay that the Government of Travancore had intended to institute proceedings for sedition under the ordinary law, but growing violence had forced the government to bring the Criminal Law Amendment Regulation into operation. It was quickly pointed out that the violence had broken out only *after* the Regulation had come into force. More and more people were asking why Sir C.P. did not withdraw the Criminal Law Amendment Regulation and prosecute the State Congress under due process of law; and they began to ask the obvious question—was he afraid to face an open inquiry?

The Maharaja's birthday, due that year on October 23rd, was always a time of great rejoicing in the state, attracting large crowds to the capital. It was also a time for major steps by the government to be announced. The Maharaja had been invested with ruling powers on his birthday in 1931, and had then announced the constitutional changes. The Temple Entry Proclamation in 1936 had been another Birthday Proclamation. Often prisoners were released on the birthday as a special act of clemency. The Action Council in Ernakulam therefore planned a mammoth demonstration in the capital for the birthday, to demand the release of the political prisoners and the immediate introduction of responsible government. It was planned with military precision; M.M. Varkey was chief of staff, and the general was to be the "Dictator" at the time. The plan was for thousands of demonstrators, all dressed in *khaddar* and wearing Gandhi caps, to be smuggled into Trivandrum before the birthday, while the Dictator was to come via Ernakulam and Madurai by train, thus avoiding danger of arrest before he (or she) arrived in Trivandrum. The Maharajah would be spending most of the day in the ancient Sri Padmanabhaswami temple in the performance of traditional religious duties, including the re-dedication of himself and the state to the god. The temple lay inside the Old Fort with its great walls and four gates, in which the rulers had for centuries resided before they sought more modern dwellings. The Fort was less than half a mile from the railway station; and the plan was for the Dictator to go in an open car to the South Gate, at which the hero Velu Thampi had presented his demands nearly a century-and-a-half earlier, to claim the ancient right of subjects to present their petitions in person to their ruler.

It was no secret that some sort of demonstration would take place. The eleventh president sent a telegram to Gandhi the previous week informing him of the plan, and also warning him that the police were organizing bogus volunteers in Congress uniforms to join the *jatha* and shout anti-royalist slogans; but he believed in a "royalist victory".[11]

The birthday fell on a Sunday, and by the previous Wednesday the demonstrators were beginning to arrive. It is impossible to make any accurate estimate of their numbers; estimates vary from the 2,000 reported by the Associated press of India to 50,000 (but that figure came from the proud husband of the Dictator of the day who was prejudiced; anyway he was inside the jail at the time). The Special Police Officer, Abdul Karim estimated there were 10,000 at the outset swelling to 20,000; as it was his business to know the size of the crowd this is probably the most reliable estimate.[12] Mrs. K.V.Eappen, John Philipose's sister, organized their lodging and their food. By Saturday there was a huge camp opposite the jail gates. The prisoners inside made a rough Congress flag out of pieces of sheeting; they used red laterite mud to stain the upper third "saffron", vegetable juice to stain the lower third green, and hoisted it proudly on a stick of firewood to flutter over the jail walls, to the joy of the campers outside.[13]

The Dictator, the twelfth president, was a young woman of 29 from a devout Syrian Catholic family, by name Akkamma Cheriyan. She was well educated, headmistress of a Roman Catholic middle school in a small town near the northern border. She was deeply religious, simple, modest, utterly fearless. M.M.Varkey called her "the Indian Joan of Arc". (But she escaped the French girl's terrible fate, and later returned to her little town, married and settled down totally unspoiled by her "crowded hour of glorious life".) On the great day, however, nobody thought of Joan of Arc; the name of Velu Thampi was on everybody's lips.

Sir C.P., well aware that the Maharaja's birthday would bring crisis, acted swiftly. On Friday, October 21st, he announced that as the signatories to the Memorandum refused to withdraw it, they would be prosecuted under the ordinary Criminal Law. On Saturday, the eve of the birthday, a proclamation was issued releasing the prisoners unconditionally, by an act of the Maharaja's clemency. The press notice ran:

"His Highness the Maharaja of Travancore, acting on the advice of his trusted Dewan Sir C.P. Ramaswamy Aiyar, has been graciously pleased to order the release of all prisoners sentenced under the Travancore Criminal Law Amendment Regulation. He has been further pleased to suspend the notifications under the Regulation".

"This Proclamation has been issued by the Travancore Government in commemoration of the Birthday of His Highness the Maharaja, and in the confident hope that those to whom the clemency has been extended will take a lesson from the recent manifestations of Civil Disobedience with their calamitous results and that, henceforth, the subjects of His Highness will confine themselves to peaceful activities".

The prisoners were to be released the following day at night, so as to avoid possible demonstrations. Sir C.P. told the Resident that the release had been staged so as to leave the Congress without a policy, and the Resident admired him for his astuteness.[14] But the general opinion was that he was terrified of the possibility of bloody carnage with such huge and excited crowds milling round the capital, and he had no alternative to releasing the prisoners.

IX.2 The Great Jatha

Accounts of the great *Jatha* are conflicting, so I have decided to use my own diary account, written on the Sunday evening, and to supplement it with Akkamma Cheriyan's account, although that was given to me in 1972, many years later, and some of what Col. Watkis told me the next day.

"*Sunday. Oct.23rd.* The place roars, and roars again. The political prisoners are free! All Saturday we waited—nothing. Going to the Durbar the streets were nearly empty, only at the gate a few hundred gathered to shout slogans. There the news trickled through: all politicals released, the State Congress and Youth League to be recognized as legal. But the Criminal Amendment Act is not repealed, and not a word about responsible government. Grudging and ungracious, is the general verdict. The Durbar was deadly: the Prince was blazing with wrath (poor child, *he* at least has judgement). The Dewan looked like a butler who has stolen the spoons and knows his master cannot but find out; the Maharaja looked yellow and ill".

"Then the morning brought the real uproar. They must have collected all night (there was a camp just outside the jail), 20,000 volunteers from all the villages, each group bringing its banners and flags, all pledged to complete non-violence and to die if necessary. Gandhi caps were everywhere as I went to church! And at eight it began, steady, organized, hammering, shouting, down at the Fort; they tell me it was amazing, the discipline they showed, 'The Police hadn't a single excuse to beat them up,' said Krishnaswamy (a young journalist member of the International Fellowship who kept me informed). For an hour it went on, then off they went to the Central Jail to fetch out the politicals. I don't know when they came out, but just now at eight Pattom went by, and somebody from his car shouted goodnight to me—while the whole place roared, and roared, and roared!"

Here is Akkamma's story. She left via Ernakulam to avoid arrest, taking 300 volunteers from her small town with her. They went by train via Madurai to Trivandrum, collecting volunteers at every station in Travancore, and arrived in Trivandrum on Sunday afternoon. A vast procession formed, with Akkamma leading it seated in an open car ("I was sailing on a sea of white") and went to the south gate of the Fort, where Velu Thampi had won his peaceful victory in 1799 in curiously parallel circumstances. There they stopped and the volunteers squatted on the ground. The Maharaja had to be smuggled in and out of the Fort by the small gate in the north-west corner. Col. Watkis came forward to ask the Dictator what she wanted, and she claimed the immemorial right of the subjects to see their ruler and present their demands. The Colonel went inside to convey the message. Meanwhile the military trucks were sent to clear a path for the Maharaja's car, but the volunteers refused to budge and the soldiers refused to drive over their own people; so some were sent on foot to kick the volunteers out of the way, but still they refused to move. Meanwhile Col. Watkis and Abdul Karim inside the palace warned the Maharaja that they could not be responsible for law and order unless he took swift action; it is said (but this is unconfirmed) that he ordered the immediate release of the prisoners. Col. Watkis returned to Akkamma to tell her they must make an appointment with the Private Secretary to the Maharaja; she insisted on an immediate interview. Col. Watkis in a flash of anger put his hand to his revolver; and warned her he would have to shoot to disperse the crowd; she stood up in the car and replied: "These are my volunteers—shoot me first!" He turned on his heel and went back to the palace.

According to Akkamma's account the procession returned to the railway station to await the released prisoners, who arrived there very late at night. According to K. Velayudhan Nair, who was in charge of the prisoners' mess, the order for release came at about four o'clock; but the food was cooking, so he said: "Have your last meal at government expense!" and they left towards 8 p.m. The crowd reached Pattom Thanu

Pillai's house in triumph (passing my house) and then must have gone to the railway station. One could trace its progress by the noise.

On Monday there was a monster meeting—the biggest crowd yet—and Akkamma Cheriyan handed back the office of president to Pattom Thanu Pillai amid delirious rejoicing, and the villagers went home happy.

But the leaders were not happy. It was nobody's victory; nothing was resolved. It was a temporary victory for the popular forces; the government could not risk those great crowds getting out of hand and jail delivery was the only possible course in face of them. The leaders had no illusions; like the officials who had whispered to each other behind their hands at the Durbar, they knew that the release of the political prisoners was grudging and ungracious, and they prepared themselves to renew the struggle.

IX.3 Labour and Youth Movements

Separate consideration should be given to two movements running parallel to the Travancore State Congress, independent of it but linked in many ways, both in the persons who comprised them and their activities in the civil disobedience movement of August to October 1938. These were the labour movements and the youth movements in Travancore. But they had a momentum of their own, and their activities diverged more and more from those of the State Congress. Two things about these movements were important for the later history of Kerala. One was that they had strong links with their counterparts in Cochin and British Malabar and strengthened the all-Kerala sentiment. The other was that the communists chose these movements for their special field of activity in the later thirties and forged strong links between labour and youth, mainly through the Youth League.

Trade unionism, as we have already seen, was well established in the coastal towns by the early thirties, and in the agitations of 1930 and 1931 Congress workers began interesting themselves in the conditions of the workers. At some time in the thirties the Congress socialists moved in; we find one P. Krishna Pillai, secretary of the All-Kerala Congress Socialist Party, active in the movement in Alleppey. Krishna Pillai was later a declared communist but at the time the communists were for the most part working closely with Congress under the epithet "Congress socialist". The Travancore Communist Party was only started in December 1938 and many of the former socialists moved into it. It was V.K.Velayudhan and P.K. Kunju, neither of them socialists, who had brought the labour movement into the Congress; but when these and other moderate leaders went to jail the communists took the lead, and the workers began to take their own line under their guidance They organized strikes in the course of the first civil disobedience movement. There were two major strikes, one of the canal boatmen and the other of the coir factory workers; and a general strike was planned for the eve of the Maharaja's birthday.[15]

The organization of water transport along the canals and backwaters of Kerala was peculiar. The main means of transport of goods was heavy canoes known as *wallams*, poled by muscular boatmen, which was incredibly slow and incredibly cheap. The boats were almost all owned by the boatmen themselves, who had to obtain a government license to operate. They formed an association to protest against the increase of license fees by the Travancore Government, and to demand recognition as a trade union (which, strictly speaking they were not); and when their demands were refused they went on strike on October 11th. They all came out and brought boat traffic between Quilon and Ernakulam to a virtual standstill; even motor boat crews were persuaded or bullied into joining the strike.

On October 21st the coir factory workers came out. By now the communists had trained volunteers and supplied them with red shirts and red Gandhi caps, and when the usual procession marched to the meeting place it was preceded by a red flag, and red-shirted volunteers acted as marshals. The president, V. Atchuthan, was a Congressman; his speech was largely political. After fifteen years of trade unionism, he said, their grievances were unredressed, and would remain unredressed until responsible government put power into the hands of the workers. Other resolutions demanded the release of the political prisoners and an impartial inquiry into the shootings at Alleppey. Industrial demands included a minimum wage of Rs. 30 a month and a 48-hour week, old-age pensions, free medical services and paid maternity leave.

Next day, the eve of the Maharaja's birthday, the coir factory workers' strike broadened into a general strike, the purpose of which was definitely political. Some of the red-shirted volunteers had already left for Trivandrum to join the great *Jatha*; others helped to organize the local demonstrations. In spite of the employers' conciliatory attitude on the industrial demands, and also in spite of the news of the release of the prisoners, the strike continued. Police reinforcements were sent; on Monday large numbers of workers marched on the police station armed with wooden spears and hatchets and carrying red flags; they attacked the police station and burnt a factory belonging to a member of the

Travancore Nationalist Party. Estimates of numbers are notoriously unreliable, but the figure of 40,000 has been given. The police made *lathi* charges, but the rioting crowds were too big for unarmed police to handle and the troops were called out. The crowds attacked with stones and hatchets and the troops had to fire; two demonstrators were killed and several wounded. Fifty-one arrests were made, including those of the labour leaders, and a ban on labour meetings was imposed for two months.

The labour troubles in Alleppey, the deaths by firing and the arrests, all contributed to keeping alive the agitation against the government. As the State Congress leaders, now free to move about, went on their rounds of meetings, resolutions were passed condemning the *lathi* charges and firings, and demanding an impartial inquiry, and money was collected for the strikers and their families. Trade unions as far afield as Cochin and Calicut in British Malabar held protest meetings and sent donations to the strike fund.

The Youth League was particularly active in helping the strikers, organizing meetings and collecting funds. A large group of Youth League volunteers came from British Malabar to help. By mid-November the strikes were over, in spite of the efforts of the Youth League to have them continued. The boatmen were successful; their association was recognized as coming under the Trade Union Regulations, so that they could consolidate their position. The government appointed a Labour Inquiry Committee consisting of a government-nominated chairman, and two representatives from both the employers and the workers. The Coir Factory Workers' Union predictably nominated two of their leaders who were under arrest for their share in the disturbances.

By now the Communists were well in the saddle in the Travancore trade union movement, and linked it with the whole Kerala movement. At the end of November the president of the All-India Trade Union Congress, Dr. S.C. Banerjee, visited Travancore and addressed a meeting in Alleppey under the auspices of the Youth League; and it is significant that he was accompanied by a well-known Malabar communist, A.K. Gopalan, and a local communist, G. Sreedhar. Alleppey became the bridgehead for later communist activity.

The youth movements in Travancore in these exciting times took a number of different forms, but all were animated by an intense nationalism, and certainly in the earlier stages they were informed by Congress ideas and ideals.

The Youth League itself began as the most Congress-minded of the youth movements. Not itself a Congress body, it was run by young Congressmen, mostly of a left-wing persuasion. Its moving spirit was K.C. George, a brilliant young Syrian Christian lawyer who, having gone to jail as a Congressman in the first civil disobedience movement, moved rapidly to the Left and emerged as an influential communist.

Another small but influential group was the Young Kerala Society. It had been founded on an inter-religious basis; most of the members belonged to the International Fellowship but considered that body too indeterminate in its views. Though it was non-political, most of the members were Gandhians; it studied political and social questions from the religious point of view; it encouraged deep and sober thinking. This remarkable group survived all the upheavals of ensuing years to become the Fellowship of the Friends of Truth which still flourishes.[16]

Among university students the Christian organizations were the oldest and best organized. The Student Christian Movement (S.C.M.) was of very long standing in India, and particularly strong in Kerala because of the large number of Syrian Christian students. All over India the S.C.M. was bringing Christian students into the broad stream of national awakening, encouraging them to look less to the West for leadership and more to their own country. The secretary for Kerala, K.A.Mathew, himself a Syrian Christian from central Travancore, had a great influence on Syrian Christian youth. He made his headquarters in Trivandrum with its concentration of university students. He kept in touch with the new stir of national life, though he was himself non-political until a crisis in 1944 brought him fully into Congress politics. He laid stress on the fundamentals of the Christian faith and their relevance to social action. The Syrian Christians had hitherto (with rare exceptions) an inward-looking attitude, concerned mainly with safeguarding their narrow communal interests and preserving untouched their ancient culture; but now the young had become critical of this narrow outlook and clamoured for social action based on Christian principles, reaching out to the whole community.

Some found a good field for wider thinking and action in the Student Inter-religious Fellowship.[17] Its first general secretary, M.A.Thomas, also made his headquarters in Trivandrum. He quickly built up a considerable organization, and he acquired a Hindu colleague, K. Janardhanan Pillai. They found there was no provision for encouraging Hindu students to study their own religion and set up a special Hindu students' study group. Sir C.P., suspicious as he was of the Student Fellowship as a whole, was delighted with this development, and helped it with a small grant for many years. By April

1937 the Student Fellowship was able to organize a conference. "Rajaji" (about to become premier of Madras) was its chief guest and spoke on the present value of religious scriptures; its other speaker was the rural secretary of the International Fellowship, "Brother Dick" Keithahn, who spoke of social service. It was heavy stuff for youngsters whose experience of education had mostly been confined to dictated notes and learning by heart.

The Waifs and Strays Home in the slums, run by M.A.Thomas and M.M.Thomas, became the centre for the students' social service activities. Students of all religions met there to run a play centre for the slum children, do health propaganda, discuss religion. It was this group that provided the volunteers for the Trivandrum meeting of the International Fellowship conference in December 1937, where they listened to more heavy stuff. A group under M.A. Thomas held a village camp in the hot weather of 1938, where among other marvels they enlisted the services of the local youth in the building of a five miles long motorable road (quite easy on laterite soil); the first vehicle to use it was the Rockefeller Health Unit cinema van, to show films about hookworm and other gruesome health subjects. The group also undertook a village survey for the Y.M.C.A. Rural Reconstruction Centre in the hot weather of 1939. And, to the embarrassment of the members of the senior group, they provided the chief organizers of the student demonstrations in the troubles of 1938. Some became communists, some dedicated Gandhian workers, some Christian social workers; few remained unchanged.

Another group arose out of the ferment of those years, the Youth Christian Council of Action.[18] Needless to say, the Thomases and K.A.Mathew and his wife were among them. At an S.C.M. camp in May 1938, the group who clamoured for social action decided to form the Council of Action, and this attracted the keenest young Christian men and women. It was backed by an indigenous Syrian Christian religious community, the Society of St. Thomas (it includes men, women and married couples), the centre of which was a Christian ashram just outside Kottayam, the Christavashram. Here they ran a small Boys' Town, and also produced a modest journal devoted to religious and social questions. The ashram had close links with the S.C.M. and the International Fellowship, and offered a home to the office of the Y.C.C.A. and a means of publicity in its journal.

Opportunity for practical action arose almost immediately. A considerable number of persons had been killed and wounded in the disturbances of the first civil disobedience movement, but the government had ignored all requests for an inquiry and refused cooperation with the unofficial inquiry committee set up under Changanacherry Parameswaran Pillai, which perforce dissolved itself. The new-born Y.C.C.A. set up its own ad hoc Relief Committee, not to inquire into the causes of the shootings and *lathi* charges but to seek out the victims and administer relief. The ad hoc committee was not specifically a Christian body; Mrs. Parameswaram Pillai was its chairman and it had Hindu and Muslim as well as Christian members. It was mostly members of the Y.C.C.A. who undertook the actual work. M.A. Thomas undertook the touring to find out which sufferers needed relief and to set up local relief committees, while M.M. Thomas was the office secretary. The findings of the Committee were that there were 20 deaths by military and police firing, one police constable killed by a rioting crowd in Kadakkal (this, it may be remembered, was not a political riot but a riot against excessive market dues); the number of wounded was 145, 141 by firing and 4 by *lathi* charges. Over Rs.7000 was collected and distributed to those in need, including the widow of the murdered police constable.[19]

The report was printed in Cochin—no press in Travancore dared to touch it. It was banned by the government but smuggled in by the energetic young Christians. The police seized many copies; M.A. Thomas hid his supply in a friendly Ezhava neighbour's mud hut, where they were eaten by white ants. Only one copy seems to have survived; it is a valuable document, for it is the only reliable record of the casualties of the 1938 disturbances.

IX.4 Renewed Agitation

The release of the political prisoners was hailed as "an act of gracious clemency" throughout India and it was expected—as would have happened in British India—that some real constitutional advance would follow. Gandhi summed up the general feeling in *Harijan* of 29th October when he wrote: "I extend my congratulations to His Highness, Her Highness and the Dewan for the general amnesty granted to civil disobedience prisoners in Travancore on the Maharaja's birthday. It is to be hoped that in order to make the amnesty fruitful and peace permanent it will be followed up by the appointment of a committee of inquiry into past events and another into the nature of responsible government to be granted under the aegis of the Maharaja". And he repeated his suggestion for the withdrawal of the allegations against the Dewan.

The local people were more realistic: they knew their Dewan. Sir

C.P. had been forced to realize that the Travancore State Congress commanded huge popular support, but he was still determined to discredit it and crush the movement. He had no intention whatever of giving an inch on responsible government.

The State Congress leaders realized that the only success of their movement had been to show the size of popular support; they had gained no advance either in the field of civil liberties or constitutional reform. They realized there could be no worthwhile civil liberties as long as they had the same Dewan, and now put the achievement of responsible government in the forefront. But they were uncertain of the next step, and were divided on tactics and above all on the Memorandum.

The next twelve months were therefore a confused period—a period of shifting policies, inconclusive moves and abortive negotiations. At this time both sides were courting Gandhi, whose influence on the course of events was crucial, however much he claimed that he confined himself to friendly advice which people were free to follow or ignore.

The Working Committee of the State Congress met at once to decide on a course of action. They determined to go on with their campaign for responsible government and to renew civil disobedience if it were not granted immediately; but they were prepared for negotiations at any time. Far from withdrawing the Memorandum they were prepared to add a supplement. They decided to send a delegation to Mahatma Gandhi.

The leaders made a tour through Travancore to Ernakulam, where they took the train to Wardha; and were received everywhere by huge and enthusiastic crowds; new branches were being formed, groups of volunteers were enrolled—both men and women. In all their speeches the leaders put the emphasis on responsible government.

Gandhi received them warmly but his advice was not altogether palatable. He commented that they could either concentrate on the fight against the Dewan or withdraw the Memorandum and concentrate on the fight for responsible government; but he himself "could not be a party to the conduct of a struggle about a personal matter". Secondly, he advised that if violence broke out in a renewed civil disobedience campaign they should at once suspend it. Finally, he appealed to them to take up the "constructive programme" of the Congress—hand spinning and weaving, cottage industries, prohibition, literacy and health campaigns—a programme which, he said, was "an instrument of permanent value".

When the delegation returned, the Working Committee held another meeting to chalk out their programme in the light of Gandhi's advice They disagreed so deeply about the Memorandum that the question was shelved; but they agreed to adopt the "constructive programme" and to begin with prohibition. They decided to stage peaceful demonstrations during the Viceregal visit due to take place in January, to hold the first All-Travancore Conference of the State Congress at a place just outside Trivandrum, Vattiyoorkavu, on December 22nd and 23rd, and to organize volunteer corps for both men and women. Akkamma Cheriyan, now a member of the Working Committee, was appointed Captain of the women volunteers or *Desa Sevikas* (servants of the country).

Meanwhile Sir C.P. embarked on his own plan of campaign to check the movement by dividing and discrediting it. His first response to the resolutions of the Working Committee on October 30th was to state that in no circumstances would a committee be appointed to consider responsible government, and he refused to deal with the State Congress in its present mood.

Arrests went on; in fact the "gracious act of clemency" had been only partial, and hundreds of convicted and under-trial prisoners still remained in jails and police lockups. These were prisoners arrested for violence or under the security sections of the Penal Code. More arrests went on, especially of labourers and others connected with the Alleppey general strike. On November 14th Miss Anne Mascarene, who had remained outside Travancore during the civil disobedience movement and had now returned, was arrested and tried on charges of sedition, and given a year's simple imprisonment. Even those who had been released had been in no sense pardoned. Their disabilities under the Criminal Law Amendment Regulations were not removed; lawyers, for example, were debarred as convicted criminals from practising in the courts for three years after release.

Sir C.P. continued to build up his supporters. The Travancore National Congress was again put forward as the true Congress organization of Travancore, and a "powerful body". A deputation of them went off to Wardha on the heels of the State Congress to acquaint the Mahatma with the true state of affairs in Travancore; the Mahatma received them but further ignored them (so for that matter did the Dewan). They held a conference at Alleppey attended by "a large gathering", at which the State Congress was denounced as communalistic and anti-royalist; but nobody was deceived.

Sir C.P. also encouraged the Hindu Mahasabha, the fanatical Hindu group who believed India should be an entirely Hindu country. Sir C.P.

had welcomed its president, V.D.Savarkar, in Travancore in October, and had blessed his efforts to form a local branch "in order to infuse among the Hindus the consciousness of a pan-Hindu solidarity and strength".[20] What he had learned in Travancore appeared in his presidential address to the Hindu Mahasabha annual conference at Nagpur in December, during which he dismissed the Christian minority in India as a whole as no danger; they could be politically assimilated though their proselytising activities should be checked and the work of reconversion should go on. "Only in Travancore", he continued, "the Christians seem to cherish political designs against the Hindu state and it is only there that we shall have to treat them with some political distrust by not allowing them too much latitude in state affairs and offices, till they cease to be political suspects to the Hindus".[21] This statement drew the wrath of the president of the Travancore State Congress, who saw it as an example of "false and malicious propaganda against our movement, which was entirely non-communal, and an attempt to foment discord in Travancore". The Travancore branch of the Hindu Mahasabha however never amounted to more than a handful of Brahmans and Nayars who backed Sir C.P.

Sir C.P. attempted to get the backing of a far more powerful entity, the Paramount Power.[22] Early in November he went to Bombay to consult with the Chief Ministers of other states troubled by Congress agitation, and they agreed to ask the Paramount Power for an unequivocal declaration that the Government of India did not intend to insist on the grant of partial or complete responsible government as a sine qua non of Federation.[23]

On his return from Bombay Sir C.P. once more went on the attack. On December 8th, a proclamation was issued amending the Criminal Law Amendment Regulation, mainly directed against voluntary organizations of a political character, the wearing of uniforms and the organization and training of bodies "intended to be employed in usurping the functions of the police or armed forces". (It was copied from a recent British law passed to cope with fascist organizations in the United Kingdom.) A few days later the District Magistrate of Trivandrum prohibited the holding of the State Congress Conference there until after the Viceregal visit on the grounds of the danger to public peace and tranquility. The State Congress was however able to point to hundreds of meetings held since the release of the political prisoners without any violence arising, and claimed their rights of free speech and went on with their preparations.

Meanwhile the government took steps to ensure that clashes would occur by a method which had already had considerable success. A new force was instituted (or rather regularized, they had functioned in earlier disturbances) called the Special Police. This impressive title was given to a body of untrained men who were given Rs.5 a month, wore no uniform and were attached to the local police stations, to be used in "dispersing unlawful gatherings". In practice the worst rowdies and drunkards were recruited; there are many accounts of how they broke up meetings with catcalls, drumming, throwing sand and mud. They tried the patience and the non-violence of Congressmen to the utmost.

Finally, on December 13th, a special tribunal was set up by proclamation to try the signatories to the Memorandum against Sir C.P. on charges of sedition. The Travancore High Court was to be invested with original jurisdiction, a special judge was to be appointed to the High Court for the trial. The trial could be held in camera, and certain witnesses could be exempted from appearing in person in court. There was to be no appeal from any sentence except to the Maharaja. By December 19th all the signatories had been arrested.

They were on the horns of a dilemma. If they stood by the allegations they would lose Gandhi's support, yet they would not get any opportunity to prove the allegations in court as the charge was sedition. Nor would they get any publicity for what they could say as the trial was to be in camera. If on the other hand they withdrew the charges they would be discredited, and the impression would be created that they were unable to prove them. Sir C.P. had them just where he wanted them.

A.K.Pillai, their best adviser, wrote from Madras approving their stand on the Memorandum. The whole proceedings would be "a huge farce"; the judge (not yet appointed) was not likely to be independent, the whole thing stage-managed by the chief culprit. Their only course was to refuse to defend the case—a course which the signatories decided to adopt.

But Gandhi wrote and telegraphed them to withdraw, and even suggested the wording in a lengthy telegram: "Memorandum unreservedly withdrawn in the interest of larger struggle for representative government stop. But whilst withdrawing allegations we would be untrue to ourselves to the cause and to the public if we did not state that the allegations were made by us with a belief in them".

The prisoners followed his advice, and withdrew them without any expression of regret or acknowledgment of error. At the same time the Working Committee accepted Gandhi's advice on the projected Viceregal visit and announced that they would not stage demonstrations during it. The Dewan accepted the withdrawal, dropped the prosecution, and after a fortnight, released them on January 5th, just before the Viceregal visit.

Sir C.P., in another of his lengthy letters, explained to the Resident that he had dropped the matter as a gesture of clemency as he did not wish to appear vindictive; in any case the accuseds' refusal to defend themselves made it very difficult for the prosecution to prove Sir C.P.'s innocence of the charges against him. But the withdrawal of the Memorandum was an empty gesture, and the cloud continued to hang over Sir C.P.'s reputation. The Resident commented rightly to the Viceroy, "The failure of the Travancore Government either to clear themselves of the charges against them, or to enquire judicially into the facts and causes of the recent disturbances, is bound to tell against them in the long run".[24]

The release of the prisoners was also an empty gesture; but it was widely regarded as a tactical victory for the Dewan. He had achieved two of his aims: the avoidance of an open and impartial inquiry into the actions of the Travancore Government and his own, and a deep split in the ranks of the Congress Party, into pro-Gandhians and anti-Gandhians. Not all of the latter, it should be observed, were left-wing; some of the moderates like A.K. Pillai were also disillusioned with the equivocal role played by the Mahatma. But it was mostly the younger element who turned against Gandhi and the moderate leadership of the local Congress. And there was no change in the Government's policy of repression. "The present policy of the Government", wrote G.Ramachandran in *Harijan*, "seems to be to avoid a frontal fight and all sensation in their policy of repression. Arrests are made without fuss and in cases almost unnoticed". Some three months after the "act of gracious clemency" there were, according to State Congress calculations, some 300 political prisoners in jail.

At least the All-Travancore Conference at Vattiyoorkavu went forward, though Gandhi, in his fear of violence, had advised cancelling it. The Working Committee went on with their plans as before, and a list of acting presidents was drawn up, in the expectation of arrests to come, each one to nominate his successor as he was arrested. Resolutions were drawn up in jail and smuggled out.

In fact two conferences were held, one at the original site and one at the railway station *maidan*, to which large numbers of delegates came by train; identical resolutions were passed at both conferences. The Vattiyoorkavu conference site was occupied by soldiers; the state Forces had orders to disperse the crowds, by firing, if necessary. But Col.

Watkis calmly ignored the orders and had his men policing the grounds, thus effectively keeping out the rowdies prowling on the outskirts. The meeting was noticeably well-conducted.*

The two conferences chalked out a plan for a campaign of "direct action", which was to include the holding of prohibited meetings, the non-payment of taxes, and the offering of *satyagraha* at the palace gates—such a campaign to be launched by the president at a time he thought fit. At the same time it was decided, following Gandhi's advice, to go on with the "constructive programme" of the Congress, and to concentrate on a prohibition drive to be launched the following month.

Immediately after the conference the president, A. Narayana Pillai, was arrested. So were Akkamma Cheriyan, now commandant of the *Desa Sevikas*, and her sister Rosamma; they joined Anne Mascarene in the Central Jail, where they were badly treated, insulted and bullied—another cause of public indignation.

The prohibition campaign had only limited success. It was intended to establish mass contacts; but it hit one community very hard, namely the Ezhavas. They were traditionally the cultivators of coconuts, tapping the palms for their juice and fermenting it into toddy, the local beer. As a result many Ezhavas became less than enthusiastic about Congress, and Sir C.P. had little difficulty in detaching some of their leaders from it.

In January 1939 the Viceregal visit went off well with no demonstrations. But the Palace failed to convince His Excellency that the Christians were the most troublesome element of the population. In spite of their efforts to stop him, he went off to the Y.M.C.A. Rural Reconstruction Centre at Marthandam, 25 miles south of Trivandrum; and came back full of enthusiasm for the wonderful work of the Christians in uplifting the villages.[25]

It was about the time of the Viceregal visit that the split in the Travancore State Congress became apparent.[26] Many Congress supporters, both inside and outside the state, had been against the withdrawal of the allegations against the Dewan, and were critical of the Gandhian policy of caution. One prominent young Syrian Christian, E.John Kuruvilla, went so far as to draw up another Memorandum, with supplements, and to collect signatures. The Youth League was specially impatient. They supported the new Memorandum (which was

---

* Note by the Author: Col. Watkis's own account, given that evening to the small group of keenly-interested European officials at the Trivandrum Club.

sent to the Maharaja and never heard of again.) They formed their own War Council, of which K.C. George was secretary, and planned their own demonstrations for the Viceregal visit. George wrote bitter letters to Pattom Thanu Pillai denouncing the inaction of the leaders, criticizing the prohibition campaign as quite unsuitable for Travancore with its large *Ezhava* community and angry with the Working Committee for ignoring the hundreds still in jail. For the time being, however, the Youth League were still prepared to accept the lead of the State Congress.

In fact the Working Committee were planning a second civil disobedience campaign, and at the meeting on January 17th announced that they would launch it on March 1st if their demands were not met. These demands were reasonable in themselves or at least open to negotiation: they were a repetition of previous demands; but the government was not in a conciliatory mood, as the next step showed.

The Legislature was due to meet in the middle of February. A week before the opening, a government communique appeared disqualifying nineteen legislators for their criminal activities which had earned them sentences of at least six months' imprisonment. There was an outcry all over the country. In Trivandrum, 22 leading citizens, none of them Congressmen, called a public meeting which drew a huge crowd; Changanacherry Parameswaran Pillai was in the chair. There was anger that not only had the nineteen legislators been disqualified without notice but that nineteen constituencies had been disenfranchised, for there had been ample time to arrange by-elections. "The Legislature", said Parameswaran Pillai, "consists of wooden hands which will rise to support government policy at a word from government". A government press note replied that the offending legislators could have applied for the removal of their disqualifications but had failed to do so, hence there was no room for complaint against the government.

This inclement act was the last straw for Parameswaran Pillai; at last he joined the Travancore State Congress. In a long press statement he explained that the Memorandum had stood in the way of his joining earlier, and when it was withdrawn he rejoiced, for he hoped that it would lead to a conciliatory policy on the part of the government. But repression had continued and he could no longer remain a silent spectator. The government's answer was to suspend his pension on the grounds of "his grave misconduct in associating with a subversive movement".

IX.5 Intervention by Gandhi

Gandhi once more intervened. March 1st 1939 had been fixed for the start of the second civil disobedience movement, but he persuaded the Working Committee to postpone it until March 25th as there were possibilities of negotiation, and to begin only when he advised them to do so. He still needed time to study the situation, and advised them meanwhile to go on with the constructive programme. John Philipose, whom Gandhi kept at Wardha to advise him on Travancore affairs, begged him to go to Travancore to see for himself; but he neither went himself nor listened to John Philipose. Meanwhile, on March 18th, the five most important leaders of the State Congress were arrested— Pattom, T.M. Verghese, C.Kesavan, V.K.Velayudhan and P.K. Kunju. The leaders remaining free therefore indefinitely postponed civil disobedience.

Gandhi was very pleased and issued a statement a few days later on the subject of Travancore. It was, he said, a special case. His chief motive was fear of violence which might result from the use of untrained men as special police. Time was also needed to mobilize public opinion in favour of liberty and for the Travancore Government to reconsider the situation. In a typical Gandhian conclusion, he wrote that the disappointment gave opportunities to discipline themselves, and they must have faith that all was for the best.

The movement was now irretrievably split. Many of the youngsters became communists and devoted themselves to working among the factory labourers and the landless labourers in the Alleppey and Shertallai area. Some left the movement in disgust. A leading Nayar, whose wife had succeeded Akkamma Cheriyan as commandant of the *Desa Sevikas*, wrote bitterly to Pattom Thanu Pillai that the policy of drift among the leadership was "nothing but a cruel betrayal of the masses. The Travancore State Congress has completely surrendered itself to outside leadership". The leaders themselves were adrift; all they had left was the constructive programme; but prohibition had been a failure, and the *khadi* and cottage industries programme achieved very little. "The Civil Disobedience campaign having been suspended", ran a report of the Constructive Work Committee of April 26th, "workers are generally groping in the dark without fully realizing what has to be done under the present circumstances".

How was it that Gandhi usually a shrewd judge of men and situations and a keen bargainer, could so fail in judgement? How could he believe that the Travancore Government would in time "reconsider the situation"? Fear of violence played a large part in his decision. Many Christians believed he had been won over by Sir C.P.'s reiterated statements that the Travancore Congress was essentially a Christian movement designed to undermine the hindu character of the state. This may be ruled out; anti-foreign-missionary he was, explicitly anti-Christian he was not. His chief mistake was to trust in Sir C.P.'s words in face of all the evidence of his unreliability. He believed him because he wanted to believe him; and he wanted to believe him partly because, in Gandhi's eyes, he had never lost the halo of the Temple Entry Proclamation.[27] But it was partly because (and this I suspect is the key) Sir C.P. had, early in their exchanges, raised the matter of a new constitution for Travancore which would go some way towards meeting the aspirations of the people.

We first hear of it in February 1939 at the meeting of the All-India states Peoples' Conference at Ludhiana, when Dr. Pattabhi Sitaramayya told a Travancorean delegate that Sir C.P. had already drafted a constitution "which he had shown to some Congress leaders and which, of course, might have moved Gandhiji for withdrawing the Memorandum".[28] That would put it back to at least as early as December 1938. We do no know. Letters are lost or not available; no definite proposals emerged until 1946, when they turned out to be a travesty of the American constitution. But a new constitution was continuously talked about in 1939, as pervasive as Harvey, the non-existent rabbit.

The mountain did, however, give birth to one little mouse, i.e. an alteration in the electoral rules. The Nayars had been dissatisfied with the Habibullah reforms of 1936, which had deprived them of their privileged position, and felt themselves an aggrieved minority. Sir C.P. had played on this sense of grievance to build up the Travancore National Congress, mainly from the Nayar Service Society members. A deputation from the latter waited on the Dewan in early November to ask for a change in the voting system, and in April their proposals were adopted and a communique issued, well in time for the 19 bye-elections still to be held. They applied to the multi-member constituencies, which under the Habibullah rules had reservation of seats for minorities; now each elector was to have as many votes as there were seats, and the representatives of minorities were those who secured at least 60% of the votes of the members of their own community. In other words, electors had to be labelled as belonging to this or that community, and the new system was an open invitation to return to communal politics. The Working Committee of the State Congress saw it as "an attempt to destroy the measure of communal agreement built up by the Travancore

State Congress". Pattom Thanu Pillai, in a strong statement, drew the conclusion that the government did not propose to consider responsible government at all. And he went off to consult Gandhi.

It was the Mahatma who started fresh discussions in June, when enthusiasm was at such a low ebb that a conference planned for that month failed to materialize. He had been exchanging telegrams with Sir C.P. and holding long conversations with Pattom, T.M.Verghese and John Philipose. In an article about the situation in Travancore in *Harijan* of June 9th 1939, he defended the suspension of the civil disobedience campaign though his critics asserted that suspension had led to even greater repression. It was advised in order to avoid popular violence, and also to pave the way for an honourable understanding with the authorities. The time had now come to open direct negotiations. "Hitherto", he wrote, "the State Congress people have talked at the authorities and the latter at them. Now the time had come for an honourable understanding. . . . It might be necessary to lower the key of such an approach; in any case the atmosphere in the state is not propitious for immediate responsible government".

The State Congress made the first approach, and on July 7th three delegates (Pattom, T.M. Verghese, and V.K. Velayudhan, i.e. a Nayar, a Christian and an Ezhava) met the Dewan. He read out a prepared statement in which he made three points: first, while subjects had the right to approach His Highness or his advisers with regard to any subject, intervention from outside was not to be countenanced; second, they were to give up any idea of civil disobedience; third, there was no intention on the part of the Travancore Government to establish a responsible government in the sense of the responsibility of the Executive to the Legislature. In spite of this unpromising beginning they agreed to meet again.

The Working Committee met to discuss the Dewan's terms and decided not to seek outside help but reserved the right to seek outside advice, and also to seek another interview. It was two months and half-a-dozen reminders later that they secured one. Meanwhile the Mahatma became indignant about the "humiliating conditions of non-intervention" imposed on the State Congress, and the Dewan tried to smoothe him down by explaining that they could seek advice but not put themselves under the mandate of an outside person or body (which they had never done or intended). To Pattom, who took his stand on the right to conduct constitutional agitation, the Dewan replied that no scheme of reforms had been decided, and no scheme could be brought into operation unless all parties were prepared to work it. Pattom assured the Dewan of the Congress' intention to work any agreed scheme; it was not their intention to accept a scheme "only in order to wreck it".

Another inconclusive interview took place on September 5th. But war had already broken out, and it gave the Dewan an excuse for putting a stop to all further negotiations. On that day the Defence of Travancore Rules were promulgated, which enabled the Government of Travancore to drop its critics into the waste paper basket of detention without trial. So ended the only attempt at an agreed solution to the problem of constitutional advance in the state.

Chapter X

THE ATTITUDE OF THE PARAMOUNT POWER

The relations of the Paramount Power with Travancore in the troubled years of 1938-1939 form a case history of the exercise of Paramountcy.

The essential dilemma of British policy in India at this time—the reconciliation of promotion of democracy in the provinces of British India with upholding of autocracy in the Princely states—has been discussed in the first chapter. Provincial autonomy in the period 1937 to 1939, during which Congress governments were in power in eight of the eleven provinces, only sharpened the horns of the dilemma. In the first place, popular agitation in the states, stimulated by the sight of self-government in the provinces, had greatly increased. Secondly, when Congress governments were in the saddle, they could not be relied on to back up the efforts of the British to check agitation in the state or support of these movements directed from British Indian provinces. The governor of Madras complained to the Viceroy, in a letter of November 15th 1938, that the Madras premier had refused to cooperate in controlling the publication of articles in the English medium press critical of the repressive policy of the Travancore Government. The Premier had taken the point of view that as the articles were in English they could not possibly incite the masses. Both "Rajaji" and the governor were perfectly well aware that at the time practically the whole of the Travancore agitation was being carried on in English; but the exasperated governor did not think the point worth a fight.[1] Worst of all, to quote a note by the Political Secretary on the dilemma: "Some of the states have shown a disturbing tendency to make friends with Mammon". The rulers in many of the states had been badly shaken by Congress activities, and even began to fear that the Paramount Power, in an effort to keep on the right side of Congress, was preparing to throw them to the wolves. The Raja of Aundh (a tiny state near Poona) had "made his submission" to Gandhi and divested himself (at least on paper) of all his governing powers and handed them to a popular government. It was all indeed disturbing.[2]

The correct policy to be pursued among these shifting sands was the subject of much discussion between the Viceroy, the Political

Department, the Residents and Agents* and the governors of the provinces; the Secretary of state for India was kept fully informed, for in the last analysis he was responsible for laying down the broad lines of policy. There was much concern for the smaller states which were by their nature unable to bear the financial burden of an efficient administration; nonetheless, they should be encouraged "not merely to refrain from misrule but to make sacrifices of prestige at any rate in the interests of the welfare of their subjects", as Lord Zetland, Secretary of state for India wrote to Lord Linlithgow, on 16th December 1938. "If the initiative is not to pass to Congress", he added, "they could no longer postpone a policy of insisting on reforms".

One frank critic of British policy towards the states was G.D.Birla, the *khadi*-clad, millionaire Congress industrialist, host to Gandhi when he visited Delhi, who nevertheless kept close contact with British officials, and through his sincerity kept their friendship. He was aware of the Political Department's distrust of Congress activities in states, and in a letter of 18th December, 1938, to the Private Secretary to the Viceroy to be conveyed to His Excellency, he wrote: "This distrust is to a very large extent unjustified". He pointed out the success of the Congress governments in the provinces where trust between Congress and British officials was growing "largely due to personal contacts. If there be greater sympathy and understanding I have no doubt that the question of the Indian states can be settled with ease and (with) less bitterness. As soon as real responsibility is offered you will find hesitation to accept it without full preparedness. On the other hand the clamour for this will increase if it is opposed". In conclusion he added: "Even from a purely utilitarian point of view I feel it is desirable to secure friendship with the Congress. But I would ask His Excellency to treat the question on a higher plane; cannot we pin our faith on a policy of trust?"[3]

But such wisdom and realism went unheeded—till Mountbatten came with a fresh view and swept the old policy away like a house of cards.

---

* Note by the Editor: In 1923 when political supervision of the states in southern India shifted from the Government of Madras to the Government of India, the name "Resident" was changed into "Agent to the Governor-General for the Madras States." In 1937 the name changed again to "Resident for the Madras States."

X.1 The Political Service

When G.D. Birla wrote "Trust begets trust, largely due to personal contact", he put his finger on one of the major difficulties: the character of the Political Service of the Government of India. It was the very nature of the machinery for dealing with states' affairs that was responsible for misinformation and misconceptions.

By the Government of India Act of 1935, the Viceroy had two distinct functions. In respect of British India he was the governor-General; in respect of the Indian states he was the Crown Representative. Theoretically the two functions could have been performed by two persons; but in practice they were combined in the same person for severely practical reasons. As Crown Representative he was served by the Political Department and the officers of the Political Service. There was a Political Adviser (not necessarily a member of the Political Service); there was a Political Department at headquarters with its political secretary, staffed by members of the Political Service. There were 12 Residents to major states or groups of states, and a number of Residents to smaller states and groups. The Crown Representative was of course responsible to the Secretary of state in Whitehall; and the India Office had its own Political Department to advice on states affairs, consisting largely of retired members of the Political Service with long experience of the Indian states.

The Political Service had two departments: the External Affairs Department which dealt with the countries on India's borders, and the Political Branch which dealt with the Indian states. The political officers were drawn partly from the Indian Army and partly from the Indian Civil Service; they had therefore very much the same social background of public school and either Varsity or Sandhurst, and very much the same outlook by whatever route they reached the Political Service.

The position of a Resident or Political Agent was quasi-diplomatic; he was as it were the representative of the Crown Representative at the court of the ruler, and had to observe strict protocol. His social position as a kind of ambassador inhibited him from making any real contacts with Indians outside the narrow circle of the palace and the higher officials; least of all could he make contact with the local politicians. (There were exceptions: one Resident joined the Trivandrum International Fellowship; another, more original, took lessons in yoga from a local Congressman.) One is tempted to perpetrate a parody, and describe the Political Service as one "where civilians speak only to

Army, and Army speak only to God". But that is an exaggeration, for political officers mingled freely with what one may call the upper castes of the British community—officials, bank men, planters, those in wholesale trade. Those in retail trade were untouchable and not admitted to the European clubs. As for the missionaries, they were almost literally unseeables; if they were quite often elected honorary members of the European clubs, they rarely came except for tennis or the Christmas children's party. As they did not drink or play cards for money, they were unable to participate in the prescribed rituals of British social life; so (apart from the Red Cross, Boy Scouts and similar socially acceptable good works) their contacts with "the club crowd" were minimal. Yet if any Europeans knew India it was the missionaries; they spoke the local language, they taught and nursed and healed the Indians, looked after the widows and orphans and lepers; they welcomed Indians into their houses and were received in Indian homes. They would have had much to tell the Residents which could not easily have been gathered from the other restricted channels of information open to them. It was true that in the last two decades of the British *Raj*, Indians were being admitted to some of the clubs; but these would be mostly high officials or Indians holding the King's Commission in one of the Services. They would be to some extent Westernised.

The result of such insulation was that the political officers found it difficult to have any broad understanding of the people of the states in which they served. In the smaller states they often had an understanding of such troubles as excessive taxation or *begar* (forced labour without payment), the simple troubles of an oppressed peasantry, and were able, by discreet handling of the big stick of possible Viceregal intervention, to put right crying wrongs. But it was extremely difficult for them to understand the point of view of the growing professional classes in the towns, the very people who wanted a bigger share in the government of the state and the guarantee of their fundamental civil rights: there was no means of contact. The Political Service moreover had no intelligence service of its own; in certain cases it relied on the Criminal Investigation Department from British India to investigate a special problem. For example, when in 1941 it was considered important to investigate the infiltration of communists from British India into Travancore and Cochin, the Resident and the two Dewans concerned called in the Madras C.I.D. The Residents had to pick up what they could, and frequently turned to the police of the state and to the Dewans for their confidential information. Bias was inevitable.

Sir William Barton's book *The Indian Princes*, published in 1934, reflects the point of view of the older generation of the Political Service, who had considerable influence on the India Office in Whitehall. Sir William had entered the Political Service via the I.C.S. in 1899, and after a long and distinguished career in the states he retired in 1930; he continued for several years as an adviser to the India Office. The historical account of the relations between the British and the Princes is sound; but the states are regarded almost entirely from the point of view of the rulers. Indian India, he claims, views politics from a different angle; it does not approve of a free and irresponsible press or of popular agitation. But the people are happy under their princes; the traditional form of government suits them; they love the colour and pageantry of life in the states. "In most Indian states", he writes, "the link between dynasty and subjects is so strong that the people would find it difficult to contemplate a change of regime". Democracy does not suit them; it is too much a matter of the urban intelligentsia. Sir William, in fact, considered the Congress a group of "power-hungry politicians", coming into the states from British India to exploit the grievances of the people for their own selfish ends. He developed this theme in a lecture to the East India Association in London in July 1939. "The artificiality of the agitation in the states is shown by the attacks on such states as Mysore, Travancore and Cochin, where the people are practically self-governing, and the administration is as efficient as in British India. Obviously in such states the Congress had not the good of the people in view".[4] Unaware as he was of the local origins of the popular movements in the southern states, he considered—and in this he was not alone—that "the Princes are unquestionably the strongest party in all the political manoeuvering, and it may be said that the key still lies in their hands. They are the most stable factor in political India at present, and their importance in the Indian empire of the future can hardly be overrated".

The rapid collapse of the Princely states after Independence was almost entirely unforeseen by the very people who were regarded as experts on the subject.

All generalizations about Indian states are dangerous; any one state, if "typical" at all, is typical only of its own area. Travancore provides a clear case of the failure of the Political Department to grasp what really was going on; but one cannot apply conclusions reached about Travancore to the totally different circumstances of, for instance, the Rajputana states or those of the Central states Agency. In Travancore and its sister state Cochin, there were a high level of literacy, strong political consciousness, and a long history of checks on the rulers' power dating from feudal times. Above all, the degree of constitutional advance which they had achieved spurred them to ask for more; they needed no stimulus from outside. Such conditions hardly existed elsewhere. It is doubtful also whether anywhere else in states was there such a close link between the politicians and journalists and the people, so close that politicians were often known by the name of the place with which they were associated and which they represented in the Legislature, such as Pattom Thanu Pillai, Changanacherry Parameswaran Pillai, Nedumangad Kesavan Nair (Nedumangad was his birthplace and for years his constituency).

The Residents' attitudes can be traced in the fortnightly confidential reports which were sent to the Political Secretary and forwarded to the India Office, and also in the special reports and correspondence concerning special events and problems. Of course, the attitude varied greatly with different Residents. In 1921, when the "old Maharaja" was seeking permission from the Viceroy to introduce considerable constitutional reforms, the then Resident, Mr. H.M.Burkitt, wrote a long special report which shows close knowledge of Travancore, in which he concludes that Travancore was fitter for reforms than any other part of India. "With the exception of Cochin, no province or state in India approaches Travancore in respect of political eligibility, if we take the usual criteria employed—literacy, the diffusion of Higher Education and the general level of culture".[5] But on the whole the Residents' reports show intimate knowledge of palace affairs (admittedly very important to the well-being of the state) and considerable ignorance of the people, particularly of those outside the capital city.

In the troubled years of 1938 and 1939, the Residents' reports, shrewd about the palace, show grave misjudgments of the whole situation. There was a tendency to accept the Dewan's version of events and people, and to forward the official communiques and press releases. Apart from his condemnation of the police excesses at the time of the student demonstrations (when he had the evidence of the commandant of the state Forces and the vice-principal of the Arts College to supplement his own observations on the spot)[6], the Resident at no time questioned the Dewan's official versions, which were often at variance with the statements of his critics; these latter were dismissed as a tissue of deliberate lies and calumny. At no time therefore was the Viceroy or the Secretary of state for India informed of the strength of popular feeling, the indigenous origins of the movement, or the solid social standing of the leaders. Protests and warnings from Carl Heath, the well-informed chairman of the India Conciliation Group (a largely

Quaker body), Dr. Stanley Jones, the famous American missionary known all over India but not to the Political Department, and C.F.Andrews himself, were brushed aside as contradicting the information of the man on the spot.[7]

A few examples will suffice. The Resident's reports for March 1938 state: "In Travancore there is nothing to report". Yet the whole state from the Dewan down to the clerks on the remotest tea estates were tremendously excited by the formation of the non-communal state Congress. In June the submission of the Memorial and Memorandum to the Maharaja is mentioned, and the Resident comments on the signatories, who were in fact the Working Committee of the Travancore state Congress: "The Nayars are a disgruntled minority, the Christian signatories, all members of th Syrian Christain church, include no representatives of the large Catholic community, the Ezhavas belong to one of the several non-caste Hindu communities of the state. The claim of the signatories to represent the whole population can thus be judged". There is no hint of the standing in the community of Pattom Thanu Pillai, respectable and respected; no realization that the greater part of the Syrian Christians were Roman Catholic, though not Latin Catholics (they used the Syrian rite); P.J.Sebastian, a Romo-Syrian, was general secretary of the Kerala Catholic Congress, the only woman member of the Working Committee, Miss Anne Mascarene, was a pioneer woman lawyer and a well-known Latin Catholic. The Ezhavas comprised 18% of the population; their powerful organization, the S.N.D.P. Yogam, had put itself solid behind the state Congress. No hint is ever given of the police use of *agents provocateurs* in stirring up trouble. The state Congress is repeatedly accused of inciting the students to commit acts of violence such as stone throwing; their successes in calming the students down are never mentioned.[8] Of the Neyyattinkara riots, the first in which lives were lost, the Resident writes: "The Dewan has definite evidence of the connection between the state Congress leaders and those of the mob". G.Ramachandran, "whose niece is betrothed to Gandhi's grandson" (and who spent the day in state Transport buses to get them safely past the mob), "cannot be absolved from responsibility for what occurred on that day".

No Resident, however, was under any illusion about those who came almost daily under their observation: the Ruling Family and the Dewan. Both Mr. Skrine and Mr. H.M. Todd, Resident in 1944, wrote their "Impressions of Travancore" for the information of the Viceroy, and they concurred that the course of events was directed by two powerful personalities, the Junior Maharani and Sir C.P. Both were greedy for power and acclaim, vain, susceptible to flattery, utterly intolerant of criticism and opposition. One of Skrine's judgements is open to question, not for itself but for the reason supporting it: he considered Sir C.P. "incorruptible by money", and based his judgment on the assumption that the directors of the Travancore National and Quilon Bank would have bought Sir C.P. if they could. He misjudged the whole situation; it was war to the knife between the directors and Sir C.P.; the directors would never have offered a bribe, nor would Sir C.P., out to crush the Syrian Christian leadership, have accepted it.[9]

X.2 Sir C.P.'s Memorandum[10]

Many of the Princes, confronted with provincial Autonomy on the one hand, and with Lord Winterton's declaration that the Paramount Power would not obstruct constitutional advance on the other, sought assurances that they would be protected. It was towards the end of 1938, when the disturbances in the states were at their height, that Sir C.P. took the initiative in calling a meeting in Bombay of the Dewans of some of the leading states, and drew up the Memorandum (already referred to in the previous chapter) on "Congress agitation and policy in respect of the administration of Indian states". This was submitted, with suitable modifications for each state, by the several Dewans through their respective Residents, who wrote covering letters. Sir C.P.'s Memorandum was the first to reach the Viceroy who concluded that he was the original author.

The Memorandum followed a line which would appeal to the Political Department. It referred to the drive against the Indian states recently initiated by the Indian National Congress "in furtherance of their programme to capture power in the forthcoming Federation". In pursuit of this policy, Congress were trying to force the pace by agitations engineered from outside. The states, declared the Memorandum, did not wish to repress the aspirations of their people or deny their civil liberties, but objected to "revolutionary methods which derive their impulse and power from the regimented activities of the Congress High Command". This concerted attack was based on the conviction that the Paramount Power would bring pressure to bear on the states to alter their systems of government and their methods of choosing representatives to the Federal Legislature.

The main proposal in the Memorandum was for an unequivocal declaration that it was not the intention of the Paramount Power to insist on constitutional changes in the states. If this were done, "the agitation will almost immediately lose its all-India character and the present mass attack would cease". Of course some agitation would continue, but the Indian states relied upon the Paramount Power "for their moral and in the last resort material support in their endeavour to maintain their historic traditions and their forms of administration and Government".

In the file enshrining this document, there is a note in Lord Linlithgow's handwriting: "What a pity, then, that the author of this able and illuminating memorandum compelled H.M.G. to disclaim any intention of *preventing* the states from carrying through internal political reforms by trying to lay the burden of responsibility for what was essentially a decision resting entirely with Travancore upon the shoulders of the Paramount Power!" His Excellency had no illusions about the brilliant Dewan of Travancore.

The comment itself (once its syntax is disentangled) is illuminating. His Majesty's Government would have preferred to leave the whole question undefined, in the hope that the horns of the dilemma would become less uncomfortable, or perhaps the beast might even go away. Nonetheless, the Memorandum started off a long discussion in the inner circles of the Political Department and in the correspondence between the Viceroy and the Secretary of state for India. The upshot was that the Viceroy and the Secretary of state arranged for a question to be asked in the House of Commons by a conservative member, and between them drew up both the question and the reply by the Under-Secretary of state for India.[11]

On 16th December 1938, a conservative member submitted a question: "To ask the Under-Secretary of state for India in what way the attitude of His Majesty's Government towards constitutional reform in Indian states has recently been modified; and what is the policy of His Majesty's Government towards the present agitation in various Indian states?"

The answer of the Under-Secretary was: "His Majesty's Government adhere fully to the statement made by my Noble friend the Member for Horsham* in his reply on 21st February last on this subject. The Paramount Power will not obstruct proposals for constitutional advance initiated by Rulers. But His Majesty's Government have no intention of bringing any form of pressure to bear upon them to initiate

---

* Note by the Editor: Lord Winterton was the member for Horsham. The conservative member of the House of Commons who had asked the question (December 1938) was Sir John Wardlaw Milne.

constitutional changes. It rests with the Rulers themselves to decide what form of Government they should adopt in the diverse conditions of Indian states.

With regard to the second part of the question, the obligations of the Paramount Power to the states extend to protecting Rulers against violence and disorder and to advising and assisting Rulers in remedying such legitimate grievances of their subjects as may be found to exist".

When Sir C.P. visited the Viceroy in Delhi a few days later, he expressed himself satisfied with the parliamentary reply. But his conversation with the Viceroy showed that he was not. It was in connection with the forthcoming state visit of His Excellency the Viceroy to Travancore, arranged for January 1939. Now the climax of such Viceregal visits was usually the state banquet at which the ruler, in his speech welcoming the guest, set forth the moral and material progress of his state, while the Viceroy often used these occasions to make statements of policy, or to exhort the Princes in general to carry out their duties to their subjects in an exemplary fashion. These speeches were thoroughly discussed beforehand and carefully disinfected of anything objectionable or embarrassing to either party. Sir C.P. proposed that His Highness, having reviewed the remarkable achievements of the present administration, should conclude that in his opinion "that represents the maximum which can safely and properly be given in this state at the present time". Such a statement in the Viceroy's presence would be tantamount to His Excellency giving his blessing to the point which constitutional advance had reached in Travancore; and His Excellency had no intention of doing so. He carefully explained to Sir C.P. that he had to consider the all-India implications of anything he said. "My strength lay in manoeuvre and freedom—conditions were too fluid for any final judgment to be made" (Linlithgow to Zetland, 20th December 1938). The embarrassing paragraph was deleted.

X. 3 Responsibility for Seeing Justice Done: The Bank Case[12]

The failure of the Travancore National and Quilon Bank in June 1938 has already been described as one of the major causes of the disturbances of that year. But it is of special interest also in a discussion of the relations of the Paramount Power with the states, for it raises the question of the responsibility of the Paramount Power for justice in the states. In the smaller states miscarriage of justice was one of the accepted reasons for Viceregal intervention; but how far could he

The photograph of Sir C.P. Ramaswamy Aiyar, Dewan of Travancore, with a group of Aides at the time of the Cabinet Mission of 1946. Reproduced with permission, from a collection of albums once belonging to A.H. Joyce, Principal Information Officer to the Cabinet Mission of 1946, the British Library, Oriental and India Office Collections.

Her Highness Setu Parvati Bai, Maharani of Travancore. Reproduced with permission, from *The Madras States Directory 1930,* Cochin: Pearl Press 1930, the British Library, Oriental and India Office Collections.

intervene in the internal affairs of a full- powered state if it was patent that an injustice had been done? This question was thrashed out in the controversy over the Travancore Bank case.

The Resident to the Madras states became involved immediately, first unofficially and later officially. In May 1938, when it was clear that the bank was in difficulties, the chairman of the bank, Mr. K.C. Mammen Mappillay, visited the Resident who was then holidaying in Ootacamund in the Nilgiri Hills, to ask for his good offices in saving the bank. Mr. Skrine arranged a meeting between Sir C.P. (also holidaying in Ootacamund) and the directors, and tried to arrive at a solution of the bank's difficulties. But the Resident, reporting to the Political Secretary in Simla, complained of Sir C.P.'s "implacable hostility" to the Directors, especially to Mr. C.P. Matthen, "his most determined political opponent", and of Sir C.P.'s determination to bring about the collapse of the bank. The Reserve Bank refused assistance and the bank closed its doors on June 21st.

The directors kept away from Travancore and took refuge in Madras. But Sir C.P. was determined to have them brought for trial for their crimes in a Travancore court, and applied to the Resident for an extradition warrant on behalf of the District Magistrate of Trivandrum on charges of issuing a false balance sheet and of conspiracy to defraud. The liquidator's preliminary report was also submitted, and the Resident, convinced that there was a prima facie case against the directors, issued the warrant, by which the directors could be arrested in Madras in British India and handed over to the Travancore police at the frontier. Convinced they would not get a fair trial in any Travancore court, the accused appealed to the Madras High Court against the extradition order; and when their appeal failed, took it to the Judicial Committee of the Privy Council, which also rejected the appeal. The Viceroy suggested that a judge from British India should be imported to try the case; but Sir C.P. objected strongly since to do so would amount to an admission that the charges levelled against the Travancore judiciary were justified. The Resident however obtained from the Dewan a verbal promise that "if the accused were convicted in the Trivandrum Sessions Court and appealed to the Travancore High Court, the Travancore Government would consider the advisability of the appeal being heard by a High Court Judge from British India appointed temporarily to the Travancore High Court".

The trial was duly heard in the Sessions court in Trivandrum. K.S. Ramanujam was released after he turned approver; another was acquitted and released. Four who were found guilty were given long sentences of hard labour. On appeal to the Travancore High Court the sentences were reduced but were still very long. C.P. Matthen, the former managing director and Sir C.P.'s most persistent opponent, was given five years' hard labour.

We are not concerned with the rights and wrongs of the case, nor with the conduct of the trial. The report of the liquidator (an Englishman of unimpeachable integrity) showed that their essential crime, apart from cooking the accounts, was the failure to keep their assets liquid; they had lent too much against property which could not easily be turned into cash. But the trial presented some curious features, and Mr. Noel Barwell, who defended K.C. Mammen Mappillay (also an Englishman of unimpeachable integrity), was "morally and intellectually convinced that none of the accused had committed the crimes with which they were charged". But the High Court of Travancore was a court of final appeal, and no appeal from its decisions could be made to the Federal Court or to the Privy Council. It appeared then that the accused would have to work out their sentences to the end. One of them—an old man with a weak heart—died in jail.

C.P. Matthen's wife was determined not to let the matter rest, and took her husband's case to the highest authority in India, the Viceroy. She seized the opening given by the Extradition Rules under which extradition warrants were issued, and maintained that Rule 7 had not been observed. Now this Rule ran as follows:

"The Political Agent shall satisfy himself that the accused receives a fair trial and that the punishment is not excessive or barbarous; and if he is not so satisfied, he shall demand the restoration of the prisoner to his custody pending the orders of the governor-General in Council".

Mrs. Matthen first obtained a legal opinion from the Advocate General to the Government of India, Sir B.L.Mitter. He examined the evidence and the judgement of the Travancore High Court and came to a damning conclusion:

"It is impossible to resist the impression that it is a case of conviction first and reasons in justification, however feeble, flimsy or far-fetched, afterwards. . . . The conviction of Matthen was founded upon inadequate evidence. . . . Relevant evidence was kept back, witnesses who could have given useful information were not called. . . . What struck me most was the desperate anxiety of the prosecution to secure a conviction and not to unravel truth. In my opinion the conviction of Matthen was illegal and was secured by means which by no decent standard could be called fair".

Armed with this legal opinion, Mrs. Matthen addressed a memorial on 26th June 1941, to the Viceroy, not as Crown Representative, but in his capacity as governor-General in Council, based strictly on rule 7. It was an appeal not for her husband's release, but for an order that the prisoner be taken back from the state custody in Travancore, to be dealt with in any manner as might seem fit to His Excellency. It was forwarded through the Metropolitan of India, Dr. Foss Westcott, to make sure that the Dewan of Travancore, through his spies and agents scattered throughout India, should not have the letter intercepted.

The case, backed by such formidable legal opinion and presented under such auspices, received the Viceroy's careful attention. The relevant papers were sent to the Political Department for a discussion of the constitutional issue, and to the Legal Department for a discussion of the legality of the trial and the appropriateness of th sentence. In a note on the file, the Joint Secretary to the Political Department clarified the position of the Paramount Power in relation to the Travancore courts:

"The Ruler of Travancore exercises full civil and criminal jurisdiction and has the power to make his own laws. The Paramount Power therefore cannot arbitrarily entertain appeals against the judgement of the Travancore High Court. . . . In the case of an accused extradited from British India to an Indian state, the Political Agent is however empowered to demand the restoration of the prisoner committed by a Court of an Indian state, if he is satisfied that the trial was not fair, pending the orders of the governor-General in Council. Moreover, by virtue of Paramountcy, the Crown Representative may entertain a petition on any affair arising in an Indian state, irrespective of whether there are specific limitations on the powers of the Ruler of the state or not".

Mr. S. Lal, of the Legal Department, examined the records of the trial, and on the strength of the evidence before the court concluded that the conviction of the accused was justified and no substantial or grave injustice had been done. But he added: "The sentence is not discreditable or barbarous but I have not the slightest hesitation in calling it excessive". He pointed out that three separate sentences, adding up to five years, had been given for what was actually the same offence, described under slightly different words, of inflating assets and concealing liabilities in the balance sheet, and that the maximum sentence for that offence was two years. The sentence was therefore grossly excessive, particularly in face of the fact that the accused had been an under-trial prisoner for more than a year. He added significantly: "It is nobody's case that the accused had personally benefited by the commis ion of the offences".

Sir George Spence of the Legal Department supported the opinions of his colleagues in both the Political and Legal Departments, adding that the Crown Representative was competent to intervene in any case, apart from the Extradition Rules, in which in his opinion there had been a gross miscarriage of justice. Sir George also suggested the procedure in the case under review for intervention: the intervention might in the first instance take the form of a tender of advice to the Maharaja or his government to reduce the sentences of imprisonment on all three convicted. "If the advice is rejected, it might be intimated that the Crown Representative, while anxious to refrain from affronting the state by the open issue of orders, would be constrained to adopt this course if the refusal to accept his advice were maintained". His Excellency approved the procedure suggested; and on the 7th September 1941 the Secretary of the Political Department wrote to the Resident with the necessary instructions to broach the matter to the Dewan; but if there was any tendency on the part of the Travancore Government to resist compliance, to warn him that it was very probable that formal advice would be offered.

Sir C.P. (who must somehow have been apprized of what was going on) had already acted before the Resident received the letter from Simla, let alone interviewed the Dewan. On the 8th September he informed the Resident that two of the accused, K.C. Mammen Mappillay and his son K.M. Eapen, were released on confession of their errors which led to the collapse of the bank. They had petitioned for pardon and release on the grounds of health, and the government, while not granting a pardon, had remitted the balance of their sentences and the fines. Sir C.P., in a lengthy letter to Col. Murphy, the Resident, explained that he was informing him of these circumstances in view of the considerable interest the case had aroused. It was not however proposed to release Mr. C.P.Matthen "as he has adopted a defiant and contumacious attitude throughout, and has been the main instigator of the frauds and irregularities which had brought ruin on thousands of families all over India". The Paramount Power was firm: C.P. Matthen had to be released. The Dewan said he would be prepared to advise the Maharaja to remit half the sentence provided it was made clear to Matthen that the conviction as such was not disturbed. The Crown Representative insisted on the letter of his instructions; the Dewan stalled. Eventually the release was postponed on various excuses for some three months. The Resident was inclined to put the blame for the delay on "the palace" (meaning the Junior Maharani). What was happening (unknown to the Resident) was that Sir C.P. was putting pressure on Matthen to admit his guilt, or at least to write a letter begging for his release.[13] Matthen was not to be caught; he emerged triumphant, protesting his innocence, and eventually restored the family fortunes. After Independence he became an ambassador for India.

Mrs. Matthen of course made great capital of her husband's release and of Sir B.L. Mitter's strictures on the Travancore Judiciary. Sir C.P. was disturbed by all the adverse publicity, and approached the Resident for permission to make public the fact that the Viceroy upheld the conviction. His Excellency ruled that the Travancore Government could do so provided they publicly admitted at the same time that they had acceded to His Excellency's advice to reduce the excessive sentences awarded. The matter was skirted round by an evasive statement that the point at issue was whether the sentences on the three charges should have been concurrent or consecutive, but the conviction itself was fully justified by the evidence before the court. The Political Department decided to let this prevaricating statement pass—it was a small crumb of comfort to Sir C.P.

There is no doubt that the two Residents concerned—Mr. C.P. Skrine and Colonel Murphy—failed to carry out their duties under rule 7 of the Extradition Rules. At the time of the sessions trial, Matthen's Lawyer had approached Col. Murphy to exercise his right to scrutinize the trial, which he claimed was being misconducted; but the Resident had refused to act until the accused had exhausted all the resources of local justice.[14] He failed to check on the second trial or the sentences passed, even though Sir C.P. had broken his promise to consider appointing a High Court Judge from British India to conduct the trial. The reason is not far to seek. Both Residents had accepted, without any questions, the opinions expressed by Sir C.P. on the Syrian Christian directors of the bank, as fraudulent and dishonest; unscrupulous men who were backing the state Congress and the Youth League in order to distract attention from their own misdeeds. Skrine wrote to the Political Secretary: "They are little better than crooks, out to loot an ever-widening circle of depositors".[15] He obviously considered that they were getting no more than they deserved, and Col. Murphy accepted this opinion. It was a prejudgement of a case still subjudice; at no time in either trial did it emerge that the directors had diverted any funds to their own use, though it is true that they had lent to their own relatives against the security of fixed assets. K.C. Mammen Mappillay was no crook; he was a great newspaper editor with a long record of public service—membership of the Sri Mulam Popular Assembly, service on a number of government committees.* His newspaper, the *Malayala Manorama*, was no scurrilous rag; it had even then a circulation of over 200,000 and in the world of Malayali journalism approximated to the *Manchester Guardian*. His brother K.C. Eapen, manager of the Trivandrum branch of the Bank, was a well-known public figure, president of the local Y.M.C.A., active in all good causes** C.P. Matthen was more of a business man, but he too had served on a number of government committees. Nor were they Congressmen. Mammen Mappillay had long been critical of the Indian National Congress; he had given his powerful support to the Joint Political Congress, and had insisted that its movement should be called the "Abstention" movement, to distinguish it from Congress activities which were called "Non-cooperation", to make quite clear it owed nothing to the National Congress. He had, it is true, been one of Sir C.P.'s greatest opponents but for the purely local reason that Sir C.P. favoured caste Hindus against Christians, Ezhavas and Muslims.[16] His paper was cool towards the Travancore state Congress at first. It was the failure of the bank, and the conviction that Sir C.P. had engineered it, that made Congressmen of them.

The basic question remains: should the Paramount Power have intervened more actively in the troubled state of Travancore? There was a clear case for intervention in the trials of the bank directors; but by no means in the general administration. The state was considered well-administered, as on the whole it was. There was no gross maladministration, no open scandals, no financial misdoings. The rulers were not extravagant, and kept within a modest privy purse. There was no widespread perversion of justice (except in political cases), the usual cause of intervention by the Paramount Power. The one case of excessive punishment brought to its notice was dealt with firmly.

Nevertheless the politically-minded Travancoreans (and that included most literate Travancoreans and a good number of illiterates who had the papers read to them regularly) were critical of the Paramount Power for upholding the hated Dewan. They knew that Delhi had been

---

* Note by the Editor: Mammen Mappillay was also twice a member of the Travancore Legislative Council representing Commerce and Industry. Apart from his banking concerns he owned extensive plantations and started various industrial ventures, like the Malankara Rubber Produce Co. Ltd.

** Note by the Editor: Together with the author, Miss Louise Ouwerkerk, he belonged to the founding members of the Trivandrum International Fellowship.

consulted about the appointment of all Dewans before that of Sir C.P.; and in appointing him without even a show of consulting Delhi the Maharaja had broken the spirit if not the letter of Clause 9 of the Treaty of 1805.[17] Many thought that if the Crown Representative had intervened then to prevent the appointment, it would have saved a great deal of trouble later on. But there were really not sufficient grounds for Viceregal intervention.

Indeed, Skrine, in his "Impressions of Travancore" written in 1938, did consider the idea of having Sir C.P. dismissed. There were two alternatives, he wrote: supporting the Maharaja and his Dewan in their firm policy towards the state Congress disturbances—with the provisos (a) that the shortcomings of the police should be remedied and there should be less favouritism and communalism in making appointments and promotions, (b) that the sedition issue should be settled by means of a proper trial or inquiry—; or getting rid of Sir C.P. Skrine rejected the second alternative. The Maharaja and his mother were so convinced of the rightness of their cause and had such faith in Sir C.P., that only a direct command coming from His Excellency would move them - and this might well lead to the Maharaja's abdication. The first alternative was the lesser of two evils.

Probably the biggest mistake made by the Paramount Power in dealing with this difficult situation was the same as that made by the Mahatma on the other side of the political curtain: the failure to insist on a fair and open inquiry into the charges against the Dewan.[18] But as we saw earlier, by the exercise of what C.P. Matthen once called his "dorsal flexibility", Sir C.P. managed to evade any trial or inquiry into his doings, and continued on his way unhindered for the next nine years.

One last point needs to be considered: the issue of civil liberties. From the beginning of the states Peoples' Movement in 1927, there had been two major demands: the grant of responsible government under the aegis of the rulers, and the guarantee of fundamental civil rights. In earlier days the people of Travancore had been more concerned about a greater share in the administration and had said less about civil liberty, because—apart from the expulsion from time to time of political troublemakers and some press regulations to which they objected—they had little cause to complain. But from 1938 onwards their civil liberties were being undermined and the clamour against their violation became ever more insistent. It was after all the case against A. Narayana Pillai which brought about the formation of the state Congress. When the Maharaja banned the state Congress by proclamation, Pattom Thanu Pillai stated: "The immediate issue is wholly one of civil liberties. Every other issue pales into insignificance before this one".[19]

Yet this issue was almost entirely ignored in the reports received by the Political Department; the whole agitation was represented as a hysterical outburst against the hated Dewan exploited by the Indian National Congress for their own ends. The resentment of the people at the loss of liberty in their own country at the will of a foreigner finds no echo in the writings of the Residents. Was this because the British authorities thought largely in terms of the constitutional arrangements for the proposed Federation, and did not export to India that passion for individual liberty which informs their own history? Congress, inside or outside the states, threatened the scheme for a "balance of forces" in the Federation; Congress was a nuisance and had to be dealt with firmly, to the extent of curtailing civil liberties in the interests of order. Bearing on their shoulders the responsibility for order in that vast country, the British administrators, in spite of mistakes, were far more justified in this than their critics, both Indian and British, are even yet prepared to concede.

But that the people of Travancore reacted strongly—and under great stress violently—against the deprivation of their prized liberties did not seem worthy of consideration by the British Raj; it was the Princes who mattered.

Chapter XI

TRAVANCORE DURING THE WAR

XI.1 The Indian National Congress and the State Congress

At the outbreak of war, His Highness the Maharaja of Travancore, in common with all the other 562 Princes, put all the resources of his state unreservedly at the disposal of His Majesty the King-Emperor. The Viceroy, without consulting either his Executive Council or the Central Legislature of India, had declared that India was at war with Germany. He did however immediately invite Mr. Gandhi to Simla for discussions on the crisis; and while the Mahatma expressed his own moral support for the war against Hitler's dictatorship, he refused to speak for the Indian National Congress.

The Working Committee of the Indian National Congress met on September 14th and required an assurance, before deciding to cooperate fully with the war, that it was indeed a war for the preservation of democracy. They asked for a declaration of Britain's war and peace aims, and urged the extension of democracy to all colonial countries, and in particular to India. The Standing Committee of the All-India states Peoples' conference also met on October 11th, and associated themselves with the request of the Working Committee for a declaration of Britain's war and peace aims. More specifically, they plainly stated an aspect of the Congress dilemma which seems entirely to have escaped the notice of the British Government: while the rulers of the Indian states were profuse in their offers of support of the cause of democracy in Europe, undiluted autocracy prevailed in their states. The Working Committee therefore invited the rulers to accept the principle of responsible government in their states and to give effect to it in the largest possible measure in the immediate future.[1]

This incongruity was an important cause of Indian cynicism about the real war aims of the British, and of Indian lack of whole-hearted support for the war against Nazi tyranny. Events in Travancore threw light on this attitude; and they in their turn should be viewed against the all-India background.

By now the Travancore State Congress was divided; the Youth

League had for the most part turned to Communism; the support of the Ezhavas was uncertain. It never regained the tremendous popularity which it had during the first civil disobedience movement. But it was by no means dead; there was always a solid core of workers and supporters of all communities, and whenever repression slackened it raised its head again. Even at the height of the repression, in 1941, the Inspector-General of police had to ask for an increase in the Budget grant for police to deal with State Congress agitation; it was a mistake, he said plainly, to think it had been crushed—it was only held down by superior forces.[2]

But right through the war years and beyond, Sir C.P. remained in the saddle, hated but secure in the support of the palace and of the Paramount Power, and in control of an effective machinery of repression, which was at once brought into operation.

The Defence of Travancore Proclamation, issued in September 1939, was a copy of the Defence of India Act; its rules provided, among other things, for detention without trial to prevent persons from "hindering the effective prosecution of the war". It was used chiefly for the government's political critics, and for the internment of a group of harmless Italian Carmelite monks. At the same time a government communique called on the people to give up processions and meetings, "especially those of a controversial nature with a view to preserving a peaceful atmosphere".[3]

The State Congress had already arranged a conference at Karunagapally, in north Travancore, for September 7th. They cancelled the procession, volunteer rally and flag-raising ceremony, in deference to the government's call but insisted on holding the conference. The conference repeated the demand for full responsible government and a general amnesty for all political prisoners. The constructive programme was to continue; and the 8th, 16th, and 24th of each Malabar month were to be observed as Civil Liberties Day, Responsible Government Day and Political Prisoners' Day respectively. There was no intention of creating a conflict with the government; their programme was entirely constitutional.[4]

The government's reply was to suspend the conversations on constitutional reform because of war conditions. When Pattom Thanu Pillai wrote to the Dewan protesting that there was no justification for this decision, the government issued a further communique warning the Travancore State Congress against organized agitation at a time when there was a likelihood of increased unemployment and public excitement due to possible shortages of foodstuffs; and they were threatened with steps under the Defence Rules in order to maintain a peaceful atmosphere.[5] These threats did not deter the State Congress from deciding to continue peaceful demonstrations. They also sent a delegation to Gandhi on October 11th to discuss Travancore affairs.

A new excitement was looming on the horizon—Sir C.P.'s sixtieth birthday. Now among south Indian Hindus this is a special landmark in life, and is celebrated by a special festival called the *Shastiabdapoorthi.* Sir C.P. decided to have it celebrated on a nationwide scale; committees for its celebration were formed everywhere by government officials to arrange for appropriate ceremonies and raise funds for presentations and gifts. A group of Syrian Christians, unhappy about the odium with which the government viewed the community, proposed to erect a statue of Sir C.P., costing Rs. 65,000 in Kottayam, the chief town of the Syrian Christians, and acquired land for a park in which to set it.[6]

The *Shastiabdapoorthi* was one of the topics which the State Congress delegation raised with Gandhi, who gave his approval to a stinging resolution. The All-Travancore Congress Committee, it said after much deliberation, had decided to dissociate itself from the celebrations, and protested against the attempt to celebrate the birthday in the name of the people. The purpose was to make it appear that his administration was both successful and popular; it was neither. The Committee pointed to the suppression of civil liberties, the flat refusal to consider constitutional advance, the growing lack in the administration of justice. The Dewan should celebrate his birthday with his friends and well-wishers.

These criticisms were supported by Gandhi in a forthright article in *Harijan* of October 7th entitled "The Unfortunate People of Travancore". He expressed his disappointment at the failure of the Travancore government after the withdrawal of the Memorandum, to take one conciliatory step, and described the suspension of constitutional talks as "a bombshell". The reason for suspension was wholly unconvincing. "Indeed I venture to suggest that the offer of the state to the British Government (i.e. of all its resources in the prosecution of the war), lacks the spirit assumed to be behind the aims of the Allies, viz, the saving of democracy for the world. Viewed in this light the grant to the people of the greatest measure of responsibility consistent with their own safety becomes a first and a first class war measure so far as the states are concerned". It was his plainest criticism, set in the context of Travancore affairs, of the inconsistency of the British Raj in opposing tyranny in Europe and supporting it in India.[7]

The All-Travancore Congress Committee, having secured the full backing of the Mahatma, decided to go on with peaceful demonstrations on November 1st and 2nd. On the 2nd, the president, Pattom Thanu Pillai, the secretary and three more committee members were arrested under the Defence Rules, and the Congress office in Trivandrum was seized. Within the next six months most of the leaders were arrested, either under the Defence Rules or under the security sections of the Criminal Procedure Code.[8] In his confidential report for the second half of December, the Resident had "nothing to report" for the first time in years.

Such of the State Congress Working Committee members as escaped arrest took refuge in Ernakulam, where M.M.Varkey once more set up the office. G. Ramachandran stayed on in British India, to keep Gandhi informed of events in Travancore and to carry on vigorous publicity in Madras. Once again, friends in Cochin state helped with money, accommodation, printing presses, cars and petrol coupons when petrol rationing was introduced. The government of Cochin ignored its own press note threatening action against newspapers criticizing the administration of neighbouring states. Occasionally a virulent newspaper had its license cancelled only to reappear under a new name with a new license. Ernakulam was the base for printing pamphlets and leaflets and smuggling them over the border. Successive presidents of the Travancore State Congress, in consultation with the Working Committee, issued statements from Ernakulam and then went to Travancore to court arrest.[9]

In 1940, Sir C.P. decided to enlist the help of the Political Department in winkling the Travancore State Congress workers out of Cochin. For this purpose he adopted a new line, that the State Congress was really a communist organization, just as two years before he had tried to prove that it was really a Christian one. In taking this line he could be sure of some sympathy, as the communist Party was proscribed in British India and communist activities were being carefully watched by the British Indian Criminal Investigation Department.

On March 23rd Sir C.P. wrote to Sir Bertrand Glancy, then head of the Political Department, complaining about the support which Cochin state was giving to the Travancore State Congress malcontents, "some of them avowed communists". Sir Bertrand asked the Resident to the Madras states, Col. Murphy, to go into the matter. If the complaints were true, Cochin was much to blame, "and it should be brought home to them". It might be wise, he hinted, to defer His Excellency's order to extend Sir Shanmugham Chetty's term of office as Dewan of Cochin.

Sir C.P. accordingly furnished the Resident with lengthy police reports of the activities of the Travancore malcontents in Cochin, as well as the part played by the communists and socialists (though he made no distinction between them) in the earlier State Congress movements. His main argument was that the State Congress was "riddled with communists", and was in fact a communist organization in disguise. He drew largely on a pamphlet by K.C. George entitled *The Travancore Fight*, and quoted his claims that it was the Kerala socialist Party that had carried on the fight when the bourgeois leadership under the guidance of Gandhi was hesitating, and through its promotion of activities among the youth and the labourers had given a correct lead to the movement. There was of course some truth in part of this contention; the communists had followed the policy of infiltrating with a view to dominating, and they had succeeded in doing so in the trade unions and the Youth League (though not in other youth groups). But the main leadership was on the whole Gandhian, and no Gandhian group could be communist. The brains behind the movement were those of M.M.Varkey, a staunch Roman Catholic, whom Sir C.P. dubbed a communist since he made use of left-wingers like K.C.George. (But blood is thicker than water with the Syrian Christians, and active Christians and active communists among them have always kept up their close relationships.) Other leaders still outside the jail were staunch Catholics like P.J.Sebastian; and the devout reformist Hindus Changanacherry Parameswaran Pillai and G.Ramachandran could not be communists either.

Sir C.P. complained specifically that the Cochin government was encouraging *jathas* into Travancore, and the Cochin police were hampering the Travancore police in their attempts to collect information about the Travancore malcontents.

Col. Murphy, armed with Sir C.P.'s memorandum, saw Sir Shanmughan Chetty and pointed out the dangers to Cochin itself of "a centre of disaffection in the state which constitutes a fruitful ground for communist propaganda". He reported that he found Sir Shanmughan "amenable;" he agreed with the desirability of tackling communist agitators—all of whom incidentally came from British Malabar, not from Travancore—and promised to put down his thoughts about the Travancore agitators in writing.

The Resident found he had trodden on a scorpion. On 6th June Sir Shanmughan wrote him two letters full of indignation. The first was "demi-official". He took his stand on the fact that the Travancoreans had broken no law of the state and therefore would not be proceeded against. "The Rule of Law is established in this state and His Highness the Maharaja has never exercised his powers in an arbitrary manner". Were he to do so, it would lead to internal discontent. Cochin had been free of the political unrest which had prevailed in other states in the past two years; in fact, the Cochin Congress had offered its whole-hearted cooperation in the war effort. The Paramount Power had the power to order the Government of Cochin to expel any non-Cochinites; but then the Paramount Power must bear the responsibility for any serious consequences that might follow. In other words, he was prepared to resign on the issue. Every word was a condemnation of the policies of the Travancore Government and of the Paramount Power for supporting them. The second letter was equally venomous; it was a formal complaint, to be placed by the Resident before His Excellency the Crown Representative, about the allegations against the Cochin Government found in the unsigned memorandum prepared by the Dewan of Travancore. "I have the honour to be, Your most obedient servant.". Never was the word "obedient", in the conventional subscription, more misplaced.

Further interviews failed to bring Sir Shanmughan to heel; all he would do was to draw a red herring across the matter by arranging, in the presence of the Resident, a meeting between the Travancore Inspector-General of police, Khan Bahadur Abdul Karim, and the Cochin police Commissioner, which was also attended by an officer of the Madras C.I.D., at which methods of dealing with communism were discussed.

The Central Intelligence Bureau took up the matter of communism in the states. They found there was no regular organization worth the name, though a certain amount of communist literature was circulating in some of the states, including Travancore and Cochin. This however was "due to individual enthusiasts rather than any organized efforts and no more than the outflow from the Communist movement in neighbouring British India". There was no need to pursue the matter.

Sir Shanmugham Chetty's term of office as Dewan of Cochin was extended, and Sir C.P. found it prudent to make his peace with his opposite number. The two warring knights buried the hatchet, and by 1941 were on amicable terms. And the Travancore State Congressites continued to enjoy Cochin hospitality.

Though the Travancore State Congress within the state went more or less underground, it was by no means the silence of the grave. The younger Christians now took up the fight, mainly through the Youth Christian Council of Action.

Their first objective was to shoot down the statue project.[10] The Y.C.C.A. took the initiative in condemning the scheme. They drew up a strong statement which declared it was "morally objectionable" to raise a memorial to an officer who was still serving, before the value of his work could be judged as a whole, when he was moreover in a position to secure support for the project by inducements and threats; it was also deplorable to ask the public for such a large sum at a time of war and famine. The statement was signed by 83 leaders of the Syrian Christian community, of whom only one, E. John Philipose, was a leading Congressman. For obvious reasons it was printed in Cochin and smuggled into Travancore; M.M.Thomas and A.K.Thampi organized its distribution through their young men and women, and it was given out at church services all over the country one particular Sunday morning. The Dewan was so shaken at the extent of the criticism that he discouraged the scheme and it was dropped. The park remained; and it is one of the pleasant little ironies of history that after Sir C.P.'s abrupt departure from the Travancore scene it was renamed the K.C.Mammen Mappillai Park.

XI.2 The Shertallai Famine[11]

The problems of unemployment and food shortages arose almost as soon as war broke out, in one corner of fertile Travancore. In the coastal region of the north, from Alleppey to Shertallai and Vaikom, the coir industry had proved more profitable than agriculture, and the poor people (mostly but not exclusively Ezhavas) had taken to coconut cultivation and coir yarn spinning as a cottage industry. Coir had also developed as a factory industry, as we have seen; but less than 8,000 men were employed in factories compared with nearly 120,000 engaged in the cottage hand spinning industry. Coir became one of the biggest exports from Travancore;* at the same time, rice, the staple food of all classes, was imported from Burma. But with the outbreak of war the coir industry was at once cut off from its overseas markets; rice imports from Burma were severely reduced and later cut off altogether with the Japanese invasion of that country. Distress showed itself at once; there was widespread unemployment, starvation and even deaths from famine.

---

* Note by the Editor: From the 1870's, coconut products and plantation crops had accounted for more than 80% of the value of Travancore's total exports. On the eve of World War II coconut products alone accounted for 37% of total exports.

The Government of Travancore took prompt steps. In October 1939 a Relief Committee was set up in Alleppey, consisting of officials and representatives of both management and labour, to consider relief works and the distribution of rice to the poor and needy. Public works were planned to give work to the unemployed. The government secured orders from Bombay for coir goods, and set up a spinning centre at Vaikom to employ some of the workers thrown out of work. Unfortunately, after this promising start complacency set in, and by April the government announced that the problem was solved, and there was no starvation in the state as the government had imported sufficient quantities of rice.

But the Y.C.C.A. was in the field and acquainted at first hand with the true state of affairs. government measures had dealt chiefly with unemployment among factory workers; they had hardly touched the distress among the cottage workers, and were quite inadequate to the size of the problem. The Y.C.C.A. therefore organized appeals for relief, and got the cooperation of local Government officials, the Nayar Service Society, the S.N.D.P. Yogam, the Catholic Bishops, the Y.M.C.A. and (when they came out of prison) the State Congress leaders. They organized the feeding of both school children and pre-school infants in the worst hit areas.

A sample survey undertaken by the Y.C.C.A. workers in five typical villages revealed the extent of the poverty, starvation and even famine deaths. "Frequency of meals" was one criterion; most families had one meal a day, but there were some which had one meal in three days. "Whole and torn cloths" was another relevant criterion in a society where clothing consisted of a waist cloth and an upper cloth; in some villages *all* cloths were torn. The Survey Committee proposed more sweeping measures, chiefly the revival of food cultivation with the help of the government Agricultural Department, and the promotion of more diversified cottage industries. The findings of the Survey Committee, their recommendations, and the reports of the various Relief Committees were published in a Special Famine Number of *Arunodayam*, the organ of the Society of St. Thomas, in December 1941.

Sir C.P. was very angry about it, partly because it made no mention of government efforts (the Director of Information having ignored repeated requests for information), and partly because it showed up the inadequacy of such steps as the government had taken. In a speech to the Legislative Assembly on December 4th 1941, he accused the famine relief workers of exploiting the situation "for political, communal and religious motives", and denounced the *Arunodayam* as "mischievous and tendentious". The Christian ashram, headquarters of the Society of St. Thomas, fell under suspicion and suffered a police raid. But the facts were incontrovertible, and the government were forced to take measures along the lines proposed by the Y.C.C.A. survey.

XI.3 Government versus Christians, State Congress and Labour

Sir C.P. continued his attempts to drive a wedge between the communities of Travancore so as to isolate the Christians and undermine the State Congress. He directed his attention to the Ezhavas, who were the easiest target. The Nayars and Syrian Christians had secure positions in the traditional caste hierarchy, but the Ezhavas were socially on the way up, anxious for approval and eager for help in their educational programme and for their fair share of good jobs. They were therefore the most vulnerable to the kind of pressures the Dewan could bring to bear.[12]

At the outset of the troubles in 1938 they had stood loyally by the State Congress throughout the first civil disobedience movement. But after the withdrawal of the Memorandum and the collapse of the attempt at a second civil disobedience movement, enthusiasm waned, that great fighter C. Kesavan resigned for health reasons, and under his successor V.K. Velayudhan the S.N.D.P. Yogam began to have second thoughts. By August 1939 it dissociated itself completely from politics. Velayudhan and his younger colleague R. Sankar, who were members both of the Board of Management of the Yogam and the State Congress Working Committee had to choose, and resigned from the Board. They were among the first to be arrested under the Defence Rules in November 1939. Next month the S.N.D.P. Yogam called on all Ezhavas to give up politics and devote themselves to social and economic uplift, and the leading Ezhavas were released from jail. R. Sankar stuck to politics, but V.K. Velayudhan gave it up. Shortly afterwards he was rewarded with a scholarship to study in England, and became thenceforth a "C.P. man".[13]

A more subtle attack came through the Nayar Service Society, which celebrated its silver jubilee in May 1940. A Hindu conference was held in connection with the celebrations, presided over by V.D. Savarkar, president of the Hindu Mahasabha; he made a strong plea for strengthening the Hindu states of India, and for the consolidation of all the Hindu communities of Travancore. Sir C.P., who took an active part in the celebrations, promised all cooperation. The next week the

S.N.D.P. Yogam held their annual conference, to which a Hindu conference was also added; this welcomed the proposals made at the Nayar conference. The S.N.D.P. Yogam was now very much in Sir C.P.'s pocket; the editor of the leading Ezhava newspaper was nominated a member of the state Council, and was promised a new rotary press. In October 1940 they decided to erect a marble statue of Sir C.P. in commemoration of his part in the Temple Entry Proclamation.[14]

But one of his critics he could no longer mollify, and that was Mahatma Gandhi, whose eyes were open at last. Sir C.P. always kept the lines of communication open with the Indian National Congress, and early in 1940 he sent an agent to Sardar Patel to ask him to arrange a secret meeting with Gandhi; he was, he let it be known, anxious to be on good terms with him. "The approval which he receives from the British Government owing to his opposition to Congress is not to Sir C. P.'s liking", wrote his go-between.[15] Gandhi was not given to secret meetings but stopped his references to Travancore affairs in *Harijan* for some months; he kept in close touch with them however through G. Ramachandran and T.M. Verghese, who had avoided arrest in order to carry on publicity. When Gandhi took up the matter of a meeting he received an "extraordinary telegram" from Sir C.P. which he published in *Harijan* of 17th July 1940:

"In view of developments in India and also having regard to the close though unacknowledged connection existing between many of the T.S.C.leaders and communist activities which have come to light after the arrest of K.C. George and in view of the openly hostile activities of Mr. T. M. Verghese and Mr. G. Ramachandran who have been chosen by you to give advice as to Travancore no useful purpose is likely to be served by such a meeting". He hopes that Gandhi "will not accept versions by persons who are discredited here—most of the leading members of the State Congress have openly dissociated themselves from State Congress activities. They number over sixty".

Gandhi was no more persuaded that the Travancore State Congress was communist than he had been persuaded earlier that it was Christian. He turned to Ramachandran for his information, and learned that K.C. George was actually a critic of the State Congress Working Committee, and that there had been only two resignations from that body, of whom V.K. Velayudhan was one; the other, a Nayar lawyer, had to apologize in order to regain the right to practise law in Travancore. "I believe every word of what Shri Ramachandran says". He concluded by commenting: "This extraordinary telegram has made me conclude that

Sir C.P. has nothing against the Congress or its members except that they are patriots without reproach and without fear. He hates their philosophy and seeks to crush them".[16]

This ended the attempts of Sir C.P. to stay on the right side of the Mahatma, but he kept in touch with Sardar Patel, and with his own old Brahman friends from South India, such as "Rajaji" and Dr. Pattabhi Sitaramayya.

So *Harijan* once more gave publicity to Travancore affairs. The then 13th president of the Travancore State Congress, A. Achuthan, wrote a long report which summarized the state of affairs in 1940. Repression was largely along three lines: "legal terrorism"—a cat-and-mouse policy of arrests under the Defence Rules, so that men and women who happened to have political opinions never felt safe; "police terrorism" exercised mainly through the so-called "special police"—hooligans who were encouraged to break up peaceful meetings and terrorize peaceful citizens; and the muzzling of the local press. Communalism was blatantly encouraged in an attempt to break down the unity which the Travancore Congress had at one point achieved. The Government of Travancore threatened legal proceedings against A. Achuthan and G. Ramachandran for their malicious propaganda in *Harijan* ; nothing came of it, but it was a broad hint to the local press not to print anything from that inconvenient weekly.

The atmosphere was however changing. The government's policy had won an apparent success, and by September 1940 the government had decided that political agitation had died down sufficiently for it to be safe to release some of the political prisoners detained under the Defence Rules or imprisoned under the security sections of the Criminal Procedure Code, and seventy-nine of the ninety-one politicals were released. Of course many more who had been accused of violence remained in prison.[17]

The policy of the State Congress changed too. In August A. Achuthan returned to Travancore and courted arrest; he was succeeded by G. Ramachandran as 14th president, but he announced that he intended not to court arrest. In October he presided over a meeting of the Working Committee in Ernakulam; always more social worker than politician, he expressed his concern with the starving and unemployed in the Shertallai area. It was decided to disband the Congress Workers' training camp in Cochin state, and to send the workers back to Travancore to carry on the constructive programme in order to relieve distress.[18]

In this changed atmosphere Dr. Pattabhi Sitaramayya, now president of the All-India states' Peoples' conference, felt the time was propitious for a move towards conciliation. He asked Sir C.P. if he would have any objection to meeting Ramachandran, and obtained an assurance that he would not be arrested. Sir C.P. was prepared to meet him. G. Ramachandran therefore came to Trivandrum, saw Pattom Thanu Pillai in jail, and discussed terms with the Dewan.

The result was the release of the remaining political prisoners except those convicted of violence in January 1941, and the return of the State Congress office from Ernakulam to Trivandrum.[19]

The Working Committee of the State Congress lost no time in meeting and in issuing a predictable set of resolutions. It declared that it stood " unflinchingly by its objective of Responsible government", and asked for the release of the remaining political prisoners (of whom it was estimated there were still about a hundred) and the removal of all disabilities on those released. A new note was struck with regard to the distressed areas along the coast; two of its members, T.M. Verghese and N. Kunjuraman, were deputed to study the economic distress and to prepare a scheme of relief.[20] The president, Pattom Thanu Pillai, in his first public speech for 15 months, emphasized that the State Congress had no intention of embarrassing the government's war effort.[21]

The Dewan's reactions were also predictable. He at once announced at an interview that he had no intention of granting responsible government but the government had no objection to normal political work as long as it did not cause communal bitterness or embarrass the government's war effort.[22] But meetings were prohibited on the slightest excuse, and the Working Committee issued frequent complaints of the harassment of meetings by rowdies and obstruction by subordinate police officers, in spite of the government's declared policy. To these complaints the government retorted that the cause of the disturbances was the inflammatory nature of the State Congress, activities.[23] Nothing had really changed.

In spite of police harassment, the State Congress was able to rebuild its organization and to continue its constructive programme. The two-man committee on economic distress produced a useful report, and the Working Committee launched a new venture, a centre for the distribution of tapioca cuttings, seeds and manures in distressed coastal areas. On April 14th 1941 the Agricultural Depot and Farm was opened at Punnapra (close to Alleppey) under the auspices of the State Congress Coastal Relief Committee, and in the presence of a large crowd, and to the accompaniment of slogans of "Mahatma *Gandhi-ki-jai*!" Mr. Pattom Thanu Pillai ceremoniously planted some tapioca cuttings. There were, he said, extensive areas in the coastal regions lying uncultivated, and the object of the State Congress scheme was to help bring such lands into cultivation for the production of food crops. Government and other agencies were no doubt doing relief work but no amount of relief work would be too much. A few days later he opened a second depot at Shertallai. It was a practical contribution to the solution of the famine problem, and after a year of inaction the government took up the idea and opened its own "Grow More Food" campaign.[24]

We get an interesting glimpse of the state of affairs in Travancore from a report by the Political Adviser to His Excellency the Crown Representative, Sir Francis Wylie, who toured the three states of Mysore, Travancore and Cochin in July 1941. As it was the declared policy of the Paramount Power to encourage the rulers of the Indian states to grant more liberal constitutions to their subjects, the tour was undertaken to see if these southern states, who boasted of their advanced constitutions, had anything to teach Simla about constitutional reform in Indian states.

Sir C.P. gave Sir Francis full details of the composition and powers of the two Houses of the Travancore Legislature. "The Assembly", wrote Sir Francis, "consists of 72 members and it is boosted as the last word in liberality in Indian states. Sir C.P. will tell you with pride that only ten members of the whole House are officials. By this he would like you to understand that the remaining 62 seats are open to public elections. The case is actually far otherwise. Only 29 members are elected by general constituencies. The members elected by the special constituencies are safe as houses while the 24 nominated members are the merest yes men. The government is at all times assured of a majority and even if it was not, the Legislature has no real powers and is merely a debating society". Sir Francis pressed the great Dewan about the alignment of parties, but he was exceedingly vague. "Sir C.P. said in his rather grand way that there was in the Assembly a Nationalist Party of about 20 members. This is the State Congress Party as I heard from other sources". On this matter Sir Francis Wylie, otherwise a penetrating observer, remained surprisingly misled. Of the state Council he remarked: "The genuine elected element is very small, hardly one third".

He pressed the Dewan about the powers of the Legislature, and it transpired that they were very little. "Political peace is maintained partly by the notable prestige of the Dewan and partly by a system of strategems and balances . . . If the Legislature feels strongly over an important issue he goes against it without the slightest qualms and covers himself by playing upon the innumerable communal differences which are the most notable features of life on the Malabar coast. . . There is no Executive Council and the great Dewan is in fact the King of the Castle".

Having examined the constitution of Cochin which he also considered "eye-wash", and that of Mysore, of which he had a somewhat higher opinion, he concluded that "the three South Indian states which have boosted their reformed Constitutions so persistently during the last years have no constitutions worth the name at all, and live actually under the carefully disguised autocracy of irresponsible Dewans".[25]

It was unfortunate that in the nature of things Sir Francis Wylie could not meet the president of the Travancore State Congress, of whose existence he seems to have been totally unaware. They would have seen eye to eye about many things and Sir Francis would have learnt a great deal.

Whenever the political atmosphere in Travancore was quiet, the Dewan allowed some freedom to the politicians. Political prisoners and detenues were then released in batches, though of course they might easily be re-arrested soon after. In August 1941, in a speech to the state Council, Sir C.P. boasted of the political freedom in Travancore; there were more meetings held in the state in July, he claimed, than in the whole of the rest of India. At the same time, however, he announced that the life of the Legislature, then due for dissolution, would be extended to June 1942, and if the atmosphere was not peaceful enough for elections to be held, it would be extended further.[26] By December the Dewan announced that the peaceful atmosphere of the state made possible the release of all political prisoners and detenues, even those who had been involved in State Congress riots and labour disturbances. But in almost the same breath he announced a further postponement of elections for one year from June 1942—not this time for political reasons but for economic.[27]

The State Congress at once resumed their meetings, but they were frequently subjected to police harassment. On April 19th 1942 a meeting to celebrate "All-India States' Peoples' Day" was prohibited. The State Congress, not wishing at this crisis to create any disorder, arranged a private meeting in the Congress office, with Pattom Thanu Pillai in the chair and G. Ramachandran as chief speaker. They were arrested, tried and sentenced to six months' rigorous imprisonment.[28] They each issued a press statement protesting against the government's action, and Dr. Pattabhi Sitaramayya issued a statement that they had been arrested under a misapprehension. They appealed against the sentence, the Travancore High Court quashed it, they were released and immediately detained under the Defence Rules.[29]

Possibly because of Dr. Sitaramayya's intervention, the government did not prohibit the holding of a State Congress conference in the Nagercoil Division on the 25th May 1942. It was the first to be held since the prohibited conference at the beginning of the war, and attracted a huge crowd. Anne Mascarene was the president. Her speech was made in the face of the threat of Japanese invasion, and it bore not a trace of the "Quit India" threat with which the Congress High Command was toying at that time after the failure of the Cripps Mission. It was, significantly, a speech in support of the war effort. She called upon the Travancore Government to enlist the support of the popular organizations; at this time of crisis responsible government was not the immediate issue, but the immediate grant of responsible government would lead to harmonious cooperation between ruler and ruled; and a resolution to that effect was passed. Another resolution called upon the people to "cultivate every inch of arable land and to achieve self-sufficiency and to take up hand spinning and hand weaving in this time of cloth shortage".[30]

It was a feeler for another conference, and it might well have led to better relations. But the next day the organizer of the conference received an order prohibiting him from taking part in public meetings for three months, and Miss Mascarene was specifically mentioned in a press note castigating those who engaged in subversive propaganda under the guise of anti-Japanese activities.[31]

At the same time there were continual rumblings on the labour front. In view of economic distress, rising prices, unemployment and growing food shortages, industrial peace could hardly be expected, and there were demands for higher wages and shorter hours, and sporadic strikes. The Government of Travancore, with some truth, blamed the labour unrest on "the incursion of subversive and communistic elements into industrial life",[32] though that was by no means the whole story. True, communists worked among the industrial workers; but they did not invent the grievances which were all too real.

The question of participation in politics cropped up in every union. The Coir Factory Workers Union of Alleppey repudiated the accusation that they were engaged in political activity, but in general labourers claimed the right to participate in politics;[33] and at the All-Travancore Labour conference in Shertallai in October 1941 political resolutions were passed demanding immediate responsible government in the state and urging the Indian National Congress to launch a mass struggle to secure India's freedom.[34]

With the entry of Russia into the war in June 1941, a new note crept into labour discussions. The communist leaders were quicker to note the implications of the Russian alliance than was the Government of Travancore, and began to change sides. No longer was it an imperialist war but a war in defence of Soviet Russia and therefore to be supported by all good comrades; and they took the labour unions with them. The communist Party headquarters in Bombay changed the title of their weekly paper from *People's Weekly* to *People's War*. The local communists' attitude deepened the split between the communist-led Youth League and the Gandhian leadership of the Travancore State Congress.

It was a long time before the Travancore Government changed its attitude. The labour leaders' protest against the prohibition of carrying the Red Flag in processions was ignored, and the government continued to arrest troublesome labour leaders, especially those who organized strikes which interfered with the production of war goods. In January 1942 a press note warned labour leaders against attempts to encourage labourers to take part in politics, and prohibited some labour leaders from attending public meetings for two months.[35]

A new body now came into the open, the Soviet Friends' Association, which was promoted by the left-wing labour leaders N.Srikantan Nayar and T.V. Thomas. Like most Congress bodies and all communist bodies, it was organized on an all-Kerala basis. It functioned freely in Cochin but was viewed with great suspicion in Travancore.[36] It led to a sharp press note, issued in July 1942, containing a warning against persons who had recently been engaged in subversive activities and who were now carrying on the same objectionable activities while describing themselves as anti-fascist, pro-Soviet and so forth. A joint reply by the secretary of the Travancore Anti-Japanese Committee and the secretary of the All- Kerala Soviet Friends' Association claimed that there was nothing subversive about their meetings; on the contrary they criticized the inefficiency of the measures taken by the government to meet the crisis, which could only be met by the establishment of a national government in the state.[37]

XI.4 "Quit India"

If the entry of Russia into the war had shifted allegiances, the entry of Japan and its rapid conquest of south-east Asia altered the whole perspective of the war in Indian eyes, and quite literally brought the reality of the war home to them. The failure of the Cripps Mission in April 1942 had thrown the Congress camp into confusion, made worse confounded by the Mahatma's non-violence. Some, following Subhas Chandra Bose, were so anti-British that they became pro-Axis; some, like C. Rajagopalachari of Madras, were so anti-fascist that they put the defeat of fascism even before the demand for Indian independence; some, following the lead of Gandhi, put the demand for Indian independence before everything else. Of these many were simply pacifist and shut their eyes to the reality of the problem. If, like Nehru, they were in sympathy with the anti-fascist struggle, they considered that only an independent India could throw its full weight into that struggle. The consequence was the "Quit India" campaign of August 1942.

All these trends of thought were present in Travancore. On the whole the State Congress was in favour of supporting the war, as the resolutions of the Nagercoil conference had shown. In the same month of May the socialist wing, the Radical State Congress party, pledged unconditional support for the war.[38] The communists of course had no problem, either in Travancore or in India as a whole. But among those loyal to Gandhi there was much heartsearching as the crisis drew near. The Committee of the Travancore State Congress met early in August to arrange for the first "annual" conference of the whole Congress to be held since the outbreak of war, to take place on August 11th and 12th, at which the question of supporting the "Quit India" campaign of the Indian National Congress was to be discussed. At that time (Pattom Thanu Pillai being in jail) Akkamma Cheriyan, a convinced Gandhiite, was acting president, and C. Narayana Pillai, another convinced Gandhiite, was secretary.[39]

The Government of Travancore acted swiftly. Miss Cheriyan and C. Narayana Pillai were arrested on August 8th under the Defence Rules and detained for six months.[40] The All-India Congress Committee and the Kerala Provincial Congress were declared unlawful associations.[41] The Travancore State Congress,which had not actually declared its support for the National Congress policy, was not; the acting Dewan (Sir C.P. was in Delhi at the time), was not making any martyrs. A ban was put on all public meetings and processions for a fortnight and was renewed from time to time until March 1943, when all danger of upheaval had passed. Even then permission to hold meetings was given only to communal and labour organizations.[42]

The great conference of the State Congress could not of course take place. The Committee met on the days planned for the conference and privately endorsed the "Quit India" resolution of the All-India Congress Committee, but they made no public pronouncement. E. John Philipose announced his intention of defying the ban on public meetings on August 26th to protest against the arrest of the political leaders; but on the morning of the 26th he was himself quietly arrested, and the arrest caused no stir. Some other leaders defied the ban and were arrested. But there was no excitement; the few public meetings that were held were orderly, with no police interferences beyond the arrest of the speakers. The Resident reported to Delhi that about a hundred had been arrested in this fashion under the Defence Rules.[43]

The only trouble spot was Nagercoil, where a complete *hartal* was observed on August 12th, the day civil disobedience was due to begin in British India. In the morning there was a huge procession, mainly of students, which was dispersed by the police by a *lathi* charge. In the evening, there was a monster meeting to protest against the *lathi* charge and to demand a national government for India and responsible government for Travancore. The police left the meeting alone and made a few arrests afterwards after which the excitement died down.[44]

In the capital city the only excitement was provided by the students. Some students of the University College boycotted their classes and one earnest young man made an inflammatory speech which earned him arrest and a sentence of two-and-a-half years of rigorous imprisonment; but he was let out after a month on promise of good behaviour.[45] Educational institutions were due to close for the *Onam* holidays in any case; and after the holidays all schools and colleges reopened and worked normally. Three students of the University College tried a hunger strike in the College compound, to demand that all educational institutions should remain closed until the British gave India complete independence; they were taken into custody by the police and handed over to their guardians. The government issued a warning to parents of the consequence of indiscipline on the part of students, and that was the end of the flurry of excitement.[46]

The "Quit India" campaign in Travancore was a resounding non-event. It may be asked why Travancore, so turbulent four years ago, gave so little trouble at this time. The chief reason was that the State Congress were themselves divided; their two most ardent Gandhiites had been jailed three months before, and many of those that were free, while not going so far as the Youth League, had been more or less disillusioned by Gandhi's leadership in the crisis of 1938-39. The influence of the communists in the labour movement and among some of the younger people was another important factor. There were others:

many Travancoreans had joined the fighting forces and the Labour Corps; some were engaged in supplying war materials. For instance, E. John Kuruvilla, that former firebrand, had a big timber contract with the Supply Department of the Government of India and considerable official contacts.[47]

Sir C.P. himself had left the state—it proved temporarily—for the Viceroy's Executive Council. The details of this curious affair do not concern us. Suffice it to say he left Travancore on August 1st, promising to return when "the crisis" was over, and the Chief secretary, Mr. G. Parmeswaran Pillai (a local man) became Acting Dewan. This in itself relieved tension; and his handling of the situation was designed to keep public excitement to the minimum. Sir C.P. resigned after less than three weeks, on the ground that a possible pact between Gandhi and Jinnah would put the interests of the Princes in jeopardy and he had to be free to act in their defence; he was back in Trivandrum after an absence of four weeks and resumed the office of Dewan.[48] By that time the movement had proved a damp squib.

And behind the backs of Travancoreans there loomed the shadow of a new menace, which came to absorb attention to the exclusion of all else —the menace of famine.

XI.5 The Hunger Years 1943-44

Famine had hit the coastal area between Alleppey and Shertallai on the outbreak of war when the coir industry lost its markets; but with the Japanese seizure of the "rice bowl" of south-ast Asia, there were food shortages in all the rice-eating areas of India, particularly Bengal, Travancore and Cochin. In these areas the people were most conservative in their eating habits—rice was their staple food and they rejected other grains, such as wheat and millets until they were literally starving. None of them grew enough rice for their own consumption; the Dewan of Travancore stated in 1943 that while Travancore's annual requirements of rice were 617,000 tons, her production was only 250,000 tons.[49] The central government set up a Food Department and made allocations of grain to the deficit areas; but Travancore and Cochin were far away, and the promised grain either did not arrive, or it fell far short of what was promised, or consisted of wheat and millet which the local people did not want. That the great scandal of the Bengal famine of 1943 was not repeated on a smaller scale in the two southern states was largely due to the immense energy of the two Dewans of Travancore and Cochin. By 1942 Sir Shanmughan Chetty had entered the service of the Government of India and his place was taken by an English I.C.S. officer, Mr. Dixon; he and Sir C.P. and the Resident to the Madras states made a strong team. They kept up the pressure on the central government to send adequate supplies.

The Travancore Government started its "Grow More Food" campaign in April 1942. In December 1942 the government assumed control of the entire output of paddy and tapioca, and began to work out a rationing scheme, which was introduced step by step in 1943 and 1944 —first in the capital, then in the larger towns.[50] But the scheme met with great difficulties: not only were the allocations from the central government erratic—a black market in ration cards developed even before rationing started, the black market in foodstuffs was soon flourishing—there were difficulties in transporting the grain, which arrived in Cochin harbour, to Travancore. The "Grow More Food" campaign hung fire though in the capital officers dutifully dug up their gardens to grow tapioca and vegetables.[51] In the Legislature the Dewan pleaded for more cooperation from the people; in his budget speech he complained that while the Agricultural Department was carrying out successful experiments in improved farming the results were not being carried to the people. "We need more field work as well as file work". But a vital link was missing—cooperation between the leaders of the people and the official machinery. The leaders had been antagonized, many were in and out of jail most of the war, and it was not easy to establish contact between them and the officials.

The general election of 1944 brought a small but irrepressible State Congress Party into both Houses. Their vigorous criticism of government's handling of the food situation led to a reorganization of the government Food Committee, which now acquired representatives from both Houses of the Legislature. There was greater vigilance, controls were more strictly enforced, and black marketers were prosecuted and punished, including, it must be said, two members of the Legislature, who were each sentenced to two years rigorous imprisonment and a fine of Rs.1,000 each.

There was also much criticism of the continuing starvation conditions in the Alleppey-Shertallai area. Unemployment was still widespread here, and the people were too poor to pay for their rations. It was said that Travancoreans were quite unimpressed by the harrowing pictures of the victims of the Bengal famine of 1943 in the national press; such sights were familiar on their own doorsteps.[52] A number of outside agencies took an interest, notably the Servants of India Society who set up a relief centre in Alleppey, and through 1943 and 1944 were daily feeding some 11,000 school children. Their organising secretary was loudly critical of the Travancore Government for failing to subsidize food out of its enormous revenues (which had doubled during the war), and their criticisms were repeated by the redoubtable Kamaladevi Chattopadhyaya, now president of the All-India Women's conference, and Pandit Hridya Nath Kunzru, president of the Servants of India Society. The Dewan however refuted all the charges, attributing them to personal and political motives. It was the work of the Servants of India Society, who were joined by the Ramakrishna Mission and the Friends' Ambulance Unit, that saved the children of the distressed area from widespread famine deaths. And in this corner of Travancore, the hatred of the Dewan grew ever deeper.[53]

Here too, the communists were at work; they were at last legally recognized but still very much the object of government suspicion. The ban on *People's War* had been lifted but it was still forbidden to raise the Red Flag or sing *The Red Flag*.[54] The government ban on meetings and processions without the special permission of a magistrate continued. The Dewan also continued his warnings against subversive propaganda under the guise of their "Grow More Food" campaign. Nothing had really changed.

XI.6 The General Election of 1944

On March 1st 1944, the dissolution of the second Assembly of the Legislature was announced in a press communique. It had been given three extensions owing to war conditions. At a press conference the Dewan explained that the war against Japan was likely to last for at least two more years, and they could not wait indefinitely for a more hopeful atmosphere.[55]

If Sir C.P. had thought that the State Congress was finished because it had kept quiet for a long time, he was disappointed. It sprang into life at once, and the Working Committee held a meeting on March 5th. Its most important resolution expressed the hope that the government would remove the disqualifications to which some members were subject on account of convictions arising out of political activities; and a sub-committee was appointed consisting of Pattom Thanu Pillai, T.M. Verghese, E.John Philipose and R. Sankar (that young Ezhava who had had to choose between the S.N.D.P. Yogam and the Congress and had chosen the latter) to make representation to government on the matter.

Pattom Thanu Pillai wrote at once to the Dewan requesting an interview for the sub-committee, but received a freezing reply reiterating the strict legal position that a person convicted by a criminal court involving a sentence of six months or more, shall not be eligible for election to the Legislature for five years unless he has been pardoned. Also repeated was the assertion that the Travancore State Congress was responsible for subversive action which inevitably led to widespread violence. Therefore government would only act on the basis of "an unequivocal expression of regret by each candidate asking for pardon". Pattom replied, as he had so often done before, that the agitation was never subversive or violent, that the State Congress was pledged to nonviolence and engaged only in legitimate activities. He added that now, more than at any other time, amity and cooperation between government and people were necessary, and could be secured only if there were in the Legislature members having a real following and hold on the country. The Dewan reiterated his position and the correspondence closed.[56]

Nonetheless, the State Congress entered the election campaign. They issued a long election manifesto explaining their programme for economic, educational and social reform, their views on freedom of person, speech, association, press and worship, and their demand for responsible government. They put forward a large number of candidates, even those who they knew would be disqualified.[57] New candidates came forward, most important of whom was K.A. Mathew, the secretary of the Kerala Student Christian Movement. He had hitherto taken no direct part in politics, though he was an active member of the Youth Christian Council of Action. He was an experienced speaker and organizer—"the straightest man in politics", commented a colleague—and completely fearless. He also had his full share of the Malayali sense of humour.

On March 22nd a sad event plunged the ruling family in gloom, the death of the First Prince, the six-year old son of the Maharaja's sister. By the matriarchal system there was now only one heir to the throne, the Maharaja's younger brother, the *Elaya* Raja. It was not only natural grief that depressed the family, but the fear that the succession would pass to the descendants of the Senior Maharani, whose two daughters were capable of bearing sons and might do so before the bereaved mother. Three months of mourning for the whole family were proclaimed, while the ruling family went into mourning for a whole year.[58] (This among other things would postpone the marriage of the Senior Maharani's second daughter which had just been arranged.)

At the same time three months' notice of the elections was given, to give time for the preparation of new electoral rolls, which would be ready by the end of May. The elections would therefore be held at the end of June as that the new Houses could meet for the budget session at the end of July. A further press note stated: "It would be undesirable to conduct public meetings or demonstrations during the period of state mourning".

There were protests against the ban on public meetings. Pattom Thanu Pillai issued a press statement declaring that the holding of public meetings is "one of the most legitimate and enlightened ways of canvassing public support in an election", and he pleaded with the government to reconsider its decision. The Chief secretary to government denied that there was such a ban, but public meetings were inappropriate at such a time because they might raise public controversies and rouse public passions. All loyal subjects would be in sympathy with the government's motives but it was obvious that the State Congress had not abandoned its usual subversive tactics. Pattom decided to put the matter to the test and tried to hold a public meeting but a magistrate appeared and drew his attention to the government press note so the meeting was abandoned. Further government orders banned all processions and the flying of flags or the shouting of slogans.[59]

The Dewan entered the campaign in his own way by condemning his critics at a press conference on the 3rd of June. The communist Party, he said, had offered to help in the food crisis, but this was only a cover for the spread of their pernicious doctrines; they would not be allowed to function as a political party. He had heard with surprise stories that the State Congress and the communist Party had made common cause for the elections, and warned the Congress against "strange bedfellows". This drew a strong denial from the State Congress Working Committee. The communists also denied the story, and denied that they had broken their undertaking to limit their activities to social work; they had no intention of engaging in electioneering.[60]

Nominations took place on June 22nd and 23rd. Practically all the former legislators sent in nomination papers; the former State Congress legislators' papers were of course rejected, as were many other on various technical grounds. Even so there was an average of six candidates for every seat.[61] The State Congress alleged that there was considerable government interference in the Tiruvalla election, where K. A.Mathew, who was a local man, was standing on the Congress ticket. A press note, signed by the Dewan and the Chief secretary to government, warned the public not to vote for him as he was a dangerous agitator who had instigated student unrest. Thus recommended, he was returned with a thumping majority and became leader of the State Congress Party in the Sri Mulam Assembly.[62]

Elections took place from July 10th to 13th. The government announced that "a large majority" of the electorate had voted, though the actual figure was about 50%. The official announcement of results was given by communities, so many Nayars, so many Ezhavas, so many Christians and so on. This concealed the important fact that in spite of all obstructions and the disqualification of the old stalwarts, the Travancore State Congress had succeeded in winning eleven seats in the Assembly and three in the state Council.[63]

The existence of this Party, small as it was, imparted a liveliness to the proceedings that had been absent for years. The Dewan got in the first blow by making a statement of the government's attitude in his budget speech; he again blamed the State Congress for the disturbances of 1939, 1940 and 1941, and concluded: "government are still of the impression that the Travancore State Congress under its present leadership is trying to ally itself with the students' movement and the labour movement for the purpose of subversive activities... But as there is a body of opinion in the country represented by the Travancore State Congress, that body of opinion should be represented on the floor of the House".

It was aimed at K.A.Mathew and he took the opportunity of the debate on the budget to reply: "The country has declared in unmistakable terms in the recent elections, despite the obstacles thrown in its way, that it is behind the State Congress... Sir, I want to assure the government that our attitude will not be dictated by a spirit of opportunism or sycophancy. We are not here to sing the panegyrics of the head of the administration or of the other officer". He referred to the government's accusations against the Congress: "I wish to make it clear that the responsibility for the untoward happenings has to be laid at the door of the government. They were the consequences of the absolutely unwarranted policy of repression pursued by the government". Government had not the courage to face an inquiry into the disturbances, nor had it the fairness and sense of responsibility to see that the recent elections were conducted fairly. "We want to serve the best interests of the country. We are in earnest. We shall not equivocate. And we shall be heard. Now I turn to the Budget..."[64]

This was a voice the Dewan dared not silence; it was too well-known throughout south India. And it must be said that no attempt was ever made to tamper with the printed proceedings of the Legislature.

The little group were like gadflies. Cut motions on the Budget, adjournment motions (usually disallowed), questions in the House about the food crisis (usually ruled out of order) gave the government no peace. The debate on the police grant gave one Congress member the opportunity to state that a certain police constable had taken a week's leave during the elections so as to induce people not to vote for the State Congress; challenged to produce his name, he replied: "I must refrain from mentioning his name for fear that he might be promoted for it". This caused much hilarity and the Dewan lost his temper. In spite of the Dewan's hostility, K.A. Mathew was elected to represent the Assembly on the Senate of the University; with his knowledge of student affairs he was the obvious choice, and he used his position to oppose the Dewan in the Senate too. The tiny band of three Congress members in the state Council played the same role of ceaseless pressure on the government.[65]

But the Dewan, with his huge majority of official and nominated members and sycophantic elected members, was always able to get his own way. The budget was passed without amendments. Congress motions got the support of only the Congress group. Their chief victory was the result of their strictures on the handling of the food crisis: the reorganization of the Food Advisory Committee and the introduction of a non-official element.

Many of the older Congressmen became dispirited and felt the whole Legislature to be a farce; but the small, brave, gay band of Congress members kept a small, brave, gay flame of independence alive.

Outside the House the harassment of Congressmen and communists continued though neither body was declared illegal. For one thing Sir C.P. had his eye on the all-India scene; he wanted to stay on good terms with his Congress friends in British India in case they came in useful later on. In fact, in his budget speech he made it clear that his strictures in no way applied to the Indian National Congress or Mahatma Gandhi.

The holding of an All-Travancore conference in January 1945 was permitted, though its chief speaker, K.T.Bashyam of Mysore, was banned from entering Travancore. There were some arrests for seditious speeches made at the conference; Pattom himself, Anne Mascarene and C.Narayana Pillai, the joint secretaries, were detained under the Defence Rules but were released three months later. Arrests of labour agitators continued, and the state communist Party was forbidden to hold its conference in August 1945.[66]

But the sands were running out. The end of the war with Japan came unexpectedly, far earlier than Sir C.P., among others, had reckoned, and whatever had been static in the Indian situation began to shift. The Resident reported to the Viceroy: "Minds are turning to problems of peace which are gradually revealing their complexity and variety".[67]

Chapter XII

RENEWAL OF POLITICAL ACTIVITY AFTER THE WAR

XII. 1 The Cabinet Mission and the states[1]

Many books have been written about the last years of the British Raj in India; but nearly all of them are chiefly concerned with Congress-Muslim League relations which brought about the tragic partition of India into the two Dominions of India and Pakistan. As we are concerned with the State of Travancore, to appreciate the developments there, we should put them in the setting of the Indian states as a whole, in their relations to the all-India developments of the time.

The All-India States Peoples' Conference had been quiescent during the War; no general conference was held between that in Ludhiana in February 1939 and that in Udaipur in December 1945. But the Standing Committee remained in being and worked closely with the Congress. Dr. P. Sitaramayya, its working chairman, asked for and obtained an interview with Sir Stafford Cripps on his mission in 1942; and when the Mission failed the Standing Committee of the A.I.S.P.C. decided to support the "Quit India" Movement, and we have seen how some of the State Congress leaders and students took part in it in Travancore.

Within a month of the end of the war with Japan, the Standing Committee met and decided to hold a full conference in Udaipur in December.[2] It was largely attended; Travancore alone sent 28 delegates, of whom 18 were elected to the General Council. Travancore was in the news again; the Travancore government had just banned the hoisting and display of the national flag, i.e., the Congress flag.

Pandit Nehru's presidential address opened the post-war campaign of the states people. He paid special attention to the "autocratic conditions in the southern states" and pointed out the paradox that these states were educationally the most advanced and yet suffered the greatest repression. He declared that he was not prepared to tolerate the insult to the national flag committed by the Government of Travancore; and in order to keep in close touch with the situation there he appointed T.M. Verghese, the deputy president of the Travancore State Congress, one of the general secretaries of the A.I.S.P.C.

The chief resolution of the conference was the political resolution which defined the policy of the A.I.S.P.C. and its organization in individual states: "Any constitution-making body should have as its States' representatives only those people elected on a wide franchise which should approximate to the franchise at present prevailing in the Provinces."[3]

The A.I.S.P.C. kept up its pressure during the ensuing 20 months, claiming to represent the entire 90 millions of the states' people. There were frequent meetings of the Standing Committee and of the General Council, and another all-India conference in April 1947 at Gwalior. Pandit Nehru, as president of the conference, gave frequent public utterances to the states peoples'demands. But all these activities were largely ignored by the Princes and the Paramount Power. The report of the A.I.S.P.C. for 1945 to 1947 noted the uncompromising attitude of all the states except Cochin, whose Maharaja announced his intention of sending popularly-elected representatives to any constitution- making body. The rule of the other Princes was denounced in the report as "irresponsible and unbridled autocracy".

The Labour government elected in 1945 was pledged to the independence of India, and in March 1946 the Cabinet Mission led by Lord Pethick-Lawrence arrived to renew the negotiations. Its discussions with the Princes and their advisers turned on the question of the part they should play in the proposed Constituent Assembly which would draw up the constitution of a Federal Government of India. The possibility of the partition of India was constantly in the background although no final decision had yet been taken on it.

Very divergent views were expressed. The Chancellor of the Chamber of Princes, the Nawab of Bhopal, wanted the states to continue with the maximum amount of sovereignty consistent with membership of a federation. He went further: if two Indias were to be created, why not three? He first raised the possibility of a Rajastan as well as a Hindustan and a Pakistan, a loose federation of the Princely states which would negotiate with the new government or Governments of India. Hyderabad, the premier state of India in size and wealth, went even further; the Nizam's representative, the Nawab of Chatari, said that if the country were partitioned "it would be impossible for Hyderabad, for geographical reasons, to join Pakistan, and for ideological reasons, to join India;" and Hyderabad would therefore remain an independent country. Sir C.P. Ramaswamy Aiyar took a completely different line; at his interview with the Cabinet Mission he pleaded for a strong centre with wide powers.

On May 16th the Cabinet Mission Plan was published; it still envisaged a united India and rapid strides towards self-government under a federal constitution to be drawn by Indians themselves in a Constituent Assembly. Its proposals in relation to the states mainly followed the lines of the Government of India Act of 1935, as developed by the Cabinet Memorandum of 1943. In the first place, Paramountcy could neither be retained by the British Government nor be transferred to the successor government or governments, and would therefore lapse at the end of the interim period before complete independence was achieved. In the proposed Federation the states would retain all subjects and powers other than three specifically ceded to the Union, namely foreign affairs, defence and communications. Arrangements for the representation of the states in the Constituent Assembly were proposed at first by a Negotiating Committee of the Chamber of Princes, and later by not more than 93 seats in the Assembly. The method of selection of members was to be determined by consultation between the parties concerned. Finally, the Princes were advised to take active steps to place themselves in close and constant touch with public opinion in the state by means of representative institutions.

The Princes were not enthusiastic. The Nawab of Bhopal wrote to the Viceroy asking for assurances that the states would retain the right to control their own forces and internal revenue. Lord Wavell gave a non-committal reply and advised him to discuss these matters with Sir Conrad Corfield. In June Sir Conrad met representatives of the Princes in Bombay, and urged the Princes to set up the Negotiating Committee advised by the Cabinet Mission. He hoped to see them develop as real constitutional monarchs, and urged them to develop a loyalty and local patriotism in their subjects which would reduce outside dictation from British India or from the Crown Representative.

His exhortations came too late. The people of the states had been ignored by the Cabinet Mission. When the question was raised at a press conference in Delhi, Lord Pethick-Lawrence had said that they had to accept the structure of India as it was. "The Cabinet Mission cannot but proceed on the basis that as at present constituted the Indian states are constitutionally represented only by the Maharajas and their advisers". Nehru, in his capacity as president of the A.I.S.P.C., sent a letter to the Cabinet Mission drawing attention to their failure to meet representatives of the states subjects; this letter also had no effect. Nehru complained at a press conference that the views of millions of the people of India were being ignored.

At the same time that the Chamber of Princes was meeting in Bombay, the General Council of the A.I.S.P.C. was meeting in Delhi. There were nearly 200 delegates, T.M. Verghese of Travancore being one of the chief speakers.[4] In a strong speech Pandit Nehru laid down the main lines of policy: "Sovereignty resides in the people", he said; therefore the representatives of the states should be chosen by the people. The Council passed a number of resolutions: they criticized the failure of the Cabinet Mission to make any reference to the internal structure of the states; after independence Paramountcy should rest with the Federal Government of India. The people of the states would not recognise any decision taken without their approval and consent.

In pursuance of this last resolution, the Standing Committee of the A.I.S.P.C. appointed its own expert Committee under the chairmanship of Nehru to prepare materials and draft proposals on behalf of the people of the states. The Standing Committee considered the A.I.S.P.C. was more truly representative of the states than any Negotiating Committee the Princes might choose to set up.

It proved very difficult to get the Princes' Negotiating Committee appointed and working. The Nawab of Bhopal and his group became progressively more reluctant to enter the Constituent Assembly at all; the Nawab still favoured the idea of Rajastan;* but Sir C.P. Ramaswamy Aiyar wrecked it by declaring that he could not envisage the Maharaja of Travancore taking part in a confederation in which some other Prince would be his superior and would give him orders. Nonetheless, Sir C.P. joined the Nawab of Bhopal in his desire to stay out of the Constituent Assembly and to negotiate with the future Union of India on equal terms. Another group, led by the Maharaja of Bikaner and the Maharaja of Patiala, who was Pro-Chancellor of the Chamber of Princes, took a point of view which was at once more patriotic and more realistic. They realized that the future of themselves and of their people lay with the Indian Union, and they were prepared to enter the Constituent Assembly and give it full cooperation. Sardar K.M. Panikkar has described the scene at the historic meeting at Faridkot House in Delhi some time in August 1946, when the question was thrashed out at a largely attended meeting of the Chamber of Princes.[5] A notable speech was made by an old Brahman, Sir T. Vijaya-raghavachari, who had served in three states and was too old to have any

* Note by the Author: Rajastan refers to an independent federation of Princes, closely linked to a Federal India consisting of the former Provinces of British India.

personal ambitions. The tall old Brahman, with his white hair, looked like a Hebrew prophet; he said that after eight hundred years the chance had come for India to be independent and united. 'And if you Princes, who claim descent from the Sun and the Moon, now stand in the way of independence, your names will be cursed from generation to generation by the people of India.... The independence of India is coming like a great wave, and withstanding it will only lead to your own destruction." This speech had such a great effect that the Nawab of Bhopal had to adjourn the meeting.

The decision to set up the States' Negotiating Committee was taken shortly afterwards. The members included both points of view, the Nawab of Bhopal, Sir C.P. Ramaswamy Aiyar and Sardar Panikkar being among them. The Chamber of Princes drew up the terms on which it was willing to negotiate, based on the recommendations in the Cabinet Mission Memorandum. But the Negotiating Committee from the Constituent Assembly upheld the position taken by the A.I.S.P.C. that the sovereignty of the people of the states must be recognized. Nehru, speaking on the resolution of the Constituent Assembly which set up their own Negotiating Committee, frankly regretted they would have to meet a committee of the rulers, when it ought to have contained representatives of the people. But it could not be insisted on at this stage. As V.P. Menon comments, "It was rather an inauspicious beginning".

Nonetheless, neither Nehru nor Dr. P. Sitaramayya at this time clamoured for the abolition of the Princes, but wished to see them transformed into constitutional monarchs through the establishment of responsible government in the states. The Princes welcomed their moderation, and it made negotiations practical politics. By March 1947 a compromise was reached: Fifty percent of the total representation of the states in the Constituent Assembly would be elected by the elected members of the states' Legislatures or where no Legislatures existed, by some other form of electoral college. It was also agreed that the states should endeavour to increase the quota of elected members as far as possible.

This was the situation at the time of Attlee's historic announcement of a new policy on February 20th 1947, which altered the pace of progress towards Indian independence, and led to dramatic developments in Travancore.

XII. 2 Renewal of Agitation in Travancore

During the war, political activity had never entirely died down in Travancore. Promptly after the war agitation revived, and the fourth "annual" conference of the Travancore State Congress was held in Quilon in October 1945.[6] Sir C.P. was in conciliatory mood; the use of the government *maidan*[*] was permitted, and the conference was held in a calm atmosphere. Pattom Thanu Pillai took the chair, and made a conciliatory speech. Congress was not against the government; it was an organization which supported the people's demand for responsible government. Temple entry had been won by powerful agitation; similarly the object of the State Congress was to attain responsible government. He welcomed the government proposals for compulsory primary education, but pleaded for a more sympathetic attitude to the Christians' desire to run their own schools. Travancore he said, should take its rightful place in a united India; and the conference passed a resolution approving the affiliation of the Travancore State Congress with the All-India States Peoples' Conference.

Sir C.P. also appeared fairly conciliatory. In a speech in the February 1945 Sri Mulam Assembly he had clarified the government's attitude towards the State Congress as one of toleration of all bodies or organizations following programmes designed to serve the public interest; but of treating as subversive those which were led by individuals waging a sort of personal vendetta and bringing the administration into disrepute. By now Sir C.P. was again obsessed with the danger from the communists. He had welcomed their support against the "Quit India" campaign and they had been granted a limited recognition. By the end of the war they were very active in the labour movement and Sir C.P. was aware that serious trouble was brewing.

But Sir C.P.'s conciliatory mood did not last long . The use of the national flag in Travancore was once more banned, (thus earning Pandit Nehru's wrath), and feelings at once worsened. When the State Congress gave notice that it proposed to hold a meeting to collect money for the Defence fund for the Indian National Army trials, the District Magistrate prohibited it. The old antagonisms were being revived, and it only needed a spark to set the state alight again.

It was the government proposal to control primary education that provided the spark.[7] Christians believed—and not without reason—that

---

[*] Note by the Editor: A *maidan* is a large, usually grassy, open space or square in a town.

Sir C.P. was anti-Christian, and they tended to view his every move as in some way directed against them. He was quite frank about his conviction that Travancore was a Hindu state and that conversions to Christianity were undesirable.

The government's educational policy brought matters to a head. Christian schools were the crux. Christians owned and managed some 70% of all primary schools in the state, and also nearly half the middle schools. Although no non-Christian pupil was forced to attend Christian religious instruction or Christian services, nonetheless Christian schools were instrumental in bringing about conversions. They already came under a certain amount of government control; schools were inspected by government Inspectors, and if they were pronounced efficient they could claim a small grant-in-aid towards teachers' salaries. In 1943 there were some attempts to interfere in the management of Christians schools through the appointment of head teachers; but this led to vigorous protests, especially from the Roman Catholic hierarchy. The result was the appointment of the Travancore Education Reorganisation Committee in November 1943,which reported unanimously in March 1945. Its chief recommendation was that primary education should be made free and compulsory. The Committee considered the position of primary schools under private management, and acknowledged the valuable part played by such schools; and it recommended that although government would have to open new schools to implement its policy, every help should be given to private managements to improve existing schools and to open new ones, and recommended a more generous grant-in-aid to cover 75% of teachers' salaries. The Committee concluded that "religious education is an essential part of education, which should form part of everybody's schooling".

But the government pursued a different policy and introduced it by arranging for a resolution to be brought forward in the Sri Mulam Assembly on August 8th 1945.[8] A Hindu member proposed a resolution requesting the government to assume the management of all primary schools for the purpose of enforcing compulsory education. In spite of protests from Christian members most of whom voted against it, the resolution was carried the following day by a large majority. Even those official members, for instance the Director of Public Instruction, who had signed the report of the Education Reorganisation Committee only three months previously, had to vote now for the different policy ostensibly put forward by a non-official member. When the state Council met on August 10th, the Dewan announced that the government had decided on taking over all the primary schools.The Council, presented with a fait accompli, duly debated the matter but of course voted for it by a large majority. Again the Christian members mostly voted against it, though Christian officials had no choice but to vote for it.

A government communique was issued on August 31st setting out the new policy by which government would assume control of all primary schools; it claimed that the policy was that recommended by the Educational Reorganisation Committee as amended by the Legislature, which had approved the new policy by a large majority. There was a place for private schools, and they could get recognition but they would not get any financial aid from the government; and the government undertook not to close them or to interfere with their management.

A storm of protest broke out from Catholics both inside and outside the state, and also from Syrian Christians. The Anglican and London Mission Christians accepted the situation as inevitable. The government issued another statement on the 12th September explaining that religious education catering to particular religious faiths would be permissible outside school hours, (as had always been the practice). But the Catholics were not mollified, and persisted in regarding the new primary education scheme as an anti-Catholic move on the part of the government. The Syrian Catholic Bishop of Changanacherry sent out a pastoral letter calling on the people to fight the scheme "with their purses and with the spiritual sword". government called on him to withdraw the letter and express regret for having published it, or government would have to take action. The Bishop refused to withdraw or to apologize. Nothing happened to him. A body calling itself "The Travancore Peace Bloc "issued an aggressive pamphlet setting forth the Dewan's moves against Christians detrimental to their interests in every field, and this provided ammunition for prominent Catholics all over south India to attack the Travancore government's educational policy. Support for it came however from south Indian Hindus.

Rather surprisingly, the Travancore communists came forward to support the Catholic agitation; their motives are not clear, but the "unholy alliance" (as the Resident called it in his report to the Political Secretary) gave the Dewan a talking point against the Catholics. Protests poured in to the Viceroy from every kind of Catholic body all over India. Here is a typical example from Travancore itself: "Travancore Government officials especially police are compelling civilians to attend meetings in all important towns and villages for supporting new education policy and giving them money to send telegrams to Crown Representative. Very few attend such meetings but advertised as mammoth meetings. "Catholic Action General Secretary". Other telegrams came from Hindu bodies in Travancore, all similarly worded: "Travancore Catholic Priests and Communists oppose and criticise Travancore government assumption of responsibility for free primary compulsory education in the state implementing resolution passed by an overwhelming majority in both houses of Legislature stop but non-Catholic Christians, Muslims, Nayars, Ezhavas, scheduled castes all welcome government decision stop agitation mischievous and personal and with selfish motives. Secretary Sreenarayana Smarka College Committee." And there were rather unexpectedly six telegrams from various Hindu bodies in the north which were identically worded. "Wholeheartedly support Travancore government decision entire Hindu India and intelligent Indian opinion solidly behind the measure any pressure on State to give up measure will be viewed with suspicion and resentment and will lead to countrywide agitation. Sanatanadharma Pratinidhi Sabha Punjab."

An anonymous letter on cheap paper in an uneducated hand, preserved in the Political Department files, somehow rings truer than the telegrams, and passages from it are worth quoting:

"Your Excellency,

The Christians of Travancore cried to you for some consolation...but you the representative of the Christian Emperor turned your back to the persecuted Christians and sided with Sir C.P. Ramaswamy Aiyar. Understand your folly... your silence in the Travancore question has made all Indian Christians side with the Congress. C.P. cannot help you against the united cry of the Indians. Now you are losing the Christians to the Congress.

Are you not in the know that Travancore is ruled by a Dictator more Satanic than Hitler? A toy king and an adulterous mother is a curse for Travancore.

A Sympathiser."

It was the authentic voice of the common man.

The Catholics organized an enormous conference at Palai in north Travancore near the border of Cochin, attended, it was said, by 200,000 people from Travancore, Cochin and beyond, on January 21st 1946, presided over by a distinguished Catholic from Madras, Dr. M. Ramachandra Rao. The main resolution was on the educational policy of the Government of Travancore, but the whole field of Christian grievances was revised—discrimination in jobs,* refusal of permission to acquire land for churches and cemeteries, and many more.

The refusal of permission to open Christian churches and cemeteries was a real grievance. Behind it lay an interesting history, going back to 1821. A Christian church for new converts had been erected along a route used by a particular Hindu procession; but of course the converts were untouchables and so polluted the roads, and the then Maharani Regent ordered the route of the procession to be changed. In order to avoid similar difficulties she issued a proclamation prohibiting all classes of her subjects from erecting places of worship without previous sanction of government, which in its turn undertook to provide sites for places of worship in such localities as would not interfere with the religious interests of others. It was a wise measure in a multi-religious society. But it had undoubtedly been utilized by the government to prevent the erection of churches and the provision of cemeteries. Frequent complaints by the Catholic hierarchy had solid grounds; a question by a Christian member in the assembly in 1946 elicited the information that between 1939 and 1946, 193 applications for erecting new churches and 8 for new cemeteries had been received, and permission had been granted for 57 churches and one cemetery. More than half the applications were from Catholics.

The Palai conference did not confine itself to religious matters but went on to politics. The conference denounced the banning of public meetings and processions and the gagging orders served on several public men, and the ban on the entry of some leading Christian newspapers into Travancore. It also passsed a long resolution on the proposals for constitutional reform, the so-called "American Model" constitution which had been published in Trivandrum on August 16th. The resolution was in very similar terms to that which had been passed by the Working Committee of the State Congress at Nagercoil three days previously and was probably modelled on it.

All these resolutions were embodied in a memorandum to the British parliamentary delegation then visiting Travancore, in spite of the Dewan's public statement that the parliamentary delegation as such had nothing to do with Travancore as Parliament had no jurisdiction in the

* Note by the Editor: Christian members of the legislature kept complaining of underrepresentation in the public services. In reply to these entreaties the Dewan put forward that the Christian share in the services was really higher than their numerical strength warranted and that Christians held 44% of appointments in the Education Department and 43% in the Medical Department. (Press confrence 1-3-1944).

internal affairs of an Indian state. This statement was challenged by the Christians on the ground that the Treaty of 1805 gave the Paramount Power the right of intervention in the internal affairs of the state. In this matter the Christians were right and the Dewan wrong, as he very well knew from the Travancore Bank case; gross injustice would have brought "advice" from the Paramount Power.

Agitation went on—conferences, meetings, student demonstrations. The Travancore Catholics saw to it that the Catholic press in England was kept informed on the Dewan's iniquities. The Archbishop of Bombay addressed an appeal to the Viceroy expressing the concern of Catholics over developments in Travancore. "The Dewan", he wrote, "exercises an intransigent and autocratic power and has complete control of every weapon of publicity and propaganda in the state." Christians were helpless. "In the atmosphere of fear and suspicion no one dares to speak out."

The whole question of Christians' grievances was considered by the officials of the Political Department in consultation with the Resident in Travancore. It was decided that while developments were not above suspicion, the discrimination was not sufficiently serious to justify advice to the Maharaja.

But Sir C.P. realised that he had to tread warily, and was glad to accept the mediation of the Apostolic delegate, Monsignor Kierkels, a genial old Dutchman with no political interests, when they met in Ootacamund in the hot weather holiday of 1946. Eventually, by an agreement signed on February 19th 1947, the Government of Travancore was to take over the primary schools, but where any denomination felt strongly on the matter, it could keep its own school provided admission was limited to children belonging to that denomination. Such schools were eligible for government grants. There were enough Catholics in Travancore to ensure their schools had sufficient pupils.[9]

The Catholic schools agitation was the first large-scale agitation in Travancore since the end of the war, and it showed that the people were ready for renewed struggles. As it went on the struggle took on more and more a political character and it is significant that political interest broadened from Travancore affairs to all-India questions. At the All-Kerala Catholic Congress of 9th June 1946, the usual resolutions were repeated but it was much more openly political on all-India questions. For instance it denounced the Cabinet Mission Plan for ignoring the people of the states and failing to provide for their representation in the proposed Constituent Assembly; it complained that there was no protection for fundamental civil rights, which should be made a central subject; and it urged Catholics to take an active part in politics.

XII. 3 The Dewan's *"American" Constitution*[10]

The Cabinet Mission sent to India by the Labour Government of Britain in 1946 was preceded by an All-Party Parliamentary Delegation which came to study conditions for itself. Sir C.P. met them in Delhi and invited them to Trivandrum, where they were due to arrive on January 20th.

Talk of constitution-making was in the air. It was in these circumstances that Sir C.P. produced the draft of a constitution for Travancore, about which he had talked so much in the latter part of 1938 and thoughout 1939, but about which he had never been specific. In a speech at Quilon in May 1939, he had expressed a preference for the American model with its separation of the powers of the Executive and the Legislature, as more suited to Indian conditions than the Westminster model; but that was all that was known of his views, and most people had forgotten them.

When on January 16th a full-fledged constitution sprang from his head, embodied in a government communique of that date, it came as a surprise and created a sensation.

The communique begins with a preamble extolling the progress of Travancore in all aspects of public life, and states that His Highness has now decided the time is ripe for a large-scale measure of constitutional reform, involving among other features the adoption of universal franchise. But "the rights and privileges of His Highness the Maharaja will be unaffected by these arrangements." It came to be known as the "American Model".

The Legislature was to consist of two Chambers, the first a Legislative Assembly popularly elected, the second a "facultative" body, composed of representatives of various bodies, interests and professions. There was to be universal suffrage, with no reservation of seats or other methods of securing the representation of minorities. The two Chambers were to have co-equal status.

The Executive was to have a Dewan at its head. The Dewan was to be appointed by the Maharaja and to hold office at his pleasure. He would not be a member of the Legislature, but could address them or send messages to them to initiate financial or legislative measures. He could remit decisions of both the Houses for reconsideration, and he would have the power of veto. Neither the Dewan nor the other high officials, who were to be appointed through a Public Services Commission, would be removable by a vote of the Legislature.

The courts would be independent; the judges of the High Court would be nominated by the Maharaja, and the subordinate judiciary by the Executive. The judges of the High Court would have the power to pronounce on the constitution. The constitution would be promulgated by royal proclamation.

A comment at the end of the communique stresses that the continuity of executive administration was essential for development. "The position of the Dewan vis-à-vis the Legislature and Judiciary will be approximated to that of the president of the United states of America subject always to the rights, privileges and prerogatives of the Sovereign."

Five days later in a *Gazette Extraordinary*, the Dewan's term of office was extended by five years.

The Resident received the draft constitution first and at once complained to the Dewan that it came as a complete surprise, though he appreciated the need for hurry in view of the forthcoming visit of the British Parliamentary delegation. But "I may say that the Political Department expect to be informed before any far-reaching constitutional reforms are finally decided upon."

Sir C.P. in one of his lengthy letters, replied he had often discussed the substance of the communique with previous Residents, with Political Advisers, and with Lord Linlithgow and Lord Wavell, and he had always made it clear that His Highness and his government considered that the Westminster system of responsible government would never work in an Indian state or even in British India, especially in view of the communal and religious cleavages in India. He pointed to the unhappy experience of France and drew attention to the introduction of universal suffrage as a major advance. He also complained that the Parliamentary delegation had, without any reference to the Travancore government, received a deputation from the Travancore State Congress, who had endeavoured to prove the state was governed not by the rule of law but by tyranny; therefore, as he had already expressed his views in public on these reforms, he felt it essential to publish the proposed constitution "to forestall any obiter dicta by the Delegation".

The Political Department searched their records but found nothing about the alleged discussions with Viceroys or political officers. They were unimpressed by the proposed constitution, as is revealed by their confidential notes on the file. They were critical of the analogy drawn with the Anerican president; the Dewan was irremovable by popular vote. The Maharaja, described as "the Sovereign", was not sovereign but under obligation to the Paramount Power. The Political Department was at that time dealing with the grievances of the Christians, and was strongly suspicious of the absence of any provision for the representation of the minorities. The Political Department must be convinced that the minorities were getting a fair deal; otherwise intervention by the Crown Representative might become necessary to prevent discontent.

The proposed constitutional reforms had a mixed reception in the Indian press. There was much enthusiasm, especially among the National Liberal Federation, which Sir C.P. had joined after his break with the Congress in 1921. Sir Taj Bahadur Sapru wired: "Congratulations Maharaja's name will live forever in Indian history". Some, while welcoming universal suffrage and approving the separation of executive and legislature on the American model, expressed doubts about the irremovable character of the executive. It would need high political skill to maintain a smooth relationship between executive and legislature, but that brilliant statesman Sir C.P., and his Maharaja, full of sagacity and wisdom, would be likely to achieve it.

The Congress press was critical; the analogy with the American constitution was only partial, the Dewan would remain an autocrat and the sovereign rights of the people did not exist. The extreme *National Herald* denounced it outright. The only good point was the proposal for universal suffrage, and apart from that the whole thing was nothing but a spectacular boost for the Dewan—and quite simply a fraud.

Reactions in Travancore were predictable. The Travancore National Party were ethusiastic, the deputy president of the Sri Mulam Assembly hailed the proposed reforms as "a bold and revolutionary step". The government monthly *Travancore Information and Listener* gave a summary of the provisions under the headline "Travancore Blazes the Trail". In announcing the extension of the Dewan's term of office it commented: "press and public have enthusiastically welcomed this announcement and feel the continuance of Sir C.P. in office is indispensable for the successful implementation of the constitutional and industrial reforms of the state."

This enthusiasm was not observable in State Congress circles nor at the Kerala Catholic Congress at Palai. Pattom Thanu Pillai in a statement to the press criticized the irremovable executive, and still more the failure to consult the people's representatives about the constitution. "The spirit of democracy should underlie the process of constitution making".

The Working Committee met in Nagercoil on January18th and gave the proposals careful consideration. Their statement was the most thorough and balanced commentary on them.[11] It began by criticising the manner in which they had been put forward. "In view of the recognition by the British Parliament of the right of the people of British India to frame their own constitution and the formation of a Constituent Assembly for that purpose, the introduction of constitutional reforms in Travancore without consulting the people is a violation of the fundamental rights of the people to shape their own destinies."

The Committee welcomed the introduction of universal adult suffrage and a fully elected Legislative Chamber. But these did not achieve a truly democratic constitution; there were certain defects which defeated the very purpose for which the reforms were supposed to be introduced i.e. a real transfer of power to the people. A bicameral legislature was not necessary for Travancore. The proposed second chamber was bound to be reactionary - therefore as both houses were to have co-equal powers it would render the lower house ineffective.

The chief criticism was directed to the Executive. The continuance of a Dewan assisted by an executive body more or less chosen by him and not responsible to the legislature was a negation of democracy. The right of vote was unqualified. They gave a critical examination of the analogy drawn up with the American constitution. The statement pointed out that the American president is elected for four years and if he wants to remain in office he has to seek re-election. The executive officers are appointed by the president only with the consent and approval of the Senate. There are provisions in the American constitution for the impeachment of the president. In fact, the position of the Dewan approaches rather that of the head of government (the *Duce*) in fascist Italy, who held his office at the pleasure of the King.

Admittedly the press communique gave a very incomplete picture; many details had still to be explained. But "to the extent that it is possible to judge the proposed constitutional arrangements, the Working Committee is convinced that the constitution envisaged is not only disappointing but definitely retrograde and undemocratic."

The leaders of the State Congress then rushed to the capital in the hope of meeting the British parliamentary delegation. (Possibly some Catholics among them went off to Palai, for the resolutions of the Catholic Congress followed those of the State Congress closely). The delegates arrived in Trivandrum on the 20th January, and were invited to meet the "representatives of the people" in the legislative building the next day. Various bodies including the Travancore National Party sent delegations. The Travancore State Congress applied for an invitation for their delegation but were refused. They then devised a strategem to get their statement to the Parliamentary Delegation.[12]

Next day Sir C.P. gave a tea party on the charming lawns surrounding the state Guest House in which the delegates were accommodated . To impress the delegates with the tranquil atmosphere of the capital the usual police guard was not in evidence. So during the siesta hour K.A. Mathew and G. Chandrasekhara Pillai, another Congressman, walked in and were hidden by the servants. As the tea party got under way they walked out and boldly presented a copy of the statement to the secretary of the delegation, Major Woodrow Wyatt. Sir C.P. could hardly have them arrested even if any police had been present to do the job. The delegates asked why the memorandum had not been submitted at the legislative building the previous day, and K.A. Mathew explained they had not been permitted to do so. The intruders then calmly strolled out of the gate. Sir C.P. is reported to have explained to his guests that they were members of a party which did not subscribe to the Gandhian principles of non-violence. Nonetheless, in the subsequent press release the Travancore State Congress is mentioned as one of the bodies which submitted memoranda at the legislative building on January 22nd.

In the February session of the Sri Mulam Assembly Congress members, led by K.A. Mathew, gave some non-violent trouble. On February 4th the Dewan-president gave his opening address, which was largely devoted to the proposed constitutional reforms. He read a message from the Maharaja and stated "His Highness, in the exercise of his prerogative, has made up his mind to give up some of his rights."

Congress went into the attack. At question time K.A. Mathew asked on what principle the choice of delegates to meet the British Parliamentary Delegation had been based.

Chief Secretary to government : "Those whom the government considered might usefully see the delegation. The Travancore State Congress had already met them outside Travancore." Replying to a supplementary question, he denied there had been any restraint placed on any member of the public trying to contact the delegation. The Dewan, intervening, said government would inquire into any obstruction on the part of officials; and he deplored the efforts of the State Congress to meet the delegates outside the state to present an ex-parte picture of what was happening in the state. One must remember that these debates were pretty fully reported in the leading south Indian newspapers, so the

Dewan was speaking to a wider audience than the members of the legislature. The reports could not of course convey the suppressed hilarity that pervaded the Chamber.

Five resolutions were set down on the reforms, three in favour and two against. One motion in favour was allowed; it expressed "the boundless gratitude for the unparalleled and historic lead in introducing a highly democratic constitution." K.A. Mathew put down another: "That this House records its opinion that the constitutional reforms are inadequate and disappointing". Discussion on this resolution was refused as it infringed His Highness's prerogative. Mathew commented that the motions having been admitted the president's refusal to allow discussion was "an insult to the House". The State Congress members thereupon walked out, followed by ten other members. Others were about to follow them when the Dewan adjourned the House for lunch.

This episode did not remain unnoticed by the Political Department. In a note on the file about the constitutional Reforms it was commented that the Dewan's refusal to allow discussion on the proposed reforms was "not a light affair". If the royal prerogative was invoked in such a manner, discussion in the Legislative Assembly would have no real value.

Opposition was building up, in spite of the Dewan's assurances at his frequent press conferences that the people were enthusiastic. The State Congress kept up the pressure. More important at this juncture, the communists took a hand. In the small industrial towns along the coast where they were strong, they organized demonstrations and processions and coined the slogan:

> "Merican model,
> Arabi kadalil!"
> (American model-into the Arabia Sea!)[13]

Of its subsequent history there is little to be said. It was formally promulgated by royal proclamation on April 7th 1947. But is was engulfed by the dramatic events that soon followed. The only parts to survive were universal suffrage and a fully elected Chamber. Ironically the machinery which Sir C.P. set in motion for compiling voters' lists on the basis of universal adult suffrage was utilized by the popular leaders for a far more democratic constitution.

XII. 4 Punnapra-Vayalar

1946 was a year of mounting tension and violence in India, and Travancore had its own terrible blood bath that year, in the communist-dominated coastal areas of north Travancore, which had suffered so much from unemployment and famine since the outbreak of the war. The communists, long active among the factory workers of the area, were now extending their activities among the fishermen along the coast and the farm workers further inland.

The Government of Travancore had given a grudging and partial recognition to the communists during the war after the "Quit India" movement; but in the face of growing labour unrest they returned to their attitude of extreme suspicion of the communists. It might be said that the obsession which Sir C.P. had had with the Christians was now tansferred to the communists. A government press note issued on February 3rd, 1946 prohibited strikes and lockouts without notice, and instigating of persons to take part in strikes was also forbidden.[14] These prohibitions incidentally were made under the Defence of Travancore rules, which were not withdrawn after the war.

The uprising in the Alleppey-Shertallai area, usually known as the Punnapra-Vayalar uprising, after the two villages most concerned, is the subject of controversy. There are sharply divergent versions of the whole affair. The government version, expounded at length in press statements, was that it was a communist plot, part of a wider plot backed by the Communist Party of India, to overthrow the Government of Travancore and establish independent communist rule in that area. Communists' accounts go into the causes of the uprising, which they give as the terrible hardships suffered by the toiling masses, their exploitation by their employers, the harassment by hooligans co-operating with the police, and the political unrest caused by the continuance of "Dewan rule". The government case that it was all a politically motivated plot backed by the Communist Party of India does not bear examination; the leaders of the C.P.I. were intelligent men who would not have supported any such crack-brained scheme. The communists 'explanation of the underlying causes of unrest deserves examination.[15]

The factory workers in the coir industry, whose trade unions were well-established and recognized by the government and the employers, still had many reasons for discontent in 1946. In spite of their strong union, with committees in many factories, there had been little improvement in their conditions. A Government of India report on the coir industry, published in May 1946, refers to low earnings, bad working conditions, lack of security, no pension scheme, no medical care beyond first aid boxes in the factories. It refers to the strong trade union in Travancore; the government had set up an Industrial Relations Committee which had succeeded in abolishing the iniquitous contract system of labour by which a contractor undertook to provide labourers at so much a head and made a big commission in the process. But there was much room for improvement.

Behind the coastal strip of sand and lagoons lay the flat water-logged lands of the "rice bowl" of Travancore. These lands were in the hands of big landowners who operated a kind of share-cropping system with their labourers, ten shares going to the landlords and one to the labourer. These agricultural labourers were the most oppressed class of labourers in Travancore; most of them belonged to the lowest of the untouchable castes, some were little better than serfs, and were so regarded by their landlords. The labourers were often cheated in the allotment of their shares by the landlords' agents, but centuries of oppression had broken their spirit. The communists began to work among these impoverished and neglected outcastes, organizing them into a union and giving them political education.

By March 1946, when the second rice crop was being gathered, the government realized that unrest was spreading among these hitherto spiritless labourers, and issued a press note warning agricultural labourers against taking any strike action for higher wages at harvest time, which would be serious in view of the general shortage of food. The press note added that government could have no objection to "duly constituted unions."[16]

The communists did not stop at organizing the agricultural labourers to stand up for their rights; they also took up the land question, and sent a memorial to the Dewan proposing a redistribution of the land. As a basis of discussion, the memorial quoted a figure: if all the cultivable land of Travancore was divided equally, each person of the population would have 13 cents, and they proposed the redistribution of land on this basis.

The landowners took alarm at this memorial. They were also alarmed at political demonstrations by their labourers, who started going about in procession shouting such slogans as "Down with Dewan rule!"—something quite unprecedented. They took a leaf out of the government's book and hired hooligans to attack the demonstrators. Communist accounts of the troubles also mention mass evictions from the workers' dwelling places, rape of women and so on. Party workers began to set up camps in which they trained volunteers in self-defence.

Another development was the organization of the fishermen into a union. Along the whole length of the Kerala coast there are fishing villages nestling under the coconut palms. The fishermen were too poor to own their own boats; they hired them from landowners and priests, who took a proportion of the catch as their rent. The women often worked as servants for the landowners, and the fishermen's huts also belonged to the landowners. The communists began to work among them, organized their union and set up union offices in every fishing village.

Official accounts usually take the attitude, both with regard to Congressmen and communists working among the poor, that they were entirely politically motivated and exploiting the poor for their own selfish ends. But Gandhian and communist workers alike were often deeply concerned to better the lot of the poor; they lived with them, shared their poverty, and won their love and respect.

Wherever they went, of course, the communists engaged in political education. They claimed that they were the true leaders of the people, and that Pattom Thanu Pillai and his men were bourgeois who were secretly supporting the Dewan. Pattom, they said, had declared that "the American model should be tested". This canard was contradicted by the forthright rejection of the proposals by the Working Committee statement of January 18th 1946; but the communist version remained current for years, and helped to turn the workers against the Congress.

Another cause of disturbance was the unrest in the armed forces, in which many Keralans were serving or had served.[17] As servicemen they were demobilized and returned to their homes, they brought a spirit of unrest with them, and some found an outlet for their discontent in communist activities. This was particularly true in British Malabar where communists were very active.

By August labour unrest was sweeping all over Travancore, and was worsened by a railway strike on the South Indian Railways and talk of a general strike in Madras. In a statement on labour unrest in the Sri Mulam Assembly of August 5th, the Dewan referred to a strike in the government rubber factory in Trivandrum, and another in the Punalur Paper Mills, where the government had requested the management to shut down the mill rather than give in to the strikers. The Dewan blamed the communists; the unrest was all part of a communist plot which was spread all over India. Four days later in the State Council, a member put down a motion referring to the difficulties of agricultural labourers; the Dewan repeated his statement about the communist plots, and the motion was withdrawn.

All official reports and newspaper accounts of the Punnapra-Vayalar uprising begin with the events of October 24th, when the demonstrations of factory workers and procession of ex-servicemen in Alleppey clashed with armed police. But they do not go into causes, nor offer any explanation of the fact that armed police were already camped in the area. Communist accounts go deeper, analyzing the causes of the outbreak, and putting the beginning of violence several weeks earlier. The following account is based on information supplied by Mr. K.C. George, former Minister in the Kerala government, supplemented by that supplied by comrade K.P. Chandranandan, who led the resistance at Punnapra.

Trouble arose along the beach near Alleppey sometime in August. A sick woman who had failed to go to her work at a landowner's house, was dragged out of her hut by the irate housewife, beaten and locked out of her hut. Union workers came to the rescue, so did the police who made some arrests. This caused a riot and the fishermen burned the landowner's house. Consequently reserve police set up a camp nearby and started arrests and beatings. The communists also set up a camp for volunteers among the fishermen; at some time they began to train the workers in self-defence and ex-soldiers came from Malabar to direct the training. This included the making of weapons—bamboo spears with sharpened ends, home-made bombs, country guns.

The landowners, already alarmed by political demonstrations among their labourers, and by the fear that the communists would actually seize their lands and redistribute them among the landless labourers, began to take their own measures. One Jewish landowner who had a thousand share-cropping tenants, sent a telegram to the Dewan, who sent a detachment of troops to protect them. Communist accounts accuse the troops of starting a reign of terror, destroying huts and raping women. In revenge, the workers seized one of the hooligans employed by the landowners and beat him to death.

The communists became impatient of the inaction of the State Congress, whom they accused of doing a deal with the Dewan to crush the "true revolutionary forces", and began to plan their own direct action. This was to be launched by a general strike, and a meeting of the All-Travancore Trades Union Congress was held at Alleppey on September 10th to plan it. This meeting was attended by two Congressmen, C. Kesavan, who as an Ezhava from a poverty-stricken background had much sympathy for the factory workers, many of whom were Ezhavas, and a young Nayar, K. Sanku Pillai. The Trades Union

Congress wanted to start the general strike on September 15th, but Kesavan persuaded them to postpone it until the State Congress Working Committee had met on October 9th as he hoped to get the support of the Congress for the strike. Kesavan and Sanku Pillai were however arrested before the Working Committee meeting and so the question was never discussed. But Pattom Thanu Pillai so abhorred violence that it is very doubtful that he would at this stage have been prepared to negotiate with them; but, according to communists' accounts, he gave the Dewan one month's notice before starting any direct action on the part of Congress.

The Trades Union Congress did not wait for the Congress, but decided to start a general strike on the Maharaja's birthday, which that year fell on October 24th; their demands were to include the end of "Dewan rule", the establishment of responsible government, and the withdrawal of the police camps. Further training was given to workers in self-defence. A big camp was set up in Vayalar, an apparently safe retreat in the water-logged area, approachable by land on only one side; here the workers drilled and piled up their home-made weapons.

The first outbreak of violence occurred on October 19th, due to some trouble among the fishermen near Alleppey, which brought a police party marching on the local fishermen's union office. But a party of volunteers, headed by a Catholic ex-serviceman, faced them so determinedly that they withdrew—only to return with five police vans which swept the beaches from Alleppey to Aroor, a distance of nearly thirty miles, destroying all the union offices. The next day the volunteers collected in the camps, which the local people stocked with food and other necessities.

October 24th was His Highness's birthday, and in far away Trivandrum he was entertaining the Governor of Madras, Sir Archibald Nye, and his Lady, who were full of admiration for the progress of Travancore. But in Alleppey there were violent clashes and bloodshed. There were two processions to inaugurate the general strike, one of ex-servicemen and another of factory workers armed with bamboo spears and stones, both shouting the slogan "Down with Dewan rule!" Armed police tried to disperse the ex- servicemen and two demonstrators were killed.

At Punnapra, not far from Alleppey, there was a camp of armed police under a Sub-Inspector, and several workers' *jathas*, led by K.P. Chandranandan, converged on the camp to attack it. The sub-inspector ordered them to disperse; but Chandrananda stood his ground, and appealed to the police to leave the camp and join the people. The sub-inspector ordered the police to fire, but the volunteers, as they had been trained to do, dropped on their bellies and crawled towards the camp. A worker hurled a bamboo spear at the sub-inspector which killed him instantly, and a number of constables were also killed (the communist accounts give twenty, the government figures three); a number of workers were also shot (the official figure is 27 but the communist figure is "hundreds"). The rest of the police fled and the workers seized their guns and withdrew.

When the news reached Trivandrum Martial Law was declared in the two disturbed *taluks* along the coast, and the Commandant of the state Forces, Major-General Parameswaran Pillai, was put in charge of both military and police forces. It was the military who came in their vans to Punnapra, collecting the dead bodies, took them to a roadside burial place, poured petrol over them and burned them.

Refugees pouring into Ernakulam in their hundreds reported that there were thousands of workers on strike; but when reporters tried to reach the area they found it cut off. Culverts and major bridges had been broken and telephone and telegraph wires were cut.

The General Officer Commanding surveyed the area by helicopter, and on October 27th the soldiers came to Vayalar in motor boats, completely surrounding it, and attacked. The workers were unable to stand up to well-armed troops; there was a short sharp attack, hundreds were killed, the volunteers were dispersed and the camp broken up. With this swift action the uprising was crushed. The following day the Travancore Coir Factory Workers' Union was banned and two days later the All-Travancore Trades Union Congress was also banned. The resistance was broken; the G.O.C. reported the situation was calm, only small pockets of resistance remaining to be mopped up. By November 11th Martial Law was withdrawn.

The government official reports give 167 killed at Vayalar; the communists estimated the dead numbered over 600. They collected the bodies and took them to Punnapra to be burnt alongside the dead of Punnapra. The spot became a place of pilgrimage, and in 1957 the communist government of Kerala erected a martyrs' memorial there.

Verbal warfare broke out even before the shooting stopped, as all parties strove to make political capital out of it.[18] The State Congress Working Committee denounced both communist incitement to violence and government repression, and accused the communists of deliberately creating an atmosphere of violence so as to destroy any State Congress campaign based on non-violence. The Dewan blamed the State Congress for its talk of direct action which encouraged subversive activities, and accused the State Congress of having communists among its members. The State Congress denied that it was itself communist, and pointed out that the government had kept silent about its own acts of terrorism in the Alleppey-Shertallai area. "A government that cannot protect the lives and properties of its people without martial law has no right to function", and concluded with a demand for responsible government.

The final government report was issued on December 2nd. It denied the assertions of the communists that some 700 had died; only 190 rioters had been killed. Fortunately the trouble was isolated; the rioters had gone to a water-logged area for participation in armed insurrection, but this had been evacuated by peaceful people. "All casualties as such are confined to the really guilty".

But Sir C.P. was not allowed to forget the matter.[19] In Bombay, where thousands of Malayalis lived, a Travancore Defence Committee was organized, with the venerable Professor P.A. Wadia as its president, and M.M.Cheriyan, a former member of the youth Christian Council of Action, now turned communist, as its secretary; funds were collected for the victims of the shootings, and the Committee published weekly cyclostyled news sheets containing the news of Travancore kept out of the national press, some of which found their way back to Travancore.

And when Sir C.P. came to address a brilliant gathering in Bombay, to inaugurate the Indian Institute of International Affairs, a thousand Malayalis demonstrated outside the Town Hall with posters bearing the words Punnapra-Vayalar and the number of the dead. He had to leave by the back door. Hatred was swelling to bursting point.

One result of Punnapra-Vayalar was to deepen the rift between the State Congress and the communists. The communists continued to accuse Pattom Thanu Pillai of secretly approving the Dewan's American Model constitution; Pattom continued to deplore the violence of the communists.

But two of the leading Congressmen were not wedded to non-violence. C.Kesavan and T.M.Verghese were convinced that the help of the communists was essential to get rid of Sir C.P. and that in the last resort violence would have to be used—and they kept in touch with the communist leaders, both in Travancore and in Bombay.

Chapter XIII

FINAL STEPS TO FREEDOM

XIII. 1 The All-India Background

The Indian scene was transformed by the announcement of a new policy by the British Prime Minister, Mr. Attlee, on February 20th, 1947. The British were to withdraw completely from India by a definite date, at that time envisaged as June 1948, and a new Viceroy, Lord Mountbatten, was to carry out the new policy. It gave a sense of urgency that had been lacking before, and sharpened all divisions and all controversies.

As far as the states were concerned, the Government stayed by the policy of the Cabinet Mission: "His Majesty's Government do not intend to hand over their powers and obligations under Paramountcy to any Government of British India." Nor was it intended to bring Paramountcy to an end before the transfer of power.

The very sense of urgency deepened the divisions among the Princes. The Nawab of Bhopal increased his effort to keep the Princes out of the Constituent Assembly; but an influential section led by the Maharajas of Bikaner and Patiala decided to send their own representatives to the Constituent Assembly, and Patiala made arrangements to have his representatives elected. But both Hyderabad and Travancore announced their intention of remaining independent sovereign states after June 1948; and Sir C.P. Ramaswamy Aiyar resigned from the states Negotiating Committee and the states Constitutional Advisory Committee.

The All-India States Peoples' Conference met at Gwalior on April 17th-18th. Nehru had to meet strong criticism for the compromise he had accepted at the joint meeting of the two Negotiating Committees on March 2nd, that 50% of the states' representatives should be popularly elected. Nehru defended the compromise as "not what was desirable but what was possible and practical." But he spoke with his usual forthrightness about the states which refused to come into the Constituent Assembly. They would be regarded as "hostile states and would in future have to bear the consequences." The conference finally ratified the agreement reached by the two Negotiating Committees about the representation of the states in the Constituent Assembly.

On June 3rd 1947 it was finally announced that India would be divided into the two Dominions of India and Pakistan, and that the date of transfer would be August 15th 1947. The policy of the British Government would remain unchanged; Paramountcy would lapse, the sovereignty ceded by the Princes would return to them, but Paramountcy would continue until the actual transfer of power.

Events now began to move at breakneck speed. The Nawab of Bhopal immediately declared that Bhopal would be assuming an independent status as soon as Paramountcy was withdrawn, and would negotiate directly with the future Governments of India and Pakistan. He resigned his office as Chancellor of the Chamber of Princes.

The Nizam of Hyderabad issued a *firman** on June 6th declaring his intention not to send representatives to the Constituent Assembly. On August 15th he would be entitled to resume his status as an independent sovereign.

On June 11th Sir C.P. Ramaswamy Aiyar announced that Travancore would resume its ancient independence as from August 15th. He also announced his intention of sending a trade agent to Pakistan.

The All-India states People's conference considered Partition a "bitter pill," but they realized that Partition made a strong centre at Delhi all the more necessary. The Standing Committee, like the All-India Congress Committee, expressed its fears of the "Balkanisation" of India; the accession of the states to the Union was therefore all the more urgent.

The Interim Government under Pandit Nehru also realized the need for a strong line towards the states. A meeting took place on June 18th between the Congress leaders and the officers of the Political Department. The meeting was stormy; Nehru claimed the right of the successor government to assume the Paramountcy which the British were allowing to lapse, and that the states had no right to declare their independence. The Political Department had already begun to dismantle itself (there was a major row about their burning their files). It was finally agreed to set up a new states Department under the Interim Government. Sardar Patel, who was intimately associated with the All-India states Peoples' conference, was to be the minister, and V.P. Menon became the Secretary.

Sardar Patel adopted the policy, in which the Viceroy fully concurred, of persuading the states to accede to the Union before independence, on the basis of the three subjects already defined by the

---

* Note by the Editor: A *firman* is a royal decree

federal provisions of the Government of India Act of 1935, namely Defence, External Affairs and Communications. Many had already done so, led by the enlightened and patriotic Princes of Bikaner and Patiala; by the time the new states Department was publicly announced on July 1st, some fifteen states had already acceded to the Union, and forty more were in favour of doing so.

Sardar Patel's first act was to put out a conciliatory statement that Congress was no enemy of the Princely order, which mollified the Princes to some extent. But it needed the personal intervention of the Viceroy to win over larger numbers. He had one meeting only with the Princes, on July 25th, and it was a personal triumph for him. He could charm the birds off the trees, and the Princes into their constitutional cages—cages that later were gilded with substantial pensions. By a mixture of appeals to reason and genial threats he persuaded them to accede to the Union. By August 15th all except three—Hyderabad, Kashmir and Junagadh—had acceded to the Union. The story how these three eventually came into the Union is outside the scope of this book; our concern is with Travancore.

It had a unique history. Sir C.P. Ramaswamy Aiyar was the first to announce the intention of Travancore to remain independent, at a press conference on March 15th; and a more formal announcement came almost immediately after the June 3rd Plan.

But, just as Sardar Patel had foretold in an argument with Lord Mountbatten, the people rose, got rid of the Dewan, and Travancore joined the Union. In the end it was the first Princely state to set up a completely democratic government.

XIII. 2 The Proposed Independence of Travancore

Sir C.P. Ramaswamy Aiyar changed his mind several times after telling the Cabinet Mission in 1946 that India needed a stronger centre than they were proposing. In December 1946 he had announced that he was resigning his post of Dewan of Travancore; he wanted to be free to write, speak and take part in the discussion on the future constitution of India; he would continue to take part in the States Negotiating Committee and in the Consultative Committee of the Chamber of Princes.[1] The Maharaja persuaded him to stay on as Dewan a little longer, to guide the state through the inevitable constitutional changes. But with the announcement of February 20th, he realized, along with many others that the new policy, by setting a time limit to the British presence in India, was an open invitation to the Muslim League to obstruct the work of the Constituent Assembly, until the date by which the British would leave, and Pakistan would become inevitable.[2] The Indian Union would be Congress-dominated. He at once made up his mind. At a crowded press conference on March 15th, which lasted three hours, he announced that on July 1st, 1948, when the British would have left and Paramountcy would have lapsed, Travancore would be an independent state.[3]

His statement began with a long review of the relations of Travancore with the British. It was as an independent state that Travancore had made the Treaty of 1795, which was a treaty of alliance to defend Travancore from foreign enemies; the later Treaty of 1805 was one of friendship, the ruler only conceding "certain powers of advice." There was no question of conquest or the assumption by the British of sovereignty as such. On July 1st, 1948 therefore, Travancore would revert to the status of 1795 as an independent state. Of course some agreements would have to be made with the Government of India with regard to matters like customs, trade, railways and so on; but they were matters to be settled by treaty and not by dictation.

He claimed that Travancore had the resources to be independent; she had wide trade with countries outside India, and she was becoming self-sufficient in food. Her smallness did not matter; independent countries like Norway and New Zealand had much smaller populations. He spoke of Travancore's relations with Congress. He declared he believed in the unity of India. He paid tribute to Congress for the great battle it had been fighting for the independence of India, of course Travancore had always made common cause with Congress in this battle. Travancore might even use the machinery of the Constituent Assembly if it suited them. But "in the whole of the future constitutional discussions let it be remembered that we are dealing as an independent state - which state can remain independent if the people and the Sovereign work together and give no room for outside interference."

In a later statement from New Delhi (where he had gone to meet the new Viceroy) he justified his decision further.[4] Travancore would have come into an India with a strong centre and would voluntarily have handed over a number of subjects; but if a strong centre did not come into being, she would retain complete liberty of action in relation to other powers. Sir C.P. raised the matter of Travancore being accorded Dominion Status both with Lord Mountbatten and in a letter to Mr. Attlee; but he was given no encouragement. He announced later that the matter was not fully decided, but he planned to go to London to see Mr. Attlee and other British ministers to discuss the constitutional position of Travancore.[5] Meanwhile he resigned from both the States' Negotiating Committee and the States' Consultative Committee, and refused to have any more dealings with the Constituent Assembly.

At the press conference on March 15th he also announced that the new constitution would shortly be promulgated. It had been formally published for discussion on January 27th, and the Dewan promised a number of modifications as a result of discussions with individuals and organizations; the powers of the Dewan would be considerably curtailed. The new Constitution was promulgated in a Royal Proclamation on April 7th, the Travancore Reforms Proclamation Act of 1122 M.E. (1946-1947).[6] The preamble stated: "It is intended to give the people complete control of the Government subject to efficiency and continuity." The constitution followed much the same lines as that first published in January of the previous year which had already aroused so much opposition from Congress and communists alike. The "modifications" were not likely to mollify them. The clause fixing the life of the legislature at four years had the modification that the Dewan could dissolve either chamber earlier or extend its life, for reasons to be given in writing. Another new clause ran: "Our Dewan may take any measures which in his opinion shall be necessary for the safety and tranquillity of the state."

The promise of independence had much the same reception as the American model constitution: the Dewan's followers were laudatory, his opponents furiously in opposition. He was now getting support from the Ezhava community; V.K. Velayudhan, back from his government-sponsored studies in England, became the Labour Commissioner; the editor of the Ezhava paper, the *Kaumudi*, was a genuine admirer. The S.N.D.P. Yogam, mindful of past favours and hopeful of more, supported "Independent Travancore," and received a grant of land for a new college.

But the mass of the people were still against him. The new American model was even less attractive than the old. Moreover the idea of United Kerala was taking powerful hold as the Malayalis saw the prospect of Kerala becoming one of the states of the future Indian Union. It gained a powerful recruit in the person of the Maharaja of Cochin (already Congress-oriented), who agreed to inaugurate a Kerala convention in Cochin state. Dr. John Matthai, finance minister in Nehru's Interim Government and a Travancorean, was one of the chief speakers.[7] It was a clear indication that Keralans did not find the idea of an independent sovereign Travancore palatable, and indeed they showed themselves prepared to help the Travancoreans in their fight against it.

The Travancore state Congress organized a conference in Nagercoil on April 9th in which the main topics were the American Model and the independence of Travancore. It was presided over by a Congress minister from Madras, and speakers came from Cochin, British Malabar, Madras presidency and even Pudukottai, the little state surrounded by Madras territory. As it was at that time only a proposal, "Independent Travancore" was not yet a burning issue, but there was great enthusiasm for a linguistic province of Kerala, which speakers emphasized would constitute a "formidable unit". In fact the citizens of Nagercoil, who were almost entirely Tamilians, boycotted the conference and held black flag processions in protest.* Nothing however dampened the enthusiasm of the Malayalis.[8] The other burning topic was the American Model; it was again condemned as totally inadequate, and the conference asked for the formation of an interim government and a constituent Assembly for Travancore, elected on the basis of universal franchise. There was also a resolution that only popularly elected representatives should be sent from Travancore to the Indian Constituent Assembly.

A new Working Committee was elected with Pattom Thanu Pillai still the president, and plans for a new campaign were discussed. Pandit Nehru's threat to states staying out of the Union heartened them, as did the resolutions passed at the Gwalior conference of the A.I.S.P.C. which drew attention to the large number of deaths at Punnapra-Vayalar, and described the detention of over a hundred communists as "a serious curtailment of civil liberties in Travancore." They were sure of the backing of the Indian National Congress and the A.I.S.P.C. in their struggle against the Dewan.

The new campaign, directed mainly against the American Model, was planned for May. It was opened by the most unexpected person, Mannath Padmanabhan, president of the Nayar Service Society, first president (in 1938) of the Travancore National Congress, and hitherto one of Sir C.P.'s most consistent supporter. Mannath was no rat deserting a sinking ship; he did his best for his community. Even in 1946 he began to realize which was the winning side, but he did not declare himself until well into 1947.

At some time (there are no written records) he approached the state

---

* Note by the Editor: There was a separate Travancore Tamilnadu Congress which, according to some accounts, was sponsored by Sir C.P. in order to weaken the hold of the State Congress over the Tamil-speaking population of south Travancore.

Congress leaders and declared his willingness to throw in his lot with them. There was a secret meeting at a house in Parur near the border of Cochin; Mannath was invited and came. They talked far into the night; by 2 a.m. they had decided to start a direct action campaign, which was to be strictly non-violent.

Mannath had hitherto been Sir C.P.'s man, and now he had heard all their secrets. So they bound him to them by the ancient brotherhood oath of the Nayars. A naked sword representing the goddess Durga* was placed before a lighted lamp, and they took an oath to stay together to achieve their aims—in this case to drive out the hated Dewan and to bring in responsible government, or die in the attempt. From this time onwards Mannath was with them heart and soul.

He resigned the presidentship of the Nayar Service Society. In a statement to the daily *Malayala Rajyam* (the Nayars' communal newspaper, for long a supporter of the Palace and the Dewan) he said that he had served the Society for thirty-two years, first as general secretary and then as president.[10] But now he wanted to serve all communities and he was therefore joining the state Congress. He did not resign from the Society, and many Nayars followed him into the Congress. The whole Society became somewhat pro-Congress, and followed the lead of the state Congress in refusing to serve on the Franchise and Delimitation Committee which was to carry out the details of implementing the American Model Constitution.[11]

Mannath began by making a Congress speech in Neyyattinkara, a Nayar stronghold, and the District Magistrate issued an order restraining him from making public speeches for two months. On May 25th the actual campaign opened at Karthikapally, not far from Quilon with a seasoned Congressman, K. Velayudhan Nayar, in the chair. The main point of Mannath's speech was a strong attack on the Dewan; he challenged the theory that criticism of the Dewan was sedition, yet this was the charge on which he jailed his critics. He characterized the Dewan's rule as Ravana Raj (*Ravana* being the black-faced king of the demons), and this phrase caught on as a slogan. Mannath was arrested and tried on a charge of sedition, and sentenced to two years' rigorous imprisonment. A new argument was part of the charge - that his speech might undermine military and police loyalty.[12] Military and police were largely Nayars—was the new charge a straw in the wind?

The immediate effect of the June 3rd Plan of 1947 in Travancore was

---

* Note by the Editor: *Durga* (or Kali) is the goddess of death and destruction.

to make the proposal for an independent Travancore official policy. At one of his lengthy press conferences on June 11th, the Dewan formally announced that, as a result of the decision to divide India, Travancore would become an independent state from August 15th.[13] He repeated all the arguments he had used at the earlier press conference on March 15th when he first put forward the idea, and added "Travancore wants to live its own life. Travancore wants to pursue its own ideals. It is distinct and separate from the rest of India in its culture." This statement would not have been accepted by the bulk of Travancoreans who felt a cultural unity with the rest of Kerala, but Sir C.P. shrugged off the idea of a united Kerala. "This will die a natural death;" Christians and Muslims would be in a worse minority, so Christians and Muslims were against it, "even though Mr. Verghese may say that he will lead an army from United Kerala." Independence would be financially favourable to Travancore; Congress wanted a strong centre which would have extensive powers of taxation, which would reduce the revenues of Travancore to a third. He admitted there was some difference of opinion about the independence of Travancore; but all officials had to work for it, and if they had different views they should resign. His Highness had made his decision and the people must stand by him.

The next day (although the budget session was nearly due) the Legislature was dissolved, and the District Magistrates placed bans on state Congress meetings. When he was criticized for the dissolution of the Legislature, Sir C.P. replied that the dissolution was part of the programme for setting up the new constitution. He now began a series of press conferences and statements to the press defending both the decision to keep Travancore out of the Union and the new constitution. He reiterated that the vast majority of the people of Travancore were in favour of the declaration of independence made by the Maharaja of Travancore; "it is only the group following the mandates of the States Peoples' Conference that wishes to subordinate Travancore to the fluctuating policies of that conference."

A further step towards the effective independence of Travancore was the appointment of a Trade Commissioner to Pakistan (which did not yet exist) in the person of Khan Bahadur Abdul Karim. He had retired from the service of Travancore a few years earlier, but was now recalled ostensibly for a different role.

The Resident, Lt. Col. G.N. Edwards, still attempted to exercise some control over events.[14] On June 17th, he informed the Dewan of the decision to set up the states Department; as a preliminary the states governments should agree to receive agents of the successor governments in their territory and should send their representatives to the appropriate successor government. Sir C.P. refused to discuss any interim arrangements until the independent government of Travancore could freely negotiate with the new Dominion governments; there would have to be quite different arrangements—for instance, Travancore would have complete control of railways in her own territory, (a sore point, this). The Resident sent the Dewan the agenda for the meeting of Princes and their advisers with the Viceroy on July 25th, mainly concerning accession to the Union. Sir C.P. rejected the whole idea of accession as contrary to the declaration of the British Government that with the lapse of Paramountcy the states would be free to enter into federal relationships with a successor government or enter into a particular political relationship. Travancore was perfectly prepared to negotiate after independence, but there was no point in sending representatives to the meeting on July 25th.

Sir C.P. might claim that the "overwhelming majority of the people are behind me;" but inside and outside the state opposition was building up. It might be said that the majority of the people of India, from the Viceroy and the state Department to young school boys in the Travancore villages, were bent on frustrating his schemes.

On all sides there was criticism. The All-India Committee of the A.I.S.P.C., at its meeting on June 12th, declared: "On the lapse of Paramountcy sovereignty resides in the people of the states, and the Princes can only be constitutional rulers embodying the people's will." In a long resolution on Travancore, it criticized the sudden dissolution of the Legislature which made it impossible for any elections to the constituent Assembly to take place through that body. The Committee challenged the Dewan to hold a referendum on the issue of independence for Travancore.[15]

Mahatma Gandhi, at his prayer meeting on June 11th, complained that Travancore had taken Partition as the signal for the Balkanization of India; he too challenged Sir C.P. to hold a referendum. He also wanted to know if there was a ban on Congress meetings in Travancore.

The Dewan had ready answers for his critics. There was no ban on meetings, but District Magistrates banned meetings in places where a breach of the peace was feared. The only people who had been arrested were fourteen Congressmen who had defied the orders. He claimed all communities in the state were in favour of Travancore's independence, and only the state Congress was opposing it (he did not mention Mannath Padmanabhan and his Nayars). The sole decision for the ruler and his people was "whether they prefer outside dictation or will stand together in vindication of honourable independence."

And now the Travancore state Congress made the final plans for resistance, confident of the support of the people of Travancore and of help from outside. Pattom Thanu Pillai and T.M. Verghese went off to Delhi—not now to Gandhi but to Sardar Patel, the "iron man" of the Congress. Even before taking charge of the state Department he was keeping in close touch with states' affairs. What was said is not known; but when Pattom gave a press conference in New Delhi he envisaged a "mighty conflict", though a strictly non-violent one. Government repression would be great but the people were prepared for suffering. There was no constitution in Travancore now; the former one had been repealed, and only a Franchise and Delimitation Committee was in existence which would take years to prepare the electoral rolls. The people were in favour of a United Kerala, but the question could not be settled until Travancore joined the Union.[16]

At a press conference in Madras, on his way back, Pattom was asked if it were true that the Congress High Command had given the "all clear" for an all-out struggle against the Dewan's decision to remain independent, and also if three Committees had been formed in Delhi to raise volunteers, finance and other things for the struggle. Pattom refused to confirm or deny: "I would say that certain arrangements are being made from outside Travancore, particularly from Travancoreans living outside the State."[17] It was the first indication of a conspiracy, of secret plans.

Condemnation of "Independent Travancore" continued from outside. The Kerala Catholic Congress described the Maharaja's "policy of isolation" as detrimental to all Travancoreans and Catholics in particular. The Kerala Provincial Congress Committee urged the National Congress to make it possible for the K.P.C.C. to take part in the Travancore struggle. The Council of the Mar Thoma Church, prudently meeting in Madras, pointed out the damage to Christians if the state were isolated; they would be deprived of opportunities of serving India as a whole. It was a good point as rumours were afloat that if Travancore remained independent, Travancoreans would be dismissed from Government of India service. Even Nehru's cabinet would be affected, for his minister of Finance was Dr. John Matthai, E. John Philipose's brother-in- law. A great meeting was held in Madras addressed by G. Ramachandran to inform the public of events which were not allowed to appear in the press. V.K. Krishna Menon, himself a Keralan, said the Travancore issue was now an all-India one, of a free Travancore in a free India.[18]

The two leaders, Pattom and Verghese, now separated. Verghese stayed on in Madras, while Pattom went on to Ernakulam where the Working Committee met. There he made another statement on June 27th in which he admitted that he had tried to work out a compromise with the government on the American Model, but he had found no statesmanship or respect for the people. Now there was an end to compromise. The projected constitution was a sham, so were the hundreds of telegrams and messages supporting independent Travancore which were extorted by Sir C.P.'s officials with threats and oppression from ration card holders, contractors, bus owners and others dependent on the goodwill of the government. The "five-rupee" police had been revived to disturb meetings, as had happened in 1938.

The leader outlined the programme to be followed: meetings were to be conducted everywhere, both where there was a ban and where there was none, all prohibitory orders were to be disobeyed in a peaceful manner; special attention should be paid to extending passive resistance in the villages; further instructions would be given.[19] The atmosphere of conspiracy deepened.

Within Travancore the struggle intensified. Sir C.P. was determined to drive through his will and to crush all opposition ruthlessly. All Government officials were ordered to hold meetings supporting independent Travancore and to extort letters, resolutions, telegrams by any means in their power; he held so many press conferences that they became a joke in the rest of India. There was an even tighter control of the press.

The state Congress needed no Pattom Thanu Pillai to give them instructions. They held meetings in season and out of season. Literature was smuggled in; the Travancore Defence Committee in Bombay was still smuggling in bulletins cyclostyled in communist Party headquarters; the Working Committee in Ernakulam was also smuggling in bulletins giving reports of meetings within Travancore. It was impossible to prevent the Travancore people from getting news.

K.A. Mathew tells the story of what went on in Tiruvalla.[20] In June a government official, by the name of Tampi, called a meeting in the Town Hall to support "Independent Travancore." K.A. Mathew and his merry men came early and occupied the hall; Tampi and his small band arrived at the correct time to make it almost full. K.A. Mathew was voted to the chair by his supporters, Tampi by his; they both took their seats on the platform. The Congressmen passed a resolution calling for union with India, which was passed by a large majority; Tampi and his party adjourned to a tree in the compound and passed a resolution in favour of independent Travancore; and only the latter was sent to the Dewan. The five-rupee police were not yet in operation. At a later meeting on July 7th hooligans broke up the meetings, and K.A. Mathew, going to the rescue of a young man, was cut about the face, seized and beaten. He was then arrested by the police, who were standing by, and tried and convicted for creating a disturbance.[21] The local people seized the ruffians, who confessed they had been instigated and paid by the police.

There were so many meetings that the District Magistrate gave up trying to stop them; but shortly after they could look to the Special Police to break up meetings. A secret bulletin issued from Ernakulam in the first half of July lists the meetings that were held in different places.[22] In two places the local police inspector told the Congress workers that talks were going on between the government and the Congress leaders and they should cancel the meetings; but the organizers ignored them and went on with their meetings. Abdul Karim was touring the state, organizing the "Special Police" and trying to persuade Muslims to support independent Travancore. The Attorney-General was touring the state also; his meetings were attended only by officials.

XIII.3 Plots against the Dewan

About this time we enter a period of dark plots, secret meetings, secret compacts. By its very nature documentary evidence is not available and one has to rely on verbal accounts, and hints in speeches and newspaper articles. Sir C.P. produced titbits of information at his press conferences; but his intelligence services were not always reliable, neither was he, and one cannot give credence to all his statements. Lord Mountbatten and Sardar Patel were more reliable sources; they certainly knew something of the plotting.

The split in the Congress began to be important. They had already lost the communists some years earlier; but now a second split developed between those who were wedded to Gandhian non-violence, and those who regarded non-violence as a technique of resistance and not a philosophy of life. The truly Gandhian group was led by Pattom Thanu Pillai, and included G. Ramachandran and Akkamma Cherian. But T.M. Verghese and C. Kesavan were not true Gandhians; and it is significant that they had been prepared to work with the communists at the time of the general strike in October 1946.

As the day of independence approached, the sense of urgency

increased, and all agreed that Sir C.P. must be driven out before August 15th so that Travancore could accede to the Union, establish a truly democratic form of government for herself, and eventually join with her fellow Malayalis in a United Kerala. They realized they had to take action amounting to a rebellion, but disagreed about the methods to be used. Pattom adhered to his non-violent principles; but T.M. Verghese and C. Kesavan were prepared to adopt violent methods, and they were supported by a number of the younger Christians, T.A. Abdulla, a leading Muslim lawyer from Alleppey, and some of the younger Nayars.

To complicate matters, it had been discovered that one of the Working Committee (a respectable citizen now, and doing excellent social work, so why drag in his name?) was passing information to Abdul Karim—his messenger had been intercepted with a note on him, but allowed to continue on his errand. So two sets of meetings were held, one which passed relatively harmless resolutions, and one of the inner ring which did the real plotting.

We can distinguish, though not fully describe: (1) a non-violent plot to get rid of Sir C.P. and his government; (2) a violent Congress plot, supported by the communists, to get rid of him; (3) some Army plots, very nebulous, which may simply have been wild talk by hot-headed young officers; (4) what I can only call a semi-non-violent plot which was the one that worked. Of course very few can be dated with any accuracy; but it appears that while some plots were initiated in June, the pace quickened in July, certainly after Pattom Thanu Pillai returned to Travancore after his visit to Delhi, dropping hints on the way, and told his followers in his press statement of June 24th: "Further instructions should be followed when they are issued."

The idea of the non-violent plot, headed by Pattom Thanu Pillai, was to create a "parallel government" to take over post offices, police stations, magistrates' courts and other government offices non-violently.[23] They were confident that the people would support such a move and the officials and police come over to them. This plot was to be put into effect on August 15th if Travancore had not by then acceded to the Union. There were open plans to celebrate August 1st as "Travancore People's Day," and to launch a campaign of civil disobedience on that day. Sardar Patel was kept in close touch with these plans, which he must have discussed with Pattom on his visit to Delhi in June; and this must have inspired Pattom's references in Madras to "certain arrangements" to get help from outside.

All these plans were made in Akkamma Cheriyan's house in North

Travancore from which they could make an easy getaway into the dense forests and find their way to the Cochin frontier. Nothing was written down. It was understood that the leaders were to avoid arrest during the open demonstrations. They knew the rest of India would be with them, and they were cheered by the story (quite unauthenticated but it may be true), that when Sir C.P. had said on June 11th that Travancore could only be forced into the Union by a defeat in war, Jawaharlal Nehru had commented: "If Sir C.P. wants a shooting war, we shall be over the border in five minutes."

T.M. Verghese headed the violent plot. These plotters believed that Sir. C.P. was too well entrenched to be dislodged by non-violent means, and planned a violent uprising. Their first step was to get in touch with E.M.S. Nambudiripad and other local communist leaders at a secret meeting (date unknown), and obtained their undertaking not to start action on their own but to support the Congress leaders from underground.

This was the plan: if Sir C.P. kept Travancore out of the Union after August 15th, there would be an armed uprising in Travancore. The first outbreak would take place in the forests of north Travancore with help from Malabar and Cochin; there would be attacks on government offices, demolition of major bridges and other acts of sabotage. It was expected that the Travancore state Forces would be sent north to put down the rebellion; then the Indian Army (by then of course under the control of the independent government of the Indian Union) would have an armoured division ready in Madurai to enter Travancore by the Shencottah Gap (which has both a railway and a good motor road) on the pretext of "restoring order," take over the capital, dismiss Sir C.P., and instal a popular government.[24] The plot was so much of the same pattern as what happened in Junagadh and Hyderabad that it sounds feasible; but in fact the Indian Army seems to have known nothing about it. Moreover, Sardar Patel was in touch with Pattom Thanu Pillai, whom he liked and trusted, and not with T.M. Verghese.

Sir C.P. was certainly aware that something was afoot, as his remarks at press conferences indicated. In June he boasted that he had reliable information that T.M. Verghese and Pattom Thanu Pillai were contacting the communist leader K.C. George with a view to starting a campaign against the state - also that Verghese had been saying that the Indian National Congress had promised him military help after August 15th and he himself would lead an army into Travancore. On July 5th Sir C.P. complained of a subtle campaign of whispers, insinuations and threats, for instance that an industrialist had made a sum of Rs. 5 lakhs available to T.M. Verghese for propaganda. Another sensational story published by the Free press Journal of Bombay was that a thousand armoured vehicles had been despatched to Travancore on the orders of Army headquarters in Delhi.

No smoke without fire. T.M. Verghese went to Bombay some time early in July, contacted a fellow-Mar Thomite, M.M. Cheriyan, at communist Party headquarters, and they arranged a meeting at the Y.M.C.A. for state Congress supporters. T.M. Verghese asked for money to purchase arms for the "parallel government." It is clear that the "violent" party were aware of the plots of the "non- violent," but intended to supplement them by what they considered the only effective methods. Cheriyan also arranged for T.M. Verghese to meet the communist leaders P.C. Joshi and S.S. Mirajkar of the Bombay Textile Workers' Union, and they promised to collect money for Travancore.[25] T.M. Verghese then went to Delhi in order to meet Patel, but there is no indication that he did so. He next surfaces at the Delhi Y.M.C.A. on July 26th addressing a meeting on Travancore, apparently quite unaware of the dramatic events of the previous day in Trivandrum.

Preparations to implement the "violent" plot certainly went on within Travancore; local leaders were appointed and they were given their secret orders by "friends" who appeared in the middle of the night and disappeared as mysteriously. The "small fry" were trained in the manufacture of small grenades, country guns, acid bombs, guerrilla tactics were planned, also the seizure of government offices, to be handed over to the "parallel government." They planned to encourage defection and mutiny in the ranks of the armed forces and the police, and to smuggle arms from military stores. The "small fry" did not know the whole of the plan, and of course the majority of the Congress leaders were kept in the dark about all these activities.[26]

No full picture is possible, as events overtook these plans, and the success of the semi-non-violent plot made all others superfluous. But they are worthy of mention, as showing the determination of the people of Travancore to win the only kind of freedom for which they cared.

How loyal were the armed forces to the Government of Travancore? There was disaffection in the Indian armed forces, as was shown by the mutiny in the Royal Indian Navy in February 1946, the excitement about the Indian National Army trials, and the existence of a secret society, the *Jawahar Sangh*, among young Indian army officers (but the extent of such secret societies cannot be known). The Travancore state Forces, who had served as units of the Indian Army, may well have been affected by these undercurrents. As early as 1938, the Adjutant to the state Forces, Major Leonard Handley, had complained about the disaffection among the Nayar troops; and the communists claimed to have started a cell in the state Forces that year.

When the Nayar Infantry returned from its war service, the policy of enlargement of the state Forces was announced, to prevent unemployment; and they were not reduced or disbanded. There was a different motive behind the enlargement: the Political Department had advised the Princes to build up their forces against any possible uprising. H.V. Hodson tells the story in *The Great Divide* that when Lord Mountbatten first seriously turned his attention to the states problem and discussed it with Sardar Patel, the latter told him not to bother about the states, as after the transfer of power the states' people would rise, depose their rulers and throw in their lot with the Congress. But the Viceroy reminded him that the states had their own forces, ranging from a division in Hyderabad to personal bodyguards in the small states, who would shoot down the rebels. Sardar Patel said he would think about it. The matter was never put to the test in Travancore, but it may be remarked in passing that when the Indian Army invaded Hyderabad, the State Forces surrendered with suspicious speed.

If the extent of disaffection among serving soldiers is impossible to estimate, the extent of disaffection among ex-servicemen was obvious. Ex-servicemen had drilled volunteers of the Punnapra-Vayalar uprising, and some formed bodyguards for the state Congress leaders. There has come to light a remarkable document, "An Appeal to Ex-Servicemen: shall we fight for Sir C.P.?"[27] It was written by Lieutenant J. Mani, a Travancorean and a communist, serving with the Royal Indian Navy; it was duplicated at communist Party Headquarters and smuggled into Travancore. The document is an eye-opener, relevant to more than Travancore.

It begins by referring to "our benevolent Dewan". At a meeting in Trivandrum on 27th June 1947, to honour the brave sons and daughters who had returned to the states after meritorous war service, he had called on them for their active support in the impending struggle for independence. But Lieutenant Mani pointed out that the Dewan had misruled the country, organized the black market (a frequent but unconfirmed accusation), concealed the appalling conditions of famine in the country, which left the choice to the young men to die of starvation in Travancore or to die fighting for the white man with a full stomach. Now he was trying to fool them by painting them as great heroes to fight and die for maintaining him in power.

"We must see through his sinister game. The Travancorean ex-servicemen will NOT strike a blow in his favour. We shall join in our thousands the Freedom movement in this country and fight the battle for real freedom. Shall we ignore the call to Freedom of our beloved leaders Mahatma Gandhi, Pandit Nehru, and others?... Shall we not respect the wishes of our dear Netaji Subhas Chandra Bose and work for the idea of a united India?" He reminded his readers of the martyrs of August 1942, the I.N.A., the Royal Indian Navy Mutiny of 1946, and "all the other Freedom battles fought for this dear land of ours."

"Ex-servicemen, the time for action has come at last. We must break the chains of slavery now. We want immediate union with the Great Sovereign Republic of India. Let us muster in our thousands, fall into step and march. Forget political and religious differences—if any. The Dewan's press conferences are but eye-washes—don't be carried away. The Dewan repeatedly says he doesn't believe in non-violence. Let him know that there are others who do not believe in non-violence. Give us half the arms and ammunition Sir C.P.'s mercenary army and police hold and then the Dewan's yes-men will search in vain for their present leaders."

At the bottom of the page is typed: "Read, translate, circulate. Time is short."

XIII.4 Exit the Dewan

Time was short. Government of India officials were tearing leaves off specially printed calendars, each page marked "so many days to Independence." Sardar Patel officially took charge of the new state Department on July 1st and Lord Mountbatten turned his attention to states' affairs; they determined to get as many states as possible to accede to the Union before independence.

In Travancore the Dewan, aware that only a swift campaign of ruthless repression could save him and his schemes, intensified his repression; the five-rupee police were revived, his press conferences multiplied and he looked round for his supporters. The S.N.D.P. Yogam were prevailed upon to declare publicly their support for "Independent Travancore."

Deserted by the leading Nayars, he even (rather late in the day) made overtures to the Syrian Christians. This led to a curious episode. K.C. Mammen Mappillay was back in Kottayam, but leaving affairs more and more to his eldest son K.M. Cheriyan. The family wanted to restart the *Malayala Manorama* ; and K.M. Cheriyan, who had taken no part in politics and was acceptable to Sir C.P., went to Trivandrum to begin negotiations. Sir C.P. received him cordially; he was prepared to give him permission to re-open the press, but he made conditions. K.C. Mappillay should express regrets for the reports in the paper on state Congress activities which had led to the seizure of the press in September 1938, and the policy of the paper should be so framed as to support "Independent Travancore." Then he blazed: "If you do not comply, I shall see that you are ruined worse than before!" K.M. Cheriyan said he would consult his brothers.

The family held a council; the old lion roared: "I'll eat mud first!" They decided to make no answer to these conditions, nor to a later telegram. Then Sir C.P. sent a cousin, one of his few Syrian Christian supporters, to ask for an answer within a fortnight. Mammen Mappillay said he would reply within the fortnight, and made arrangements to move his entire family to Madras. But before the fortnight was up it was Sir C.P. who was fleeing to Madras.[28]

The Congress made its preparations; the leaders decided to come out into the open and risk arrest. In Calicut K.A. Damodara Menon organized a bodyguard of 72 volunteers for the leaders; some of them were policemen dismissed for going on strike, some were ex-servicemen—all of them were smart and well-drilled and made the hooligans think twice before getting near them.[29] But the violent and non-violent wings' secret preparations went on; and among the latter a plot within a plot was being hatched.

On July 3rd Pattom Thanu Pillai came out into the open in Kottayam, where he addressed a huge meeting. He hammered away at the twin themes of responsible government and Travancore's joining the Indian Union (United Kerala could wait); the *Hindu* reporter wrote: "He was heard in a pin-drop silence and loudly cheered at the end of the meeting."[30]

On July 5th the Trivandrum Bar Association joined battle with the Dewan. It recorded its view that the proposed declaration of independence of Travancore was detrimental to the best interests of the people of the State. It added its main reason for expressing its views: "The Association views with grave concern that the propaganda started by the Dewan and carried on now by the officials of the state is undermining the fundamentals of the rule of law which have been prevailing in the state for one century or more."

On July 6th the state Congress arranged a meeting at the railway *maidan* to be addressed by Pattom Thanu Pillai; but it was suddenly cancelled. He had heard a story about the plot of the platoon of the

Nayar Infantry who were ordered to disperse the meeting. They had signed on for guard duty at palace, fort and railway station, put in substitutes dressed in their uniforms and carrying dummy rifles with which the recruits usually drilled, while the platoon proposed to go to the meeting dressed in their ordinary clothes, with their rifles and ammunition concealed under their loose shirts, ready to defend the state Congress leaders. Pattom refused to endanger lives and cancelled the meeting in the name of non-violence. He arranged no further meetings.[31]

For a few days nobody dared to call a meeting for fear of the police and their rowdies. But a student found this silence intolerable and called a meeting on his own initiative. Kalathil Velayudhan Nayar was in the chair and C. Narayana Pillai was the chief speaker. It was held on July 13th on the Pettah *maidan*, an open space about a mile from the railway station; about 5,000 people came to it. There were a good many hooligans and drunks in the crowd, and heckling started as soon as Velayudhan Nayar began to speak. Narayana Pillai was also heckled but held his audience. In the course of his speech the Assistant Superintendent of Police arrived with about sixty reserve police armed with *lathis* and rifles. They had clearly expected the meeting to be disorderly by now, which would have given them the excuse to break it up; but the A.S.P., without giving a warning to disperse, ordered his men to charge with *lathis*. Chairman and speaker protested and were beaten for their pains. The people dispersed in panic, and the police were ordered to fire on the retreating crowd. Caught in a narrow lane, three people were killed and some fifteen were injured by bullet wounds. One of the killed was a student called Rajendra—the *maidan* is now called Rajendra *Maidan* in his memory.[32]

Pattom Thanu Pillai collected the facts and issued a statement, which concluded: "Such incidents will not cow down the people. It will only strengthen their resolve to end autocracy in the state."

The government put out its own press note, blaming the state Congress for training volunteers to deal summarily with hecklers and inciting the crowd to throw stones at the police. It was this that led to the *lathi* charges, and the firing was ordered when the crowd became violent. "The situation is now quiet, but these incidents show that the state Congress are definitely embarking on a campaign of violence. They are also inciting students in the colleges to strike." These were the old accusations of 1938; they were no more believed than they were then.

The statement concluded with an appeal to "Patriotic citizens...The question of independence is no longer a live issue and in the course of the next few days the Independence of Travancore will be recognised by the Parliament and the Crown." Public meetings were once more banned and the Trivandrum colleges were temporarily closed "in order that students should not be embroiled in breaches of the peace."[33]

Public opinion both inside and outside the state showed no hesitation in deciding which version of the Pettah shootings to believe. The Trivandrum Municipal Council adjourned on July 15th as a protest against the shootings. "The Mayor hopes the Government will realize the depth of feeling in the country and try to satisfy the popular demand." The Trivandrum Bar Association passed a resolution on July 16th condemning the police firing. The Chief Justice therefore ordered the closing of the Association room in the High Court building to prevent its being used for political purposes. So the Association met at the home of K.P. Abraham (C.P. Matthen's lawyer) to protest against the undertaking required by the Chief Justice not to hold political meetings in the premises of the High Court, and re-affirmed their "inherent rights of free speech, free expression of opinion and free association within their own Association room." The Alleppey Bar Association shared their protest, and students everywhere observed a *hartal*. There were indignation meetings in Madras. News of protest came from as far away as Singapore, where 3,000 Malayalis gathered to condemn the Dewan's policies.

Sir C.P. went on with his policies undisturbed. At a press conference the day after the Pettah firing, referring to the passing of the India Bill in the House of Commons without a division, he repeated his intention to make a treaty with the Indian Union after August 15th. "Travancore having its own state Forces and Police will not ask for any help in the matter of internal security, but is willing to place its forces at the disposal of the rest of India to resist external aggression."

On July 19th the Maharaja broadcast the independence of Travancore from the Trivandrum radio station:

"On and from 15th August 1947, the close and friendly relations that have subsisted for over a century and a half between the British Crown and Travancore will be formally terminated by reason of the renunciation by His Majesty of his suzerainty in respect of the Indian states."

He declared his intention to associate his people with him in the tasks of Government; the material and human resources of the state were abundant and promised a happy and prosperous future. "At this auspicious moment, I call upon all my beloved people to rejoice with me and join me in dedicating ourselves to build anew and in fuller amplitude the fabric of a greater Travancore."

The Maharaja called in vain. The *Travancore Information and Listener* might describe in its "March of Events" column the "rejoicings throughout the state," but the reality was that his beloved people were grimly planning a united effort to destroy the Dewan's castle in the air of an Independent Travancore governed by the American Model constitution, by any means in their power.

The state Congress Committee met in Alleppey on July 20th to make its final plans for the campaign of Direct Action due to start on August 1st. They condemned the iniquities of their tyrannical Dewan, who was suppressing public opinion by "means which no civilized country would adopt. . . But he cannot achieve his ends with the help of hooligans. Popular demonstrations cannot be put down by the use of police and military. The Government of Travancore has lost all moral right to conduct the governing of the state."

It demanded the immediate dismissal of Sir C.P. Ramaswamy Aiyar, the introduction of responsible government, an Interim Government to be set up, a constituent Assembly popularly elected to frame the constitution for Travancore; finally Travancore should join the Union and the Indian constituent Assembly. "The state Congress appeals to all communities to take part in the last fight to remove despotic government and misrule. All people should take care that the struggle is carried on in a non-violent manner. . . . It appeals to the people to abide by the directions given by the president."[34] Sardar Patel was kept fully informed of the decisions of the Committee.

The Dewan however was not in Travancore at this auspicious moment; Lord Mountbatten had invited him to Delhi and he was on his way. In the world of the Princely states he was an elder statesman of considerable stature, and his decision to keep Travancore out of the Indian Union was dangerous. His arguments in the correspondence with the Resident could have serious repercussions: they might well influence those rulers who were not in favour of acceding to the Union. The Viceroy therefore made another effort to win him over.[35]

Sir C.P. was in New Delhi from July 20th to the 22nd, and had a series of interviews, two with the astute Secretary to the states Department, V.P. Menon, and two with Lord Mountbatten. Both played skillfully on his vanity and his fears, and undermined his case for an Independent Travancore.

On July 20th Sir C.P. had an exploratory talk with V.P. Menon, who pointed out the advantages to Travancore of accession. But Sir

C.P. argued that it would be a disadvantage to Travancore as a maritime state, because the centre would take over customs, import and export duties which would take away half Travancore's revenues. V.P. Menon warned him that Travancore and Cochin were hotbeds of communism, and pointed out that if Travancore did not accede to the Union she would be completely on her own after August 15th; communism was a threat to India as a whole, and could only be effectively combated by a strongly integrated political and economic system. Let it not be said of him that at India's critical hour he had failed to make his contribution to the building of a united India when he had the power to do so. Sir C.P. promised to think it over.

Next day he had an interview with the Viceroy. Overnight he had returned to his old position. He began by producing a big file of newspaper clippings and cartoons of himself, then declared that Travancore would never accede to India. Lord Mountbatten played on his fears; he said he had heard that a big industrialist had donated Rs. 5 lakhs to Travancore state Congress funds only that morning. (This was not inherently impossible; T.M. Verghese was in New Delhi at the time). He also played on his vanity; it was a golden opportunity for Travancore to play its part; its accession would be hailed as a great act of statesmanship, and Travancore could have great influence through its representatives in the Dominion Legislature to shape the future of India. But Sir C.P. would not agree to accession, but only to an agreement with the Dominion of India after Independence.

On July 22nd V.P. Menon went to work on him again. An agreement was not enough; signature of the Instrument of Accession was essential. At first Sir C.P. was adamant, but after a second interview with Lord Mountbatten (and there are many stories about what His Excellency said to him) he agreed that accession was inevitable. He asked the Viceroy for a personal letter to the Maharaja setting out the proposals so that he could ascertain His Highness's pleasure; and he returned to Trivandrum with the personal letter and a copy of the Draft Instrument of Accession. He told the Viceroy he had an important engagement in Trivandrum connected with the centenary celebrations of Swati Thirunal, a Maharaja of Travancore who was also a famous musician, on July 25th. He promised to return for further discussions on July 27th. But he failed to keep the appointment. Before that date Travancore history took a sudden lurch.

XIII.5. The Semi-non-violent Plot

"We did not mean to kill him," hissed one of the conspirators to me long afterwards, "killing was too good for him. We meant to send him away from the state humiliated and disgraced—and we succeeded." He added, as he explained the details of the plot: "We knew he was a coward (this was totally unjust; the little man had the reckless courage of a terrier), from his behaviour at the great *Jatha* of 1938,so we knew that it was enough to give him a fright to send him scuttling out of the state."

At the end it was the ancient traditions of the martial Nayars curiously modified by the Gandhian philosophy of non-violence,which gave the final push to the liberation of Travancore from its tyrant. It had been mainly the Nayars who had bound Mannath Padmanabhan by the ancient Nayar oath of brotherhood. Their ancestors, the fighters of feudal times,had always been ready to check tyranny and oppression in their Rajas and get rid of evil advisers. And so, in July 1947, after a century and a half of subordination to the British and exposure to the influences of Western civilization, the spirit of Velu Thampi walked again and they set about freeing their Maharaja and their country from the presence of another hated foreign Dewan.

It was a plot within a plot. Pattom Thanu Pillai and his followers were busy with their non-violent open plans for civil disobedience on August lst and secret plots for the parallel government after August 15th; T.M Verghese and his followers were busy with their plot for a violent uprising if necessary after August 15th to supplement the Gandhians, with the help of the forces of the new Indian Union. But in Trivandrum was an inner circle within Pattom's inner circle, who formed the plot to attack the Dewan himself.

It was largely, though by no means entirely the Trivandrum Nayars whose ancestors had served the *Rajas* for generations and who had close connections with the palace. But I heard the details or at least some of them, on condition I name no names: so against my instincts as a historian I must maintain the cloak-and-dagger atmosphere.

They found a young man to do the deed. They will tell you in Trivandrum that nobody knows who did it; but when you say "Oh but it was so-and-so", they will go into details. Suffice it to say he was a Brahman, and he had a sword-stick. Two days before the festival in honour of Swati Thirunal, he practised on a bust of Sir C.P in front of the Poor House which was the Dewan's pet project, and neatly sliced off its nose. On the day itself they sent Pattom Thanu Pillai off to

Nagercoil with two British journalists to look at a camp for "five-rupee" police. It would make a good story they said. That evening the young man dressed himself in black and blacked his face and hands, and set off on his bicycle, prepared to die in the attempt. He leaned his bicycle against the high wall which surrounds the Music Academy, and climbed over. After the concert, as Sir C.P. came down between the two rows of chairs to get into his waiting car, he leapt forward and attacked him. The brave little man defended himself and his devoted secretary interposed himself between the Dewan and his assailant. Just then Trivandrum was plunged in darkness as all the lights went out (not part of the plot but just an ordinary failure not unfamiliar to Trivandrum residents) and the young man escaped, unaccountably leaving behind a pair of *khaki* shorts as well as his knife. He scaled the wall again, got on his bicycle and pedalled off to a junction where a lorry was waiting for him. He and his bicycle were hauled on board the lorry and they roared off through the night to Madurai. There he took the train to Bombay and turned up at communist Party headquarters, where he had an old classmate who he was sure could arrange for him to go underground.[36]

The police investigated and found out who had done the deed and quietly dropped the case. After all, to do a great right he had done a little wrong, and deserved well of his country. When the dust had settled he returned to Trivandrum and thereafter lived a blameless life, his anonymity protected by a grateful people.

In Trivandrum that night all was excitement and confusion. Sir C.P. was rushed to the General Hospital for preliminary treatment. The Maharaja was informed at once, and immediately ordered the arrest of all members of the state Congress Working Committee. Pattom returning home about 9 p.m. after his fruitless visit to Nagercoil, was astounded to find the District Magistrate and Assistant Superintendent of police waiting to arrest him; he was snatched from his weeping wife and children without any idea why he was being arrested. But Sir C.P. from his bed in the hospital ordered Pattom's release; whatever he said in public, he knew Pattom could have had nothing to do with the affair; and he was home again by midnight. Next morning he issued a press statement deploring the attack, which could only cause grief to those who believed in non-violence, and stressed that the state Congress was wedded to non-violence. But he pointed out the evil effects of the government's attempts to create a terrorist and violent atmosphere, and hoped better counsel would prevail.

The Inspector-General of Police issued a press statement describing the attack as "a deliberate and cold-blooded attempt at assassination for political purposes." Political agitators had recently foresworn non-violence and were planning violent action. Precautions had been taken but a cowardly attack was not anticipated in that part of Trivandrum. (This incidentally drew attention to the fact that the police that night were everywhere except at the scene of the outrage.)

The news made headlines all over India. Lord Mountbatten telegraphed: "My wife and I are shocked at dastardly attack. I trust you will be well enough to continue the profitable discussion we have been having about Travancore and India."[37]

But further discussion was unnecessary. On July 26th, the day after the attack, the Maharaja wired his accession to the Union. It was an event of all-India importance. Lord Mountbatten wrote in his next report to the Secretary of state of India : "The adherence of Travancore after all C.P.'s declarations of independence has had a profound effect on all the other states and is sure to shake the Nizam."

Sadar Patel wired Pattom Thanu Pillai to call off the campaign of Direct Action due to start on August 1st. But the local leaders had won only one of their four battles; those for responsible government, civil liberty and united Kerala were still to be won. They had no intention of stopping the fight simply because Patel and V.P. Menon had landed Travancore in the Union bag. And Sir C.P. was still the Dewan of Travancore.

It appeared nothing had changed. On July 27th arrests and detentions of Congressmen were resumed, but now in connection with the threat of Direct Action. Pattom himself was re-arrested on that day, and by the 29th the whole Working Committee all over the state were inside. But on July 29th Sir C.P. was flown off to Madras for plastic surgery, and on the following day it was publicly announced that His Highness had acceded to the Union. On the 30th all state Congress leaders, a total of 41, were released from jail; and on August 1st "Travancore People's Day" was celebrated with public meetings, without any interference from the police.

There was no moderation of Congress demands. On his release Pattom Thanu Pillai issued a statement which welcomed the decision to join the Union, but the agitation of the state Congress would continue until all their demands were satisfied. Travancore People's Day should therefore be observed with complete non-violence. The situation was still grave. Pattom then left for Delhi to meet Sadar Patel who had sent for him; but whatever was said made no difference to his determination.

On August 15th Travancore should in theory have been celebrating its own independence as a sovereign state in a suitable manner. But Sir C.P. was still in Madras and the government made no arrangements. This did not prevent the Congress people celebrating the birth of the Indian Union, of which they now felt themselves to be part; they held meetings and hoisted flags everywhere. It was the forbidden flag of the Indian Union which fluttered from the flagstaffs, and the police did nothing.

On August 19th Sir C.P. returned from Madras. His last act was to give a farewell party to Col. Edwards, the Resident, and Mrs. Edwards, who had waited to say goodbye to him. He issued his final press statement as Dewan, and resigned on August 19th. The press statement was his apologia; in it he listed his achievements as Dewan, which were many. He had at least set the state on the road to industrialization, and founded a university; these were permanent achievements. He ended with the achievement of Travancore in retaining its position as a sovereign and independent state.

"Long live His Highness and his dynasty; may Travancore always be in the vanguard of progress in all directions!"[38]

That same day he left Trivandrum by plane for Madras, and did not return.

And so the great Dewan passed off the small stage of Travancore into the shadows, to become a forgotten man. From the wings he watched those men who had once been his colleagues in the Indian National Congress, but whom he had for long opposed and criticized, step out into the brilliant light of world history.

XIII. 6 From Union to Responsible Government

On August 20th, 1946, the Maharaja appointed P.G. Narayanan Unnithan to be officiating Dewan. He had a long solid official career, had been Excise Commissioner and was appointed Administrative Secretary to the Dewan, and had acted for him since the attack on July 25th. He was universally liked and trusted, and was specially welcome now as "a son of the soil." He was a personal friend of Pattom Thanu Pillai.

At what point in the story he got in touch with Pattom on political matters is not known. But as soon as he was fully in charge, he sent for him openly, and by August 23rd had initiated talks with representatives of different political and communal organizations in the state, and of different interests represented in the Legislature, such as industries, planters and commerce. He met Thanu Pillai several times.[39]

But the state Congress did not relax its efforts. The Working Committee met at Alleppey on August 20th, and decided on Direct Action to secure an Interim Government composed of popular representatives, an elected constituent Assembly to form a democratic constitution, and popularly elected representatives in the Indian constituent Assembly. Volunteers were enrolled and there were daily meetings in the capital and other centres. Various bodies joined the agitation: the state Muslim League, the Kerala Catholic Congress—and needless to say, the Travancore Students' Congress. The ban on meetings still in force—was completely ignored. The talks however were going well, and journalists in Trivandrum gave optimistic reports of a quick settlement.

On September 4th the result of the negotiations was announced in another sensational Royal Proclamation, which granted full responsible government to Travancore. Here are the relevant passages:[40]

"WHEREAS in pursuance of Our policy of freely satisfying popular aspirations, we promulgated the constitution Act of 1122 with the widest possible franchise viz. adult franchise as its main feature.

AND WHEREAS in further pursuance of such policy it is now Our pleasure that the constitution Act of 1122 should be revised with a view to establishing Responsible Government without prejudice to Our rights and prerogatives;

NOW THEREFORE We are pleased to command that a Representative Body consisting of persons popularly elected on the base of adult franchise should be constituted and they should consider and submit to Us a draft for the review or modification of the constitution Act, with a view to the establishment of Responsible Government."

A press communique issued on the same day announced that the government was appointing a small committee to be known as the Proclamation Preliminary Committee, to suggest steps to be taken for the election of the members of the Representative Body.

Nobody quarrelled now with the method of Royal Proclamation. Nobody quarrelled with anything. The people had everything they wanted. Everybody's face was saved (even, quite literally, Sir C.P.'s; the surgeons in Madras made an excellent job of it). In Trivandrum they poured into the streets and made their way to the railway station *maidan*, where there was a public meeting of about 50,000 people. The state Congress leaders compared the excitement to that which greeted the Temple Entry Proclamation.

On September 19th the personnel of the Proclamation Preliminary Committee was announced. There were fifteen names; the only official member was the Legal Remembrancer, who was on the Committee in an advisory capacity and had no vote. Half of them were Congressmen; Pattom Thanu Pillai, T.M. Verghese and C. Kesavan were together again; Mannath Padmanabhan who had in the end earned his place; T.A. Abdullah to represent the Muslims; old Mr. Govindan, president of the S.N.D.P. Yogam—a truly representative gathering.

The officiating Dewan, who won the praise of all for his good sense, helpfulness and spirit of cooperation, opened the first meeting of the Committee on September 23rd. He stressed that there was not a single official or nominated member on it, apart from the Legal Remembrancer who had no vote. The selection of members had been guided by the recommendations of important organizations. He hoped that in view of the decision to introduce responsible government, there would be a change in the programmes and propaganda of the important organizations in the state. It was really superfluous to say this; Pattom Thanu Pillai had already publicly expressed his thankfulness that direct action was no longer necessary.

Pattom was unanimously elected chairman of the Committee; it got quickly to work, and produced its report, of what was practically a draft constitution, on November 6th. This was quick work; but a draft constitution had in fact been drawn up already by E. John Philipose and T.K. Nilakanta Pillai and some others, sitting quietly in Nilakanta Pillai's house along that lonely road where he had once been set upon by Sir C.P.'s hooligans.

The Franchise Committee, which had started its work in mid-August, completed its task by mid-October; there was an electorate of nearly three million adults.

The elections to the Representative Body, the first in Indian history to be held on the basis of adult franchise, were held in February 1948. The Congress were returned by a huge majority; the following were the results :

Travancore state Congress: 97

Travancore Tamilnadu Congress (those Tamilians from south Travancore who wished to join Madras) : 14

Muslim League : 8

Independent : 1

So 111 of the 120 members were Congressmen. Even allowing for the human tendency to jump on the band-wagon, it was an impressive total. Three of the members were women; Akkamma Cheriyan, standing for Congress in her home town, was returned unopposed.

The first meeting was held on March 20th, with the officiating

Dewan in the chair. He read out a royal message of greetings. It referred to the constitutional development of Travancore since 1888 when it was the first Indian state to have a Legislative Council, down to the grant of responsible government in September 1947. Travancore was the first state to have responsible government as well as the first to introduce universal suffrage.

After the swearing in of members, the House proceeded to the election of a president. The officiating Dewan announced that there was only one nomination, that of A.J. John, and he was duly declared elected. The Dewan vacated the chair, and Pattom Thanu Pillai led the veteran Congressman to the chair.

The first act of the Representative Body was to pass a bill establishing an Interim Government. By its provisions the Representative Body was invested with the powers and functions of a Legislative Assembly, and a constitutional Monarchy was established. The relevant clauses of the Travancore Interim constitution Act, passed in the name of the Maharaja, state that the executive authority of the state shall be exercised by the Maharaja on the advice of a Council of Ministers; and any bill passed in the Legislative Assembly shall be submitted for the royal assent. The bill was submitted to His Highness on March 23rd who signed it and it became law.

A press note issued the same day announced : "The administration of the state is entrusted to a cabinet of three Ministers. The Prime Minister and the two Ministers newly appointed by His Highness the Maharaja have accordingly today taken the oath of office and assumed charge of their duties. The Dewan has relinquished charge of his office. The Ministers will function as a Cabinet or Council collectively responsible to the Legislature : . . . . Mr. Pattom A. Thanu Pillai is the Prime Minister, and the other Ministers who form the Cabinet are Mr. T.M. Verghese and Mr. C. Kesavan."

The long fight was ended. Almost exactly ten years after the Travancore State Congress was founded to fight for responsible government under the aegis of His Highness the Maharaja of Travancore, the leader of the fight took office as the first prime minister of the state of Travancore.

Chapter XIV

POSTSCRIPT

The people of Travancore, of whom the Travancore State Congress had been the chief mouthpiece, had achieved two of their aims by 1948, union with India, and a fully democratic constitution under the aegis of the Maharaja. He became Governor of the new state of the Union, with the courtesy title of *Raj Pramukh.** He was a model constitutional monarch.

Soon the people of Travancore achieved their third goal of a United Kerala. It was developed in two stages. In 1951 Travancore and Cochin were merged into one state of the Union, Travancore-Cochin. The old Maharaja stepped down in favour of the younger Prince,** and His Highness of Travancore became the *Raj Pramukh.* In 1956, with the reorganization of India into linguistic states, Travancore-Cochin and Malabar were joined together to form the state of Kerala, and the southern Tamil-speaking tip of Travancore was cut off and attached to Tamilnadu. Thus the artificial division of the Malayalam-speakers was healed, and a unit with its own distinctive language and culture emerged. At this point the Maharaja retired from public life and the governors of Kerala were nominated from New Delhi.

The Maharaja, then, became in effect a private citizen, though retaining his titles and privileges until 1972. After the fall of Sir C.P. Ramaswamy Aiyar, the Maharani took no part in the political life of the country, and devoted herself to the care of her family. All Princely titles, privileges and pensions were swept away in 1972. The Maharaja's sister, known as the First Princess, had only daughters. Her husband became Director of the Tourist Bureau of Kerala, and her elder daughter took a degree in French and became lecturer in French at the Women's College in Trivandrum. The Maharaja's younger brother, the Elaya Raja, took himself and his family off to Bangalore, where his

---

* Note by the Editor: The title of *Raj Pramukh*, constitutional monarch, was generally given to rulers who continued to be governors of their own states after independence.

** Note by the Editor: The "old Maharaja" refers to the ruler of Cochin and the "Younger Prince" to the ruler of Travancore. Personal relations were strained between them, especially at the time of the merger.

aunt the former Maharani Regent was already comfortably settled, and started a plastics factory. The younger generation of the erstwhile royal family are indistinguishable from the other charming young things that make up the smart set of Bangalore.

The massive unity displayed by the people in their final struggle for freedom did not last. Sir C.P. Ramaswamy Aiyar was unquestionably right in the contention that the American type of constitution was more suited to Travancore than the Westminster model, and his reference to the unhappy state of French political life was all too apt. Within six months the State Congress Party was riven with dissension and broke up into a number of smaller parties. Travancore, and later Kerala, became noted for the instability of its ministries; and it was largely disillusionment with the Congress Party that brought about the Communist Government of 1957. But never again (apart from the Muslim League) did party divisions fall along communal lines, and although communalism still exists, it has never returned to the bitterness of the thirties.

Pattom Thanu Pillai took part in the shifting politics of Travancore and later Kerala for several years; but he was too accustomed to the older ways of governing to be a success as a premier. He would have made a very good Dewan, just as Sir C.P. would have made a very bad premier: for the two men had been brought up in the tradition more than two thousand years old, of authoritarian rule under the Rajas. He ended his days as Governor of Andhra Pradesh, respected by all.

His former comrades, T.M. Verghese and C. Kesavan, both took their turn at being chief minister of Travancore. Akkamma Cheriyan also remained in politics for some years, until it became too corrupt and petty for her; she married a man who, like herself, had been too involved in the freedom struggle to think of matrimony, and they lived happily ever after, as the fairy stories say—poor, but content to have made the sacrifices which brought freedom to their country.

G. Ramachandran, never as at home in politics as in social services, got back to the service of the rural poor; and with his doctor wife, and Dick Keithahn, rural secretary of the International Fellowship, and his doctor wife, started a rural reconstruction centre called Gandhigram, which has grown into a great institution for training rural social workers, a beacon light to a whole area in Tamilnadu. K.C. Mammen Mappillay revived the *Malayala Manorama*, and after his death his son took it over and it is still run by the family. Its circulation is roughly equal to that of the *Manchester Guardian.*

And Sir C.P. himself? When his wounds were sufficiently healed, he went to Delhi to stay with his old friend Sardar Patel. After a suitable interval he began to feel his way towards some distinguished post in the service of his country. President S. Radhakrishnan was sympathetic; they were old friends and fellow south Indian Brahmans—an ambassadorship perhaps? But the Prime Minister of India was adamant. They had been joint secretaries of the Indian National Congress in 1916. "This man's perfidy," he said, "is too recent to be overlooked". So they gave him the Vice-Chancellorship of Annamalai University; and he displayed the same energy and devotion to his task as did Cardinal Wolsey as Archbishop of York after he lost the favour of Henry VIII. He finally retired to Ootacamund to write his memoirs, and became the greatest ornament of its society, loved by all, retaining to the end his brilliance and charm. He died in London at the age of 87, while on a lecture tour of England. A marvellous old man.

And so the whirligig of time brings its revenge.

NO ELEPHANTS FOR THE MAHARAJA

EPILOGUE

1972. An ancient Rolls-Royce leaves the palace on the hill above the town, where the grass grows high on the once trim lawns, and makes its way down to the ancient temple in the old city of Trivandrum, capital of Kerala, state of the Indian Union. In it is a slight elderly figure with a lined face; nobody takes the slightest notice of him. A leading communist who had frequently been put in jail by the former Government of Travancore, but has since been a minister in the Communist Government of Kerala, comments with an amusement in which there is no malice or vindictiveness: "There goes His Ex-Highness, still going to present his job-card to the Almighty, as he did every morning when he ruled the State."

But now a popularly-elected government rules the state. The pomp and ceremony of Princely rule are gone; the gorgeous Durbars and religious processions are only a fading memory. And now there are no elephants for the Maharaja.

NOTES

For background material on Travancore I have used chiefly three books. The *Travancore State Manual* (1940), by T.K. Velu Pillai, is a mine of information, though as it is a Government publication, its presentation of political events tends to be one-sided. *The Census of India 1931*, Volume XXXVIII, Travancore, is another important source of information. I have chosen the census for that year because it is nearest in time to the troubled decade of the thirties. A. Sreedhara Menon's *A Survey of Kerala History* (Kottayam, 1967) gives an admirable survey of social and cultural history as well as of political history, except that in his account of recent social reforms he omits significant changes in the Syrian Christian communities. The gap however is adequately filled by *The Indian Churches of St. Thomas*, by C.P. Mathew and M.M. Thomas (Delhi, 1967). K.M. Panikkar's *A History of Kerala* (Annamalai University, 1960) is another most valuable history. Thurston's *Castes and Tribes of Southern India*, written in 1908, remains an authority on the subject.

CHAPTER I

Chief books consulted :

Barton 1934.
Cambridge History of India 1964.
Sitaramayya 1946-47, vol.2.

CHAPTER II

1 Letter from the Resident, Lt.-Col. E. Cadogan, to the Governor of Madras, 1832.
2 Panikkar 1960.
3 Ambedkar 1945.
4 Mathew & Thomas 1967.
5 Panikkar 1960.

CHAPTER III

From about 1830 the Reports of the Residents to the states of

Travancore and Cochin become valuable sources of information. Reports were made fortnightly, and special subjects, such as the character of a new Maharaja in 1885, or the proposed constitutional reforms in 1932, were dealt with in longer special papers. These are to be found in the papers of the Government of India Political Department (Political and Secret).

1 From a prayer in a Christian ashram.
2 Political Department: Council of Madras Presidency, Paper no. 7 of 1859. Minute by Mr. Walter Elliot, 3 March 1859.
3 Paper no. 7 of 1859 (see previous note).
4 Mahadev Desai 1937 and Andrews 1929.
5 Madras Residency Records : Letter from the Resident to Travancore to the Dewan of Travancore, 9 September 1886.
6 Resident's Fortnightly Report for the first half of December 1924.
7 Mathew & Thomas 1967.
8 I have relied almost entirely on newspaper reports for this subject, which cries out for fuller research.
9 Madras Residency Records: Resident's report of 24 August 1885.
10 Ramakrishnan Nair 1964.
11 Madras Residency Records: Note on the Administration of Travancore, 3 June 1914, by Dewan P. Rajagopalachari.
12 Madras Residency Records: Paper on the Legislative Council Regulation of 1921, G.O. 399 dated 25 August 1921.
13 Ibid.
14 I am indebted to Miss Doris Watts for this legend; she was a mine of information about the Ruling Family.
15 Proceedings of the Sri Mulam Popular Assembly, 28 February 1928.

CHAPTER IV

The Resident's Fortnightly Confidential Reports (F.R.) to the Government of Madras, and later to the Political Secretary of the Government of India, form a useful foundation of facts on which to build the remainder of the material. The most valuable book on the development of the communal problem, though inevitably biased, is that published by the All Travancore Joint Political Congress, *Travancore: The Present Political Problem* (Calicut, 1934). The

Travancore Government publications, *The Travancore Public Service Recruitment Committee Report*, 1933 and the *Travancore Service Recruitment\Manual*, 1937, deal adequately with the communal problem in the Public Services.

1 Author's diary.
2 *Madras Mail*, 7 November 1931.
3 Author's diary, together with the Resident's "Impressions of Travancore" (Pol. Dept. No. 739 P(S) 1938). These are shrewd assessments of character, but necessarily superficial, compared with my knowledge of them as their servant. I take full responsibility for the opinions expressed.
4 Author's diary.
5 Political Department File "Impressions of Travancore" (see note 3).
6 Resident's Fortnightly Report for first half of November 1931.
7 Political Department File No. 400 P(S) of 1938.
8 Author's diary.
9 Namboodiripad 1967.
10 *Travancore State Manual* 1940, Ch. XXXVI.
11 All Travancore Joint Political Congress 1934.
12 Madras Residency Records: letter from Resident to Governor of Madras, 31 July 1891.
13 Joint Political Congress (Note 11).
14 Madras Residency Records: G.O. No. 158 of 5 December 1932.
15 Joint Political Congress (Note 11).
16 This is fully described in the Political Agent's Fortnightly Reports.
17 Government of Travancore communique.
18 *Travancore Service Recruitment Manual* 1937.
19 Government communique.
20 *Report of the Commission for Franchise and Delimitation* 1937.
21 Proceedings of the Sri Mulam Assembly, 21 June 1937.

CHAPTER V

On the Temple Entry Proclamation the chief book is Mahadev Desai's *The Epic of Travancore* (1937). Dr. B.R. Ambedkar's *What Congress and Gandhi have done to the Untouchables* (1945) is savage but probably justified, and the facts can be relied on. *The Report of the Temple Entry Enquiry Committee* (Trivandrum: Government Press, 1935) is of interest far beyond the immediate question. The Resident's Fortnightly Reports, 1932-1937, Mr. Gandhi's weekly *Harijan*, the *Madras Guardian*, a Christian weekly, the Church Missionary Society's periodical *Outlook* for the years 1936 to 1939, contain insights from different points of view.

1 Keer 1961.
2 Proceedings of the Sri Mulam Popular Assembly, 1921.
3 *Report of the Temple Entry Enquiry Committee*, 1935.
4 *Times of India*, 10 November 1932.
5 Stuart 1936.
6 Desai 1937.
7 *Harijan*, 9 May 1936.
8 Author's diary.
9 Author's diary. Many of my colleagues in the Government Women's College were caste Hindus.
10 See *Outlook* 1936-1939.

CHAPTER VI

1 This section is based on the author's diary, personal letters, and correspondence with A.A. Paul.
2 Madras *Guardian*, October 1936.
3 Resident's Fortnightly Report, first half of May 1937.
4 Proceedings of the Sri Mulam Assembly.
5 The *Malayala Manorama*.
6 Proceedings of the Sri Mulam Assembly.
7 I am indebted for this inside information to Mr. J.W. Tolson, member of the "European Planters' Association," who gave us a blow-by-blow account of the debate at the European Club each evening. He himself was approached but did not vote.
8 Author's diary.
9 "The Way Through," the report on the Council Meeting, Madras, 1938. I have also drawn on my diary.

CHAPTER VII

The History of the Indian National Congress by P. Sitaramayya is a valuable reference book, as are the files of *Harijan*. The Madras daily

The Hindu gives considerable space to Congress activities in the southern Native States from 1921 onwards.

1 This was in fact G. Ramachandran.
2 Political Department File No. 307 P(S) 38.
3 *The Hindu*, 29 July 1921.
4 Resident's Fortnightly Report, first half of April 1925.
5 This was very fully reported in *The Hindu.*
6 Fortnightly Report for the first half of September 1937.
7 Political Department File No. 739 P(S) 38.
8 Ibid.
9 Political Department File No. 89-IA of 1937.
10 Proceedings of the Sri Mulam Assembly, 29 July 1937.
11 Fortnightly Report to Viceroy, August 1937.
12 Author's diary.
13 Proceedings of the Sri Chitra State Council, 1 December 1937.
14 Proceedings of the Sri Mulam Assembly, 25 January 1938.
15 *Travancore Today: Her Struggle for Freedom*, 1938.
16 Proceedings of the Sri Mulam Assembly, 2 February 1938.
17 *Travancore Today*, supplemented by author's diary and letters home, and by interviews with leading politicians.

CHAPTER VIII

In a propaganda war accounts tend to be one-sided. But I must necessarily depend on my personal judgment of the characters of the leading contestants, all of whom I knew well, in assessing their factual accuracy and honesty of interpretation. The major source book is *Travancore Today: Her Struggle for Freedom* (Cochin 1938). The facts, insofar as I could check them, are correct, but I have no means of assessing the accuracy of the accusations against the Dewan. I have drawn largely on my diaries and letters home for this and the next chapter. My sympathies were strong for the State Congress, but I trust time has corrected any bias.

Newspaper accounts must be treated with caution: the *Madras Mail* accepted the accounts of the Associated Press of India, which received a substantial subsidy from the Government of Travancore; *The Hindu* was favourable to the Congress, and on the whole gave the Congress version. Government communiques were very distorted, State Congress statements somewhat less so. The Resident was inclined to base his confidential reports uncritically on the Dewan's version of events. His account of the episode at the Science College on July 15th is excellent; he witnessed much of it himself and got fuller details from Colonel Watkis and myself. C. Narayana Pillai, whom I interviewed several times in 1972, was compiling a source book of documents on the history of Travancore State Congress; his statements are reliable.

1 C. Narayana Pillai, interview; Akkama Cheriyan, interview.
2 C. Kesavan, interview.
3 Details supplied by his sister, Mrs. Mariam Eappen.
4 All India States Peoples' Conference (A.I.S.P.C., Nehru Library, New Delhi). Letter from K. Kumar to Dr. P. Sitaramayya, 21 April 1938.
5 A.I.S.P.C. papers (undated and unsigned).
6 Mannath Padmanabha Pillai, Autobiography.
7 *Harijan*, 9 July 1938.
8 Pattom Thanu Pillai Papers (Nehru Library, New Delhi).
9 Author's diary.
10 *Travancore Today.*
11 Pattom Thanu Pillai Papers.
12 Both the *Madras Mail* and *The Hindu* give full coverage.
13 *Travancore Today.*
14 Ibid.
15 Ibid.
16 Fortnightly Report for second half of May 1938. *Madras Mail*, 13-17 May 1938.
17 C. Narayana Pillai, interview.
18 *Travancore Today.*
19 Political Department File No. 476 P(S) 38, parts I and II.
20 C. Narayana Pillai, interview.
21 *Harijan*, 14 January 1939.
22 Political Department File No. 330 P(S) 38, parts I and II.
23 C.P. Matthen, *I Have Borne Much* (privately printed).
24 Fortnightly Report for July 1938 (I kept a full record of events and talks in my diary).
25 Proceedings of the Sri Chitra State Council.
26 Author's diary.
27 Author's diary.

CHAPTER IX

The Resident's Confidential Fortnightly Reports (F.R.s) give the factual framework of this complex period, but they need to be supplemented from other sources, such as the files of *Harijan*, the Pattom Thanu Pillai papers, and the accounts given me many years later by a number of the participants on the State Congress side. The secret files of the Political Department concerning agitation in the states in the years 1938-39 are invaluable; but it is striking that at no time were the Political Department of the Government of India—and therefore the India Office in London—apprised of the real character of the State Congress leaders.

1 M.M. Varkey, interviewed by author.
2 Political Department File No. 476 - P(S) 38, part II.
3 Fortnightly Report (F.R.) of first half of September. See also *The Hindu*.
4 Ibid. also see author's diary.
5 F.R. and author's diary. Report of Y.C.C.A.'s Relief Committee.
6 F.R. and author's diary.
7 F.R. and *Malayala Manorama.*
8 *The Hindu.*
9 The *Malayala Manorama*. The editor, interviewed by author in 1972.
10 F.R.
11 M.M. Varkey, Akkama Cheriyan, interviewed by author.
12 Author's diary; figures supplied by Police Commissioner.
13 M. Velayudhan Nair, interviewed by author.
14 F.R.
15 K.C. George, interviewed by author.
16 G. Ramachandran, interviewed by author.
17 *Madras Guardian*, passim. Author's diary.
18 John 1972.
19 Report of the Ad Hoc Relief Committee, 1939. I am indebted to Mr. K.N. Karunakaran Nair for arranging the translation from Malayalam.
20 V.D. Savarkar Papers (Nehru Library, New Delhi).
21 Ibid.
22 Political Department File No. 476 P(S) 1938, part II.
23 Political Department File No. 647 P(S) 1938.

24 F.R. for second half of December 1938.
25 Author's diary. I received accounts of the visit from both the Resident and Dr. Hatch, who accompanied him.
26 Pattom Thanu Pillai papers.
27 Pyarelal Nair, Gandhi's personal secretary, interviewed by author.
28 A.I.S.P.C. papers (Nehru Library, New Delhi).

CHAPTER X

The chief sources for this chapter are the Secret Papers of the Political Department, including the Residents' Fortnightly Reports on the Madras States. The Memorandum of the Political Department of the India Office for the information of His Majesty's Government is also most illuminating. Sir William Barton was then one of the Advisers to the India Office on matters concerning the Princes, and his views, set out in his book *The Princes of India*, written in 1934, have clearly influenced the Memorandum. On the Travancore Bank case, C.P. Matthen's book *I Have Borne Much* (privately printed in 1943), though biased and in some places inaccurate, contains much useful information. The chief sources are however the two files on the case to be found in the National Archives of India, New Delhi.

1 Political Department File No. 307 P(S) 1938. Congress activities in the States.
2 Ibid.
3 Ibid.
4 *Asiatic Review,* 1939: 706.
5 Madras Residency Records. Note on the proposed Bill for the Extension of the Legislative Council, 11 July 1921.
6 Resident's Fortnightly Report for first half of July 1938.
7 Political Department File No. 476 P(S) 1938, part II. Agitation in Travancore.
8 Author's diary.
9 Political Department File No. 739 P(S) 1938. Impressions of Travancore.
10 Political Department File No. 647 P(S) 1938. Congress Agitation and Policy.
11 Ibid.
12 Political Department File Nos. 330 of 1938 and 1(35) of 1941.

13 Matthen, *I Have Borne Much.* 1943: 155.
14 Ibid. Appendix 5. Appeal by Mrs. C.P. Matthen.
15 *Travancore: The Present Political Problem.* 1934.*
16 Political Department File No. 330 P(S) 1938.
17 Political Department File No. 400 of 1936. Correspondence on the appointment of Sir C.P. Ramaswamy Aiyar as Dewan of Travancore.
18 Political Department File No. 476 P(S) 1938, part II.
19 *The Hindu*, August 27 1938.

CHAPTER XI

The Resident's Confidential Fortnightly Reports (F.R.s) form, as always, a useful framework of facts, and in this period are more reliable and unbiased than in the previous period. The secret files of the Political Department are also important. A new publication of the Government of Travancore, started in 1940, the monthly *Travancore Information,* blossoming into the *Travancore Information and Listener* in 1943 when Travancore started its own radio station, is the source of much information; its non-political articles are excellent, and it contains the full text of Government Press releases and communiques; but anything touching political matters tends to be biased. A recent book, *The Youth Christian Council of Action*, by G.M. John (Bangalore, 1972) throws light on the big part played by the Christians both in social service and in keeping alive the Travancore State Congress. Many old freedom fighters gave me much information, otherwise unobtainable.

1 Sitaramayya 1946-7, vol. 2.
2 Proceedings of the Sri Mulam Assembly, July 1941.
3 F.R. for first half of September 1939.
4 Travancore State Congress, Working Committee Statement to the Press, 27 March 1940.
5 *Harijan*, 7 October 1939.
6 John 1972.
7 *Harijan*, 7 October 1939.
8 Papers of the All India States Peoples' Conference

* Note by the Editor: Some kind of error seems to have crept into this reference since Skrine did not become Resident before 1936, while the bank crash took place in 1938 only.

(A.I.S.P.C.).
9 Political Department File No. 16 (28) P(S) 1940 and 46 (2) P (Secret).
10 John 1972.
11 F.R.s and the special Famine Number of *Arunodayam*, Nov. - Dec. 1941.
12 F.R.
13 Information supplied by the editor of *Kaumudi*, an Ezhava newspaper.
14 F.R.s.
15 Political Department File No. 11 (35) P(S) 1940. Intelligence reports regarding Madras States.
16 *Harijan*, 21 October 1940.
17 F.R.
18 Ibid.
19 Ibid.
20 *The Hindu*.
21 Ibid.
22 Ibid.
23 F.R.
24 *The Hindu*.
25 Political Department File No. 62 P/41 (Sec) of 1941.
26 F.R. for first half of August 1941.
27 F.R. for second half of December 1941.
28 F.R. for second half of April 1942.
29 F.R. for second half of October 1942.
30 A.I.S.P.C. papers.
31 F.R. for first half of July 1942.
32 F.R. for first half of June 1941.
33 F.R. for first half of October 1941.
34 F.R. for second half of November 1941.
35 F.R. for second half of January 1942.
36 F.R. for first half of May 1942.
37 F.R. for first half of July 1942.
38 F.R. for first half of May 1942.
39 C. Narayana Pillai interviewed by the author.
40 Ibid.
41 F.R. for first half of August 1942.
42 F.R.s from August 1942 to March 1943.
43 Political Department File No. 12 (12) P(S) 42. Congress Agitation in Madras States.

44 Ibid.
45 F.R. for first half of August 1942.
46 Political Department File No. 12 (12) P(S) 42.
47 Ibid.
48 Sitaramayya 1946-47, vol. 2: 377 ff.
49 *Madras Mail*, 23 August 1943.
50 F.R.s for 1943 and 1944. Detailed reports of the food situation in the two states of Travancore and Cochin were regularly appearing during the famine.
51 F.R.s for 1944.
52 F.R. for first half of September 1943.
53 F.R.s for 1944.
54 *Travancore Information and Listener* (*T.I.L.*), July 1944.
55 *T.I.L.*, March-April 1944.
56 Ibid. The correspondence is given in full.
57 F.R. for first half of April 1944.
58 *T.I.L.*, May 1944.
59 Ibid.
60 F.R. for second half of June 1944.
61 The *Deepika* (The Light) of Kottayam, 24 June 1944.
62 K.A. Mathew, interviewed by author.
63 F.R. for second half of July 1944.
64 Proceedings of the Sri Mulam Assembly.
65 Proceedings of the Sri Mulam Assembly and Sri Chitra State Council.
66 F.R.s for 1944 and 1945.
67 F.R. for second half of August 1945.

CHAPTER XII

Most of the matter of this chapter is well documented. But anything written or said about the Punnapra-Vayalar riots and their bloody suppression comes from sources which were by no means objective. I have had to do my best with what I could gather. The powerful hatred against the Dewan they engendered is however an incontrovertible fact.

1 I have used Phadnis 1968 and V.P. Menon 1956 for this section.
2 A.I.S.P.C. papers (Nehru Library, New Delhi).
3 Phadnis 1968.
4 *Madras Mail*, 13 June 1946.

5 K.M. Panikkar, interviewed at Oxford, 1958 (tape recording at St. Anthony's College, Oxford).
6 *Malayala Manorama* archives.
7 This section is based chiefly on the Political Department File No. 26 (43) IA/45 of 1945, "Christian Grievances re: Primary Education". I have also drawn on a pamphlet by Mr. Joseph Thaliath, retired Chief Justice of Travancore, *Truth about the Travancore Educational Policy*, Trivandrum, 1946, and the pamphlet (undated) of the Travancore Peace Bloc, Note on the *Present Position of Christians in Travancore.*
8 Thaliath 1946.
9 *The Hindu*, 26 February 1947.
10 Political Department File No. 239 P(S) 46 of 1946.
11 I am indebted to Mrs. V.V. Varkey (Akkamma Cheriyan) for an original paper.
12 I am indebted to Mr. K.A. Mathew for the details of this episode; the *Deepika* also published the story.
13 This has become a folk memory in Kerala.
14 *Travancore Information and Listener (T.I.L.)*, March 1946.
15 I am indebted to P.K. Chandrananda for this information; he wrote a paper for me on the whole subject.
16 *T.I.L.*, March 1946.
17 See following chapter, p.264.
18 This verbal warfare is fully reported in the *Madras Mail*, between 29 October and 1 November 1946.
19 I am indebted to Mr. M.M. Cheriyan, Advocate, for this information.

CHAPTER XIII

For the all-India background H.V. Hodson's *The Great Divide* (Hutchinson, 1969) is invaluable. *The Travancore Information and Listener* (*T.I.L.*) faithfully records all the Dewan's speeches and much else besides. I have drawn very largely on what was told me by those who had actually taken part in the events described, and lent me documents of the time. *The Hindu* gave full coverage of Travancore affairs.

1 *T.I.L.*, December 1946.
2 Ibid. March 1947.
3 Ibid. April 1947

4 *The Hindu*, 23 March 1947.
5 *The Hindu*, 8 May 1947.
6 *T.I.L.*, May 1947.
7 *The Hindu*, 3 April 1947.
8 Ibid. 11 April 1947.
9 The information was given me (at different times and places) by two Congressmen who took part in the ceremony. It has become part of folk history.
10 *Malayala Rajyam*, 22 May 1947.
11 *T.I.L.*, June 1947.
12 *Malayala Rajyam.*
13 See *T.I.L.*, for all the Dewan's statements.
14 Pattom Thanu Pillai Papers.
15 *The Hindu,* 14 June 1947.
16 Ibid. 20 June 1947.
17 Ibid. 23 June 1947.
18 *The Hindu* reports all these meetings.
19 *Malayala Manorama* archives.
20 I am indebted to Mr. K.A. Mathew for this story.
21 *The Hindu*, 11 July 1947.
22 *Malayala Manorama* archives.
23 Mr. and Mrs. V.V. Varkey's report on the plots in Travancore including the "parallel government" plot.
24 Information supplied by two of the local leaders involved, and supplemented from Mr. M.M. Cheriyan's diary.
25 Mr. and Mrs. Varkey's report.
26 Ibid.
27 Mr. K.A. Mathew gave me a copy. Mr. M.M. Cheriyan indentified it as one he had duplicated at the Communist Party Headquarters.
28 Mr. K.M. Cheriyan related this story to me; it was confirmed by other members of the family.
29 Mr. K.A. Damodara Menon, interviewed by the author.
30 *The Hindu.*
31 Mr. Kalathil Velayudhan Nayar, President of the Nayar Service Society, who was to have been present at this meeting, has permitted me to quote him as my authority for it.
32 The incident and the controversy about it are fully reported in *The Hindu.*
33 *T.I.L.*, August 1947.
34 Printed report, kindly translated by Mr. K.A. Mathew.

35 V.P. Menon 1956.

36 I was given several accounts, all of which tallied (except that the police account mentions a loincloth which was left behind, and the conspirators say it was a pair of shorts).

37 *The Hindu* also reported these events fully.

38 *T.I.L.*, September 1947.

39 *T.I.L.* This government monthly henceforward gave full publicity to the doings of the popular party.

40 *T.I.L.*

BIBLIOGRAPHY

A. OFFICIAL SOURCES: UNPUBLISHED

1. *National Archives of India, New Delhi.*
   a) Secret Files of the Foreign and Political Department, 1921- 1947.
   b) Fortnightly Reports of the Resident to the Madras States.
2. *India Office Records, London.*
   a) Secret Files of the Foreign and Political Department, 1921- 1947.
   b) Fortnightly Reports of the Resident to the Madras States.
   c) Madras Residency Records.
   d) Private Documents: the Skrine Papers, 1937-1939.
3. *Nehru Memorial Museum and Library, New Delhi.*
   a) All-India States Peoples Conference Papers.
   b) Pattom Thanu Pillai Papers.
   c) V.D. Savarkar Papers.
   d) Rajkumari Amrit Kaur Papers.
   e) K.B. Menon Papers.
4. *Kerala Regional Records Survey Committee, Trivandrum.*
   a) Report of the Ad Hoc Famine Relief Committee, 1938 (secretly printed).
   b) Correspondence between Dr. P. Sitaramayya and Sir C.P. Ramaswamy Aiyar.

B. OFFICIAL PUBLICATIONS

1. *Government of India.*
   Census Reports of 1901 and 1931.
2. *Government of Travancore.*
   a) Census Reports, Travancore: 1921, 1931, 1941.
   b) Travancore State Manuals:
      1. *Travancore State Manual*, 1906. V. Nagam Aiyar, Trivandrum.
      2. *Travancore State Manual*, 1938. T.K. Velu Pillai, Trivandrum.
   c) Official Communiques and Reports.

1. Government of Travancore: Official Communiques
2. *Travancore: Memorandum for the Indian States Committee.* Trivandrum: Government Press, 1928.
3. *Travancore Public Service Recruitment Committee Report, 1933.* Trivandrum: Government Press, 1934.
4. *Commission for Franchise and Delimitation,* Chairman, E. Subramanya Aiyar, Trivandrum: Government Press, 1937.
5. *Temple Entry Enquiry Committee, 1934.* Trivandrum: Government Press, 1935.
6. *Travancore Service Recruitment Manual* by N. Kunjun Pillai, Chief Secretary to Government; with an introduction by G.D. Nokes, Public Service Commissioner. Trivandrum: Government Press, 1937.
7. *Kerala District Gazetteer:* Trivandrum. A. Sreedhara Menon. Trivandrum: Government Press, 1962.

d) Proceedings of Representative Bodies.
1. *Proceedings of the Sri Mulam Popular Assembly,* 1904-1932.
2. *Sri Mulam Assembly Proceedings*, 1933-1946.
3. *Sri Chitra State Council Proceedings*, 1933-1946.

e) Official Periodicals.
1. Government of Travancore, *Administration Reports*, M.E. 1104 (1928-1929) to M.E. 1122 (1947-1948).
2. *Travancore Information,*1940-43.
3. *Travancore Information and Listener*, 1943-8.

C. NEWSPAPERS AND PERIODICALS

1. *Daily Newspapers.*

a) English.
The Hindu, 1929-1947.
The Madras Mail, 1929-1947.
The Bombay Chronicle, 1938-39, 1946-47.
The Statesman, Calcutta, 1938-39, 1946-47.
The National Herald, Allahabad, 1938-39, 1946-47.

b) Malayala.
The Malayala Manorama, Kottayam. Selections.
The Deepika, Kottayam (a Catholic daily). Selections.

The Mathrubhumi, Calicut, 1947. Selected passages.

2. *Periodicals.*

Harijan, M.K. Gandhi's weekly, published in Wardha.

The Madras Guardian, a Christian monthly published in Madras.

The International Fellowship, organ of the Federation of International Fellowship. Madras. Editor, A.A. Paul.

Outlook, London. Published by the Church Missionary Society.

D. BOOKS AND ARTICLES

1. *General:*

a) Indian History.

-Ambedkar, B.R. *What Congress and Gandhi have done to the Untouchables.* Bombay: Thacker & Co., 1945.

-Azad, Maulana Abul K. *India Wins Freedom.* Calcutta: Orient Longmans, 1959.

-Brecher, Michael, *Nehru, A Political Biography.* London: Oxford University Press, 1959.

-Edwardes, M. *The Last Years of British India.* London: Cassel, 1963.

-*The Evolution of India and Pakistan 1858-1947.* Ed. by C.H. Philips, London: 1962, vol. IV, Documents.

-Ghoshal U. N., *A History of Indian Political Ideas.* London: Oxford University Press, 1959.

-Glendevon, John. *A Viceroy at Bay.* London: Collins, 1971.

-Hodson, H.V. *The Great Divide.* Hutchinson, 1969.

-Jaipur, Maharaja of, *Indian States' Forces.* Orient Longmans, 1967.

-Johnson, Campbell A. *Mission with Mountbatten.* London, 1951.

- Keer, Dhananjay. *Dr. Ambedkar, Life and Mission.* Bombay, 1961.

-Majumdar, R.C. (Ed.) *History and Culture of the Indian People.* Bombay, 1969. vol. XI, The Struggle for Freedom.

-Moraes, Frank. *Witness to an Era.* London: Weidenfeld & Nicholson, 1973.

-Moreland, W.H. & Chatterji, A.C. *A Short History of India.* Longmans Green, 1936.

-Mosley, J. *The Last Days of the British Raj.* London: Weidenfeld & Nicholson, 1961.

-Nair, Balakhrishna. *The Dynamic Brahmin.* Bombay: Popular Book Depot, 1959.

-Sitaramayya, Pattabhi. *The History of the Indian National Congress.* Bombay: Padma Publications, 1946-47, 2 vols.

-Tendulkar, D.G. *Mahatma.* Bombay: Times of India Press, 1951, 8 vols.

-Thurston, E. *Castes and Tribes of Southern India.* Madras: Government Press, 1909, vol. 5.

-Tisserant, E. *Eastern Christianity in India.* Orient Longmans, 1941.

-Trevelyan, H. *The India We Left.* London: Macmillan, 1972.

-Venkataraman, S.R. *Temple Entry Legislation.* Madras: Bharat Devi Publications, 1946.

-Woodruff, P. *The Men Who Ruled India, vol. 2, The Guardians.* London: Jonathan Cape, 1954.

Zinkin, M. & T. *Requiem for Empire.* London: Chatto & Windus, 1964.

b) The Princely States.

-Barton, Sir W. *The Princes of India.* Nisbet & Co, 1934.

-*Cambridge History of India.* Ed. by H.H. Dodwell and R.R. Sethi. Cambridge University Press, 1964, vols. 5,6.

-Corfield, C. *The Princely India I knew.* Madras: The Indo-British Historical Society, 1975.

-Fitze. K. *Twilight of the Maharajas.* Murray, 1956.

-Lothian, A. *Kingdoms of Yesterday.* Murray, 1953.

-Menon, V.P. *The Story of the Integration of the Indian States.* Madras: Orient Longmans, 1956.

-Munshi, K.M. *The End of an Era.* Bharatiya Vidya Bhavan, 1957.

-Phadnis, U. *Towards the Integration of Indian States.* Bombay: Asia Publishing House, 1968.

-Wint, G. *The Third Killer.* 1965.

2. *Travancore and Kerala.*

-All-Travancore Joint Political Congress. *Travancore: The Present Political Problem.* Calicut: The Empire Press, 1934.

-Andrews, C.F. *Mahatma Gandhi's Ideas*. London: Allen & Unwin, 1929.

-Brown, L.W. *The Indian Christians of St. Thomas*. Cambridge: Cambridge University Press, 1956.

-Coatman, Ph. "Reform of the Depressed Classes," in *Asiatic Review*, Jan. 1933.

-Crowley, E. *Champion of the Outcaste: Lester Hooper of Travancore*. Highway Press, 1941.

-Desai, Mahadev. *The Epic of Travancore*. Ahmedabad: Navajivan Press, 1937.

-Fic, Victor M. *Kerala, the Yenan of India*. Bombay: Nachiketa Publications Ltd., 1970.

-Gopalan, A.K. *Kerala, Past and Present*. Laurence & Wishart, 1959.

-Handa, R.L. *History of Freedom Struggle in Princely States*. New Delhi: Central News Agency, 1968.

-*History of the Freedom Movement in Kerala*, The Regional Records Survey Committee. Trivandrum: Government Press, 1970, vol. 1.

-John, George M. *The Youth Christian Council of Action 1938-1954*. Bangalore: Christian Literature Society, 1972.

-Joseph, S.C. *Kerala: The Communist State*. The Madras Premier Co., 1959.

-Keralaputra (K.M. Panikkar), "Responsible Government in Indian States," in *The 20th Century*, March 1939.

-Keraliyan. *G. Parameswaran Pillai: The Father of Political Agitation in Travancore*. Trivandrum: Radh-Ind. Publications, 1948.

-Kottayam Municipality. *Golden Jubilee Souvenir*, Kottayam, 1971.

-Kuruvilla, K.K. *A History of the Mar Thoma Church and its Doctrines*. Madras: Christian Literature Society, 1951.

-Mankekar, D.R. *Red Riddle of Kerala*. 1965.

-Menon, A. Sreedhara. *A Survey of Kerala History*. Kottayam: Sahitya Pravarthaka Co-operative Society Ltd., 1967.

-Namboodiripad, E.M.S. *Kerala: Yesterday, Today and Tomorrow*. Calcutta: National Book Agency, 1967.

-Nataraja Guru. *The Word of the Guru*. Cochin: Pai

Publishing Co., 1952.

-Padmanabha Iyer. *Souvenir of the Sastiabdapurthi of Sir C.P. Ramaswamy Aiyer.* Trivandrum, 1940.

-Padmanabha Menon, K.P. *A History of Kerala.* Published privately, Trivandrum.

-Panikkar, K.M. *A History of Kerala.* Annamalai: Annamalai University Press, 1960.

-Perumal, Nilkan. *A Hindu Reformation.* Madras: R.J. Ram & Co., 1937.

-Pothan, S.G. *The Syrian Christians of Kerala.* London: Asia Publishing House, 1963.

-R. Ramakrishnan Nair. *Constitutional Experiments in Kerala.* Trivandrum: Kerala Academy of Political Science, 1964.

-Ramanath Aiyar, S. *A History of Travancore.* Madras, 1938.

-Sekhar, G.P. *Select Writings and Speeches of G.P. Pillai.* Trivandrum, 1964.

-Stuart, T.G. "The Ezhava Movement in Travancore", in *East and West Review,* 1936.

-*Travancore Today: Her Struggle for Freedom.* Working Committee of the Travancore State Congress. Cochin: Union Press, 1938.

-Watts, M.E. "Travancore," in *Asiatic Review*, 1930.

E. PRIVATE PAPERS

1. *Akkamma Cheriyan (Mrs. M.V. Varkey) papers.*
   a) Autobiographical note.
   b) Statement on proposed prosecution of the Memorialists, 21.10.38.
   c) Statement on students' strike, 21.10.38.
   d) Demands of the State Congress, by the 11th President, 21.10.38.
   e) Statement at Madura, 22.10.38.
   f) Account of the demonstration on 23.10.38.
   g) Speech delivered at Trivandrum Railway Station, 23.10.38.
   h) Resolutions of the Working Committee, 28.11.38.
   i) Instructions to *Desa Sevikas.*
   j) P.J. Sebastian, letter to Akkamma Cheriyan, 17.10.40.

k) Appeal for constructive work, 26.10.40.
l) Presidential address, by Akkamma Cheriyan, 11.8.40.
m) Statement on "American Model," by Working Committee, January 1946.
n) Presidential address by Pattom Thanu Pillai (1946?)
o) Statement by Pattom Thanu Pillai on "Independent Travancore," 1947.
p) Bulletin for first half of July 1947 issued by State Congress.
q) Varkey, Mr. and Mrs. V.V. Report on the preparations for a violent uprising in August 1947, among the "small fry" 1972. Prepared for the author.

2. *Author's Diaries and Letters.*
   a) Diaries, 1929-1946.
   b) Tour Diary and Notebook, 1971-1972.
   c) Letters to author's mother, 1929-1941.
3. *M.M. Cheriyan Papers.*
   a) Diary for 1947.
   b) Accounts of the Punnapra-Vayalar riots.
   - Chandrananda, P.K. "The Punnapra-Vayalar Riots."
   -Thandar, N.P., M.L.A. "Unforgettable Memories."
   (These papers were written for me in 1972 and translated by M.M. Cheriyan.)
4. *International Fellowship Papers.*
   a) Correspondence between A.A. Paul and the author, 1936-1938.
   b) "The Way Through." Report of the 6th Biennial Meeting of the Council of the Federation of International Fellowships, 27-31 Dec. 1937. Ed. A.A. Paul, Madras, 1938.
5. *K.A. Mathew Papers.*
   a) *A Statement Against the Erection of a Statue to Sir C.P. Ramaswamy Aiyar by Christians*, signed by 64 Christians, 1939 (secretly printed and circulated).
   b) *A Social Manifesto of the Church*, undated (secretly printed and circulated).
   c) Report of the Meeting of the Travancore Working Committee, Alleppey, 20.7.47.
   d) Mani, Lt. J., Royal Indian Navy. "A Call to Ex-Servicemen," 1947 (duplicated at Communist Party Headquarters, Bombay and secretly circulated).

6. *Malayala Manorama Archives.*
   a) Presidential address of Pattom Thanu Pillai at the 4th annual session of the Travancore State Congress, Quilon, October 1945.
   b) *Weekly State Congress Bulletins*, June-July 1947 (printed in Ernakulam and smuggled into Travancore).
   c) Cherian, K.M. Negotiations with Sir C.P. Ramaswamy Aiyar re: reopening of *Malayala Manorama*, article in *Malayala Manorama Year Book* (summarized translations supplied by P.K. Abraham of the *Manorama* staff).
7. Matthen, C.P. *I Have Borne Much.* 1943 (privately printed for private circulation).
8. Thaliath, J. *Truth about the Travancore Educational Policy.* Trivandrum, 1946 (privately printed).
9. The Travancore Peace Bloc. *Note on the Present Position of Christians in Travancore,* undated (privately printed).

F. INTERVIEWS

1. *From author's travel notebook.*

T.A. Abdulla. Leader of *Samyuktha* Movement and of State Congress, member of Working Committee.

K.C. Alexandra (Mrs. Chinnamma Anthony). Active in Students' Inter-Religious Fellowship, Secretary of Ad Hoc Committee for Famine Relief.

K.K. Chandy. Member of Society of St. Thomas, later its head. Active in Youth Christian Council of Action.

K.M. Cheriyan. Son of K.C. Mammen Mappilay. Editor of *Malayala Manorama.*

M.M. Cheriyan, Advocate. Active in Students' Inter-Religious Fellowship and Youth Christian Council of Action. Later became Communist, in charge of Press section of Party Headquarters in Bombay during war years.

K.A. Damodara Menon. Active Congressman, member of Kerala Pradesh Congress Committee, helped organize struggle in Travancore from Ernakulam. Editor of Cochin edition of *Mathrubhumi.*

K.R. Elankath. Active member of Travancore State Congress, member of Sri Chitra State Council.

K.C. George. Active in Young Kerala Society and Youth League, active in Travancore State Congress, but later joined Communists and became leader. Member for Education in Communist Government of Kerala, 1957-59.

K. Janardhanan Pillai. Active in Youth movement, especially Hindu youth movement. A Gandhian social worker.

Dr. C.K. Kareem. State Editor *Kerala Gazetteer.*

K.P. Kesava Menon. Grand Old Man of Kerala politics. Founder of *Mathrubhumi* and its first editor. Took part in Vaikom Satyagraha.

C. Kesavan.

R. Kesavan Nair. In the State Congress from the beginning. Member of Trivandrum International Fellowship. Member of Sri Chitra State Council, 1937-39.

M.K. Kumaran. Active in Trades Union and Communist movement.

N. Kunjuraman. Ezhava from poor family, but studied in Trivandrum and became a Lawyer. In State Congress from the beginning, member of Working Committee. Minister of Education 1948-51.

P.K. Kunju Sahib. Muslim leader, joined State Congress and Samyukta Party, became member of the Working Committee.

K.A. Mathew.

K.P. Madhavan Nair. From Parur near north Travancore border. Moved to Ernakulam, helped Travancore State Congress 1938-1947. Family house used for secret meetings.

C. Narayana Pillai. Journalist. Trivandrum agent of the *Indian Express*. Member of Travancore State Congress Working Committee. Author of A *History of the Travancore Freedom Movement* (mostly collection of source material).

Father Victor Narively. Editor of *Deepika*, Roman Catholic daily.

K.P. Nilakanta Pillai. Advocate. Member of State Congress Working Committee from the beginning.

Mannath Padmanabha Pillai.

John Pellissery. On editorial staff of *Malayala Manorama.* Editor of Year Books and supplements.

Dr. R. Prasannan. Secretary to the Kerala Legislature in 1972.

Pyarelal Nair. Gandhi's personal secretary and biographer.

G. Ramachandran.

Kuttanad Ramakrishna Pillai. Advocate. An old Congress fighter, member of Legislative Assembly for many years. Author of the life of K.C. Mammen Mappillay.

D. Ramachandran Potti. A schoolboy during the first Civil Disobedience Movement. A student during the "Quit India" movement and expelled from the Law College. Later a Gandhian social worker.

K.Sukumaran. Managing Editor of *Kerala Kaumudi*. Joined India National Congress in 1921. Studied in Trivandrum. In State Congress from the inception but left on issue of the Memorandum. Supported Sir C.P. on issue of "American Model."

Mrs. A. Thanu Pillai, Widow of Pattom A. Thanu Pillai.

Dr. M.A. Thomas.

Dr. M.M. Thomas.

A.P. Udaybhanu. Resident Editor, *Mathrubhumi*, Calicut. Ezhava. Active in State Congress. Member Legislative Assembly in Travancore 1944.

M.M. Varkey. Journalist. Secretary of Travancore State Congress from the beginning.

Mr. and Mrs. V.V. Varkey. Mr. Varkey is a journalist, in State Congress since its inception.

J. Vedasiromani. Principal, St. John's College, Palayamkottai. Formerly from Nagercoil, the Tamil-speaking area of Travancore which was later merged with Tamilnadu.

Kalathil Velayudhan Nayar. Advocate, Ernakulam. President of the Nair Service Society after the death of Mannath Padmanabha Pillai.

2. *From the author's diary of 1973.*

V. Sankar, I.C.S. (retired). Deputy Secretary, Home Department of the Government of India during War (he handled the file on author's internment 1940-41). Private Secretary to Sardar Vallabhbhai Patel in States Department in 1947.

Lord Trevelyan, formerly of the Indian Political Service.

3. *Taped Interviews with K.M. Panikkar;* "The Princes and the Transfer of Power." Recorded in 1958. Tapes in St. Anthony's College, Oxford.

INDEX*

---

* For obvious reasons of convenience some ultra-frequent entries don't record their page numbers, and content themselves with the laconic indication *passim*.